CONGRESS AND THE SHAPING OF THE MIDDLE EAST

CONGRESS AND THE SHAPING OF THE MIDDLE EAST

Kirk J. Beattie

Seven Stories Press

NEW YORK • OAKLAND

A SEVEN STORIES PRESS FIRST EDITION

Seven Stories Press
140 Watts Street
New York, NY 10013
sevenstories.com

Library of Congress Cataloging-in-Publication Data

Beattie, Kirk J.
Congress and the shaping of the Middle East / Kirk Beattie.
 pages cm
ISBN 978-1-60980-561-6 (hardback)
1. United States. Congress. 2. Pressure groups—United States. 3. United States—Foreign relations—Middle East. 4. Middle East—Foreign relations—United States. I. Title.
JK1021.B43 2015
327.73056—dc23
        2015004643

Printed in the United States of America

9 8 7 6 5 4 3 2 1

*I dedicate this book to my loving and supportive wife,
Elizabeth Hagge Beattie, and my wonderful daughters, Zoë and Taya.*

CONTENTS

ACKNOWLEDGMENTS

Research and writing for this book was spread out over nearly ten years. My primary method of investigation was that of personal interviews, as detailed in the book. I have many people I need to thank for their assistance with this book, but my first thoughts go to all of the Senate and House staffers who granted me some of their precious time. To garner honest and illuminating responses, I had to guarantee these interviewees complete anonymity. I only wish that circumstances enabled me to thank the staffers by name, especially those who demonstrated keen insight and allowed me to return to them for follow-up conversations. I also wish to thank the handful of congresspersons with whom I conducted interviews, especially former congresspersons Sen. Lincoln Chafee (Rhode Island), Rep. Marty Meehan (Massachusetts), and Rep. David Obey (Wisconsin). Two other current House members requested anonymity.

Numerous interviewees at off-the-Hill lobby shops or Middle East–focused organizations were particularly helpful. They included past and present directors and/or staff at Americans for Peace Now, especially Lara Friedman; M.J. Rosenberg, while he was at the Israel Policy Forum; Kate Gould at the Friends Council on National Legislation; James Zogby and two aides at the Arab-American Institute; former Amb. Warren Clark and others at Churches for Middle East Peace; Janet McMahon, former Amb. Richard Curtiss, and former Amb. Andrew Killgore, all at the *Washington Report on Middle East Affairs*; Mary Rose Oakar, Christine Gleichert, and Raed Jarrar of the American-Arab Anti-Discrimination Committee; Todd Deatherage at the Telos Group; Amb. Philip Wilcox at the Middle East Initiative; Clayton Swisher, then director of the Middle East Institute; Rob Levy at Brit Tzedek v'Shalom; George R. Salem, lawyer and D.C. political consultant; a J Street staffer who preferred anonymity; the Washington, D.C., office directors of the United Nations Relief and Works Agency; Jerry Madison, aide to Rep. Obey; and longtime friends and Middle East NGO hands John Viste and

Elaine Strite. Former State Department official Aaron David Miller also graciously shared his views with me, as did former congressional staffers David Dumke, Michael H. van Dusen, and Ellison M. Heath. I would also like to thank the former ambassadors of Egypt and Syria, the director of the Palestinian Authority office in Washington, D.C., and the political consul at the embassy of Iraq in Washington, D.C., for their assistance. Several individuals helped me with the collection of information, such as former Simmons students Megan Conlin and Amanda Skuldt. Many thanks to Kristin Hagge for the steady supply of articles and information over the years; and to Dr. Youssef Cohen for his thoughtful observations; and kudos to Dr. Andrew Brown and my Simmons College colleague Dr. Benjamin Cole for assistance with methodological concerns. I am also very grateful to Dr. Stephen Walt for reading the manuscript and providing feedback. I am also heavily indebted to the veteran staffers who, collectively, vetted all of the chapters of this book and provided insightful feedback, especially to the anonymous senior staffer who provided valuable commentary on matters relating to Appropriations, and two other former senior staffers for their comments on numerous chapters of the book. Due to the highly conflictual nature of this issue area, I want to state that I requested an interview with any representative of the American Israel Political Affairs Committee in 2006. I did not receive a response. Given their reputation for efficiency and professionalism, I elected not to call again.

At Seven Stories Press, thanks to former publicity manager Anne Rumberger, who first took an interest in the book. And very special thanks to my editor and publisher at Seven Stories Press, Dan Simon, who exhibited great patience, skill, and keen insight in guiding me to the finish line with this book. Thanks also to the other members of the Seven Stories team who each contributed in important ways, especially copy editor Ben Rowen, managing editor Liz DeLong, editors Jesse Ruddock and Lauren Hooker, art director Stewart Cauley, and, in the publicity department, publicity director Ruth Weiner and senior publicist Ian Dreiblatt. All errors of commission and omission are mine and mine alone.

PROLOGUE

Events of great significance have occurred since the first full draft of this manuscript was sent to the publisher roughly midway through 2014. The Israel–Palestine conflict erupted in the summer of 2014, once again producing widespread death, dislocation, and destruction. Just months later, in November 2014, American voters went to the polls for a new round of congressional elections. The Republicans registered a resounding victory, acquiring control of both chambers of Congress. Emboldened by their lopsided victory, they went on the offensive, challenging Pres. Obama on numerous fronts.

Nowhere was congressional contestation of executive branch policy any greater than on matters relating to US Mideast policy. Beginning in December, Republican hawks spoke in shrill voices, threatening to cut aid to the Palestinians and/or the UN should the Palestinians either be granted statehood or permitted to join the International Criminal Court. Within months, they invited Israeli Prime Minister Benjamin Netanyahu to speak before a joint session of Congress on March 3, 2015, providing Netanyahu with the opportunity to decry Pres. Obama's efforts—made in concert with British, Chinese, French, German, and Russian officials—to strike an accord with the Iranian regime over its nuclear program, a deal designed to block Iran's development of a nuclear weapons capability. The invitation, not to mention Netanyahu's speech, caused great rancor among US congresspersons, including criticism by some of Israel's staunchest lifelong supporters, who denounced Republican leaders for what they saw as a blatant attempt to politicize US foreign policymaking and undermine Pres. Obama's diplomacy. Netanyahu's hardline speech before Congress, in addition to his March 16 announcement rejecting the establishment of a Palestinian state, contributed to his surprise victory in Israel's election on March 17, a win that seemingly crushed all hopes of resolving the Israeli–Palestinian conflict in the near future.

Meanwhile, before any agreement with Iran was hammered out, some forty-seven US senators took the extraordinary measure of penning a letter to Iran's leaders, forewarning them that any deal struck by Obama and his foreign allies would meet with fierce opposition from Congress. The acrimonious relationship between the American president and his own Congress was played out under the klieg lights of global media. It highlighted the strong bond between many members of Congress and Israel, the power many members of Congress possess to obstruct presidential foreign policymaking, and those congresspersons' willingness to exercise that power when it comes to matters affecting the Middle East. In short, all of these points serve to reinforce the value of arriving at a deeper understanding of Congress, and what motivates the behavior of US congresspersons who are shaping US Mideast policy.

Introduction

IS CONGRESS BROKEN?

In this book, I examine the behavior of members of the US Congress with respect to the major Middle East conflicts involving Israel. As a political scientist specializing in Middle East and North African (MENA) affairs, I have long been interested in the Arab-Israeli conflict. It's a subject I have taught in the classroom for more than three decades. In fact, I've taught the course for so many years that its very name, the Arab-Israeli (A-I) conflict, has become a misnomer. The A-I conflict has morphed into an imbroglio with three principal, interconnected, conflictual axes: Israel-Palestine (I-P); Iran-Israel; and the Arab states (Syria, Lebanon, Iraq, Saudi Arabia, etc.) still not at peace with Israel. Egypt and Jordan, longtime Arab protagonists in the A-I conflict, remain deeply affected by and involved in today's conflicts despite peace treaties with Israel signed in 1979 and 1994, respectively. (A fourth axis, Israel-Turkey, emerged after the arrival of the Islamist AK Party in power in Turkey, but will be given shorter shrift in this book.)

Due to my long-standing interest, I have steadily tracked US policies—adopted by both the executive and legislative branches—that deal with these Middle East conflicts. My interest and concern for doing so was greatly reinforced by the events of September 11, 2001, and ensuing US government efforts to defeat Islamist extremism because of its connection to the A-I conflict. After all, the man who conceived the September 11 plan and sold the idea to Osama bin Laden—Khalid Sheikh Muhammad—was motivated heavily by his hatred of US support for Israel in its conflict with the Palestinians and other Arab nations. And as is well known, the hatred of US government policies by bin Laden himself, as well as by Ayman al-Zawahiri—the Egyptian doctor who served as bin Laden's éminence grise and replaced bin Laden as head of al-Qa'eda—was kindled by events such as Israel's crushing defeat of Arab forces in the 1967 war. Zawahiri and many others were further hardened into extremist positions by the torture they experienced, years later, while imprisoned in Egypt, whose authoritarian leaders were steadily rewarded with heavy US military and economic support for making and sustaining Egypt's 1979 peace treaty with Israel.

The US "special relationship" with Israel figures prominently in this calculus because it has enabled Israel's continued occupation and settlement of Arab lands, including Palestine. What makes the continuation—or even deepening—of this relationship so problematic is that since 1977, with perhaps two exceptions (March 1992–November 1995 and March 1999–July 2001), increasingly right wing Israeli governments have embraced policies decreasing the prospects for peace with Israel's neighbors. While it is a reality that many people around the world hate Israel because they are anti-Semites, a far greater measure of regional and international opprobrium has been generated by Israel's continued occupation of Palestinian and Arab lands, including right wing Israeli governments' active promotion of settlement activity on lands that the entire international community recognizes as the home of a future Palestinian state. Israel's aggressive policies would be far less likely without the unwavering military and economic assistance provided by the US government, in which the US Congress has played a major contributing role. Although successive US presidents hold considerable responsibility for these policies, the US Congress has proven an even more consistent, unrelenting agent in making Israel a regional behemoth impervious to worldwide criticism of its long-lasting violations of international law. Congress has become something akin to a win-at-all-costs horse trainer, "buting up" or "doping" his horse, Israel, to perform powerfully, but in a manner that is both illegal and potentially injurious to the long-term well-being of "the horse" itself.

This book's primary objective is to explain congresspersons' behavior with regard to Middle East policy formulation, with greatest attention given to policies affecting Israel's Mideast (IME) conflicts. As my research progressed, however, the book acquired a secondary objective. The more I studied congressional policymaking on IME conflicts, the more I came to see that policymaking as impaired by many of the same factors plaguing congressional activity across a broad range of issue areas. For many years, numerous issues have fueled perceptions of Congress as broken and dysfunctional. The health care debate; the home mortgage debacle; the economic crisis—with the meltdown of the financial system and the bailout of banks and other major corporations; attempts at gun control in the aftermath of the Tucson (Rep.

Gabby Giffords) and Newtown, Connecticut, tragedies; the "fiscal cliff"; the sequester: all of these events and issues have produced legislative wrangling that has left the majority of American citizens both depressed and frustrated by congressional outcomes. This frustration is reflected in US public opinion polls, with poll after poll demonstrating citizens' deep dissatisfaction with Congress.

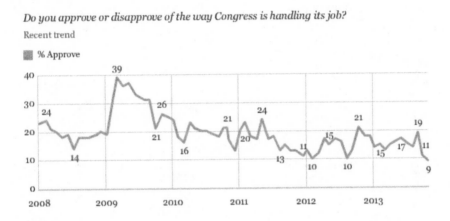

Do you approve or disapprove of the way Congress is handling its job?

Recent trend

GALLUP

No matter how angry or disappointed citizens may have been with the performances of former Pres. George W. Bush and Pres. Barack Obama, Congress has regularly "bested" them with its even lower popularity rankings. The nadir of Bush's public opinion poll was recorded at 20 percent in a CBS survey conducted between October 31 and November 2 of 2008. Obama's low of 38 percent was recorded by Gallup over a three-day period in October 2011. But as Gallup reported in November 2013,[1] Americans' approval of Congress reached an all-time low: 9 percent.

So far, fortunately, there have been no signs that Americans have reached the point of repudiating their belief in the value of the overall system; their faith in liberal democracy and liberal democratic institutions remains firm. As a staunch believer that democracy is the best of all political systems, despite its many flaws, I see this continued faith in democracy as a good thing. But the crisis in confidence is real. Partisan identifications have withered, with citizens characterizing themselves as independents consistently outnumbering those who identify as Democrats or Republicans, as indicated in the Gallup poll below.[2] In addition, there has been an increase in citizens mobilized by protest movements such as the Tea Party or MoveOn.org, not to mention those responding to mass mobilization by political comedians like Jon Stewart and Stephen Colbert. These developments serve as strong indications that citizens are fed up with the major parties and Congress's inadequacies, and that they are voting with their feet to launch new political movements to achieve serious reforms.

Party Identification, Yearly Averages, 1988-2013

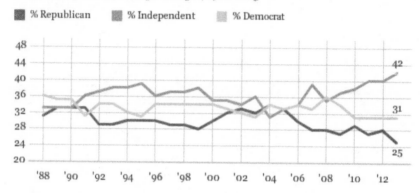

Based on multiple day polls conducted by telephone

GALLUP

So what is going on here? Why is Congress regularly performing in a manner that merits such low marks? And so what? What difference does this make to the nation's welfare? How does it happen that 90 percent of the public clamors for gun control legislation, for example, and Congress fails to act? And importantly for this book, has US foreign policymaking also been affected by deficiencies in the US system of government? In this book, I seek to shed light on several of the most critical factors producing a negative impact on Congress and its ability to serve more efficiently and effectively the national interest. I also hope to draw attention to the severely negative consequences of this country's inability to address these shortcomings and defects. I seek to make these points in the context of examining and analyzing the role Congress has played in shaping American foreign policy with regard to the Middle East, and in particular with regard to the region's conflicts surrounding Israel.

TAKING A BRIEF LOOK AT THE BIG PICTURE OF CONGRESS'S FAILURES

If one steps back to take a broad perspective, it's clear that Congress's difficulties in recent times are manifestations of historically deep-seated problems in US governance. Much ink has been devoted to the influence of "special interests" in the electoral process, with early warnings issued by Elizabeth Drew (1983) and Amitai Etzioni (1984) on the nefarious role of political action committees (PACs). Other astute observers of American politics have pointed out defects in the legislative process itself. For example, William Greider, the highly acclaimed journalist, made the following observation in 1992: "Most political inquiries focus their analysis on campaigns and candidates, the techniques of persuasion and of assembling electoral majorities, the contest of slogans and ideology and so forth. . . . [but] beyond elections [are] the practical questions of how and why some interests are allowed to dominate the government's decision making while others are excluded. After all, this is the realm of politics that matters to people in their everyday lives. And this is the realm where we will find tangible explanations for their discontent."[3]

Greider's analysis was remarkably prescient; it wasn't until 2005–2006 that congressional difficulties and derivative popular discontent attracted greater public attention. According to John Dean, whose *Broken Government* was published in 2007: "A check of the record for the past ten years in LexisNexis and several other databases . . . revealed only one commentator writing about 'broken government' at the federal level: Harlan Ullman, a former naval officer, a senior associate at the Center for Strategic and International Studies, and a columnist for the Washington Times."[4]

Although Greider's book was published just two years prior to the stunning Republican revolution of 1994, whatever hopes this change brought for its believers did not last much beyond one decade. Rather, the latter 1990s and early 2000s yielded a bumper crop of cases of large-scale corruption among Republican power holders, and the elections of 2006 served up a stinging rebuke of Republican control of the executive and legislative branches.

By the time John Dean was putting the finishing touches on his book, Congress had became so subservient to the interests of Republican President George W. Bush, elected in 2000 and reelected in 2004, as to prompt two of the nation's best-known specialists on the US Congress, Norman Ornstein and Thomas Mann, to publish their highly acclaimed study, *The Broken Branch*.[5] In their analysis of the demise of Congress, these preeminent scholars highlighted the debilitating effects of the major parties' ideological polarization and congresspersons' inability to deliberate and define solutions to the nation's crises. Contributing mightily to this failure, in their learned opinion, was the major party leaders' recourse to other means of increasing loyalty among their members. Two of these, according to their study, were for party leaders "to play a more central role in congressional elections, especially in their financing, [and] to enlist sympathetic interest groups and their lobbyists to the partisan cause."[6]

With the exception of mega-rich candidates like former US Senator Jon Corzine of New Jersey, who might be able to eschew external sources of support to finance their own campaigns, "special interests" are clearly crucial to the first half of Mann and Ornstein's equation; after all, hardly any of the campaign finance funds harvested by party leaders and then redistributed to fellow party members are really coming from their own pockets. Rather, those funds are provided primarily by "special interests." Through these practices, both parties' leaders and congresspersons in general have become increasingly incapable of ignoring the demands of "special interests," and less adept at designing policies beneficial to the nation in general.

There is broad agreement that the common culprit undermining the ability of Congress (and the executive branch) to address issues to the benefit of the general public is the power of "special interest" groups.[7] Lawrence Lessig's 2011 work *Republic Lost*[8] has helped to focus concerned citizens' attention on the debilitating impact of "special interests" on Congress. He cogently demonstrates how lobbyists play a critical middle role, using the special interests' money to influence electoral campaigns, thereby furthering the objectives of those "special interests." Lessig notes:

> As I write these words, Gallup's latest "confidence in Congress" poll finds only 11 percent who have confidence in this Congress. Eleven percent. At what point do we declare an institution politically bankrupt, especially an institution that depends fundamentally upon public trust and confidence to do its work? When the czar of Russia was ousted by the Bolsheviks, he had the confidence of more than 11

percent of the Russian people. When Louis XVI was deposed by the French revolution, he had the confidence of more than 11 percent of the French. And when we waged a Revolutionary War against the British Crown, more than 11 percent of the American people had confidence in King George III.[9]

In this book, I hope to go beyond Lessig's work in analyzing the depth and complexity of the crises afflicting Congress. My own understanding of the negative influence of "special interests" crystallized over time as I witnessed developments across a broad array of issues and became increasingly aware of attendant "special interest" influence. Let me share a few vignettes to make this case, beginning with a quick look at financial sector lobbyists' efforts to influence Congress at the time of the late 2000s banking crisis. Just how big were their efforts? Matt Taibbi estimated that over a three-year period, 2008–2010, some $600 million was "hurled" at Congress by industry lobbyists in a "legislative orgy" aimed, successfully, at derailing efforts to produce serious reforms in the financial sector.[10]

In the January 2011 "Tucson Tragedy," a deranged man took the lives of six people and wounded thirteen others. Among the thirteen was US Rep. Gabrielle Giffords, who was left in a perilous state, having taken a shot to the brain. Many citizens had reason to believe that members of Congress, having seen one of their own gunned down, might finally legislate against the easy purchase of rapid firing guns. Not so fast, said an otherwise highly sympathetic Chris Hayes of MSNBC and The Nation, who quickly and correctly predicted that the 4.3 million members of the National Rifle Association (NRA) would have no problem countering the wishes of the broad American public. This was followed by the late 2012 Newtown slaughter, and still Congress failed to respond with gun reform laws despite calls for action by Pres. Obama and support from the overwhelming majority of the American public.

If one examines the 2008–2009 congressional debates over reform of the housing crisis or the health care system, one sees the same debilitating factors at work. In the health care debate, over 100 lobbying firms spent over $100 million to at least dilute, if not defeat, the newly elected president's proposals. Both parties shared the blame; for all intents and purposes, Sen. Max Baucus (D) blocked any meaningful Senate debate on Republican proposals to cut health care costs by introducing restrictions on medical malpractice suits.

All of these examples, and so many others, helped either to first stimulate or reconfirm the need to compare these developments with the powerful role played by "special interests" in my own area of specialization: Middle East politics and US Middle East policymaking. Prima facie evidence that there were important parallels across a broad range of issue areas appeared compelling.

"SPECIAL INTERESTS" AND MIDDLE EAST POLICYMAKING

My research effort has enabled me to bring important insights to this conversation in two critical areas. First, I have chosen to explore Congress's problems through extensive interviews with congressional staffers. This approach enabled me to write something akin to a primer for anyone interested in the behavior of congresspeople and the tremendously important role they play. The interviews offer the reader a window on the great structural and functional deficiencies in congressional procedure. This "congressional procedure" template suggests how and why difficulties are encountered in other issue areas, such as health care, gun reform, and others. Second, there is a dearth of empirical evidence on Congress's role in Middle East policymaking; my research helps fill the gap and has enabled me to explore how Congress really works. This is of great importance when one recognizes that Congress's Mideast policymaking directly affects America's standing in the "War on Terror."

That "special interests" weigh in heavily in the shaping of US Mideast policy is no surprise to anyone who has studied the history of US policymaking as regards Israel's Middle East conflicts. However, the general public remains ignorant of the extent to which "special interests" hold sway over foreign policymaking in the United States, and its ignorance makes a difference. There are several plausible explanations for the public's lack of awareness. First, most Americans are inclined to see a high degree of congruence between American and Israeli interests. After all, this is the message they are consistently fed by most major American and Israeli political figures, as well as the American mainstream media. Most Americans see Israel as a kindred liberal democracy, a small country historically surrounded by authoritarian regimes (Egypt, Jordan, Syria) and a highly problematic democracy (Lebanon), and they feel a sense of commitment to defending Israel's security. Most Americans are oblivious to the formal presence and participation of racist parties and politicians—the likes of which are not tolerated by the broad American electorate—in all of Israel's recent, right wing coalition governments. Second, an important segment of American society, comprised of Christians and Jews, feels a strong attachment to Israel motivated by religious and/or ethnic considerations—for them, Israel is both the natural homeland of the Jewish people, granted to them through their covenant with God, and a state that affords a safe haven to the Jewish people.

Other important factors are also at work. For example, the general public is largely ignorant of the origins and dynamic of IME conflicts, the motivations and actions of its principal protagonists, and the role the US government has played, over time, in the Middle East. Also missing is a higher level of education and/or exposure to alternative viewpoints, which serves as a backdrop to the fact that most Americans would have considerable difficulty imagining that "special interests" might trump the "national interest" in the formulation of foreign policy. Finally, there is in general a strong (if not inexplicable) tendency for foreign issue-oriented "special interests" (or at least the ones in this issue area) to be left out of scholarly and most mainstream journalistic investigations of "special interest" influence in Congress. To present just one example, the excellent book by Lawrence Lessig[11] mentioned earlier includes no reference to the lobbyists discussed in this book despite the fact that one of the groups—the American Israeli Public Affairs Committee (AIPAC)—has long been considered among the most successful and influential lobbies in contemporary American political history. Such "errors of omission" have led, in turn, to lesser public awareness of this reality.[12] Whether or not this absence of coverage is due to the likelihood that authors critical of Israel incur a high risk of getting slammed and smeared with the ugly and often unjustifiable charge of anti-Semitism, as has happened to many, I will leave to others to decide.

Of course, work has been done on the impact of "special interests" on US foreign policymaking, including study of the Arab-Israeli conflict. Most noteworthy is *The Israel Lobby* by Drs. John Mearsheimer (University of Chicago) and Stephen Walt (Harvard University), both major figures in International Relations.[13] First posted as a lengthier monograph on Harvard University's John F. Kennedy School website and then published in abbreviated form as a long article in *The London Review of Books*,[14] their denunciation of the Israel lobby's influence in Washington, D.C., prompted one of the greatest firestorms in academe and among political cognoscenti in recent memory. Indeed, I felt fortunate at the time that I had completed all but a handful of my entire first round of interviews prior to the 2006 *London Review of Books* publication. As matters turned out, however, little "damage" had been done to my research environment. In fact, the interviews I conducted after publication of their article were not only intrinsically beneficial but also "instructive" in that they demonstrated the extent to which congressional staffers live in an "ivory tower" of their own, a tower from which their view is obscured by the daily communications blizzard. To wit, few staffers had even heard of Mearsheimer and Walt's original study or follow-up article, and many stated they didn't have the time to read it. I can, therefore, happily state with great confidence that my entire 2005–06 round of interviews was not affected by their publication, and I doubt for comparable reasons that it had much impact on the 2011–13 round as well. At any rate, Mearsheimer and Walt's work did not attempt to document the manner in which "special interest" influence exerts itself in Congress as I do here; that is, through the use of primary research. So I believe I am making a significant contribution to the literature on US Mideast policymaking with this book.

A BRIEF, HISTORICAL BACKGROUND SKETCH

In the following chapters, staffers and others make frequent references to major developments relating to IME conflicts and other important regional developments. These matters are so complex, and the history so long and deep, as to render any fuller-blown discussion here spatially impossible. However, it's important to provide a brief sketch of major historical developments so that the reader may contextualize and better comprehend references invoked by my interviewees.

Let's take the creation of Israel as a starting point. After decades of Zionist Jews' colonization of Palestine, on balance made possible by British Mandate control of that land from 1920 to 1948, the Zionist leadership unilaterally declared Israel's independence in May 1948. This brought to a head the recurring armed conflict between the Zionist settlers and the indigenous Palestinian Arab population, which had sought its own sovereignty, and resulted in the latter's defeat and mass expulsion and exodus from Palestine. Some 750,000–780,000 Palestinians became refugees. The 1948 war also induced the conflict's regionalization. Official armies and private militias from Egypt, Syria, Jordan, and Iraq were involved in the fighting and lost. No Arab states recognized Israel's right to exist, and major wars ensued in 1956, 1967, and 1973. The 1967 war was especially important in that it ended with Israel occupying all of Egypt's Sinai Peninsula, the Egyptian-administered Gaza Strip, Syria's Golan Heights, and the West Bank, which had been under Jordanian administration since 1948. The war also created another 125,000 Palestinian refugees; Palestinians in Gaza and the West Bank came under Israeli military administration, and West Bankers and their descendants remain so until today. The Golan Heights were formally annexed by Israel's right wing Likud government in December 1981, prompting UN Security Council Resolution 497, which denied the legitimacy of the Israeli move.

Under Egypt's President Anwar Sadat, a major change to the conflict occurred due to his pursuit of peace with Israel in November 1977. A peace treaty with Israel, the Camp David Accords, was reached in March 1979, bringing full recognition of Israel by the Arab world's largest nation-state. In spite of great contestation of this peace by many Egyptians, other Arabs, and most Muslim nations, and in spite of the treaty serving as a motivating factor in the October 1981 assassination of Sadat, that peace has held until this writing. Even the "Arab Spring" and revolutionary change in Egypt in early 2011, the election of a Muslim Brotherhood president, and his ouster in a 2013 "revocoup"[15] spearheaded by Egypt's military and police did not overturn the Camp David peace. Both Israel and Egypt became major recipients of US largesse—military and financial aid to the tune of $3.2 billion and $2.2 billion, respectively, over many decades—as a reward for making and preserving this peace.

The year 1979 had already proven momentous for the region due to changes in another demographically weighty but also resource-rich country: Iran. There, the January 1979 overthrow of the shah of Iran, a stable US ally, eventually brought the arrival in power of a radical Shi'ite Islamist regime—a regime that placed the US and Israel at the top of its list of foreign foes. Iran's Islamists would seek to project their revolutionary credo to other Shi'ite populations in neighboring Iraq, Lebanon, and the Gulf, and to curry favor with the secular regime in Syria, where a son of the Shi'ite derivative Alawi community, air force officer Hafez al-Assad, had claimed control of the country in 1970. Over time, strong links were forged between the Iranian regime and

Shi'ites in Lebanon, namely with the early-1980s' radical Islamist Shi'ite organization named Hizballah. Backed by Iran, and assisted by Syria, which used
Hizballah as a proxy in its conflict with Israel, Hizballah would grow into the
strongest armed force in Lebanon. In due time, Iran also built close ties with
and strengthened the Palestinian, Sunni Islamist organization Hamas. Both
Hizballah and Hamas became major headaches for Israel along its northern
and southern borders, respectively.

After nearly four decades of fruitless efforts by a host of Palestinian organizations—from diplomatic initiatives to the use of terror tactics—Palestinians in
the Gaza Strip and West Bank rose up against the Israeli occupier in late 1987.
This uprising, the First Intifada, lasted several years, and fostered activity by
major international powers and the UN to bring peace. Ultimately, Palestine
Liberation Organization (PLO) representatives and Israeli officials hammered
out an agreement in Oslo, Norway, and Pres. Clinton's government stepped
in to chaperone the 1993 Oslo Peace Accords, signed in Washington, D.C.
Never had peace seemed so close at hand. But just over two years later, its
Israeli signatory, Prime Minister Yitzhak Rabin, was assassinated by an Israeli
religious fundamentalist. The accords were further undermined via terrorist
attacks by Palestinian extremists in Israel, which engendered an atmosphere
fraught with heightened insecurity and led to the May 1996 election of PM
Benyamin Netanyahu of the right wing Likud party. Netanyahu would lose
the premiership three years later to Ehud Barak, and Barak would enter
into peace talks with the Palestinian leader Yasser Arafat at Camp David in
summer 2000. Once again, there was a glimmer of hope for peace, but those
talks failed and were accompanied by widespread perceptions, painted by
Pres. Clinton, that Arafat was to blame. Despite this, in the waning days
of the Clinton administration, yet another effort was undertaken to bring
together the principal protagonists, and the January 2001 Taba Accords established what most moderates have long recognized as the basis for a resolution
of the I-P conflict. Sadly for those who saw the possibility of peace, aggressive actions undertaken by its opponents once again scuttled the effort. Right
wing Likudnik and former general Ariel Sharon took his historic "walk" on
the Temple Mount, or Haram al-Sharif, in Jerusalem on September 28, 2000,
causing Palestinian outrage and triggering a launching of a second Palestinian
intifada, which would last until early 2005.

All of these tensions made their own contribution to the watershed event of September 11, 2001. 9/11 begot the US attack on Afghanistan, after its Taleban government refused to bow to pressures to yield Osama bin Laden. Arch-pro-Israeli, American neoconservatives, now driving the Middle East foreign policymaking of Pres. George W. Bush, convinced the latter it was high time to topple Iraq's Pres. Saddam Hussein from power on the later-proven-false pretext that he, too, was connected to bin Laden's heinous attack. By March 2003, the US had entered Iraq, and what was initially presented by the neoconservatives as a "walk in the park" military operation turned into the protracted nightmare and costly loss of precious blood and treasure that Americans came to know all too well.

Just as I was beginning the research for this book, in the mid-2000s, the US found itself deeply embroiled in Iraq, suffering significant casualties. Elsewhere in the region, Yasser Arafat, longtime leader of the PLO and PA president, died in November 2004, amidst claims that he had been poisoned by Israeli operatives. In many Western capitals, officials hoped that his moderate successor, Mahmoud Abbas, would be more conciliatory in the pursuit of peace. Israel's government, led by PM Ariel Sharon, fulfilled its decision to remove Israeli settlers and troops from the Gaza Strip in August and September 2005. Some 8,500 Israeli settlers had been living in the tiny enclave alongside 1.5 million Palestinians. But Israel retained tight control over air, land, and maritime access to Gaza, and if any peace dividend was expected from this withdrawal, none was gained.

January 2006 saw two significant developments. First, early in that month, Israeli PM Sharon suffered a massive stroke and was placed in a medically induced coma that would last eight years until his death. For optimists, his departure was lamentable in that his hawkish, military past and overall stature might have enabled him to make peace with moderate Palestinians, in a "Nixon went to China" manner; and the pursuit of a "two state" solution would prove unattainable by his weaker successor, PM Ehud Olmert, and seemingly undesirable by PM Netanyahu. Second, later in January 2006, Israel's more implacable Palestinian adversary Hamas emerged with a small plurality of the vote in the first democratic election held by the Palestinian Authority. Opposition to Hamas's leadership of the Palestinian government soon brought open fighting between Hamas and the more secular Fatah party, and a de facto split of the occupied territories resulted, with Hamas taking control of the Gaza Strip and Fatah controlling the West Bank. Meanwhile, along the Israeli-Lebanese border, clashes with Hizballah convinced Israeli decision makers in summer 2006 to launch large-scale military operations that targeted not only Hizballahis and Palestinians, but vital Lebanese infrastructure. Israel's path of destruction was wide and deep, but not without significant loss of life to its own soldiers, as Hizballah's fighters proved phantom-like and lethal.

The "black eye" suffered by the Israeli Defense Forces (IDF) in 2006 perhaps strengthened subsequent Israeli leaders' resolve to turn any future military engagements into ones that left their own deadly mark on their opponents. Thus, when the firing of rockets by Palestinian Islamist elements caused Israel to retaliate in the three-week Gaza War of late 2008 and early 2009, Israel not only demonstrated its military superiority, but also utilized banned weaponry, such as white phosphorous bombs, to deadly advantage. As a consequence, the war left a lopsided 1,400-plus Palestinian to 13 Israeli (four by "friendly fire") death toll. Still, if there was a lesson to be learned, these developments neither prevented serious clashes from recurring along the Israeli-Lebanese border in 2010 and 2012 nor discouraged Hamas and the Islamic Jihad movement from lobbing rockets into Israel from the Gaza Strip during the same time frame. All of these events, and more, presented grist for US congresspersons and their staffers during the period of my study.

HOW I CONDUCTED THE STUDY

With the partial exception of the two chapters dealing with candidates' election and reelection to Congress, the material in this book is based heavily on interviews with congressional staffers, "off-the-Hill" lobbyists, and congressional cognoscenti. Congressional staffers are the lifeblood of the legislative process. No member of Congress alone would be capable of tackling, in any serious and credible fashion, the myriad requests and torrent of information from constituents, concerned citizens in general, the media, interest associations, other governmental institutional actors, foreign embassies, and international organizations. As shall be detailed in this book, the flow of information can create a veritable communications whiteout. In consequence, the staffers' work—their handling of phone calls and office visits; their sifting through regular mail, blast faxes, and emails; and their provision of written and oral advice to their "boss" on current developments—is all of enormous importance. To reinforce this point, one need look at only one aspect of congressional lawmakers' workload. As shown in the "Interim Resume of Congressional Activity" from the December 29, 2010, *Congressional Record—Daily Digest*, the Senate and House were in session for 158 and 127 days, respectively, between January 5 and December 22, 2010. With these numbers in mind as mathematical denominators, contemplate the figures that follow. In the Senate, 1,506 measures were introduced during this period in 2010; 3,098 were introduced in the House. These measures included 1,139 bills and 320 simple resolutions on the Senate side, and 2,158 bills and 788 simple resolutions on the House side. And of course keep in mind that the range of issue areas covered by these bills and resolutions is enormous. So even this partial view of legislative activity, which totally ignores time spent in the home district or state to meet with constituents and pursue fund-raising, provides ample insight into a congressperson's workload, as well as an appreciation for the amount of work that falls on the shoulders of congressional staffers. (The current, 113th "do-nothing" Congress of 2013–14, with its lower level of legislation passed, is considered an aberration, its legislative inactivity being chalked up to partisan/ideological gridlock.)

To gain permission to interview congressional staffers, I had to promise them anonymity. In most offices, anonymity was imposed on the staffers as part of standard operating procedure in their offices. In bowing to this condition, I hoped to obtain, and sincerely believe that I received, frank and honest responses to my questions.

To guarantee a representative sample, I assigned a number—from 1 through 435—and computer-generated a random numbering of these representatives to create my House sample. I then proceeded to work my way down this list, beginning with the "#1" representative's office. During my initial survey, I contacted a total of 334 House offices, out of which I was able to conduct 106 interviews with House staffers. In 68 of the offices that I contacted, the staffers declined to cooperate due to "office policy." In most cases, this meant that the House member had established an office ban on responding to requests for interviews by any scholar or individual seeking information for the purpose of a study. There were a few instances, however, in which the individual staffer intimated that she or he was invoking "office policy" because they were disinclined to speak, usually because of a lack of familiarity with the topic. (I will make additional comments about this in the text.) In another 160 offices, contact was established, but no interviews were completed due primarily to my own time and financial constraints. On balance, as I will demonstrate later, I feel confident that I obtained a highly representative sample of respondents in the House. In only a very small number of offices did individuals decline to participate because of the sensitivity of the issue area, although I did encounter some people who were circumspect.

On the Senate side of the Hill, I entered all 100 Senate offices. During my 2005–2006 rounds of interviews, I was granted interviews in 29 Senate offices, with 16 rejecting my request on the basis of "office policy," and 55 left "untapped" due once again to my own time and financial constraints. Again, I feel that these 29 interviews constituted a solid representational sample.

For one week in February 2011, and for two weeks each in the spring of 2012 and 2013, I conducted additional interviews. For methodological reasons, I returned primarily to offices I had visited earlier to see how things had changed. In many of those offices there were already new staffers in place. During this second round, I conducted an additional 30 House interviews and 10 additional Senate staff interviews. Again, the purpose of these visits was to ascertain how much the "state of play" had changed, if at all, from the time of my first set of interviews. But this also provided the opportunity to make cross-time comparisons, looking at the mid-2000s to the early 2010s. In the end, the only states for which I failed to contact a House member were Alaska, North Dakota, South Dakota, and Wyoming—all of which had just one representative—and Mississippi, which had four representatives. Put differently, I contacted at least one staffer from 45 states, whose combined number of representatives constituted over 98 percent of the total number of reps in the House.

In addition to the interviews conducted with congressional staffers, in all of the aforementioned time frames I also interviewed key individuals in numerous lobbies, interest group associations, think tanks, other US governmental institutions, three foreign embassies (Egypt, Iraq, and Syria), and the formal representatives of the Palestinian Authority (PA) to hear their perspectives. Last but not least, I also interviewed several members of Congress and several US diplomats, both active and retired, as part of my data collection effort.

Finally, I analyzed the backgrounds of my interviewees' makeup as opposed to those staffers whose "office policy" precluded an interview, as well as the group of staffers with whom I was unable to finalize an interview where "office policy" was not a stated obstacle. I did find a slight—but only slight—bias along partisan lines, with staffers working for Democrats being a little more willing to comply with my request than were staffers in Republican offices. However, the difference was slight enough that I do not consider it problematic in terms of my findings. There simply were too many Republican staffers from a host of backgrounds who were happy to help out.

I am, therefore, satisfied with the pool of data I was able to generate. It would have been preferable, obviously, had I benefited from even greater time and resources to interview more people, and perhaps to interview a greater number of congresspersons themselves. All told, I believe these data have enabled me to arrive at many solid observations, generalizations, and assertions with regard to the questions under analysis.

ORGANIZATION OF THE BOOK AND A FINAL CAVEAT

Chapter one offers a view of what goes on during congressional elections, with particular attention to the role played by "special interests." Chapter two is comparable, but focuses on congresspersons' reelection concerns. Chapter three examines House offices and House staffers and how they tackle Middle East issues; chapter four looks at how these matters are taken care of in Senate offices by Senate staffers. Chapter five involves an analysis of House and Senate members' behavior. Chapter six focuses on how House members legislate on IME issues; chapter seven does the same for the Senate. In both of these chapters, particular attention is paid to the roles played by their foreign affairs committees. Chapter eight presents a view of how House and Senate Appropriations Committee members and staffers deal with IME issues. The book ends with a brief conclusion.

There is one important caveat. I had no control over the terms my interviewees and others used to characterize the individuals and groups at the center of this study. As the reader will see, staffers, other interviewees, and media sources are prone to speak in terms of "pro-Israel groups" versus "pro-Arab and pro-Palestinian groups" and interests. This binary appellation of the protagonists is highly problematic. First, all of the predominantly Jewish American groups discussed in this book are pro-Israel, but significant differences exist between them over what policies are in the best, long-run interest of that country. These differences parallel historical disagreements in Israel between right and left wing Zionists, much of which has to do with land.

Right wing Zionists have long argued that the Zionist enterprise was short-changed by Great Britain's division of Palestine to create Transjordan in 1921. The right wing Zionists have desired control of more land, inspired by a combination of religious sentiments (control of the "promised land" of ancient Israel for colonization and population absorption), national security (control of the Golan Heights, West Bank, etc.) and water security (West Bank aquifers). Liberal, and especially leftist, Zionists have been more willing to retain less land in exchange for peace with their Arab neighbors. These differences have a direct impact on two grand policy debates: (a) should Israeli governments more actively pursue a "two state solution" to the I-P conflict, a solution acceptable to moderate Israelis and Palestinians alike, and trade land for peace with Syria; and (b) should the US government pursue policies designed to pressure Israeli governments to meet this objective.

Second, there is not a single noteworthy "lobby" discussed in this book, no matter what its membership's composition, that seeks Israel's destruction. In fact, during the time of this study (and until today), there was not even any noteworthy "special interest" group or lobby on Capitol Hill pursuing a "unitary state" outcome; that is, a group seeking a solution in which Israelis and Palestinians share equal citizenship rights in a single, territorial unit encompassing all of present-day Israel, the Gaza Strip, and the West Bank. Thus, groups or interests described as "pro-Palestinian" or "pro-Arab" in this book are, generally speaking, pursuing the same "two state solution" sought by many Jewish American groups and Israelis. Third, even the "pro-Palestinian" and "pro-Arab" appellations are too simplistic because these pro-peace, pro–two state solution groups prefer to deal with Arab and Iranian actors willing to live in peace with Israel and distance themselves from actors calling for Israel's destruction.

For these reasons, I have taken recourse to referring to those individuals and groups that do not actively seek a "two state solution," as described above, as "right wing pro-Israel" actors; their sentiments and actions place them in alignment with right wing elements in Israel—individuals, groups, and parties that have not actively pursued a "two-state solution" and appear intent to proceed with Jewish Israeli settlement of the West Bank, not to mention the Golan Heights. The moderate individuals and interest groups in Washington that favor a "two-state-solution" and promote Palestinian human rights, including the right to self-determination, are described accordingly.

To sum up, the initial focus of my research was on the Arab-Israeli conflict and related policymaking, and broadened to include Israel-centered Middle East conflicts. However, I hope and fervently believe that this study also sheds light on how Congress works and will in many ways shed light on how other major issue areas are dealt with by US congressional actors. In a March 14, 2011, *Time* magazine piece by the well-known political commentator Fareed Zakaria, the author asked "Are America's Best Day's Behind Us?" In response to his own question, Zakaria wrote:

> The key to understanding the moves by both parties is that, for the most part, they are targeting programs that have neither a wide base of support nor influential interest groups behind them. (And that's precisely why they're not where the money is. The American political system is actually quite efficient. It distributes the big bucks to popular programs and powerful special interests.) . . . It's not that our democracy doesn't work; it's that it works only too well. American politics is hypersensitive to constituents' interests. And all those interests are dedicated to preserving the past rather than investing in the future. There are no lobbying groups for the next generation of industries, only for those companies that are here now with cash to spend. There are no special-interest groups for our children's economic well-being, only for people who get benefits right now.[16]

This book will provide ample opportunity to gauge the accuracy of Zakaria's thinking based on the results of my empirical research.

Chapter One

THE "COSTS" OF GETTING ELECTED

Before anyone can play a role in Congress, she or he must—exceptional guber-natorial appointments aside—be elected. As nearly all concerned Americans know, the cost of congressional campaigns has become exorbitant, imposing onerous constraints on the electability of prospective candidates. While I shall address the implications and consequences of these campaign costs for simply getting elected, I also want to impress upon the reader what the broader "cost" of this campaign finance burden is in terms of policymaking at the national level of government. Specifically, I'll demonstrate why it's essential to examine how the game of electoral politics is played, to determine how it's affected or influenced not just by the candidates' behavior or their political parties, but by other concerned citizens and organizations, such as domestic interest groups or mega-rich individuals. After all, if even a small number of people can influence the election process, they can potentially "predetermine" the outcome of congressional action.

Two political scientists, Peter Bachrach and Morton Baratz, long ago high-lighted this aspect of democratic politics in presenting their concept of a "mobilization of bias."[17] Extrapolating from the logic of their argument, and to offer a hypothetical example, if pro–Costa Rica interests were able to get an over-whelming majority of congressional candidates to commit to a pro–Costa Rica agenda prior to getting elected, so that pro–Costa Rica candidate X would be competing against pro–Costa Rica candidate Y in most congressional districts, then clearly everyone could expect a more pro–Costa Rican agenda to be taken up by the newly elected Congress. If newly elected congresspersons subsequently failed to deliver once in office, thereby violating their prior campaign pledges, one would also expect a greater likelihood of there being "hell to pay" during the next electoral cycle. So the simple question one may pose here is: are such factors at play in the US electoral process with regard to the Middle East issues under study? I pose this question here; the answer will appear in ensuing chapters.

HOW ARE CONGRESSIONAL CANDIDATES' VIEWS SHAPED BEFORE ASSUMING OFFICE?
Is There a Widespread, Pro-Israel Bias?

Political socialization is the process by which individuals acquire their knowledge, sentiments, attitudes, opinions, and ideological orientations about political matters. There is a long list of possible "agents" of political socialization: the family; one's peers; institutions of formal education; the visual and print media; religious institutions; ethnic groups; communities; regions; historical factors (an economic depression, a war); contact with political systems, political parties, and institutions; and so forth.

I will begin by asserting that most Americans have been politically socialized in a manner that has produced a pro-Israel bias. Far fewer in number are those Americans brought up to feel greater sympathy with various Arab or Iranian protagonists. Many factors are at play here, but the more important ones include the following: (1) Throughout nearly its entire history, Israel has been a democracy, however imperfect, surrounded by authoritarian states or troubled democracies (like Lebanon), and most Americans have an affinity for democratic nations. (2) Both the United States and Israel share a comparable narrative in terms of their early histories—persecuted religious minorities colonizing, with the use of great guile and force, territory held by another people. (3) Most Americans are Christians, and the Judeo-Christian tradition has created a sense of spiritual connectivity between Christians and Jews. (4) Continuous sensitization of the American populace about the Holocaust has occurred through films, television shows, and public school programs; this has produced a desire to protect Israel as a safe haven for the Jewish people. (5) For some older Americans in particular, there are feelings of guilt due to inaction by the US government to impede the Holocaust and the heinous slaughter of millions of Jews by Hitler's Germany. Support for Israel serves as a form of atonement. (6) Israel and the US assisted one another during the Cold War. (7) There has been a constant demonstration of support for Israel by most American political figures and the two major political parties, which in and of itself constitutes an important source of political socialization for

American citizens. (8) For many Americans, Israel is seen as fellow victim of Islamist extremists, as well as an ally in the post–September 11 "War on Terror."

This pro-Israel bias is clearly corroborated by survey research findings, like those found in Gallup polls conducted on an annual basis over many years.

In the Middle East situation, are your sympathies more with the Israelis or more with the Palestinians?

Based on yearly averages from 1988 to 2013

■ % Israelis   % Palestinians

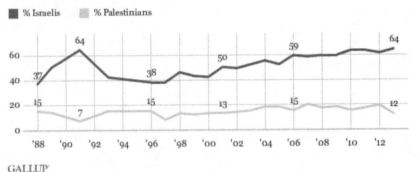

GALLUP'

Favorable Views Toward Israel, the Palestinian Authority, and Iran

% Very/Mostly favorable

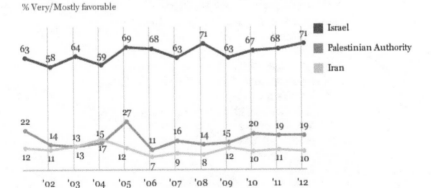

GALLUP'

Sympathy for Israelis vs. Palestinians in Mideast Situation, by Party ID
% Sympathize more with Israelis

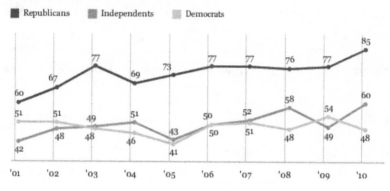

GALLUP'

Next, I'd like your overall opinion of some foreign countries. What is your overall opinion of [country]? Is it very favorable, mostly favorable, mostly unfavorable, or very unfavorable?
Feb. 7-10, 2013

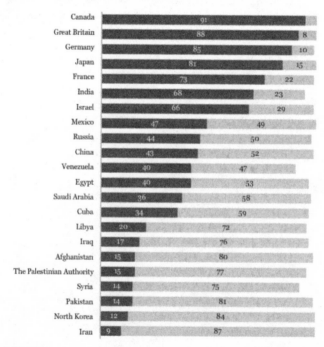

GALLUP'

Country Ratings Showing Significant Age and/or Partisan Gaps
% Total favorable

	18 to 34 years	35 to 54 years	55 and older	Republican	Democrat
	%	%	%	%	%
China	62	38	34	39	45
Cuba	39	32	22	23	37
Egypt	72	60	47	57	64
France	75	63	55	52	76
India	76	67	60	64	69
Iran	18	10	6	9	13
Israel	63	67	70	80	53
Mexico	60	52	38	46	55
North Korea	30	11	6	11	18
Pakistan	34	22	17	25	24
Russia	61	47	38	40	56
The Palestinian Authority	28	17	15	12	25
Yemen	35	22	10	17	26

Feb. 1-3, 2010

GALLUP

The polls show a clear and constant difference in collective sympathy, with pro-Israel sentiment stronger than sympathy for Arabs, in general, and Palestinians and Iranians, in particular. There are times when aggressive behavior by Israel's government, such as the 1982 invasion of Lebanon, causes a decline in sympathy for Israel and a simultaneous increase in sympathy for the Palestinians and/or others, but even in those moments Israel has retained a greater measure of sympathy.

At the same time, let's not exaggerate the level of sympathy for Israel. As surveys comparing sympathy for Israel with that of other countries also clearly demonstrate, Israel has never really ranked among the "most beloved" of nations in Americans' minds. That category is reserved for Canada and the United Kingdom, and even for former WWII enemies Germany and Japan. Further, France, a country many Americans use as a punching bag of sorts, has ranked near or at times above Israel in terms of its favorability.

Because nearly all American congresspersons were born and raised in the United States, most have shared a pro-Israeli political socialization experience with their fellow citizens. As shall be discussed, some congresspersons' lives have been touched by other—even alternative—socialization factors due to the trajectory of their personal lives: their family histories, religious beliefs, contacts with peers, and so forth. These factors will be discussed in greater detail later. For now, suffice it to say that most congresspersons, given the environment in which they grew up before seeking political office, are more likely to hold a greater fondness for Israel than for any of the other nation-states of the Middle East.

ETHNO-RELIGIOUS COMMUNITY-BASED BIAS

Only a small minority of Americans live in communities with strong ties to the Middle East. None of the most "organic" ethno-religious constituencies—Arab Americans, Jewish Americans, and perhaps some Muslim Americans—constitute a particularly large segment of the American population. Americans of Arab descent represented only 0.42 percent of the American population according to the 2000 census, and this figure had risen by only one or two hundredths of a percent by the turn of the 2010 decade.[18] In addition, the tiny Arab American community is weakened politically by divisions along both religious (Christian vs. Muslim) and national lines. Lebanese Americans have long constituted the most sizable Arab American community, roughly one third of the total, followed by Syrians, Egyptians, Iraqis, and others. On a country by country basis, a disproportionately high percentage of these people are Christians, not Muslims, and on top of this, they come from disparate Christian denominations: Maronites, Orthodox, Roman Catholic, Copts, Chaldean Catholics, Anglicans, etc. Moreover, in contrast to their status in the Arab world, Christian Arab Americans, historically, have outnumbered Muslim Arab Americans. One only need contemplate Lebanon's destructive civil war—itself a partial derivative of the Arab-Israeli conflict—or the discrimination suffered by various Christian and Muslim communities in the Arab countries Iraq, Lebanon, Syria, and Egypt to understand how divisive events there have been for the Arab American community writ large.

Although the number of Muslim Americans, now about 2.1 percent of the population, surpassed Jewish Americans a number of years ago, the Muslim

American population has been bolstered by African American converts to Islam, as well as by the arrival of many Muslims of non-Arab descent. While most Muslim Americans do hold a certain affinity for Israel's adversaries for a host of reasons, concerns about economic matters and/or the socio-cultural discrimination they experience greatly outweigh their focus on the A-I conflict.

There is an ongoing debate over the exact size of the Jewish American community, with the percentage of the total US population ranging from 1.7 percent on the low end to 2.1 percent on the high end. But here, too, there is great diversity of focus and opinion. The US Jewish community is not a monolith. It's divided into numerous branches: Reform, Conservative, Orthodox, Hasidism; and it includes secularists, as well as agnostics and atheists. Members in each of these groups feel individually determined notions of "Jewishness." Surveys conducted by the Public Religion Research Institute or financed by the American Jewish Committee (AJC) consistently show American Jews are far and away most concerned with the American economy, health care, taxes, or social equality, and not with Israel or Middle East issues. In politics, American Jews have historically exhibited a strong penchant for liberal values and for support of the Democratic Party. Pres. Obama received 78 percent of the 2008 Jewish vote, and 69 percent in 2012, at a time when his popularity in Israel was in single digits. According to one report, only 4–4.5 percent of voting American Jews considered Israel the most important issue for them in 2012.[19] Another report put the figure at 10 percent.[20] An even smaller percentage—1.3 percent—considered how a US president would handle Iran's nuclear weapons program as the most determinative issue for their presidential vote.[21] So let's do some math here. Of the 2.1 percent of Americans who are Jews, about 80 percent are eligible to vote.[22] If all 80 percent, roughly five million people, do vote, that's 1.68 percent of the total population.

Jewish Americans who are highly supportive of Israel are not alone, as will be demonstrated at great length and multiple reprises in this book. Another, bigger base of support comes from the Christian evangelical community, which, as any person with a passing knowledge of contemporary American politics knows, has been very influential, especially within the Republican Party. Some 26.3 percent of the US population sees itself as evangelical/born again Christian.[23] That's huge. However, as will be discussed later, most of these people's votes are far more affected by issues such as abortion, school curriculums, and the economy. Only a tiny fraction is most concerned about Israel's fate.

My point here is simply to show that in the aggregate, national level, only a very small percentage of Americans are politically motivated by concern for Israel. The reader must keep this in mind as I attempt to decipher why members of Congress display such great concern for Israel's fate and demonstrate collective, unflinching support for the policies of right wing Israeli governments.

BIAS INDUCED BY "SPECIAL INTEREST" GROUPS

Moving beyond these background factors, we can start to focus on how American political actors are often targeted for additional socialization. To wit, special interest group leaders are always on the lookout for individuals who appear to have the "right stuff" for political competition. On the basis of my research, right wing pro-Israel groups, especially AIPAC, are highly skilled at "discovering" and nurturing putative hot prospects. Their searches often target people before they are even considering running for a US congressional seat. Talented individuals are approached and vetted while they are serving in state or local political politics. Potential "rising stars" and solid prospects then often find themselves being offered an all-expenses-paid trip to Israel. As one congressional staffer put it, "Usually the people who come knocking on the doors of political officeholders are trying to get something from these political figures, not offering to give them something. But when someone comes along offering you a free trip, like an all-expenses-paid visit to Israel, it's pretty hard to say no." In addition, as another staffer said, "Because most politicians are not likely to have formally studied the politics of the Middle East prior to any such trip, their brains are relatively clean slates upon which their Israeli hosts can make an important impression." Indeed, some recipients of the free trips spoke to the impact they can have. In a telephone interview I conducted, a New York City Council candidate, who went on a sponsored trip to Israel, said, "Yes, the trip had a very powerful impact on my thinking about the conflict, and definitely made me more sympathetic to Israel's situation."

On balance, the trips make a difference, and the paucity of competition from other organizations is of significance. The now defunct Washington, D.C.–based National Association for Arab Americans (NAAA) once provided trips on a fairly regular basis, and various Arab American chambers of commerce coordinate such trips with foreign embassies. As will be discussed more fully later on, other Arab-based organizations provide comparable trips, as have new groups like J Street, but all have done so for far fewer individuals and for far less time than have right wing pro-Israel organizations.

For many years, nothing spoke more loudly to the significance of these congressional trips than the reluctance of either party to curb them by truly serious campaign finance reforms. Trips to Israel were seen as likely to create great empathy for that country, because short drives or helicopter excursions would quickly impress upon visitors the country's small physical size and apparent vulnerability to hostile neighbors. One staffer with experience living in Israel told me that "the termination of such trips would be ruinous to pro-Israel interests." Accordingly, alarm bells were sounded in many circles in January 2007 when reform-minded Democrats swept into power, in part due to voter outrage over serious ethical violations, including congressional "junkets" by Republican congresspersons. The Democrats' much ballyhooed reforms, embodied in the Honest Leadership and Open Government Act of 2007, included curbs on earmarks, the use of corporate jets, and gifts and travel, and took aim at the Republicans' K Street (lobby shop) Project. But the alarm bells quickly fell silent. Although travel restrictions were put in place, the new regulations did not effectively constrain the provision of travel opportunities for lawmakers by lobbyists. AIPAC, for example, simply passed this task to a new, affiliated, tax-exempt organization, the American Israel Education Fund (AIEF). The AIEF

spends the bulk of its $24 million budget paying for congressional trips to Israel. According to the Web site LegiStorm, "When Congress was working on strengthening the travel ban in 2006, reports indicated AIPAC lobbied for an exemption from the ban on lobbyist-sponsored travel. The organization did not receive a specific exemption, but the loophole on allowing non-profit travel allows the organization to continue to sponsor travel." The non-profit AIEF simply certifies that it "does not retain or employ a registered federal lobbyist." That this was no accident was confirmed, perhaps inadvertently, by Melanie Sloan of Citizens for Responsibility and Ethics in Washington. In a 2009 C-SPAN interview, host Brian

Lamb asked about the 2006 travel rules adopted as a result of the Jack Abramoff scandal whereby an "institution of higher learning" can sponsor trips. "Well," Sloan responded, "this was initially even called the AIPAC exception, there was this exception that 501(c)(3) organizations and universities could, in fact, still sponsor trips." To Lamb's characteristic "Why?" she replied, "That was the compromise that was reached in the House. They didn't want to ban all private travel and they thought that these were the kind of trips that were more easily explained and didn't have the same kind of appearance of corruption."[24]

Of course, AIEF is not alone. Just to give a few additional examples, the Republican Jewish Coalition paid for a trip to Israel for Senate hopeful Carly Fiorina of California in 2010, and comparable trips to Israel by both parties continue to this day, reportedly to great effect. Meanwhile, the number of trips to the Israeli occupied territories and Arab countries that are sponsored by "pro-peace," "pro-Arab," or "Muslim" organizations has been small, historically, in comparison to those sponsored trips promoting strong support for Israel alone. Nonetheless, groups such as the American-Arab Anti-Discrimination Committee (ADC), J Street, and the Telos Group emulate AIPAC's AIEF in one form or another and have gained some ground in recent years.

What are members of Congress and congressional staffers likely to learn on a "pro-Israel" sponsored trip like those of AIEF? Here is a view presented by Richard Silverstein of the well-known publication *Tikkun*, a pro-Israel, pro-peace, liberal publication.

In defending their propaganda tours of the Promised Land, the Israel Lobby grasps at any straw to distinguish them from [Jack] Abramoff type junkets: "It's broadly understood that the Israel sojourns—grueling 6:30 a.m. to 11 p.m. affairs—hardly count as junkets."

But what they conveniently omit is the fact that these Israel trips, while not as blatantly corrupting as the Abramoff outings, are toxic nonetheless in their impact on US-Israel relations in terms of the Congress. Members get an entirely distorted perspective on Israeli political discourse. They only hear from the rightist security hawks like [Benyamin] Netanyahu or [Nathan] Sharansky. If they do hear from so-called moderates like Shimon Peres or Tzipi Livni, the political message conveyed is much more conservative than the message such politicians would convey to an Israeli audience. In other words, the Israeli sources tailor their message for what they perceive as Aipac's hard-line views of the Israeli-Arab conflict.[25]

On the basis of my interviews with congressional staffers, Silverstein's comments are largely on target. While numerous staffers described the trips as beneficial to their bosses and/or themselves, an equal number were quick to note the heavily biased picture presented to trip recipients. I will return to discussion of lobbyists' use of trips later in the book.

HOW AND WHAT CANDIDATES "LEARN" ON THE CAMPAIGN TRAIL

Once candidates enter the electoral fray, they encounter numerous "hoops" deployed by interest groups. These "hoops" are designed to get candidates to embrace a clear-cut position on those groups' issue(s) of greatest concern. This "pre-testing" and "orientation" of candidates takes on several forms, but some of the more prominent ones brought to my attention were the following.

First, there is what congressional staffers call "the litmus test." Many staffers noted that candidates are presented a set of questions by certain interest groups in order to ascertain their attitudes with regard to the Arab-Israeli conflict and its major protagonists. While some Arab American and Muslim interest groups engage in such "testing" through entreaties to present position papers, I obtained very little empirical evidence that this is widespread. By contrast, a great number of staffers noted that right wing pro-Israel interests do vet candidates in this fashion. This practice has been made clear by publications' references, such as those in the *Near East Report*,[26] to candidates' "position papers"; that is, their preelection positions on Israel and related matters.

Second, there are direct, personal contacts by private individuals or very small groups, either by letter or through face-to-face encounters. Potential donors often employ this approach, seeking to feel out the candidates' orientations prior to making a gift of whatever size. Private citizens will call a candidate's headquarters, "dropping" the names of well-known, wealthy individuals from the congressional district while inquiring about a politician's stance on specific issues. Representatives of a variety of interests engage in this type of activity, but again references to the overall number of interest groups and to the overall donations of a right wing pro-Israel nature, in contrast to that of "pro-Arab" or strong "two state" solution advocates, attest to the overwhelmingly greater strength and potential influence of the former. Indeed, not a single staffer interviewee mentioned the name of a wealthy Arab American individual or family, whereas references by interviewees to wealthy Jewish Americans were commonplace.

Third, there are invitations to candidates to present and discuss their views with concerned constituents, either by themselves or in a debate with their opponent. Debate situations are most frequently conducted in an institutional setting, whereas individual candidates may also be invited to private homes. The number of Muslim Americans surpassed the Jewish American population several years ago, but far more staffers discussed invitations that their bosses received to speak at synagogues than at mosques or Arab Christian churches. Staffers added that it was clearly the objective of many attendees to call out the candidate (or incumbent) with regard to his or her views on the A-I and I-P conflicts. According to several of my interviewees, one strategy employed by "pro-Israel" groups is the ambush debate. Candidate X is invited to speak before a predominantly Jewish audience, let's say at a temple or synagogue. The candidate arrives and discovers, without prior notification, that his or her opponent has also been invited. The candidates are then entreated to speak on the issues, including matters relating to the conflict. As one veteran staffer recounted, "They arranged a debate at a synagogue—behind closed doors—between the congressman and two of his opponents. There was no point of contention here vis-à-vis Israel, but it was a very interesting choice of venues; it was set up there to make sure they hear what the congressman says. It was a very large, influential group of people; there was no way our opponent could oppose us on this issue."

Whatever the nature of the encounter, all of this behavior must be considered part and parcel of the democratic process. One must simply ask the question of whether or not the existence of any consistent bias, or the absence of any significant countervailing influence, creates an overall environment in which candidates feel pressured to adopt positions contrary to what might be deemed—based on analysis liberated from the pressure of such domestic influences—in the country's best interest.

THE PRESSURES OF CAMPAIGN FINANCE

"Money is the mother's milk of politics."
—Jesse M. Unruh (former California state treasurer)

"Just don't talk about the money."
—a Jewish American staffer's advice to this book's author

The Democrats sought to curtail lobbyists' influence by legislation enacted in 2007, but as the *New York Times* reported at the time, "The ethics rules do not address the most valuable gifts that come from lobbyists and others interested in legislation: campaign donations."[27] Election to the US Congress and the presidency has come to require a daunting mobilization of people and cash. In 2012, almost $6.3 billion dollars were spent. Money has become of tremendous importance to mobilizing voters because of the dazzling cost of media coverage, especially television ads. According to campaign finance expert Joseph Cantor, candidates rely on four major sources to fund their campaigns: (1) individual citizens making direct contributions; (2) the candidate's political party; (3) interest groups, such as PACs; and (4) their own personal resources.[28] In the run-up to the 2008 presidential election, Barack Obama revolutionized the process of campaign fund-raising, amassing an enormous campaign war chest by garnering donations from millions of small donors. However, for most national-level candidates even after the introduction of Obama's strategy, parties and interest groups have come to play increasing roles. With the Supreme Court's 2010 ruling in the *Citizens United* case, which struck down many provisions in the 2002 Bipartisan Campaign Reform Act, wealthy individual donors and group interests have reentered the campaign donation scene with a vengeance. An April 2014 Supreme Court ruling, *McCutcheon v. Federal Election Commission*, further consolidated change in this direction by striking down caps on federal election campaign donations.

Just how expensive had running for a congressional seat become during the time frame of this study? In the 2004 electoral cycle, House candidates, on average, raised $1,147,930 dollars and spent $1,033,538.[29] By 2012, the average spent by House members was $1,689,580.[30] The total amount of campaign finance money spent in 2010 was a staggering $1,081,709,237 by competitors for House seats and $741,541,251 by Senate seat aspirants!

Even for an incumbent running in a district where there is not much of a challenge, campaign costs rarely drop below a quarter of a million dollars. House incumbents feel compelled to "campaign" just to sustain higher visibility. For example, Rep. Gregory Meeks spent $679,887 during the 2003–2004 election cycle in New York's 6th district. What made this especially eye-catching was that Meeks was running unopposed! Commenting on the high costs of noncompetitive races, one veteran Republican staffer noted back in 2006, "A cheap election will cost more than $250,000. We have to spend over $1 million. Even if you don't have a race, you still have to spend. Rural areas are cheaper; you can use radio. But we've got an urban area. If a race is targeted by the AFL-CIO [American Federation of Labor and Congress of Industrial Organizations], you know you're gonna have to spend $1 million." At present, heavily contested House seats now cost well over $1 million per candidate. The most expensive battle for a House seat in 2004 was between two incumbents, Martin Frost (D) and Pete Sessions (R), in the newly configured 32nd district of Texas. The two candidates each spent over $4.5 million, with Frost spending roughly $119,000 more than Sessions in a losing effort. Jumping forward to the 2010 election cycle's most expensive race, Michele Bachmann (R-MN) spent $11,647,656 in besting Tarryl Clark (D), whose campaign cost $4,689,117. In 2012, the race between incumbent Allen West and his challenger and winner, Patrick Murphy, cost a whopping $29,279,964 in total; that is, almost double the most expensive race of the previous cycle.[31]

In the Senate, where the stakes are higher given the greater prestige and length of term in office, campaign costs are several times higher than for House seats. A "cheap" Senate seat will cost several million dollars, whereas an expensive one can "cost" tens of millions. In 2000, the average winning candidate for the Senate expended $7.4 million.[32] By 2012, the average cost per Senate seat was $10.5 million, almost ten times the average cost of a House seat.[33] In 2012's most expensive Senate race, Elizabeth Warren defeated incumbent Scott Brown, with a combined $85,429,334 spent, the majority of which was expended by Warren.

The 2010 electoral season saw some individual Senate candidates blowing past the $50 million mark, like Connecticut's Linda McMahon, who spent $50,181,464 in a losing effort against Richard Blumenthal (over $8.7 million). But as this race and others demonstrate, the biggest spender does not always win. Despite the occasional aberration, however, there is no serious debate over how important it is for candidates to be financially competitive. In all of the House and Senate races held from 2000 to 2010, the bigger spender won 93 percent of the House seats and 83 percent of the Senate seats.[34] With such widely known odds, dollar-based electoral calculations are ever present in the minds of all prospective candidates. The task becomes so onerous for so many candidates that many feel as though they spend the bulk of their time raising money as opposed to tending to the legislative affairs of the country. In 2012, some $3.7 billion was spent on congressional races!

As noted above, most candidates have come to rely heavily on political parties and interest groups, including PACs, to cover their campaign expenditures. In the 2006 electoral cycle, PACs provided nearly half (43 percent) the average expenses for each House winner—$542,397—and roughly one-sixth (16 percent) of the average campaign expenses of victorious Senate candidates.[35] In the 2010 cycle, PAC contributions to House and Senate candidates accounted for 31 percent and 12 percent of total campaign expenditures, respectively.[36]

With regard to the performance of political parties, a relatively new, interesting twist has been the appearance of Leadership PACs. Leadership PACs involve the mobilization of funds by particularly powerful, influential congressional actors. A good example from the time frame of this study would be the role played by the once superpowerful Texas congressman Tom DeLay, who used a portion of his Leadership PAC funds to finance the campaigns of less established congressional contestants. For many congressional officeholders, and especially for the newer ones, Leadership PAC money features quite prominently on their lists of sources of campaign finance funds.[37] Sen. Jim DeMint topped the list of Leadership PAC leaders for 2009–2010, having amassed over $9 million. Rep. Eric Cantor collected over $4 million during the same cycle, leading all House members in this category.[38] Leadership PACs totaled over $44 million in 2010, and $46 million in 2012.[39] The reader should thus keep in mind that candidates seeking Leadership PAC assistance are likely to think twice before endorsing policies that buck the orientation of Leadership PAC dons or their major donors.

The high cost of campaign finance provides a great point of entry into congressional politics for "special interests," no matter what the interest and related interest group. No one doubts the ability of the NRA, the American Medical Association (AMA), major trade unions, big banks, major agribusinesses, huge pharmaceutical firms, large insurance companies, and myriad other interests to curry favor with politicians by providing campaign finance assistance. They do so based on their well-founded belief that if their preferred candidate wins there will be some satisfactory return on the interest group's investment. In fact, many interest groups bet on both horses in the race to ensure some degree of access to the seat holder no matter what the outcome.

The presiding role of campaign finance was placed clearly in evidence when Congress, siding with the NRA, bucked the wishes of 90 percent of the American public in failing to pass gun purchase legislation after the Newtown, Connecticut, massacre. We might hope that, in contrast, issues of foreign policy are relatively immune to "special interest" influence. Such a hope, however, is highly naive and myopic. A whole range of foreign policy issues are fair game for influence peddling and therefore are subject to competitive bidding for the furtherance of specific interests.

Federal law prohibits foreign entities from buying influence in the United States government. Campaign contributions by foreign countries and foreign residents are illegal. In fact, if not for this legal restriction, AIPAC might not exist. Its creation came about as the result of scrutiny applied to the American Zionist Committee for Public Affairs (AZCPA), a lobbying division of the American Zionist Council set up in 1953 by former Ohio newspaperman turned Israeli Ministry of Foreign Affairs member Isaiah L. Kenen. Friends and foes alike of AZCPA were concerned and outraged by its use of international funding to influence positions taken by American congresspersons. The practice was outlawed, so a domestic agent was deemed necessary. AIPAC was born.

By contrast, no law blocks campaign contributions from flowing across state boundaries. Residents of Massachusetts or Wisconsin, for example, may back congressional candidates in Hawaii or any other state should he or she wish to do so. As we will see, national lobbying groups and individuals are able to exploit this to launch national campaigns against local candidates whose views they perceive as being against their interests.

SHAKING THE MONEY TREE

At first blush, one might assume that neither "pro-Arab" nor "pro-Israel" American interest groups would constitute campaign finance heavyweights. Neither Arab Americans nor Jewish Americans constitute a particularly large segment of the American population, and neither camp behaves in a completely homogeneous manner when it comes to the IME conflicts, as discussed earlier. What can more than make up for the small size of these camps is that the political alignment and votes of even a small number of individuals matter greatly in tight elections and "swing states." This is especially true in presidential elections due to the Electoral College. In addition, the ability of groups, and even families and single individuals, to make heavy campaign donations can also make up for the small demographic weight of any particular minority group. As has proven true in other issue domains, "one percenters" can end up playing a radically disproportionate, influential role. Both of these points will be illustrated in the following discussion, but before entering into specifics, two basic points must be registered: (1) Jewish Americans have punched well above their weight in making campaign finance contributions. (2) Arab Americans, Iranian Americans, and Muslim Americans generally have not raised significant campaign funds.

A more focused examination of campaign contributions motivated by Middle East concerns is revealing. Let's begin by looking at "pro-Israel" campaign contributions.

"PRO-ISRAEL" CAMPAIGN DONATIONS

Between the 1990 and 2002 campaign seasons, at the national level, "pro-Israel" interests made political contributions totaling $41.3 million.[40] From 1998 to 2012, per annum "pro-Israel" campaign expenditures averaged $2.87 million.[41] As Jeffrey Blankfort discovered, based on an examination of *Mother Jones* "Top 400 Campaign Donors in 2000," 7 of the top 10, 12 of the top 20, and 125 of top 250 individual campaign donors were Jewish, at which point Blankfort just stopped counting.[42] Most donations from these individuals went to Democrats, accounting for roughly 50 percent of all campaign funds raised by the Democrats.[43] In recent election cycles, discussed more fully below, these already impressive figures have been greatly surpassed. (One must quickly note that these are gross values; that is, they don't reflect narrower political ideological and/or policy differences. Some of the top Jewish American donors provide backing, for example, to more moderate, "pro-peace" candidates. But importantly, none of these donors would be perceived as "anti-Israeli" or "pro-Arab" except in the eyes of strong and extreme right wing pro-Israel elements.)

It is interesting to see how, for many years, these funds were raised. Campaign finance reforms introduced in 1974 prohibited individuals from making donations in excess of $1,000 to any single candidate per election per electoral cycle. Thus, an individual could contribute up to $2,000 to a single individual per electoral cycle to help that candidate cover his or her primary and general election expenses. These limits gave rise to the formation of Political Action Committees, or PACs, with no legal limit set on the number of PACs operating in any particular issue area. PACs were created to represent a broad range of special interest groups, trade associations, and corporations. As Neve Gordon wrote, "PACs became part of the political scene in 1974 when Congress enacted campaign finance reforms which [also] limited organized donations to $10,000 per candidate—a $5,000 primary election donation and another $5,000 during the general election campaign. According to J.J. Goldberg, PACs proliferated around the country, from 608 in 1974 to 4,681 in 1990. The total amount donated by PACs to congressional campaigns increased during the same period from $12.5 million in 1974 to $150.5 million in 1990."[44] It was the growth in power and influence of these PACs that was discussed in the books by Drew (1983) and Etzioni (1984) noted earlier. By the 2010 election year, PACs contributed a whopping $422,229,571 to congressional candidates—over $330 million for House candidates, and over $91 million for Senate candidates.[45]

What role did PACs, especially "pro-Israel" PACs, come to play on Middle East matters in US elections? As explained by Richard Curtiss, a retired US diplomat, Israel's American supporters learned early on that there was a powerful way to skin the campaign finance legal cat. Their major weapon was what Curtiss labeled "stealth PACs," which employed to great effect the now well-known practice of "bundling." Again, no law prohibits a group of individuals from lumping together or "bundling" their contributions for greater effect. Thus, a family of five in 1974, for example, could end up providing up to $10,000 in campaign contributions to a single candidate in any one electoral cycle.

The practice of "bundling" became more generally established in 1994. Checks written by individual donors are collected by a PAC or lobby representatives and then presented in a bundle to specific candidates. All kinds of "special interest" actors and groups engage in this practice. When I broached this topic in one of my college courses, for example, a nontraditional student with many years of high-level experience in banking spoke of how her workplace superiors routinely pressured her and her peers to write checks that were "bundled" for campaign finance purposes. In short, the practice is widespread and fairly long-standing

What Curtiss helped highlight was how a new set of "stealth PACs" had cropped up; that is, PACs designed to garner financial support for "pro-Israel" candidates on the down low. Curtiss drew heavily upon the painstaking research of Edward Roeder (1984) and Edward Zuckerman (1986, 1988), who were intrigued by the rapid growth of PACs in the early 1980s. Both researchers had independently discovered the presence of numerous PACs that "had neither explicit titles nor 'sponsors.'"[46] Moreover, both researchers had noticed that whereas in the 1982 elections there were many PACs with titles clearly indicating their support for Israel, these PACs had virtually disappeared by the 1984 election cycle. Roeder, for example, discovered that 54 of the "not so readily identifiable" PACs were "pro-Israel" PACs that had collectively raised more than $4 million by mid-summer 1984. By studying the flow of PAC money to congressional candidate Richard Durbin of Illinois across the 1982 and 1984 elections, Zuckerman arrived at the same conclusion as Roeder about the concealed identities of these new PACs. They then found further confirmation of their findings via scrutiny of PAC contributions to other candidates in elections of significance to Israel's supporters.

As Roeder wrote in an October 15, 1984, article in the WRMEA:

> One former official of a pro-Israel PAC, who asked not to be identified, told of being criticized and chastised by officials of another pro-Israel PAC for choosing a PAC name that merely suggested the PAC's link to American Jewry. Leaders of the other PACs appeared to be concerned about being out front with the name Jewish in it. They're afraid of the appearance of being tagged as part of the "all-powerful Jewish Lobby."[47]

By 1986, the number of pro-Israel PACs had grown to 94. They had collected some $8,154,211 in funds, and made donations totaling $4,609,984 to 420 candidates.[48] During the 1988 elections, some 78 pro-Israel PACs made $5,432,055 in direct donations to 479 congressional candidates, a figure representing 12 percent of all PAC contributions to congressional candidates.[49] As Curtiss observed, "Whereas all other PACs are limited to contributing $10,000 to a candidate in an election year, the pro-Israel PACs provide whatever they believe the candidate needs to win an election. As the record shows, contributions in the neighborhood of $50,000 to House candidates, five times the maximum that the law permits, and of a quarter million dollars to Senate candidates, 25 time the legally permissible amount, were not uncommon in 1988."[50]

It is difficult to establish exactly how many "pro-Israel" PACs have come into operation in any given year because the names foster a "stealth-like" profile by avoiding references to Israel, like the Sunshine PAC in Florida. Similar PACs are dissolved, and new ones are created with new names. One need only take a quick look at the websites of the Florida Congressional Committee PAC,[51] the Desert Caucus,[52] or the Midwest-based To Protect Our Heritage PAC[53] to get a taste of some PACs' activities, including their fund-raising success and impressive events schedule of congressional speakers. One can then think of these PACs' activities as being replicated in many parts of the country to get a fuller sense of their proliferation and nationwide level of significance. A rough estimate of the number for the 2012 electoral cycle is over 30.

Do these "pro-Israel" PACs have connections to known lobbies or "special interests"? Neve Gordon insightfully observed: "Many of the pro-Israel PACs are connected to the American Israel Public Affairs Committee (AIPAC), [described in the latter 1990s as] a 'middle-of-the-road' Jewish organization with an annual budget of about $15 million, five or six registered lobbyists and a staff of around 150 people. As with other lobbying groups, AIPAC's major objective is to pressure members of Congress to vote according to its recommendations, helping to reelect incumbents who have a 'good' voting record, while 'punishing' those who don't by funding an electable opponent."[54] And as J.J. Goldberg put it, "The pro-Israel lobby is able to wield much greater influence than any other narrow-issue interest group because the distribution of funds of many of the so-called pro-Israel PACs was—and—is coordinated by AIPAC."[55] By 2008, according to the *New York Times*, AIPAC had a $100 million endowment, over 100,000 members nationwide, and spent $1 million annually on lobbying Congress.[56] Guesstimates of its annual operating budget run as high as $70 million.[57] As discussed more fully later, AIPAC is not a PAC; it doesn't make campaign finance donations. As an organization registered as a 401(c)4 group, it is legally barred from doing so. That said, as the *Wall Street Journal* reported, many of the PACs "which draw money from Jewish donors and operate under obscure-sounding names—are operated by AIPAC officials or people who hold seats on AIPAC's two major policy-making bodies."[58]

As a current, multi-term House member told me, "Special interest groups put you through a rigorous vetting process and without a doubt the most engaged group is AIPAC and its supporters. Early on, you get a call requesting you sit down with an AIPAC member in your district, and he or she will ask your position on a long list of issues. Then you get invited to a big regional dinner, like in Boston or New York City; and it's asserted early on at these dinners that 'so-and-so' would like to have a fundraiser for you. This is how it's done."

In recent years, the Center for Responsive Politics (CRP) shook off its initial reluctance to associate AIPAC with campaign financing, despite AIPAC's long-standing insistence that it plays no direct role in such matters.[59] Practicing due diligence, the CRP staff back-checked data to track AIPAC lobbying expenditures from 1998 forward.

Perusal of the center's data for 2010 campaign spending reveals that of the $3.9 million spent by "pro-Israel" groups, AIPAC directed contributions accounting for over $2.7 million of that total. In addition, the even more hard-line Zionist Organization of America (ZOA) ponied up $299,100 in 2010, and significant donations were registered by other right wing groups as well. By comparison, the more pro-peace pro-Israel group J Street provided $520,000, while the (self-described) leftist and strongly pro–two state, pro-Israel organization Americans for Peace Now (APN) spent $80,000.[61] As the folks from CRP state—see endnote 35—these figures all potentially err on the side of conservative estimations.

While AIPAC has tried to obfuscate or disclaim its role in campaign contributions, the J Street PAC has seemingly adopted the opposite approach. According to its website, JStreetPAC had a very successful 2008 cycle, endorsing 41 candidates—33 of whom were successful. The PAC distributed more than $575,000 to its endorsees, making it the largest pro-Israel PAC on record. According to JStreetPAC's FEC filings, however, its direct contributions to 2008 candidates totaled a mere $44,521, making it the twenty-second largest pro-Israel PAC in that year. In other words, and in no way to detract from its significance, JStreetPAC only served as a conduit for more than the roughly $500,000 difference.[62]

Although the practice of "bundling" has continued until recent times, it was rendered somewhat obsolete by the 2010 Supreme Court ruling in *Citizens United v. Federal Election Commission*, in which laws prohibiting corporate and union political expenditures were deemed unconstitutional. Legal donations by individuals were also raised so that, by 2011–12, a single individual could donate $2,500 to a federal candidate per election, and make a biennial aggregate contribution of $117,000 to an individual candidate via national, state, and local party committees and federal PACs. And changes in FEC regulations in July 2010 allow new SuperPACs to spend unlimited amounts of money on elections; they simply have to refrain from providing direct support to candidates, and cannot coordinate their expenditures with the campaign staffs of the candidates.

Heavy "pro-Israel" spending does not guarantee victory, as evidenced in the aforementioned 2004 Pete Sessions versus Martin Frost contest in Texas. Interestingly, both candidates were regarded as strongly "pro-Israel," but Martin Frost had already established his pro-Israel bona fides during his 13 terms in office and, perhaps because of his Jewish roots, garnered even stronger financial support from pro-Israel backers in his attempt to retain his incumbency. Frost was fighting an uphill battle, however; the district in which he was competing was "configured" to enhance a Republican's chances of victory. So despite huge AIPAC-orchestrated support, Frost went down. Not to worry, from a right wing pro-Israel perspective; Sessions has remained a very strong supporter of Israel.

A more recent "failure" came with the campaign assistance provided by Sheldon Adelson and his wife to 2012 presidential hopeful former Speaker of the House Newt Gingrich. Although I'm now partially stepping outside the "congressional parameters" of my project, as the reader will see, the case is too enlightening to leave unmentioned because it shows how mega-rich individuals can far exceed expenditures by entire categories of donors and PACs, and how this behavior touches on Mideast policymaking.

In January 2012, Adelson, who became a billionaire through moving from computer trade shows to ownership of major casinos, provided a $5 million contribution to a pro–Newt Gingrich SuperPAC called Winning Our Future, with another $5 million kicked in by his Israeli wife, Miriam. The Adelsons eventually injected another $10 million into Gingrich's campaign. At one point, Adelson was quoted as saying that he would happily spend up to $100 million to assist Gingrich's presidential bid to oust Pres. Obama; along the way, Adelson was perhaps partially inspired by (or inspired?) Gingrich's description of Palestinians as "an invented people." With Gingrich's failure, Adelson shifted his attention to the Republican nominee Mitt Romney, whose pro-Israel views were also widely seen as more hardcore than those of Pres. Obama. The Adelsons ponied up at least $10 million to Romney's Restore Our Future SuperPAC. All told, they are thought to have spent $98 million on the 2012 election cycle, of which millions went to some 34 different candidates and groups.

In "truth is more amazing than fiction" fashion, Adelson also almost failed in another pursuit; that is, his long-standing effort to defeat Nevada Congresswoman Shelley Berkley. Of course, Berkley stands, or sits, on the wrong side of the partisan divide from Adelson's perspective, but what makes his consistent opposition to her candidacy confusing—she ran for the US Senate in 2012—is that she was easily counted among the most heavily right wing supporters of Israel in all of Congress. Personal animus was at play here, with Adelson's anti-Berkley commitment deriving in part from the fact that while Berkley was serving as Adelson's employee and legal counsel, it became public knowledge that she had allegedly encouraged Adelson to shower his largesse on local judges and political figures in hopes that they would look more favorably upon his business transactions. Adelson has apparently never forgiven this faux pas, alongside Berkley's other "negatives." But in the end, the $4 million Adelson provided Berkley's opponent, Republican Dean Heller, combined with the $6.6 million of indirect support received out of at least $23 million Adelson gave Karl Rove's Crossroads GPS SuperPAC, helped Adelson garner at least one major electoral victory. And Senator Heller has not disappointed Adelson on Israel. All told, including so-called dark money, some believe the Adelsons may have spent up to $150 million on 2012 candidates, of which, I will also note here, $6.5 million for the right wing pro-Israel Republican Jewish Coalition, $5 million for the Congressional Leadership Fund, and another $5 million for the Congress-focused YG Fund.[63]

Also worthy of commentary is the funding provided to J Street by the Hungarian-born Holocaust survivor and Jewish American billionaire businessman George Soros. Established in 2008, primarily by Jewish Americans, J Street strongly advocates a "two state solution," is critical of hard-line, right wing Israeli government policy, and has begun to provide significant funding for political candidates through its affiliated JStreetPAC. J Street initially denied

Soros's contributions, getting egg on its face when it was eventually forced to fess up to Soros's help. As noted by Ben Smith in *Politico*, "Soros's views on Israel have put him outside the mainstream of American Jewish politics for a while, both because he's left of center—though he's not alone there—and because he has no particular warmth for Israel. 'I don't deny the Jews their right to a national existence—but I don't want to be part of it,' he told the *New Yorker* a few years ago, suggesting that Jews should overcoming [sic] anti-Semitism by 'giv[ing] up on the tribalness.'"[64] Soros and his children provided $245,000 to J Street roughly two months after its founding in the summer of 2008, and another $500,000 by fall 2010.[65] Staffers discussing the balance of campaign finance forces in spring 2012 did indicate that, with time, support for J Street and other moderate, pro-peace groups could make a difference "if it was not already too late to obtain a two-state solution" for the I-P conflict.

On balance, money from Jewish American heavy donors has moved in a more conservative direction. Neve Gordon noted that, "although the majority of Jews vote for Democratic candidates, by 1996 'Jewish PAC money was going to Republicans over Democrats by a six-to-four margin.'"[66] And this shift in the direction of supporting Republicans has increased over time, as showcased by the campaign finance behavior of Sheldon Adelson and others discussed below, such as Irving Moskowitz.

"PRO-ARAB" AND OTHERS' DONATIONS: THE ABSENCE OF COUNTERVAILING INFLUENCE

Compared to "pro-Israel" funding, what "pro-Arab" and "pro-Iranian" donors bring to the campaign finance table has been peanuts. Four (out of a total of seven) pro-Arab PACs hit a contribution high of $61,147 for the 1985–86 election cycle, but never exceeded $39,000 for any of the other cycles between 1983–84 and 1989–90.[67] Not all that much has changed with the passage of time. Between the 1990 and 2002 campaign seasons, "pro-Arab" interests combined contributed just $297,000.[68] In the 2004 electoral cycle, the Arab American Leadership Council PAC—one of only two Arab American PACs at the time, and the only one to contribute—made $109,000 in contributions to some 42 candidates, with the largest contribution to an individual candidate being $6,000 for Jim Moran (Virginia).[69] For the period from 1998 to 2012, it's actually difficult to ascertain "pro-Arab" campaign expenditures because they were so small during this time frame that they did not appear on the radar of major watchdog organizations like the Center for Responsive Politics. (CRP did report that Arab American and Iranian American PACs combined contributed a grand total of $69,950 to congressional candidates in 2010.)[70] However, the staff at the Washington Report on Middle East Affairs (WRMEA) has tracked the numbers assiduously, and they noted in spring 2011 that "the small number of Arab- and Muslim-American PACs contributed . . . $36,500 to candidates in 2010; and since 1972 . . . Arab- and Muslim-American PACS have donated less than $700,000."[71]

As noted earlier, three "pro-Arab" PACs (Arab American Leadership PAC, Arab American PAC, and Americans for a Palestinian State), along with one Iranian American PAC, spent a grand total of $69,950 assisting candidates in 2010. Even if combined with the spending by J Street and APN, these totals pale in comparison to conservative, right wing "pro-Israel" contributors.

Here's how Khalil Jahshan, former director of the National Arab American Association (NAAA), discussed these matters with me in 2006.

> As I reflect on it now, this is really a structural problem not just related to this area. We've become a country where policy is for sale, but this is especially true of foreign policy. Things are not done in the national interest. But there are major reasons for Arab Americans' failure, beginning with participation—you need people and money. There are 5.3–5.9 million American Jews, with over two million active members, AIPAC, the American Jewish Committee . . . one-third of American Jews are engaged in pro-Israel activities. We are only 2.5–3 million [Arab Americans]; just one-half the size, but out of this, we don't have one out of 300 involved. Maybe at best we have 50,000–75,000 active Arab participants. Before, the religious factor—Christian versus Muslim Arabs—didn't matter, but it does now. There were complaints that most leaders were Christian, even though two-thirds of Arab Americans are Christians. But perhaps more importantly, the community just doesn't contribute. There is just $.5 to $1 million per year for Arab organizations. When NAAA folded in 1999–2000 and merged with ADC, our budget at its height was just several million dollars. The Arab community has never

been able to sustain its organizations. So you get $12–$15 million pro-Israel on the Jewish side alone to congressional campaigns versus $250,000–$500,000 per year from the Arab side. So there's no need for conspiratorial talk at all; it's just money and mobilization. For us, we're lucky if we could mobilize 40 percent of the people, but we still wouldn't get more than 5 percent making a financial contribution.

Later in our interview, Khalil Jahshan added, "Just note the increasing role of money: it used to cost $750,000 for a Senate race; now it costs $20–$30 million. There's no conspiratorial effort here, it's just the new cost of the game. When meeting with congressmen, they'd say, 'you're very persuasive, etc., but you can't compete for votes without money.' One prominent congressperson told me, 'You know, I agree with a lot you have to say, but you've got to show me your green side.' Our problem is that the [Arab American] community doesn't contribute."[72]

So as regards campaign financial assistance, pro-Arab and/or pro-Palestinian interests have offered almost no competition. While there are dozens of "pro-Israel" PACs influencing the Washington scene, there is only a handful of "pro-Arab" or Muslim competitors. For many years, there were just two organizations with a record of lobbying for the Arab and Muslim communities, the NAAA and the American Muslim Council, and neither group spent more than $14,000 in any single year between 1997 and 2001.[73] The NAAA became defunct when it merged with the American Arab Anti-Discrimination Committee (ADC) in 1999. The Arab American Leadership PAC, the political arm of James Zogby's Arab American Institute, stepped into the fray in 1996, and in 2002 was renamed the Arab American Leadership Council Political Action Committee. It remains a relatively small player. In 2009, the New Policy PAC was created, but to date it remains small, virtually unknown, and ineffectual.

Engaging in a Google search for "pro-Arab" campaign financing can yield meager, even ironic results. A few years back, one of the more prominent results I came across was a report on an article allegedly written by the celebrated *New York Times* columnist Maureen Dowd, entitled "Obama's Troubling Internet Fund Raising." Dated June 29, 2008, the article claimed that the huge influx of small donations to the Obama campaign had been orchestrated by highly sophisticated Internet users in Saudi Arabia, Iran, and other Middle East countries.[74] The article, including use of Dowd's name, was completely contrived, a total hoax.

Another prominently featured Google item, discovered during the same search, had as its headline "Arab Americans seek apology from McCain campaign." It was perhaps more emblematic of the travails of Arab American fund-raising. The article, completely factual, read as follows:

> The McCain presidential campaign made a major strategic error this week insulting the Arab American community when it cut a community leader and politically active Arab American Republican from its Michigan finance committee. The decision to remove Mr. Ali Jawad from the campaign effort came after protestations from a discredited blogger known for her hate language and ignorant rants against Arab Americans, American Muslims, the religion of Islam and American officials and public figures with whom she disagrees. . . . On Monday at 2:30 p.m., the leadership of the Arab American community held a press conference at the Lebanese American Heritage Club . . . in Dearborn to call on the McCain campaign for an apology for their hasty and insulting decision.
>
> Ali Jawad, president of Armada Oil & Gas Company and founder of the Lebanese American Heritage Club, was cut from the campaign because of rumors begun by the discredited blogger that he has ties to Hizbullah. Jawad was one of six finance committee members listed in an invitation for a $2,300-per-ticket McCain fund-raising event . . .
>
> "The Michigan Republican Party and the McCain campaign need to be reminded that the blood of Arabs is red and the color of their money is green," said Osama Siblani, president of the Arab American Political Action Committee (AAPAC).[75]

A relatively recent and comparable development occurred in conjunction with the appearance of the first successful Muslim American congressional candidates. There were reports that members of the Council on American-Islamic Relations (CAIR) provided campaign funding to Keith Ellison, perhaps in excess of $10,000.[76] Ellison was the first Muslim American elected to Congress, representing the Fifth District of Minnesota (Minneapolis and suburbs). Another report suggested that Ellison may have obtained support, perhaps in the low thousands of dollars, from American organizations with Muslim Brotherhood ties.[77] These reports also featured attempts to associate Ellison with Islamist extremists—i.e., terrorists. None of these reports was substantiated, and Ellison has so far proven capable of withstanding these attacks.

These stories remind me of another recounted to me by AAI's James Zogby, who provided greater historical context. Zogby said: "Many years ago, I contacted Rep. Ed Schau [R-California] who was running against Sen. Alan Cranston. He told me to tell the Arab community to keep away. He said: 'If I get $5,000 from Arab Americans, then Jewish Americans will spend $500,000 against me.' So I told people to forget about him; write him off."

In brief, funding for some Muslim and Arab candidates is easily and readily smeared and stigmatized, often with no basis in reality. Meanwhile, funding for right wing pro-Israel candidates, some of it from sources strongly opposed to official US Mideast government policy based in international law—such as the money provided by Sheldon Adelson to Newt Gingrich, or by Irving Moskowitz to Rep. Ileana Ros-Lehtinen of Florida—is courted and pocketed without repercussions.

This is not to say that the "Arab position" has been everywhere helpless. For example, due to congressional redistricting in New Jersey prior to the 2012 election, Democrat Rep. Steven Rothman calculated his chances of reelection to Congress would be greater if he moved out of his now heavily Republican district and attempted to defeat his erstwhile fellow Democrat and friend Rep. Bill Pascrell. Although Pascrell's pro-Israel voting record was nearly identical to Rothman's, the Rothman campaign tried to paint Pascrell as an anti-Semite and soft on Arabs and Muslims. Pascrell had stood up for the latter's rights, which had come under assault in the post–9/11 environment. Rothman's backers urged Orthodox Jewish Republicans to register as Democrats so that they could cross over and vote for Rothman in the primary.

A wealthy Palestinian American, Dr. Aref Assaf, took note and penned articles in district newspapers that went far in mobilizing Arab and Muslim constituents to register and turn out in unprecedented fashion in the district's largest city, Paterson, thereby contributing significantly to Pascrell's victory. To the best of my knowledge, the Arab American Institute assisted in this effort. This demonstrated that grassroots initiatives can still trump money the old-fashioned way, mobilizing human resources and getting out the vote. But, on balance, the barriers to congressional victory are much higher for candidates willing to criticize Israeli government policies.

ARE THESE SIGNIFICANT DONATIONS?

Are campaign finance donations motivated by Middle East concerns significant? Do they get the attention of congressional contenders? In the early years of its existence, the CRP listed pro-Israel campaign finance contributions in a category labeled "Top Industries," alongside such major donor sectors as "Health Professionals," "Lawyers/Law Firms," "Insurance," "Real Estate," "Commercial Banks," "Securities & Investments," and "Automotive." As a source of campaign funds, "Pro-Israel" actually ranks quite prominently on a number of candidates' lists. For example, in 2004 "Pro-Israel" was thirteenth on former Senator Tom Daschle's list of "Industry" contributors, twentieth on soon-to-be Senate Majority leader Bill Frist's, and seventh on Representative Steny Hoyer's. Comparable examples abound and are readily found at CRP's OpenSecrets.org website.

Illustrating just how much more "pro-Israel" PACs were contributing than PACs of other issue domains, Neve Gordon noted that, in 1990, "Some 95 pro-Israel PACs gave a total of $4,948,934 to congressional candidates, while PACs opposed to gun control [like the NRA] gave a mere $914,000, and those on both sides of the abortion issue gave $747,000.[78] Interestingly and importantly, during the 2000–2012 time frame, "pro-Israel" PACs' expenditures continued to outpace spending by lobbyists on such hot button issues as abortion policy and gun control. As regards abortion, from 1999–2012 "pro-choice" and "pro-life" expenditures averaged $1.11 million and $450,000 per electoral cycle, respectively, for an average total of $1.56 million per cycle.[79] "Gun rights" advocates contributed $1.6 million per electoral cycle on average, while "gun control" proponents averaged $100,000 over the same time period. So the *combined* contributions of proponents and exponents on each of the abortion policy and gun legislation issues averaged $1.56 and $1.70 million respectively per electoral cycle, while "pro-Israel" contributions alone averaged $2.87 million per cycle over this period.[80]

It is intriguing to note that in the 2012 election cycle, the results of which put in place the Congress that shot down the "gun control" aspirations of over 90 percent of the American public, "gun rights" advocates spent over $1.53 million backing federal candidates while, by comparison, pro-Israel PACs spent $2.98 million on federal candidates (a figure that is less than for each of the previous four election cycles).[81]

Chapter Two

GETTING REELECTED TO CONGRESS, OR NOT

*"There were real cases of incumbents being targeted, like Findley and Percy.
Or look at [Sen. Charles] 'Mac' Mathias's case. Mathias and McCloskey; they
were mainstream. Mathias, they went after him; this was in the early 1980s. See
Mathias's Foreign Affairs criticism of the lobby; he was beginning to open his
mouth and they decided to shut him up."*
—Khalil Jahshan in 2005

*"There is much talk about AIPAC's power—the McKinney and Hilliard cases.
AIPAC takes the credit. They say, 'Look, this is what we do to our opponents.'
Their strategy is to pick the weak deer out of the herd. They did pour money
against Dingell but lost. They build up perceptions of their power."*
—David Dumke (former House staffer)

It is not much of an exaggeration to state that the day after first-time vic-
tors are elected to the House of Representatives, nearly all of them begin
thinking about what they'll need to do to ensure reelection. And no matter
what advantages of incumbency are bestowed upon them, they must remain
vigilant against powerful opposition interest groups seeking to engineer their
demise just two years down the road.

How real is the electoral power of conservative, hard-line, pro-Israel
groups? As reflected in the quotes above, there are divergent views on this
question. Most cognoscenti, however, concur that the electoral power of such
groups is great. They also agree that AIPAC is far and away the group feared
most by members of Congress with alternative views.

Sen. Charles Percy; Rep. Paul Findley; Rep. Pete McCloskey; Rep. Cynthia
McKinney; Rep. Earl Hilliard. Before 2006, these are the individuals whose

names were mentioned to me most often in the mid-2000s by older staffers and longtime observers of Congress and congressional elections as object lessons. As one put it, "You cross AIPAC or the right wing, staunchly pro-Israel special interests, and you risk being made to pay a heavy price." The Percy, Findley, and McCloskey cases are now somewhat dated, but anyone would still benefit from a look at former Rep. Findley's 1985 book, *They Dare to Speak Out*, in which he discusses those cases and others. Of more recent vintage, the two most commonly cited cases of incumbents angering "pro-Israeli" interests at the time of my 2005–2006 interviews were those of Cynthia McKinney and Earl Hilliard. In the mid-2000s, both cases were immediately recognizable to any staffer interviewee with a modicum of experience on Capitol Hill.

Cynthia McKinney (D-GA) had raised the ire of Israel's right wing supporters by repeatedly adopting a strongly sympathetic posture vis-à-vis the Palestinians. (She is the only congressperson ever described to me by a staffer as being "anti-Israel.") In consequence, AIPAC and other organizations targeted Rep. McKinney during her 2002 campaign for reelection in the heavily African-American 4th district in Georgia. Pro-Israel interests provided some $52,000 in support to Denise Majette, which assisted Majette in defeating McKinney in the Democratic primary. McKinney's election woes were greatly compounded when her father, responding to media queries about her primary election defeat, waxed anti-Semitic in pronouncing that her problems could be spelled out quite simply: "Jews have bought everybody. Jews. J-E-W-S."

Pro-Israel interests' support for Majette, combined with a media campaign against McKinney, were seen by many observers as constituting major factors in McKinney's defeat.[82] Certainly, another major factor was that Georgia's open primary system allowed Republicans to cross over to vote against McKinney, and also that many voters saw McKinney as too much of a loose cannon. One staunchly "pro-Arab" spokesman even noted, "The McKinney case was actually not as decisive as the Findley and Percy ones; McKinney was a fringe member; she was too aggressive."[83] In addition, McKinney had also been one of the House's most consistent foes of the Bush administration's agenda over the free trade issue, which angered some voters. These factors noted, there is no gainsaying the significance of pro-Israel support for McKinney's challenger, and, importantly, the lasting perception on Capitol Hill that she was "done in" by pro-Israel forces.

During my 2005–2006 interviews, the second most cited case was that of

Earl Hilliard (D) of Alabama's 7th district. Hilliard earned the disapproval of right wing pro-Israel support groups by voting against full funding for Israel, as well as for opposing the criminalization of certain Palestinian political figures. In his 2002 House primary election campaign, Hilliard went down in a narrow defeat against another African American named Artur Davis, who had received an estimated $206,595 in donations from pro-Israeli groups, according to a conservative estimate made by CRP.[84] According to Eric Fleischauer of the *Decatur Daily*, "Seventy-six percent of Davis' contributions during the 2002 election cycle came from outside Alabama, most from New York City."[85] Indeed, Fleischauer noted that by May 15, 2002, Davis had received $446,821 in campaign contributions, and of the 517 individual contributors, only four were Alabamians.[86]

According to one report, there was more at stake here than Hilliard's "anti-Israel" voting record; many home voters were angered by 2001 allegations of ethics violations, and nationwide business interests teamed up against him because he was seen, much as was McKinney, as too hostile to the promotion of free trade.[87] But once again, the Hilliard case went down on the Hill as a "You cross 'em, you pay the price" phenomenon.

In response to John Mearsheimer and Stephen Walt's book *The Israel Lobby*, Jerome Slater forwarded a thorough and thoughtful examination of many of their major assertions, including the notion that candidates experience strong pressure from pro-Israel lobbyists to toe a pro-Israel line.[88] He examined nine such cases, including several of those mentioned above: Sen. J. William Fulbright (1982; Arkansas), Sen. Adlai Stevenson's gubernatorial bid (1982; Illinois), Rep. Paul Findley (1982; Illinois), Paul McCloskey (1982; California), Sen. Roger Jepsen (1984; Iowa), Sen. Charles Percy (1984; Illinois), Rep. Earl Hilliard (2002; Alabama), Rep. Cynthia McKinney (2002; Georgia), and Sen. Lincoln Chafee (2006; Rhode Island). For each of these cases, Slater found "no compelling evidence" that these candidates' losses could be attributed primarily to their having been targeted by a pro-Israel lobby, and he presented cogent arguments, citing alternative factors, to explain their defeats.[89]

As one would deduce from my discussions of several of these cases, I agree with Slater's assessment. But what Slater himself acknowledges is that the perception of creating a negative backlash from, or attacks by, right wing pro-Israel interest groups must be taken seriously, however difficult the effect of such backlash is to measure or to get candidates to speak candidly about.

Through my off-the-record interviews with scores of congressional staffers, I can assure the reader that this perception, this fear, is pronounced among a very high percentage of congresspersons. A great number of staffers either made unsolicited, explicit assertions or subscribed readily to the idea that to oppose AIPAC on recent Israeli government policy would constitute "the kiss of death" and is "simply not worth the risk." And as Slater himself wrote:

> In the final analysis, it is not easy to determine the actual power of the Israel lobby to affect congressional elections. On the one hand (as I have argued), there appear to be few cases in which the lobby's opposition to congressional candidates was clearly the determining factor in their defeat. On the other hand, it is certainly plausible that because congressmen have nothing to gain and possibly much to lose by opposing Israel or the lobby, the perception that it is to be feared evidently gives it real power—as Senator Alan Cranston put it, the defeat of Senator Jepsen in 1984 "struck terror into the hearts of senators" on Middle East issues (quoted in Israel Lobby, 158). Similarly, J. J. Goldberg concluded that the lobby's success in defeating congressional candidates "has only happened a handful of times, mostly in the early and mid-1980s . . . But that was all that was needed to make the point." In sum, then, the presumed power of the Israel lobby to swing elections clearly gives it real power in Congress; nonetheless, the Israel Lobby (and many other accounts) exaggerates its actual power to do so.[90]

Let me word this one final way: the perception of AIPAC's ability to make incumbents "pay a heavy price for crossing its wishes" is so widespread and rock solid that, even if it were erroneous, most congressional actors behave as though that perception is reality. The Arab American Institute's James Zogby was very quick to inform me that domestic factors caused Findley, Percy, Hilliard, McKinney and others to lose, but as he added: "So the myth is greater than reality, but it's enough to shape reality."

A LOOK AT OTHER CASES FROM THE 2006, 2010, AND 2012 ELECTION YEARS

The introductory paragraph of AIPAC's 2006 election guide, the *Insider*, states:

. . . our work with the Congress and Administration continues to be critically important. As a result of announced retirements by sitting members of Congress, we already know that there will be dozens of new faces in the 110th Congress. We also know that several of Israel's staunchest allies in Congress are facing tough bids for reelection. With narrow margins separating the parties on Capitol Hill and a volatile political environment, we must be prepared for any and all changes. Your willingness at this time to build relationships with Members of Congress and candidates is essential to maintaining and strengthening the relationship between the United States and Israel.[91]

The guide's contents provide a breakdown of Senate and House races categorized as "Highly Vulnerable," "Potentially Vulnerable," "Open Seats," and "Possible Open Seats." For each incumbent candidate, the guide presents a description of the candidate's position, as well as a chart indicating how the congressperson has voted over time on key letters, resolutions, and bills relating to Israel's concerns. The descriptions do not offer explicit instructions on whether to vote for or against a particular candidate, as this would constitute a clear violation of AIPAC's 501(c)(4) legal status. However, the voting record charts are widely perceived as constituting a scorecard, thereby transgressing the *Insider*'s assertion on the guide's introductory page that "we [AIPAC] do not rate or endorse candidates." In addition to these descriptions and scorecards, the guide also presents information on the candidates' status regarding funds raised, disbursed, and cash on hand. Finally, as noted on its introductory page, the guide is updated and new editions appear in the run-up to any election to keep AIPAC's membership fully informed of changes in the candidates' status. I leave it to you, the reader, to imagine how members are expected to respond to AIPAC's appeal to display their "willingness at this time to build relationships with Members of Congress and candidates . . ."

So let's look at a few cases, beginning with how Rep. John Hostettler (R-Indiana) was scored in the spring 2006 AIPAC *Insider*.[92] A staunchly conservative Baptist and Christian Coalition type, Hostettler had voted for several AIPAC-endorsed items, including the 2003 Syria Accountability Act (SAA) and the 2004 Principles for Peace Resolution, and he had even cosponsored other AIPAC-endorsed bills. But his voting record on foreign aid was "mixed"—he had consistently voted against foreign aid to Israel since 1998—and he declined to support many other AIPAC-endorsed letters and resolutions.[93] In consequence, he was targeted for defeat by right wing pro-Israel forces. Hostettler's victorious opponent, Brad Ellsworth, was on the receiving end of $48,750 from pro-Israel groups, making him the second largest House recipient of "pro-Israel" funding in 2006 (after Mark Kirk).

Rhode Island Sen. Lincoln Chafee's 2006 AIPAC scorecard similarly reflected a Bronx cheer on items of concern to AIPAC. While he signed on to several AIPAC-endorsed letters and resolutions, he voted against the SAA, a major bill, and refused to either sign or cosponsor as many AIPAC-endorsed letters and resolutions as those he supported.[94] Sen. John Sununu's 2008 scorecard also showed a bleak performance from AIPAC's vantage point. With the exception of voting for the 2003 SAA and cosponsoring the 2004 Iran Resolution, he refused to sign and/or cosponsor all the other items scored by AIPAC and voted against the 2004 Peace Process Principles Resolution.[95] Both Chafee and Sununu, who at the time were seen by staffers as #1 and #2 respectively in the Senate as most understanding of moderate Arab and Palestinians' grievances, lost their bids for reelection, and both of their opponents were recipients of significant "pro-Israel" campaign funding.

During the 2010 election cycle, eyebrows were once again raised over right wing pro-Israeli groups' election-time influence, but there was a new twist to the campaign jousting. In several races, longtime staunch supporters of Israel, congresspersons with impeccable pro-Israel voting records, had to compete against even more right wing "pro-Israel" candidates. Prime examples included Rep. Jan Schakowsky (D) of Illinois and Joe Sestak (D) of Pennsylvania. Let's look at their cases in reverse order.

Sestak, a 30-year navy veteran who retired with the rank of vice admiral, won election to the House in 2007 and launched a Senate bid in 2009. His opponent, Rep. Pat Toomey (R), presented himself as an Israeli hard-liner, blasting the Obama administration for its "unusually harsh" treatment of Israel.[96] The contest was billed by the *Jewish Week* (of New York) as a test of power pitting J Street, supporting Sestak, against AIPAC and other right wing forces, supporting Toomey.[97] During the campaign, Sestak faced repeated claims, which he termed "mendacious," against his commitment to Israel. An article written by Bryan Schwartzman for the *Jewish Exponent*, offers insight to what Sestak encountered.

A new effort to attack US Rep. Joe Sestak's record on Israel has gone viral. A debate that has long been playing out in the pages of the *Jewish Exponent* has now made its way to MSNBCs *Morning Joe*, and Web sites such as *Politico*, the *Atlantic*, *Commentary*, The Huffington Post, and YouTube. But the stakes are now higher for Sestak, the Democratic nominee going up against Republican Pat Toomey for Pennsylvania's junior Senate seat in the November election. At the centerpiece of the new campaign against Sestak is a television ad sponsored by a prominent group of Jews and Evangelical Christians calling itself the Emergency Committee for Israel. The ad . . . highlights an appearance he made before a controversial Muslim group in 2007 and criticizes him . . . for condemning Israel's blockade of Gaza in a Jan. 21 letter signed by 54 Democrats and for refusing to sign a letter drafted by the American Israel Public Affairs Committee asserting US support for Israel.[98]

Sestak responded to these attacks by meeting with a large group of Jewish leaders held by the Jewish Federation of Greater Philadelphia. He also launched his own ad campaign, asserting that "According to AIPAC, Joe Sestak has a 100 percent pro-Israel voting record."[99] Not so fast, responded an AIPAC spokesman, Josh Block: "Joe Sestak does not have a 100 percent voting record on Israel issues according to AIPAC. It couldn't be true, we don't rate or endorse candidates."[100] Could Block have forgotten about his own organization's repeated publication of the AIPAC *Insider?* In any event, "'You look at my voting record and AIPAC says it's perfect,' [Sestak had] told the Orthodox Union . . . '*There's no letter that I ever sign or don't sign that I don't contact AIPAC. That's just the way it is, you know,*' he told the Jewish group. 'My voting record is right down the line.'"[101] [Italics mine.] Sestak, despite continued backing by some pro-Israel sources,[102] lost by a narrow margin. Toomey won 51.1 percent of the vote, and it's hard to imagine that strong media support and campaign finance assistance from pro-Israel conservatives did not help tip the balance.[103] And Sen. Toomey has consistently proven his loyalty to AIPAC since taking office.

In Illinois, Congresswoman Jan Schakowsky should have had every reason to believe that she was "bulletproof" when it came to her stance on Israel. Not so. Even if she enjoyed solid support from AIPAC, challenges from even harder right wing elements were in the offing. Thus, in her 2010 House race against Joel Pollak (R), Pollak repeatedly accused her of being weak on Israel, remarking that at a debate between the two: "Schakowsky ended [one debate] by noting one common opinion she shared with Pollak: 'There is one issue on which Joel and I agree, and that is the importance of supporting the state of Israel.' In the past, Pollak had publicly challenged the congresswoman's commitment to the safety and security of Israel, a sensitive issue among the district's Jewish voters. When Pollak responded, he noted, 'She wants to appease America's enemies. I believe in standing up for our allies.'"[104]

Even after his defeat, Pollak did not relent. He accused Schakowsky of invoking anti-Orthodox (Jewish) stereotypes against him and reiterated his charges that Schakowsky was bad for Israel. The Schakowsky-Pollak campaign provided interesting insight to the new dynamic of hard right wing challenges to solidly "pro-Israel" candidates.[105]

Another interesting 2010 example came in the form of Republican Mark Reed's challenge to incumbent Rep. Brad Sherman (D) in California's 27th district. Reed, a Native American with Mohawk and Apache family roots, "chastise[d] Sherman, the consummate Israel/AIPAC loyalist, for not being Israel-loyal enough. Reed admonished Sherman for not taking the Obama administration to task for what Reed believed was Obama's disregard for Israel and its leaders."[106] Reed's website castigated the Obama administration inter alia for the following reasons:

- Support for multinational resolutions to strip Israel of nuclear weapons
- Refusal to approve any major Israeli requests for US weapons platforms or advanced systems
- For the first time in recent US history, the US government actually sold weapon technology to Muslim nations before selling the technology to Israel
- Obama's refusal to dine with Israeli PM Netanyahu or allow any photos to be taken at the White House during their first meeting in Washington
- Obama hasn't done enough to prevent Iran from getting its own nuclear weapon
- Condemnation of the building of settlements in the Jewish suburb of north Jerusalem called Ramat Shlomo
- Bowing to Muslim leaders, sacrificing Israel relations[107]

Reed's website also noted that "Brad Sherman has not publicly condemned the Obama administration for these actions."[108]

As Linda Milazzo poignantly observed: "What makes Reed's Israel allegiance so bizarre is the inescapable irony that Reed's native-American ancestors had their land taken by European colonists to form the current nation of America, just as European colonists (in this case, European Jews) drove the Palestinians from their land to form the current nation of Israel."[109]

Reed's bid failed and Sherman won, but just two years later, due to redistricting and California electoral laws, the eight-term Sherman found himself pitted against fellow Democrat and fifteen-term Howard Berman in the 2012 House election. Berman was the Ranking Member on the House Committee on Foreign Affairs, and Sherman was a longtime member of the same committee. Both were well known for their unwavering commitment to Israel. Berman, for example, had once stated in an interview with the *Jewish Daily Forward*, "Even before I was a Democrat, I was a Zionist."[110] The Berman-Sherman showdown gave witness to each candidate trying to outshine the other in his devotion to Israel, with Sherman espousing ever more hard-line positions. The far more hawkish Sherman, considered by nearly everyone on and off the Hill not to be of Berman's caliber—I will spare him here the unflattering terms many interviewees really used—was victorious. Pro-peace elements of many stripes lamented Berman's demise.

Also in 2012, in Connecticut's Democratic Senate primary, Lee Whitnum, John Kerry's girlfriend in the early 1990s, was competing against numerous, better-funded contestants. Whitnum took her opponents to task for their ignorance of the historical role played by neoconservatives in selling the war on Iraq to the American public. She also adopted a position highly critical of the close, US-Israel relationship, highlighting this on her campaign website. In an April 5, 2012, "live" NBC televised public debate, Whitnum attacked the leading candidate, Chris Murphy, as "whore, here, who sells his soul to AIPAC."[111] When I checked Whitnum's donation total at the Center for Responsive Politics in spring 2012, the figure given was zero. Her primary campaign went nowhere.

Another more serious case was the reelection bid by Ohio Democrat Sherrod Brown. Brown was attacked by far right pro-Israel elements for cutting some $2.5 million from the huge foreign aid package for Israel in order to send the money, as one keen Hill observer put it, "to the poorest of the poor in Africa." Other votes by Rep. Brown back in 2004 against certain congressional expenditures were dredged out and cited as anti-Israel votes. By taking an endorsement from the more pro-peace J Street and by showing up at a J Street conference, Brown exposed himself to further vilification by right wing elements, who painted J Street and Brown as arms of the Obama administration. But Brown, who no objective observer sees as hostile to Israel, managed to survive this onslaught.

Finally, there was the case of six-term senator and Ranking Member of the Senate Foreign Relations Committee, Richard Lugar (R) of Indiana. Although Lugar had opened himself up to strong criticism for having become too distant from his home state base, this longtime supporter of Israel was attacked by his primary opponent, Richard Mourdock, in a *Human Events* op-ed piece entitled, "Sen. Dick Lugar's History of Harming Israel Must End."[112] A Tea Party member and evangelical Christian, Mourdock was backed by out-of-state SuperPAC funding, enabling him to match Lugar's own fund-raising efforts. After culling four votes (in 1998, 2001, 2002, and 2007) from Lugar's 35-year Senate career that allegedly defined his record on Israel, Mourdock opined: "In May of this year, Lugar chose not to challenge President Obama after he called for Israel's borders to return to '1967 lines with mutually agreed swaps.' This is not surprising. Lugar was one of the first to speak favorably in 2002 of the so-called 'Saudi plan,' which called for return to the pre-1967 lines. It may have taken nine years, but ultimately Dick Lugar found a President he can work with on issues of Israel."[113]

I mention Lugar's case because a veteran staffer, very well informed about Lugar's affairs, brought Mourdock's op-ed to my attention in a spring 2012 interview, asserting that everyone on the Hill saw it as contributing significantly to Lugar's defeat. The staffer noted: "After all Lugar has done for Israel and to defang the Palestinians, this is what he gets." Interestingly, Lugar received a $20,000 campaign donation from NORPAC, a "pro-Israel" lobby that many place slightly to the right of AIPAC.[114] Not all right wing Israel supporters, it seems, wanted to throw Lugar under the bus. But under the bus he went in the Indiana primary, and staffers saw right wing pro-Israel elements as greatly responsible for his demise.

Let me be clear. Any objective, skillful analyst could examine the Sestak, Schakowsky, Lugar, and other cases and find strong, alternative factors contributing significantly to their election difficulties. But no objective observer would refute the explanatory weight of AIPAC or other right wing pro-Israel actors. Moreover, according to numerous, D.C.-based, longtime observers of congressional politics, including many lifelong supporters of Israel, the 2010 and 2012 races created a new perception on the Hill—an impression that "Nobody is safe" and that "One can't be too good for Israel." Staffers and "off-the-Hill" observers with intimate knowledge asserted that even members like Rep. Gary Ackerman—a lifetime, stalwart supporter of Israel—were affected by the 2012 election developments, causing them to exercise far greater caution in their handling of issues like the West Bank settlements.

If imitation is the sincerest form of flattery, then the Arab American Institute (AAI) has flattered AIPAC for several election cycles now by publishing its own *Congressional Scorecard* on congresspersons' voting behavior. As an AAI spokesperson told me, "Of course, we are not permitted by law to add up the pluses and minuses alongside the names and voting records of the congresspersons, but it's pretty easy for any reader to figure it out." In brief, there are organizations with alternative viewpoints now engaging in the same behavior as AIPAC, but, to date, their activities have not produced the same results in terms of campaign contributions, electoral votes, and pressure on congressional candidates to "toe the line" as have AIPAC's. Only J Street has perhaps begun to make a difference in this regard.

Adding a final note regarding AIPAC's electoral influence, here is what the celebrated journalist and nonfiction author Thomas Friedman said in London in an interview in June 2013 with his Al Jazeera interlocutor, Mehdi Hasan. As Philip Weiss of Mondoweiss reported June on 16, 2013:

> Hasan: One of the big issues cited by violent extremists in that part of the world is America's blind support some would say for the state of Israel . . . You would accept that the US is not an honest broker in the Mideast?

> Friedman: Let me put it in my terms, not yours. Let's go inside American politics for a second. What happened, and as you know, President Bush the first stood outside the White House one day and said I'm one lonely man standing up against the Israel lobby. What happened as a result of that, Mehdi, is that Republicans post Bush I, and manifested most in his son Bush 2, took a strategic decision, they will never be out

pro-Israel'd again. That they believe cost them electorally a lot. So that pulled the American spectrum to the right and it created an arms race with the Democrats, over who could be more pro-Israel.

Friedman then went on to explain, using admittedly exaggerated figures to make his point, that the 2010 Citizens United Case Supreme Court decision would enable a candidate backed by AIPAC to make a few phone calls to garner the requisite campaign finance backing, whereas his or her opponent would have to make 50,000 calls to raise a comparable amount. In Friedman's view, this has pulled the whole spectrum on the Israel question to the right in the US. How much? Friedman said:

"To the point, and this is very disappointing to me, where if you're a young political officer, you're in NEA, our Near East division of the State Department, you dream one day of being ambassador to Oman . . . You will not state publicly what is actually official US policy, that Israeli settlements are an obstacle to peace. Now when you go so many years where people won't even say publicly what is the policy, it's inevitable that people perceive us rightly in many ways not to be an honest broker."[115]

DOES CAMPAIGN FINANCE HAVE AN IMPACT ON POLICY?

"It's a lot of money."
—high-ranking House staffer

In his insightful book *Honest Graft: Money and the American Political Process*, journalist Brooks Jackson asserts that the problem with PACs in general "isn't corruption; it's more serious than that . . . money can twist the behavior of ordinary legislators. The system of money-based elections and lobbying rewards those who cater to well-funded interests . . . and it also punishes those who challenge the status quo."[116] Does this language "fit" the Israel–Middle East conflict issue area? For any objective mind, it should strain credulity to think that heavier "pro-Israel" sources of funding do not turn the heads of many members of Congress. Perhaps more importantly, it should strain credulity to believe that these campaign finance concerns do not instill an element of fear in most congresspersons' minds—a fear that any steps or statements perceived as "anti-Israel" could result in either a reduction of support for their own campaigns or increased backing for their electoral challengers.

While conducting my interviews, I considered this question too sensitive to ask in a direct, systematic manner. In part, I didn't feel my interviewees were the best qualified individuals in the office to know about such matters because they were handling foreign affairs and other portfolios, not (a few exceptions notwithstanding) serving as chiefs of staff or in capacities that would put them in closer touch with campaign finance concerns. They were obviously not working in the home district office where fund-raising activity would be a principal part of the workload. Nonetheless, on numerous occasions—usually prefaced by a cautionary note that such information was "absolutely not for attribution" (despite my having clearly established nonattribution as the ground rules for all the interviews)—Senate and House staffers, alike, stated in unequivocal terms that it was a common perception among members of Congress that questioning Israeli government policies would be politically suicidal. Again, as one Senate staffer said, it constituted a potential electoral "kiss of death." This thinking still registered high in the calculations of my interviewees when I returned to Capitol Hill in spring and summer of 2011, 2012, and 2013. Time and again, I heard the same refrain: "The threat is just too great"; "It's just not worth it to rock the boat." The only change to this widely held view came from staffers—typically working for more progressive congresspersons—who felt that the appearance of J Street, with its own (admittedly smaller) impact on campaign donations, was beginning to make a difference.

In the way of indirect, anecdotal evidence, it is interesting to read statements by former congresspersons "speaking freely" about common congressional practice with regard to the nexus between money and politics. Here are a few, insightful quotes taken from Martin Schram's *Speaking Freely* and posted on the CRP website.

> (1) Former Rep. Thomas Downey (D-New York): "I think that the process is compromised by the need to raise money. I don't think that there's any question of that."
>
> (2) Former Sen. Dave Durenberger (R-Minnesota): "I think the House is more compromisable because it takes these guys so long to get anywhere. If 70 percent of their money comes from PACs, then

you know that the PACs represent the kind of Congressman that they are. But I think it [the money] goes to their belief systems rather than to their votes."[117]

(3) Former Rep. Peter Kostmayer (D-Pennsylvania): "It's often not what you do, but what you don't do. In something like NAFTA, for example, if you're a Democrat and you've gotten support from labor but you don't like labor's position on it, maybe you just keep quiet about it. That way you don't alienate anybody. . . . [I]t's not as if it's a specific payoff, like you get a bag of money one night for voting a particular way. It's much harder to describe, and I think in many ways it's much more insidious. . . . [A] member will help a particular company or particular interest. Or get something out of the bill. Or sign a letter. Or make a call to a federal agency. And you don't then do it and then call them up that day and say: 'Well, I did what you asked me to do. Can I have a contribution?' What you do is after you've done it, come campaign time, you remember. That's exactly the way it works. Nobody ever admits it; nobody ever acknowledges it. Everybody does it."[118]

I find these disclosures instructive in and of themselves, but the reader would do well to keep them in mind when digesting the staffers' comments on their bosses' behavior in the ensuing chapters. One staffer after the next suggests money does not make a difference, then each proceeds to offer examples of how it might or did. Over the years, I have also found it fascinating that even among these candid expressions of interest group influence, I have come across few people mentioning pressure exercised by "pro-Arab" or "pro-Israel" interests. And yet, as the campaign contributions demonstrate, along with other means of peddling influence to be discussed in subsequent chapters, there are daily efforts to influence the behavior of congresspersons when it comes to Middle East affairs. It has struck me as equally intriguing that there is little to no mention of such influence peddling on IME conflicts in the major works on Congress and interest group activity. For years on end, AIPAC, in particular, has been recognized as the second most successful lobbying organization in Washington, D.C., yet only recently has it received more than passing mention in academic books exploring the importance of interest group activity in Congress in general.

To reiterate, I did not have the chutzpah to ask my interviewees whether or not quid pro quo arrangements were in effect with regard to IME conflict related policies. I can state, however, that there is very strong evidence for the claim that any congressperson who supports policies perceived negatively by AIPAC and more right wing backers of Israel believes that he or she will feel threatened. I will provide additional statements by staffers to corroborate this point later in the book.

On many occasions, staffer interviewees volunteered the names of financially prominent constituents who let their views be known on Middle East policy. Sometimes these constituents contact their representatives directly; on other occasions, individuals from the district call in to say that they spoke with Mr. X or Ms. Y recently, well-known wealthy constituents, and he or she expressed a particular point of view on a certain policy. In almost every one of these interviews, the name of the noteworthy, powerful individual or family cited was a strong supporter of Israel. Not one time did someone mention to me the name of a wealthy Arab, Iranian, or Muslim American donor.

As for the issue of quid pro quo, in spring 2013, a J Street staffer told me that "Providing campaign finance has absolutely made a difference to our group's success. But you know, sometimes we've had problems. Sometimes we've given big money to members' campaigns, then they've voted against us. I, personally, have had to go to members' offices and say, 'Hey, what's up? We helped you a lot and this is what we get?' There's no quid pro quo, you know, but . . ."

On the other side of the process, a House staffer, trying to enlighten me in summer 2013 as to how some decisions really go down, shared this: "This is a direct, recent quote by this aide concerning an item that AIPAC was pushing and that this aide and others were debating as to whether they would go along with what AIPAC wanted or not. In the midst of this discussion, the senior aide said, 'It's a lot of money.' So this shows that this is part of their decision making; that is, the pressure AIPAC could bring to bear against their bosses by AIPAC's supporters withholding their assistance in the form of campaign donations. This was not said with reference to any particular person or campaign, and is *not* to be seen or interpreted as a bribe on a particular item."

SO DOES ELECTION ENGINEERING CREATE A MOBILIZATION OF BIAS?

Just who are the major recipients of campaign funding by interest groups with "skin" in the Israel–Middle East conflicts game? Where do they sit in Congress?

The data on campaign financing are quite telling if examined with regard to individual recipients. Let's begin by examining the recipients of funding by "pro-Israel" donors because that's where nearly all the action is.

Figure X.

TOP TEN 2006 AND CAREER RECIPIENTS OF PRO-ISRAEL PAC FUNDS, IN DOLLARS

House: 2006 Cycle		Senate: 2006 Cycle	
Kirk, Mark (R-IL)	76,564	Lieberman, Joseph (D-CT)	127,093
Ellsworth, Brad (D-IN)	48,750	Nelson, Bill (R-FL)	89,861
Hoyer, Steny (D-MD)	44,500	Kyl, Jon (R-AZ)	87,000
Cantor, Eric (R-VA)	43,000	Stabenow, Debbie (D-MI)	85,796
Berkley, Shelley (D-NV)	39,250	Menendez, Robert (D-NJ)	84,835
Hastert, J. Dennis (R-IL)	38,700	Santorum, Rick (R-PA)	75,500
Engel, Eliot (D-NY)	38,000	DeWine, Mike (R-OH)	74,000
Ros-Lehtinen, Ileana (R-FL)	36,500	Whitehouse, Sheldon (D-RI)	72,000
Pryce, Deborah (R-OH)	30,000	Talent, James (R-MO)	69,510
Edwards, Chet (D-TX)	28,600	Cardin, Benjamin L. (D-MD)	66,565

House: Career		Senate: Career	
Berkley, Shelly (D-NV)	246,205	Levin, Carl (D-MI)	658,887
Frost, Martin (D-TX)	190,014	Harkin, Tom (D-IA)	520,950
Engel, Eliot (D-NY)	179,918	Specter, Arlen (R-PA)	489,973
Obey, David (D-WI)	152,100	Lautenberg, Frank (D-NJ)	434,078
Hoyer, Steny (D-MD)	136,775	McConnell, Mitch (R-KY)	377,185
Kirk, Mark (R-IL)	129,882	Lieberman, Joseph (D-CT)	363,851
Cantor, Eric (R-VA)	128,730	Durbin, Richard (D-IL)	330,421
Levin, Sander (D-MI)	122,227	Baucus, Max (D-MT)	327,648
Lantos, Tom (D-CA)	121,250	Reid, Harry (D-NV)	320,321
Ros-Lehtinen, Ileana (R-FL)	120,990	Wyden, Ronald (D-OR)	277,562

Chart by the Washington Report on Middle East Affairs[119]

As regards the 2006 cycle Top Ten, Dennis Hastert was Speaker of the House. Steny Hoyer, who by that time had taken as many trips to Israel as any other congressperson except perhaps Tom Lantos, was Minority Whip; that is, number two in the party. Tom Lantos, the only Holocaust survivor to ever serve in Congress, was Ranking Member (RM) on the House Committee on International Relations (HIRC). Ileana Ros-Lehtinen was chairwoman of HIRC's Subcommittee on the Middle East and South Asia. Eliot Engel and Shelley Berkley, veritable pit bulls in defense of right wing Israeli policies, were members of that same subcommittee. Mark Kirk, as a member of the House Committee on Appropriations, served on its crucial Foreign Operations, Export Financing, and Related Programs subcommittee; and he went on to fill a comparable slot in the Senate. Along with Nita Lowey, Kirk was perceived as one of the major "water carriers" for pro-Israel funding. Eric Cantor, on Ways and Means, was first elected to the House in 2000. He was quickly marked as a rising Republican superstar, and his meteoric rise took him to the position of Minority Whip from 2009–2011, then Majority Leader in the 112th Congress in 2011. These are all figures with tremendous clout.

For the House 2006 Top Ten recipients, Brad Ellsworth (IN) and perhaps Deborah Pryce (OH) and Chet Edwards (TX) are among the lesser-known actors. However, it's noteworthy that it was Ellsworth who defeated incumbent John Hostettler, who since 1998, as noted earlier, had established an erratic voting record on aid to Israel. Chet Edwards attracted support given his membership on the important Appropriations Committee. A repeat Democrat victor in a district that had been heavily restructured to favor Republicans in the mid-2000s, Edwards succumbed to Bill Flores in 2010. One year after taking office, Flores and his wife went to Israel as part of a six-person congressional delegation with all expenses paid by AIEF.

"'I am concerned that the Palestinians have not overtly come out and said that they support a two-state solution that recognizes Israel's right to exist as a Jewish state,' Flores said. 'That's something that, in my view, the Palestinians really need to do if we're going to find a path forward in this area. They've got to recognize Israel's right to exist as a Jewish state. I think that the United States should make sure that we never waver from that position, as well,' he added. 'Peace, prosperity and freedom for the Palestinians ultimately is connected to their willingness to recognize Israel's right to exist as a Jewish state,' Flores said. The Texas congressman believes that Israel has 'bent over backwards to try to achieve peace' with the Palestinians within the framework of a two-state solution."[120]

Rep. Deborah Pryce (R-OH) represented a seventh-term incumbent and powerful woman's voice among Republicans. In 2006, Pryce was serving in the influential position of chair of the House Republican Conference. Over her years in office, Pryce has consistently backed measures such as safeguarding Jerusalem as the "undivided capital of Israel," moving the US embassy to Jerusalem, and supporting the US war effort in Iraq.

In terms of the House's "Top Ten Career Recipients," the 2006 support to Martin Frost proved of lesser value because he failed to retain his seat, and therefore could no longer play the supportive role he had while a House member. No matter, he lost to Jeff Sessions, who as I noted earlier has proven a very strong supporter of Israel.

There is no need for redundancy regarding members appearing on the 2006 "Top House Recipients" list as well as the "Top Ten Career House Recipients." But two on the "Top Ten Career" list merit commentary here. First, Dave Obey served for many years as either chairman or RM on House Appropriations. Although Obey hailed from a district where constituents did not prioritize Middle East affairs, and although he was not knee-jerk in his support of all Israeli policies, after the early 1990s he rarely contested appropriations for Israel in any significant manner. And he certainly never returned any of the "pro-Israel" money that was sent in his direction. Second, Mr. Lantos's devotion to Israel is detailed later in this book. As either chairman or RM of HIRC, he held great power to steer House policymaking in a "pro-Israel" direction, and was thus worth his weight in gold to all forces seeking to shield Israeli governments from critical evaluation. Finally, Sander Levin was also not a noteworthy figure when it came to the issues being most heavily discussed in this book but has always been a solid, pro-Israel voter.

As for the senators, Menendez and Stabenow appeared of lesser value among the "2006 Cycle's Top Ten Recipients," but as we shall see Menendez went on to become chairman of the Senate Committee on Foreign Relations. Stabenow hailed from a state, Michigan, with a large and increasingly vocal Arab community, so contributions to her may have been well placed as a counterweight. Although Sheldon Whitehouse (D) of Rhode Island was lesser known at the time, having just been elected, his victory was heavily publicized and removed Lincoln Chafee from the Senate. Chafee had been serving as chairman of the Senate Foreign Relations Middle East subcommittee, and to pro-peace forces represented the most balanced voice in the Senate on the A-I and I-P conflicts. As for the Senate's "Top Ten Career Recipients," only Sen. Ron Wyden had lesser name recognition and clout based on the data I collected, although he has been a staunch supporter of Israeli government policies. All of the other senators on the list represented key party figures, with perhaps the slight exception of Sen. Lautenberg. Senators McConnell, Reid, Lieberman, Durbin, Levin, Baucus, Harkin, Specter: all either were or have become towering figures in their parties and in the Senate. Durbin was the man who, years ago, defeated Paul Findley, the representative who had started to question the role played by "pro-Israel" special interests. McConnell, Specter, Bennett, Harkin, and Durbin all sat—and, except for Specter, are still seated—not only on the Senate Appropriations but also on its Foreign Operations subcommittees. Durbin became Senate Democratic Whip in 2005, and then Senate Majority Whip—the second most powerful member of the Senate—when the Democrats reclaimed Senate control in 2007. Levin has alternated between chair and RM of the Committee on Armed Services, which figures prominently on all issues relating to defense, including such matters as military research and development in which Israel has enormous interest. Last but far from least, by 2013, McConnell (R) and Reid (D) had served as the leaders of their respective parties for many years running.

When I asked my staffer interviewees in 2005–2006 which members serving on the House Appropriations committee took a special interest in Israeli affairs, nearly all those "in the know" told me I should speak with Reps. Nita Lowey or Mark Kirk to gain insight. As one can see from the chart on the following page, Lowey was #6 on the list of career recipients of "pro-Israel" funding. Kirk was the top recipient of pro-Israel funding in 2006 among House members, and by the end of that year had already moved up the ladder to #6 among House career recipients of pro-Israel funding despite having only served three terms in the House. For his 2010 Senate bid, Kirk had "Kirk for Congress" written in Hebrew on his campaign website. Meanwhile, his opponent Alexi Giannoulias, whose Middle East policy "support[ed] Israeli and Palestinian equality, was harshly targeted by the National Republican Senatorial Committee (NRSC) for donating to the Committee For A Just Peace In Israel And Palestine; a peace and justice organization."[121] Kirk received heavy pro-Israel financial backing for his 2010 Senate race—indeed he was the leading recipient of pro-Israel funds in that electoral cycle. Kirk won the election by a slim margin, just 2 percent. And this assistance moved him to #10 on the Senate career recipients of "pro-Israel" funding by 2010.

TOP TEN 2010 AND CAREER RECIPIENTS OF PRO-ISRAEL PAC FUNDS
Compiled by Hugh Galford

HOUSE: CURRENT		SENATE: CURRENT	
Skelton, Ike (D-MO)	51,000	Kirk, Mark S. (R-IL)	115,304
Ros-Lehtinen, Ileana (R-FL)	45,000	Reid, Harry (D-NV)	72,700
Deutch, Theodore E. (D-FL)	43,600	Feingold, Russell D. (D-WI)	69,128
Klein, Ron (D-FL)	42,650	Wyden, Ronald L. (D-OR)	67,400
Hoyer, Steny H. (D-MD)	42,000	Inouye, Daniel K. (D-HI)	57,000
Cantor, Eric (R-VA)	41,500	Boxer, Barbara (D-CA)	50,250
Berkley, Shelley (D-NV)	36,000	Gillibrand, Kirsten E. (D-NY)	46,200
Berman, Howard L. (D-CA)	35,500	Specter, Arlen (D-PA)	46,000
Engel, Eliot L. (D-NY)	34,000	Bennett, Robert F. (R-UT)	42,000
Lowey, Nita M. (D-NY)	28,000	Vitter, David (R-LA)	40,500
		Thune, John R. (R-SD)	40,500
House: Career		**Senate: Career**	
Berkley, Shelley (D-NV)	326,055	Levin, Carl (D-MI)	728,937
Engel, Eliot L. (D-NY)	269,418	Harkin, Thomas R. (D-IA)	552,950
Hoyer, Steny H. (D-MD)	235,275	Lautenberg, Frank R. (D-NJ)	503,578
Cantor, Eric (R-VA)	217,730	McConnell, Mitch (R-KY)	485,141
Ros-Lehtinen, Ileana (R-FL)	208,740	Reid, Harry (D-NV)	393,001
Lowey, Nita M. (D-NY)	177,238	Durbin, Richard J. (D-IL)	373,421
Burton, Dan L. (R-IN)	143,336	Lieberman, Joseph I. (Ind.-CT)	368,851
Levin, Sander M. (D-MI)	132,727	Baucus, Max (D-MT)	349,648
Berman, Howard (D-CA)	124,550	Wyden, Ronald L. (D-OR)	344,962
Harman, Jane (D-CA)	123,771	Kirk, Mark S. (R-IL)	336,386

Source of Recipients Chart: Washington Report on Middle East Affairs[122]

The more it changes, the more it's the same. As one can see from the 2010 chart, the same staunchly pro-Israel supporters appear again in all quadrants of the chart: Reps. Ros-Lehtinen, Hoyer, Cantor, Berkley, Berman, Engel, and Lowey, with hard-liners Berkley and Engel moving up to occupy the #1 and #2 spots on the career House list.

The 78-year-old Ike Skelton, chairman of the House Committee on Armed Services and longtime supporter of Israel on key votes, was fighting a tough battle against a Tea Party candidate, Vicky Hartzler, in 2010. In the end, Hartzler's candidacy and victory presented no real problem from a "pro-Israel" perspective. In one of her first speeches as a congresswoman, reading from a prepared text, Hartzler expressed disappointment with President Obama's proposal for Israel to return to its pre-1967 borders, a proposal anchored in international law. She said, "President Obama's call for Israel to make more sacrifices in the pursuit of peace in the Middle East is unacceptable. . . . The borders that were established in 1967 followed three wars launched against Israel. The territory acquired by the Israelis after they were subjected to unprovoked attacks serves as a buffer between Israel and enemies intent on destroying her."[123]

Ted Deutch joined the newest members of Congress in 2011; he came from the district previously represented by Robert Wexler, a district described by some staffers as being "the most Jewish district in the nation." In his first speech on the House floor, he congratulated Israel on its sixty-second birthday and called for the US to maintain its steadfast commitment to Israel's security.[124] Ron Klein (D-FL), who had chastised the Obama administration for being too tough on the Israeli government after it thumbed its nose at Obama's criticism of Israeli West Bank settlement expansion,[125] lost to Tea Party Republican Allen West. Again, no problem. In response to Pres. Obama's statement calling upon Israel to negotiate a resolution of the conflict based on a return to the 1967 boundaries with land swaps, West put out the following statement:

> Today's endorsement by President Barack Obama of the creation of a Hamas-led Palestinian state based on the pre-1967 borders, signals the most egregious foreign policy decision his administration has made to date, and could be the beginning of the end as we know it for the Jewish state. . . . America should never negotiate with the Palestinian Authority—which has aligned itself with Hamas. Palestine is a region, not a people or a modern state. Based upon Roman Emperor Hadrian's declaration in 73 AD, the original Palestinian people are the Jewish people. It's time for the American people to stand by our strongest ally, the Jewish State of Israel, and reject this foreign policy blunder of epic proportions.[126]

The very conservative, evangelical Dan Burton made his appearance at #7 on the career House list; and Jane Harman (D-CA) appeared on the career list at #10. Harman had alternated between chairwoman and RM for the House Committee on Intelligence. The apparently tight—perhaps even scandalously tight—relationship she enjoyed with AIPAC and the Israeli government is discussed more fully below.

Among those on the Senate list, "pro-Israel" money for Senators Russ Feingold (too liberal for right wingers) and Specter (too independent-minded) did not pay off, but Senators David Vitter, John Thune, Kirsten Gillibrand, and Barbara Boxer all won. Boxer has been a stalwart supporter of Israel on the Senate Committee on Foreign Relations. Vitter is a steady signatory of "pro-Israel" letters in the Senate; Thune has initiated resolutions blocking aid to the Palestinian Authority and equating rocket attacks on Israel with September 11; and Gillibrand moved away from initially strong support for fellow Democrat Pres. Obama's handling of Middle East matters to embrace a more critical and questioning posture.

Do campaign finance recipients "perform" on behalf of their donors? Again, it's impossible to establish direct causality, but here are some examples. As detailed in an article by Neve Gordon, after the September 1993 Oslo Peace Accords were signed by Israeli Prime Minister Yitzhak Rabin and Palestinian Authority President Yasser Arafat, Rabin himself backed the creation of an international fund to help build the new Palestinian economy. Dozens of countries, including the US, financially supported the initiative. The hard-line ZOA's leaders opposed this effort and lobbied Congress accordingly. More specifically, they got Senators Specter and Richard Shelby (D-Alabama) to insert an amendment obstructing the US contribution to this fund. The Clinton administration sought removal of this amendment but failed. As Gordon observed, "Subsequently, Senator Specter became co-chair of the ZOA-initiated Peace Accord Monitoring Group (PAM) in the US Senate. Specter, one should note, has received $298,623 from the so-called pro-Israel political action committees (PACs) since 1980, and Shelby has received $135,825 from them since 1984."[127] The story offers a prime, yet far from unique, example of Congress taking a hard-line, pro–right wing Israeli position, working against the professed wishes of not only the US president but also the more peace-seeking prime minister of Israel.

Rep. Obey hailed from north-central Wisconsin, with his home base in Wausau. His district has almost no people of Middle East background and a very tiny Jewish American community. In the early 1990s, Obey, a Democrat, sided with Pres. George Bush's effort to block Israeli West Bank settlement construction by threatening to withhold $10 billion in US loan guarantees. He feared continued Israeli settlement would, over time, render a two-state solution of the conflict impossible. For this, Obey was attacked by AIPAC, but he stuck to his guns. He was convinced, with good cause, that Bush's stance helped to bring down the hard-line Likud government of Yitzhak Shamir, brought Rabin to power, and paved the way for Rabin's signing of the 1993 Oslo Peace Accords. Mr. Obey wrote very clearly about this clash in his own book,[128] but what he discusses less is his subsequent decision to assume a less confrontational role. In the opinion of many knowledgeable observers, Mr. Obey decided that it was simply not worth the fight. The closest challenge he ever experienced as an incumbent came in 1994. After that date, Mr. Obey went on to collect over a quarter million dollars in campaign contributions from "pro-Israel" sources, this while continuing to represent a district where there are almost no constituents with any strong interest in the conflict. (I am perhaps being too harsh on Rep. Obey, as will be made apparent by my lengthier analysis of his Middle East–related behavior later in the book.)

A more recent example involves one Irving Moskowitz and Florida's Rep. Ileana Ros-Lehtinen. Moskowitz was born in New York City, grew up in Milwaukee, Wisconsin, and earned a medical degree from the University of Wisconsin in Madison. He went on to amass a fortune by building and managing hospitals and owning a legal gambling enterprise in California. Over time, Moskowitz took up residence in Miami Beach, Florida, and also acquired property in Israel. Moskowitz has long engaged in numerous philanthropic activities, but having lost 120 family members in the Holocaust, he responded to this tragedy by becoming an ardent Zionist and has contributed in a major way to various right wing Zionist undertakings. The latter includes his 2007 financial backing of extensive housing development in the Sheikh Jarrah neighborhood of East Jerusalem, which was condemned by both the US and British governments. What makes Moskowitz's case particularly interesting is that he is one of the top contributors to Rep. Ros-Lehtinen, who has served as chairwoman of the House Foreign Affairs Committee and its Middle East subcommittee. He and his wife, Cherna, donated $9,600 to Ros-Lehtinen's campaign during the 2010 election cycle; they also provided $5,000 to the National Action Committee PAC (NacPAC), a pro-Israel PAC that donated $10,000 to Ros-Lehtinen in 2009–2010.[129]

As highlighted in later chapters, Ros-Lehtinen was serving as chairwoman of HIRC's Subcommittee for the Middle East and South Asia during the period that almost all of my staffer interviews were conducted. With the Republicans regaining control of the House following the 2010 elections, she became chairwoman of the full House Committee on Foreign Affairs. As a seasoned veteran, she hit the ground running, giving every indication that she would work indefatigably in defense of hawkish "pro-Israel" positions in the House: turning a blind eye to Israeli West Bank settlements; rejecting the Hamas-Fatah unity government; keeping the focus on the threat from Iran; and reacting with total hostility to Hizballah's increased influence in Lebanon. In brief, Moskowitz's investment appears to have paid off handsomely. And many of these "returns" are at the direct expense of policies being actively pursued by presidents of the United States.

A fourth, fascinating case is that of Rep. Jane Harman. Robert Naiman of the *Huffington Post* presented an intriguing look at Harman's dealings with AIPAC, congressional leaders, and the Israeli government. The gist of the allegations against Harman, made public in 2009, were based on a 2005 National Security Agency (NSA) wiretapping of a phone call between her and an Israeli agent. In that call, Harman stated that if the Israeli government would like her to become chairwoman of the House's Intelligence Committee, it could have AIPAC send this request to Speaker Nancy Pelosi, thereby enhancing her prospects of attaining that position. As Naiman wrote:

> [I]f this was Harman's actual belief about how to make things happen in Congress, it's a very significant fact. After all, Jane Harman was in a position to know. She's got many years of experience in Washington political games. She's close to AIPAC. She's close to the Israeli government. She's close to Pelosi. She knows how these actors interact.
>
> So first of all, Harman had to believe that if the Israeli government tells AIPAC to do something, AIPAC is very likely to do it, without asking for much explanation. And second, she had to believe that if AIPAC tells Nancy Pelosi to do something, Nancy Pelosi is very likely to do it, without asking for much explanation. In this case, the mechanism was allegedly that media mogul Haim Saban (financial backer of the Brookings Institution's Saban Center) would threaten to withhold campaign contributions to Pelosi. Given that Pelosi has a safe seat, this

wouldn't seem to be that much of a threat to her personally, so in order to believe that this was a credible threat Harman had to believe that Pelosi had some proclivity to accede to such a threat. . . .

But as a judgment of how people perceive the Democratic leadership, I do think the scandal has implications that the Democratic leadership should consider. The belief that the Israeli government can tell the Democratic leadership what to do is apparently so widespread that the set of believers seems to include high-ranking Democratic members of Congress.[130]

As this scandal evolved, it was widely reported that Alberto Gonzales, Pres. George W. Bush's attorney general, asked that the investigation be squelched. For her part, Harman consistently denied the allegations, and in June 2009 the Justice Department sent her a letter informing her that she was no longer under investigation. She won reelection to the House in 2010, but resigned in early 2011 to become president and CEO of the prestigious, D.C.-based Woodrow Wilson International Center for Scholars.

Any knowledgeable Washington insider knows that influence peddling and deal cutting by pro-Israel organizations in Washington is played out on a daily basis in scores of offices, typically with considerable success. By contrast, "pro-Palestinian" or "pro-Arab" players are largely absent from the field of competition. The most noteworthy counter to the influence of powerful, right wing pro-Israel forces has come over the last two election cycles, in which the pro-two-state-solution J Street has mobilized funding for certain candidates with its JStreetPAC. Two quick points are in order. First, it is significant that J Street has found senators willing to take its endorsement and financial support. In 2012, they included Senators Dianne Feinstein, Maria Cantwell, Sheldon Whitehouse, Sherrod Brown, Tammy Baldwin, Tim Kaine, and Martin Heinrich. Importantly, Sen. Durbin joined this group in 2013. Second, in 2012, J Street and JStreetPAC backed over sixty victorious House candidates, six of whom ran against so-labeled "One State Caucus" incumbents; that is, against representatives who supported Israel's settlement and annexation of West Bank, Palestinian territory. Two prominent examples were the wins by Tammy Duckworth (D) over Tea Partier Rep. Joe Walsh in Illinois, and Patrick Murphy (D) over another Tea Partier, Rep. Allen West in Florida. All told, JStreetPAC helped mobilize some $1.8 million to 71 "pro-Israel, pro-peace" candidates in 2012.

A NOTE ON THE OIL LOBBY AND CAMPAIGN FINANCE

The group or "special interest" most often cited by pro–right wing Israel supporters as acting to counter their influence is the "oil lobby." For example, as
Michael Massing pointed out in his review of the academic furor triggered
by the Mearsheimer and Walt article, numerous critics took the authors to
task for their failure to discuss the power of the "oil lobby" to determine US
Middle East policy.[131] Indeed, ironically, the "oil lobby" is regularly cited by
right wing pro-Israel supporters and leftist critics of Israel alike as effectively
offsetting the influence held by an "Israel lobby." For example, Stephen Zunes
wrote that "there are far more powerful interests that have a stake in what happens in the Persian Gulf region than does AIPAC, such as the oil companies,
the arms industry and other special interests whose lobbying influence and
campaign contributions far surpass that of the much-vaunted Zionist lobby
and its allied donors in congressional races."[132] While more will be said about
this putative source of "pro-Arab" support later in this book, it is instructive
for the purposes of this chapter to examine campaign finance funding from
the oil and gas industry for Senate and House candidates. Here are the contributions from that sector for three electoral cycles presented by CRP:

TOP 20 RECIPIENTS OF OIL AND GAS INDUSTRY
CAMPAIGN DONATIONS

2004 Election Year

Rank	Candidate's name	Office	Amount
1	Bush, George W. (R)	Pres.	$2,627,825
2	Kerry, John (D)	Pres. cand.	$305,610
3	Conaway, Mike (R-TX)	House	$275,918
4	Thune, John (R-SD)	Senate	$262,327
5	Vitter, David (R-LA)	Senate	$259,446
6	Hutchison, Kay Bailey (R-TX)	Senate	$242,070
7	Barton, Joe (R-TX)	House	$224,398
8	Burr, Richard (R-NC)	Senate	$222,552
9	John, Chris (D-LA)	Senate	$212,296
10	Coors, Peter (R-CO)	Senate	$208,439

11	Murkowski, Lisa (R-AK)	Senate	$205,163
12	Neugebauer, Randy (R-TX)	House	$202,122
13	Sessions, Pete (R-TX)	House	$190,577
14	Carson, Brad R (D-OK)	Senate	$188,069
15	Coburn, Tom (R-OK)	Senate	$175,558
16	Pearce, Steve (R-NM)	House	$146,212
17	DeLay, Tom (R-TX)	House	$145,425
18	Boren, Dan (D-OK)	House	$137,610
19	Martinez, Mel (R-FL)	Senate	$135,347
20	Cornyn, John (R-TX)	Senate	$132,400

2006 Election Year

Rank	Candidate's name	Office	Amount
1	Hutchison, Kay Bailey (R-TX)	Senate	$140,911
2	DeLay, Tom (R-TX)	House	$112,490
3	Santorum, Rick (R-PA)	Senate	$110,050
4	Barton, Joe (R-TX)	House	$109,450
5	Burns, Conrad (R-MT)	Senate	$101,575
6	Allen, George (R-VA)	Senate	$92,500
7	Hastert, Dennis (R-IL)	House	$92,000
8	Cornyn, John (R-TX)	Senate	$86,000
9	Pombo, Richard (R-CA)	House	$66,200
10	Bode, Denise (R-OK)	House	$63,700
11	Talent, James M. (R-MO)	Senate	$63,150
12	Sullivan, John (R-OK)	House	$62,500
13	Kyl, Jon (R-AZ)	Senate	$60,850
14	Cole, Tom (R-OK)	House	$52,796
15	Sessions, Pete (R-TX)	House	$50,300
16	Thomas, Craig (R-WY)	Senate	$49,000
17	Inhofe, James M. (R-OK)	Senate	$48,200
18	Pearce, Steve (R-NM)	House	$44,700
19	Tiahrt, Todd (R-KS)	House	$43,650
20	Thomas, Bill (R-CA)	House	$41,500

2010 Election Year

Rank	Candidate's name	Office	Amount
1	Lincoln, Blanche (D-AR)	Senate	$496,566
2	Vitter, David (R-LA)	Senate	$459,250
3	Blunt, Roy (R-MO)	House	$358,135
4	Murkowski, Lisa (I-AK)	Senate	$341,885
5	Pearce, Steve (R-NM)	House cand.	$322,720
6	Portman, Rob (R-OH)	Senate cand.	$310,108
7	Toomey, Pat (R-PA)	Senate cand.	$306,766
8	Fiorina, Carly (R-CA)	Senate cand.	$286,184
9	Pompeo, Mike (R-KS)	House cand.	$270,710
10	Hoeven, John (R-ND)	Senate cand.	$260,939
11	Flores, Bill (R-TX)	House cand.	$238,078
12	Boren, Dan (D-OK)	House	$231,450
13	Rubio, Marco (R-FL)	Senate cand.	$225,138
14	Buck, Kenneth R. (R-CO)	Senate cand.	$201,479
15	Angle, Sharron (R-NV)	Senate cand.	$197,658
16	Landry, Jeff (R-LA)	House cand.	$196,550
17	Cornyn, John (R-TX)	Senate	$196,225
18	Gardner, Cory (R-CO)	House cand.	$195,950
19	Burr, Richard (R-NC)	Senate	$195,500
20	Edwards, Chet (D-TX)	House	$184,930

2012 Election Year

Rank	Candidate's name	Office	Amount
1	Romney, Mitt (R)	Pres. cand.	$5,762,061
2	Perry, Rick (R)	Gov. TX	$996,674
3	Obama, Barack (D)	Pres. cand.	$828,627
4	Cruz, Ted (R-TX)	Sen. cand.	$758,118
5	Dewhurst, David H. (R-TX)	Lt. Gov.	$631,446
6	Berg, Rick (R-ND)	House	$556,669
7	Rehberg, Denny (R-MT)	House	$524,471
8	Boehner, John (R-OH)	House	$455,149
9	McConnell, Mitch (R-KY)	Senate	$431,200

10	Hatch, Orrin G. (R-UT)	Senate	$370,150
11	Brown, Scott (R-MA)	Senate	$346,350
12	Wilson, Heather A. (R-NM)	Sen. cand.	$342,400
13	Barrasso, John A. (R-WY)	Senate	$340,666
14	Allen, George (R-VA)	Sen. cand.	$338,250
15	Williams, Roger (R-TX)	House cand.	$309,108
16	Pompeo, Mike (R-KS)	House	$295,800
17	Mandel, Josh (R-OH)	Sen. cand.	$278,471
18	Boustany, Charles W. Jr. (R-LA)	House	$271,950
19	McCarthy, Kevin (R-CA)	House	$252,200
20	Cantor, Eric (R-VA)	House	$251,450

Source for tables: The Center for Responsive Politics. The author recognizes that these figures are subject to slight modifications by the CRP over time.

As anyone even slightly familiar with the American political landscape can discern, most recipients of oil and gas sector campaign finance money represent oil and gas–producing states: Texas, Louisiana, Alaska, and Oklahoma. And the campaign contributions do flow across partisan lines, even though Republicans have an advantage. Yet as will be discussed at greater length when describing the congresspersons' behavior, the only persons on these lists ever espousing a more sympathetic position with regard to Arab or Palestinian interests are Sen. John Sununu and Rep. Charles Boustany, both Republicans of Lebanese Christian ancestry. Although generally perceived as more sympathetic to moderate Arab and Palestinian positions, neither was identified by my interviewees as a strong, consistent leader on these issues while in Congress. Meanwhile, many individuals on these lists either were or remain very strong and active supporters of Israel. At a bare minimum, Senators James Inhofe, Jon Kyl, Tom Cole, Mitch McConnell, and Pat Toomey and Representatives Roy Blunt, Tom DeLay, and Eric Cantor have all been noteworthy in this regard.

More importantly, I did not have so much as a single staffer interviewee mention activity by an "oil lobby." I approached every interviewee with very open-ended questions, asking which interest groups and lobbies figured most prominently in the debate over the Arab-Israeli conflict and related matters. Not one single time did any interviewee make a reference to an "oil lobby." For this reason, I proceeded to ask explicitly if there was any pressure from an oil lobby with regard to Israel-centered, Middle East conflicts. My question always elicited pensive silence, followed by completely negative responses—as in, there was nothing there to discuss as far as activity by an "oil lobby" in these Middle East matters.

SUMMING UP

Washington insiders are of two minds when it comes to the "electoral power" of pro-Israel groups: (1) The groups are indeed powerful, and congresspersons and their staffers fear them; (2) Some groups, like AIPAC, actually successfully exploit only the myth or perception of their power. No one believes they have little to no influence. As regards the first point, staffers commonly offered candid assessments akin to the following comments. As one House staffer said, with a heavy note of irony: "[The boss] was talking to the [major home city] AIPAC guy and missed the vote today—Steny Hoyer's office called and asked if he'd voted. Any member can fill out a form—you go to the Cloak Room and tell people how you would have voted and that goes into the *Congressional Record*. AIPAC will score this vote, so his AIPAC score would go down—that's why it's in his interest to register his sentiments in the Cloak Room."

Said a Senate staffer: "There is a fear of AIPAC as a powerful constituency. We have no real concern about a challenger being financed, but you certainly don't want to agitate them and be their enemy." A second Senate staffer, a career military officer, said, "You don't want to cross AIPAC because to do so would be like the kiss of death."

With regard to the second point, regarding myths and perceptions, Khalil Jahshan asserted: "The myth that comes with the power of the lobby magnifies their power tenfold. The myth is that congressmen cannot breathe; they have no margin of maneuver; that the scary threat or prospect of the lobby coming after you is real. Friends of ours in the Jewish community know this is just a myth, but most enjoy and benefit from this."

I argue, however, that perceptions do translate into power. I am reminded of what David Dumke, a former House staffer and very astute observer of Congress, told me about former Rep. Jim Kolbe, head of the influential Foreign Operations subcommittee of Appropriations. "Kolbe is one of the cardinals (a leading figure in House Appropriations). He has real power versus the power of Ros-Lehtinen's rhetoric," noted Dumke. (Ros-Lehtinen, as we'll see, has been a leading figure on the House Committee on Foreign Relations.) Later on in the same interview, Dumke asserted: "Knollenberg wants to engage in the area, but is worried he'll get ripped apart by AIPAC. So even people who'd like to present a more balanced position on the Middle East feel stymied because of the negative reaction this would beget. They would get stopped doing their other work." One can thus deduce that even genuinely powerful actors, like Rep. Kolbe, in the end fear the consequences of actions perceived as injurious to Israel's interests by right wing pro-Israel groups such as AIPAC.

In one of my final interviews, in July 2013, a J Street staffer told me: "Personally, I'm completely against PACs. But I have to admit that our PAC, via its campaign finance work, opens doors; it makes people a lot more friendly. This is especially true with House members because they are constantly in campaign mode, and the strong belief still exists among many that to get Jewish votes you have to show you are pro-Israel, as defined by the dominant group. D.C. is a dirty town. We'd love for money not to be important, but that's just the way the game is played. We're the first peace group to play politics, and this is a major reason we've made such a big splash."

I'll conclude this chapter by sharing a quote from AAI's Jim Zogby: "This is an exceptional issue area because what you know doesn't matter. I once spoke with Congressman Conyers [D-MI] and as he said, 'The day most members get elected, the national interest goes out the window. They're only worried about the next election. Or as [former] Congressman Dellums told me, 'If I were a hero on this issue, I wouldn't be one on other issues.' The perception of getting punished for taking a principled stand begets a willed ignorance; and this is the dark secret nobody in Congress ever talks about."

Chapter Three

HOUSE STAFFERS
ON THE JOB

Congressional staffers are the lifeblood of the legislative process. They have their House members' backs during hearings and sundry other Hill activities, and without their efforts their bosses would be buried by the daily avalanche of communications and informational needs. They are, in a word, indispensable. With their crucial role in mind, it makes sense to ask who the staffers are, what they bring to their jobs, and how they deal with their onerous workloads. This dimension, I believe, has not been awarded great enough attention in assessing either Congress's shortcomings or the influence of special interest groups. So this chapter is designed to answer the following questions: Who are the staffers? What do they do? How do they do it? And why is all this relevant to a book dealing with Congress's Mideast policymaking?

A HOUSE OFFICE'S PERSONNEL STRUCTURE AND BUDGET

Besides the congressperson, the boss, the typical House congressional office contains eight to ten staffers. Presented in descending order, staffers are typically headed up by a single chief of staff, one or two legislative directors (LDs), the same number of legislative assistants (LAs), several legislative correspondents (LCs), and two or three staffers working in the office's reception area. At any given time, the office also enjoys the services of one, if not several, interns. Each House member typically has an additional four to nine staffers working back in his or her home district.

Office expenses are covered out of the budget provided to each congressperson—the Members' Representational Allowances (MRA)—which in 2006 ranged from $1,218,685 to $1,574,753, and averaged $1,335,086. In 2010, the range was from $1,428,395 to $1,759,575, with an average MRA of $1,522,114.[133]

(Variations in MRAs derive from such factors as the travel distance of one's home district to Washington, D.C., and the relative cost of renting office space in home districts among other considerations.) With at least sixty[134] Tea Party "revolutionaries" set to take office in 2011, two major budget cuts were introduced: a 5 percent cut in Fiscal Year (FY) 2011, followed by a 6 percent cut in FY 2012. I will say more about the impact of these cuts later in this chapter.

In Washington, D.C., there are minor variations in office responsibilities and the designation of work by title from one office to the next. The chief of staff, sometimes called the administrative assistant, reports directly to the House member. She or he runs the office, both weighing in on legislative action and interacting with district constituents. The LD—most often there is just one—directs the flow of work to the handful of LAs, each of whom possesses a number of portfolios as also detailed below. Many offices have a press secretary or communications director, an individual who handles the House member's communications with the media and constituents. At the bottom of the office food chain are the LCs, who respond to all constituent letters and communications; the front office staffers, who do yeoman's work in answering the phone and receiving guests; and the interns. The latter are responsible for critical legwork, information gathering, and other essential clerical work.

The pay scale varies radically from top to bottom—the average chief of staff takes home a salary of over $100,000 annually, while LCs may earn little more than a quarter of that figure. (The maximum salary for House office staffers in 2009 was set at $168,411 per annum, just under the $174,000 earned by representatives and senators.) Interns are usually not paid. As one young woman, having graduated from a nearby university, noted: "I got an internship and interned over the next four years on the Hill. I even got paid $10 per hour; it's very rare to get paid as an intern." The reader should not forget that these people are living in Washington, D.C., and its environs, one of the most expensive areas in the country with respect to cost-of-living. A veteran of the Hill commented on the low pay and high cost of living, saying, "People start in the low $30,000s. When I started [over ten years ago], it was the low $20,000s. I had $200 per month after bills back then. There are a lot of group houses—people with roommates."

When I returned to the Hill to interview staffers in the spring and early summer of 2011, 2012, and 2013, staffers were still likely to be earning roughly the same range of incomes according to rank as previously noted. Due to the cumulative 11 percent in budget cutbacks of 2011–2012, followed by the impact of the 2013 sequester, far fewer staffers were receiving salary increases and/or bonuses than had been receiving in the past. "Low-end" staffers, like those working in the reception area, could be earning as little as $18,000 per year, which one staffer perceived as "a ridiculously low amount of money to try to live off of in an area as expensive as Washington, D.C." Other staffers said that "The low pay makes it hard to get more talented young people," and that "morale is low due to press reports that make is sound like people are doing nothing up here, whereas all the staff and the congressmen are working really hard most all of the time." The budget cuts also brought pay freezes, so that "more talented staffers, even ones who've loved working on the Hill, are seeking jobs elsewhere."

CLASSIFYING THE HOUSE STAFFERS: BACKGROUNDS, EXPERIENCE, AND WORKLOADS

House staffers working on international relations in members' offices may be divided into three groups. On the basis of my office interviews, it is clear that the first, and by far biggest, group of staffers assigned the foreign affairs portfolio is made up of young LAs—roughly 75 percent of the total. A second group is much smaller, yet substantial, and made up of "older hands"—about 25 percent of the total. This group includes individuals holding a range of formal titles—from LAs to LDs and, in many offices, the chief of staff. Such LDs and chiefs of staff are motivated by various factors to take an interest in international affairs. A third, separate, much smaller group includes individuals who have been seconded to House congresspersons' offices from the Pentagon and/ or the State Department so that they can acquire experience working in another branch of government. These staffers bring ten or more years of military or State Department experience to the House offices in which they serve, usually for a period of one year. I will not provide any specific, additional commentary on this group because of its small size, other than to note the members' backgrounds afford them a broader perspective than that of most of their peers and that such staffers must produce an interesting dynamic in their congressional office work as they are much older than most of their office mates.

The response in many congressional offices to constraints induced by the 2011–2012 budget cutbacks and the sequester has been manifold. One strategy has been to reallocate human resources; that is, make changes in the number of D.C. versus home office staffers after calculating the cost differential. Another has been to introduce greater fluidity to the coverage of tasks in the D.C. office, having people of different ranks take on assignments once engaged in by others, thus transgressing the somewhat more clear-cut division of labor that was in place.

In my random sample, 14 percent of the staffers worked for women members of Congress and 86 percent worked for men, at a time when the female/male split in the House was 16 percent vs. 84 percent. Fifty-four percent of those interviewed had bosses who were Democrats and 46 percent had Republican bosses at a time when the Democrat/Republican split was 46 percent vs. 54 percent. In other words, the sample had a Democratic bias. Perhaps, on balance, staffers for Democrats were more liberal and amenable to interviews by a scholar introducing himself as hailing from a liberal part of the country—Boston, Massachusetts. I do not know for certain.

THE BIGGEST GROUP: NEW KIDS ON THE BLOCK

Perhaps the most striking thing about House staffers in the first and largest group is their age. On the basis of the extensive interviews I conducted in the House, the majority of House staffers are individuals in their early twenties. The "mean" (or average) age of my sample was 32, but this figure was strongly, upwardly biased by the presence of several older hands; the median age was 27, while the modal—most common—age, and most indicative age, was 23.

The overall youthfulness of House staffers creates a college-type atmosphere. On Fridays or days when Congress is not in session, many staffers are permitted to dress in more relaxed garb, prompting a more seasoned staffer to tell me "they often look like a bunch of frolicking frat boys and frat girls. You know, you should be here sometime on Friday afternoons. Every once in a while, you'll see staffers hauling cases of beer into a congressman's office." In the summer, the number of young interns peaks. A staffer interviewee who had worked a few years on the Senate side of the Hill and then moved to the House side disparagingly said it was like "moving from college back to high school." But he was smiling, and I don't want to give a false impression here. As I will demonstrate shortly, in general the staffers are very bright, industrious, and work very long hours for less than great compensation. They more than earn their moments of reduced stress and casual dress.

On the surface, one gets the sense of roughly equal gender representation among House staffers, but among my random sample of interviewees 28 percent were women and 72 percent were men. They came from a mishmash of colleges and universities from across the country; and for what it's worth, some 6.6 percent had studied at Ivy League institutions. Nearly all had received a B.A. in one of the social sciences or the humanities, but not necessarily in political science. Of the 106 House staffers I interviewed in 2005–2006—and remember each held his or her boss's foreign affairs portfolio—71 percent were political science majors, 29 percent had taken at least one course on Middle East politics, and 71 percent had not had a single course on that region.

In terms of recruitment channels, many of the staffers had interned on the Hill during college, enjoyed the experience, and sought out a position in a House member's office sometime after completing their undergraduate studies. Others caught their congressperson's (or a key staffer's) eye by working on the election campaign, met the House member at some social function, or came recommended by family members or friends. A good number of the staffers had invested a year or two working as a staffer in the front office or plugging away as an LC, risking carpal tunnel syndrome from writing responses to letters and emails from constituents, before advancing up the office food chain and laying claim to one of the policy-focused and policy advisory jobs as an LA. (In every office in which I conducted an interview, I was informed that every letter from a constituent received a response.) Others had paid their dues at lower posts then hopscotched into higher positions that opened up in some other congressperson's office.

With respect to on-the-job experience, my survey found that the average number of years spent working on the Hill by House staffers was 5.47 years, the median 3.13 years, and the mode just 3 years. Seventy-five percent of my House interviewees had worked just 5 years or fewer on the Hill. Of 106 first round interviewees, only 16 had worked on the Hill 5 to 10 years, 8 had worked between 11–20 years, and 3 between 21–30 years. Responding to my query about age, recruitment channels, and experience, one of my interviewees observed that, "The typical staff age is around 22; there's a huge turnover. You need to be able to multitask. There are some 'privileged' to get into the office;

for example, the kids of large campaign donors. Others, like me, have to work really hard to get here." In another office, an 11-year Hill veteran summed up his responses to my question by noting, "On our staff, we've got 3 people over 30 and one works in the reception area; the 7 others are in their early twenties. This is no way to run a country."

When I returned to the Hill in 2011–13, numerous staffers told me that the budget cuts had had an impact on the age and experience of staffers. One veteran said: "I think now there are even younger and more inexperienced people than in the past; I mean, staffers who have been here for 3 years or less. I'd say there's about the same or fewer staffers in the middle with 3–5 years of experience; and definitely fewer individuals with more than 5 years of experience." Another veteran stated: "A lot has changed since 5 to 6 years ago. We're 2 staffers short from normal—2 people at the LA level. Everybody's work has spiked; I believe this is quite widespread. I'm here until 8 p.m. every night."

On the basis of my 2011–13 interviews, I find these characterizations generally accurate. And I will quickly add that if I had been able to return to all 100-plus offices where I'd had interviews in 2005–2006, I would not have found more than a handful of my previous interviewees. When I returned to Capitol Hill in early 2011 to check on offices where I had conducted interviews five years earlier, almost all of my interviewees were no longer anywhere to be found. When I enquired about them, the most common refrain was, "Oh, I think she (or he) left several years ago." The small number who were still there were nearly all among the elite group of staffers; i.e., individuals making high five or low six figure salaries and working in key committee positions. Indeed, many young staffers in place in 2011 were no longer present when I sought them out in 2013.

I possess inadequate data to make strong statements about whether there are discriminatory hiring practices in place when it comes to the recruitment of staffers. One staffer, whose résumé listed work or association with numerous Jewish organizations, told me that one job interviewer baldly stated, "If Israel matters to you at all, you won't want to work here because AIPAC hates us." At its worst, the warning issued to the job seeker constituted blatant stereotyping, and, at its best, considerable ignorance. I interviewed numerous Jewish American staffers working for House members who are critical of Israel, or others who hold their own critical positions while working for members who are not critical of Israeli policies. In this particular case, the job seeker, who was Jewish, chose to look elsewhere and found a position in another congressional office. But beyond this staffer's experience, and returning to the bigger picture, all evidence suggests that the number of Jewish staffers is relatively high. It is certainly well in excess of the percentage of Jewish American citizens in the general population, but perhaps just a reflection of that community's predilection for higher education. Twenty of my House staffer interviewees identified themselves as Jewish, roughly 20 percent of my first-round interview sample and about ten times the size of the Jewish community in the United States. By comparison, I interviewed just three staffers who were of Arab-American ancestry, all of whom were Christians, and one black African, Muslim American. (There are roughly 3.5 million Arab Americans, and the size of the Muslim American community surpassed that of the Jewish American community several years ago, as noted earlier.) On a person-by-person level, these figures mean absolutely nothing in the sense that staffers' ethno-religious backgrounds provide no clear indication of their views on the conflict, as will be noted repeatedly.

To those unfamiliar with standard operating procedure and issue prioritization in most congressional House offices, the youthfulness of staffers working on foreign policy derives in part from the low priority assigned to foreign affairs, by both the members themselves and their constituents. Membership on what was called in the mid-2000s the House Committee on International Relations (HIRC) and what is now officially the House Committee on Foreign Affairs (HFAC) is not considered a "plum" committee assignment; it is not an "A" committee in the way that the Appropriations, Ways and Means, or Rules committees are widely perceived as "A" committees. In addition, membership on other committees, like Agriculture, Energy, or Small Business, is much more highly coveted by various House members as a function of their constituents' interests. For most House members, HFAC membership doesn't help them with their constituents because, without prejudice to cultural sensitivities, there is no "bacon" to bring home to the home district. "No pork, no play," as the Hill expression goes. It follows that the best, most seasoned staffers working for any individual congressperson are more likely to be focused on higher priority issue areas, sometimes leaving less seasoned staffers to cover foreign affairs work. Of course, some HFAC members are acutely interested and involved in international relations matters and/or have constituents who are acutely interested in certain foreign affairs issues, so they do seek foreign relations committee membership and allocate their staff resources accordingly. But they are in a minority.

A second common, and equally striking, feature is how much work the typical staffer has on his or her plate. In every office I entered, I began by stating the nature of my study and asked to speak with the staffer who assisted the congressperson with foreign policy issues, with special attention to policy-making on the Arab-Israeli and IME conflicts. However, when I interviewed the foreign affairs staffers, I also asked what other portfolios they held. The standard response included defense, intelligence, homeland security, veterans' affairs, commerce, the environment, and several other "minor issues." Substitute taxes, judicial affairs, or some other weighty portfolio for certain items from the preceding list, as I moved from one foreign affairs staffer to the next, and the reader gets a strong sense of the average House staffer's responsibilities. To quote one former staffer directly, "I do foreign affairs, defense, homeland security, intelligence, immigration, trade, justice, welfare, women's issues, animal welfare, plus two or three more issues." In another office, a chief of staff observed, "We have one LA who handles fourteen issues—he's 23 years old." Yet another young staffer said, "I work primarily on foreign policy, homeland security, immigration, trade, and small business issues. It's impossible to keep on top of all these issues." Being responsible for roughly ten portfolios, to my great surprise, was the norm.

To reiterate, when I checked back in on a great number of the same offices in 2011, 2012, and 2013 previous staffer interviewees, especially the younger ones, were almost all long gone. Their replacements and/or chiefs of staff said that the standard staffer workload had either remained roughly the same or had increased from the previous time period in 2005–2006 due to the Republicans' budget cuts. Where applied directly to office staffing, these cutbacks caused the removal of at least 1–1.5 staffers per office, and many offices had indeed chosen to reduce their D.C. staff's size. The only indication I received about positive change was that some offices had introduced electronic systems for sorting email messages from constituents, enabling them to process and respond in a more efficient, albeit less personal, way.

Faced as most House staffers are with these ridiculously long laundry lists of chores, the amount of time most can spend on foreign affairs is quite limited. During my interviews, I asked how much time they actually do spend on foreign policy issues and, more specifically, the matters relating to the Arab-Israeli conflict, broadly defined. I found an enormous disparity in the amount of time spent on such matters between the least and most concerned offices. One House staffer said he spent 2 percent of his time on foreign affairs issues in general, and the reader should remember that he holds that portfolio for his congressperson; one other House staffer (and only one) spent 100 percent of his time on foreign affairs. Time spent working on the IME conflicts ranged from 0 to 90 percent of time spent on foreign affairs in general. In the House, the average amount of time spent on foreign affairs in general was 36 percent; the median was 30 percent; and the mode was 10 percent. Of this time spent on foreign affairs in general, the average amount of time devoted by my staffer interviewees to work on the IME conflicts was 36 percent, the median was 30 percent, and the mode was 20 percent. In effect, the staffers whose responsibility it is to stay on top of these issues and provide advice to their congressperson spent on average 13 percent of their total time working on the conflict, but the median was 9 percent, and the mode—again the most common percentage and undoubtedly the more indicative figure—was 2 percent. And here, too, to reinforce the point via redundancy, the overwhelming majority of these staffers had come to their jobs with little to no knowledge of this complex issue area.

The typical "new kid on the block" staffer, burdened as he or she is by their job assignments, rolls with the punches of the legislative agenda and events on the ground. Thus, when a crisis or important event occurs, their focus can shift radically from one week to the next. "Washington goes in cycles with regard to its devotion to foreign policy issues," noted one young staffer in 2006. Or as another young staffer said in 2005, "I spent 80 percent of my time working on Iraq in the run-up to the war. Normally I spend about 60 to 70 percent of my time on transportation issues, and 20 to 30 percent on another issue area. Usually I spend about one percent of my time on foreign affairs." And, introducing a partisan angle, a third staffer commented: "Republican cuts have translated into fewer staff members. It's an outrage that there's not one person working exclusively on foreign policy because there's just so much to do."

To sum up, roughly three quarters of the House staffers working on foreign affairs are young, bright, and work hard but staffers of all ages face almost impossible odds to keep themselves well informed on such a broad range of issues. The consequences for congressional behavior are significant and are spelled out in greater detail below.

THE VETERAN STAFFERS

Although the data above include individuals from all three subgroups of staffers, it's important to spend some time talking specifically about those with greater experience. Alongside the great corps of youthful staff cadres there exists another, smaller corps of staffers who are seasoned veterans. Again, in my first-round sample, I had 27 individuals with over five years of experience working on the Hill, roughly 25 percent of the first-round total. For these individuals, the mix of psychic and material gratification provided by their congressional staff work had been great enough to keep them on the Hill. Staffers who stay on the Hill can acquire experiential learning far surpassing what they might learn in any graduate program, as one former veteran told me. She also noted that she knew young staffers who had left the Hill to go to graduate programs or law school, only to be unable to find jobs, and moreover to find themselves blocked from recovering the positions they had once held on the Hill! So many veterans can feel their choice to stay was a sound one even on material grounds.

One veteran with an excellent academic pedigree commented, "You don't get rich at this. We're more like you academic types," suggesting that one stayed on the job because of the high level of psychic gratification and a respectable income. "Members on committees will have older types," he added, "because you [the congressperson] get what you pay for. In many offices, there's a lot of poor work done due to inexperience." Most of the veterans I interviewed were found in the offices of House members serving on the full House Committee on International Relations, and even more specifically in the office of those serving on HIRC's Subcommittee on the Middle East and Central Asia. I also came across several seasoned staffers in other House offices who had considerable interest and expertise on the Middle East. This second "group" was comprised of LDs or chiefs of staff, in addition to a number of LAs. Their interest in the region was generally attributable to some combination of special constituent interest, strong personal interest (a significant number did identify themselves as Jewish Americans), or greater interest in this issue area by their congressperson. However, as noted, this number was small.

Staffers in the "veterans" group were mostly in their thirties, although a few were in their forties or fifties. Fewer than 10 of my 106 2005–06 House interviewees were over 35 years old. Most of these staffers were people with greater academic credentials than their youthful counterparts. They all have had considerable experience on the Hill—20 of the 27 had eight or more years on the Hill—and usually they had either traveled to or lived in the Middle East. A handful of these individuals demonstrated very impressive, in-depth knowledge of Middle East issues and actors; they exhibited a true command of the conflict's details.

The "veterans" are usually in a position of comparative advantage over their youthful counterparts in that, on top of their experience, they are asked and/or allowed to devote a far greater percentage of their time to studying the Middle East and tracking its daily developments. The difference here is often a function of a specific congressperson's keener interest in Mideast issues, regardless of his or her idiosyncratic motivations. "I'm one of the lucky few who can focus on foreign policy," said a "veteran" with impressive educational credentials. He spent about 80 percentof his time on foreign affairs. With a few exceptions, however, veteran staffers did not necessarily devote a significantly greater percentage of their time to foreign affairs issues or to following the IME conflicts, perhaps because their greater experience enabled them to handle a broader range of issues with greater efficiency. "Veterans" were not exempt from demanding workloads and the handling of diverse portfolios. They were, however, more likely to hold just four to six important portfolios, not eight to fourteen.

THE PROBLEM OF INFORMATION OVERLOAD

Almost every day of a staffer's life brings a torrent of communications. Staffers in the front lobby do yeoman's work in responding to phone calls, listening remarkably patiently—in nearly all cases—to constituents' concerns and complaints. (I witnessed and overheard the staffers' ends of hundreds of exchanges while waiting in the reception area for my interviews to begin.) In addition, these staffers are very adept at screening calls to higher-ranking staffers and their bosses to provide them the space they need to complete their work. I know this through experience as well, having had many interview requests I made by phone parked by those who took the calls.

But even with these screening mechanisms in play, staffers are left with heavy informational workloads. Mail, delivered three times daily, accumulates rapidly, producing daunting piles of correspondence—often several feet high—from constituents, lobbyists, nongovernmental organizations (NGOs), and special interests. It was a common occurrence for my staffer interviewees to "show off" their piles of paper communications, a "show and tell" exercise meant to demonstrate the great challenge staffers face as part of their daily routine. One staffer commented on the mass of communication, saying, "We get mail three times per day, with at least fifteen items per time. Come voting season I'll get double that. Plus you get emails and blast-faxes. It's overwhelming. There are seven to eight things going on simultaneously. You have to fly by the seat of your pants."

The burden of this imposing mass of material has been severely compounded in the new millennium by the advent of the Internet and high-speed communications. It takes virtually no time for anyone to learn how to obtain email access to a House or Senate office—all one does to reach a House member or staffer, for example, is to type firstname.surname@mail.house. gov. Office staffers find themselves on the receiving end of a veritable flood of emails from constituents, interest groups, and institutions. Of course, everyone has a computer, and many staffers would not be caught dead without their BlackBerry (in the mid-2000s) or iPhone (today), but the challenge of processing email has become one of the most vexing issues for staffers. Due to budget cutbacks and a decline in office staff in many offices, this situation had at best remained the same, if not gotten worse, by 2011–13. Although, again, there were some signs by late 2012 that electronic sorting mechanisms for email messages were providing some relief.

The electronic revolution in communications poses an extremely important new dilemma. Because congressional resources have not expanded to help offices meet this new challenge, staffers have been left in a position in which it is impossible to process meaningfully all the information sent their way. In 2006, a veteran staffer referred to a recent study by the Congressional Management Foundation that showed there had been a 100 percent increase in contacts with constituents over the past five years,[135] and noted that the problem was only going to grow. She said, "Technology makes for new issues every day, such that we don't know what we're dealing with from day to day. Everybody is throwing tons of information at you every day, so how do you filter through this, especially with the same number of staffers today as in the pre-tech period? I've come to see myself as an untrained professional. People should be trained for this work; they don't come prepared."

Other young, astute staffers put numbers to the problem. One said, "Because of the Internet, we've gone from answering 25,000 to 48,000 pieces of 'mail' per year over the past two and a half to three years." Another asked, "Have you seen a congressional in-box? There's three feet of news per day—literally three feet of paper mail per day. That doesn't include emails or letters. I get 100 to 150 emails per day. When the Dubai Ports incident [early 2006] occurred, I got 300 emails per day; almost all said the same thing."

Again, the 2011–2012 budget cutbacks did not help matters. Even in an office where the interviewee told me the "workload hasn't changed in our office," he admitted, "the volume of mail and email—it's now more email dominated—is off the charts." An older staffer, seconded from the State Department, said, "The workload is so great, you have to rely on the head-lines from newspapers because we're just so busy. The headlines dictate the crisis of the day, so you end up with a superficial understanding of things, which can be dangerous."

In terms of visual media, nearly all congressional offices contain one or two television monitors in their reception room. While one monitor is usually reserved for C-SPAN broadcasts of House or Senate deliberations, the other is typically set on either CNN or Fox News. But most staffers are buried in work in the back offices, using the reception lobby only if summoned to meet supplicants or perhaps to watch some breaking news.

The overall deluge of information has fostered a variety of coping mech-anisms. In the issue area under investigation here, the staffers' perspectives yield poignant insights. Here are two staffers' views of this issue:

> "A key thing here is to get good information on something fast. Obviously I'm not an expert on this stuff, so I need to get good info from someone and get it fast. I tend to get it from a government source, like CRS [Congressional Research Services], or the State Department's government affairs office. We hear a lot from pro-Israel groups, and [home state] Jewish groups. AIPAC comes in and I col-lect information from them, and there is a large Jewish community in our area. You have to skim everything, so in my case I discard a lot of AIPAC stuff because I know where they stand."

"Because the flow of information is overwhelming, the trust factor comes into play; that is, you pay greater attention to what are deemed as important or trustworthy sources of information."

Lest one think that the staffers' challenge of dealing with this mass of information diminishes with on-the-job training, one need only be reminded that most of the young staffers do not stick around very long. Again, because the research effort for this work extended over several years, I noticed upon making return visits to House offices, even within the same six-to-twelve-month time frame, that the staffers I had interviewed were no longer there. In general, the following formula holds: small paychecks + high cost of living = rapid turnover. So, many staffers think of "getting this work experience on their résumé to go work off the Hill on K Street" (with the lobbyists)—where they can make much more serious money. As one savvy, youngish staffer observed: "LAs average one and a half years in place before leaving. You can look at how long people stay with their bosses; if they stay, it's probably because their boss is listening to them more. Staff assistants—the ones who take the phone calls—they last about six months. LCs last about eight months. This place has the biggest burnout rate imaginable—the carrot is to make it to LA, then to become a lobbyist and make six figures." Another staffer said, "Many people work two years, then go to lobbyists to work for much larger salaries. An LA getting a lobbyist job can make in the low $100,000s; a chief of staff can get a job with a big firm making $200,000 to 300,000."

Unsurprisingly, the same pull affects the "staying power" of higher-ranking staffers. In 2006, there was a roughly $140,000 income cap for staffers. But the bottom line was that staffers could not make more than their bosses, whose pay in 2006 was $165,200 per year ($174,000 in 2009).[136] As one veteran noted in 2006, "Now there is also great change, or turnover, among chiefs of staff, too, and that's where the expertise really was before; now there's a revolving door there, also."

High burnout and turnover rates were not always a problem. A 50-something staffer with lengthy Hill experience commented, "Back in the old days, I was the odd person out being young. That was back in the 1970s and early 1980s." But this is clearly no longer the norm. Low salaries, high burnout rates, and the allure of greener pastures all keep the average age of most House staffers low. So to complete the formula: high burnout = less experienced staffers. The great majority of staffers are lacking in experience. And the reader should ponder the following: if the longer-run objective of many of the staffers is to acquire a better paying position with lobbyists, doesn't this make them less likely to create friction with the very groups and special interest organizations by whom they one day hope to be employed? (A former, veteran staffer who reviewed this text injected at the end of this observation an emphatic, "Yes!")

Returning to the informational blizzard: it's crucial for all to realize that this information overload translates into reams of mail and gigabytes of emails. Hill staffers face so much informational input that they have to go into "triage mode." Only the factors that strike the respective analysts as being most significant are taken seriously; the rest of the information will be ignored. Extremely importantly, only those organizations or interests having established a large measure of name recognition, credibility, and significance are likely to have their materials or messages read. Triage does not negatively affect letters and phone calls from most constituents, which—based again on my extensive observations—still command some measure of respect and due processing by LCs; however, almost everything else is fair game for the trash bin, the cold shoulder, or the unanswered phone call. Indeed, staffers openly admit that they do not have the time to read all the messages and reports flowing to them, even sometimes those from more influential actors. This point was confirmed to me in one particularly interesting exchange I had in an interview with two House staffers—one of whom was a former intelligence analyst—in the near aftermath of publication of John Mearsheimer and Stephen Walt's article on the Israel lobby in the *London Review of Books*. As I noted in this book's introduction, I feared the article would be quickly and widely read by staffers and might negatively affect, even contaminate, my interview pool as I neared completion of my first major round of Capitol Hill interviews in 2006. I asked the seasoned staffers if they had yet read the piece. They responded by asking me how long the article was, and when I told them that the full version posted on Harvard's John F. Kennedy School website was about 80 pages in length, one of the staffers answered, in all apparent earnest, "No; no one up here has time to read something that's that long." I was relieved insofar as my own social scientific pursuit was concerned, but troubled by the thought of what this portended for the welfare of the nation. All things considered, the informational challenge heightens the need for concerned players to obtain access through other channels, such as personal phone calls, and/or face-to-face meetings with individuals and group representatives. And one must remember, this informational overload is heaped on individuals who, for the most part, have a very slim knowledge base in this issue area. This state of affairs flings the door wide open to powerful single actor constituents and highly skilled lobbyists. The same veteran staffer who commented on the impact of the 2011–2012 cutbacks on staffing and the quality of staffer recruits added, "This does make our staff more dependent upon interest groups and lobbies, people who can help us with information." In addition, lobbyists with clout—lobbyists who cannot be ignored without paying a price—are much more likely to be paid attention to. Lobbyists who can provide what is perceived as sound information in a timely, highly professional manner more readily earn the respect and/or forbearance of most congressional staffers. Toss in free pizza, snacks, or beverages along with an information session, and the youthful, underpaid staffers are "in."

As noted earlier, a fair number of staffer interviewees came to their jobs having taken courses in politics, but only an extremely small number had a background in the arcane politics of the Middle East. I asked all of my interviewees if they had studied the Middle East, and a strong majority—64 percent—had never taken a single course on Mideast politics. Those who had studied the Middle East had usually taken just one course. Although nearly all my interviewees impressed me as highly energetic, extremely hardworking, and bright people, it would require an incredible stretch of the imagination to consider most young staffers capable of providing expert advice to their bosses on Mideast affairs. So as a group they might best be described as competent "generalists," not experts. As one of my staffer interviewees asked rhetorically, with an appropriately wry smile, at the start of the interview, "So you've come here to find out how little we know about the subject?"

In this regard, the staffers are not much different from most of their bosses with regard to Middle East matters. Most House members' educations, careers, and life experiences have left them with little knowledge of Middle East history and politics. A veteran staffer noted: "There's even a large percentage of Republicans who take it as a badge of pride that they haven't traveled. Only 10 to 20 percent of the congresspersons overall really give a damn about this [Arab-Israeli conflict] issue. Coastal members may be more knowledgeable, in general. I'd say about 5 to 10 percent of members are actually knowledgeable on these issues; and about 5 to 10 percent of staffers." As another veteran House staffer stated, "Most House members have an LA to assist them with Middle East issues because they don't know much about the area."

In light of so many staffers' own limitations, this comment should not be taken as terribly reassuring. For example, one young staffer, fresh out of college with a major in political science but with zero background on the Middle East, asserted that his boss "depends on me a lot as a resource on these issues. Foreign affairs is not her bag." The young staffer in question had been on the job for all of eight months, had no academic background in Middle East affairs, and had way too much else on his plate to acquire one! Many other staffers, with comparable backgrounds, provided similar accounts.

This widespread lack of experience and thin knowledge base leaves most staffers and congresspersons all the more dependent on alternative internal and external sources of information and counsel for the processing of many issues, including those relating to the Mideast. So let's see what staffers noted as their major sources of information.

SOURCES OF INFORMATION; GRIST FOR DECISION MAKING

I did not ask my interviewees to rank their sources of information and counsel in terms of importance. I rarely provided prompts, but did so on occasion if the interviewee seemed to have the answer on the tip of his/her tongue. So what follows is a list of those sources without, for the most part, a value attached to the order in which they were presented. For many staffers, items placed lower on this list may figure more prominently than those near the top. Whatever their weight, these sources represent critical inputs to the formulation of staffers' views and therefore to what they tell their bosses. In the end, most bosses' thoughts and decisions are affected, at least in part, by these sources.

The Print and Visual Media as Sources?

Most staffers began their response to the question about sources of information by running through a standard litany of print media sources: the *New York Times*, the *Washington Post*, the *Economist*, the *Financial Times*, the *Wall Street Journal*, the *Weekly Standard*, the *Christian Science Monitor*, *Time*, *News-*

week, US News and World Report, the *Hill, Roll Call, Politico*, and the *National Journal.* Most read a small subset of these publications, plus a local (home state or city) paper, and also turned to *Congressional Quarterly* (CQ) or the *Congressional Daily.* Many staffers noted that they just do Internet searches to bolster their understanding of various subjects, like getting updates from *Foreign Policy*'s "Daily Brief" in the 2013 time frame. However, it was interesting to see specific ideological biases on clear display in several staffers' comments. This occurred with greatest frequency among conservative staffers, who often asserted that given its "liberal bias," they would never read the *New York Times*, the paper considered by many political cognoscenti as the nation's "newspaper of record." A few liberal staffers chided their conservative counterparts, noting "R's make the mistake of only listening to Fox, or reading the *Wall Street Journal* and the *Financial Times*."

A fair number of staffers, usually ones with greater experience and a military background or orientation, plugged into the Pentagon's "Early Bird" press clippings/daily briefing. Some Democrat staffers, perhaps erring in the opposite ideological direction from the R's, noted: "Fox News, the American Enterprise Institute (AEI), and Heritage [Foundation] are all so biased I don't look at their publications any more. I don't like the Republican media; it's just a big machine. It so completely supports the president [George W. Bush] and warmongering, so I reach out to professors at [my alma mater] or others I've met here."

Overall, a very small number of staffers, just a handful, cited papers from the Middle East region, including the more liberal/leftist-leaning *Ha'aretz* and the *Jerusalem Post*—both Israeli publications—and the *Forward*—an American newspaper that addresses issues of interest to the Jewish American community. A couple staffers with experience living in Israel tuned in first and foremost to the Israeli media. "I live on *Ha'aretz* and Israeli army radio." "First I read *Ha'aretz*, then I read the *New York Times* and the *Washington Post*." A few staffers cited al-Jazeera's website, and two people in total mentioned the *Daily Star* (of Beirut, Lebanon). So, to the extent that any publication carries its own biased coverage of Middle East events, the staffers are consuming information from print media sources that affect their viewpoints. Because the most commonly cited sources—the major US newspapers—carry a moderate to strong "pro-Israel" bias, and are more likely to carry reports and/or editorial commentary supportive of right wing Israeli viewpoints, a generally pro-Israeli perspective is embodied in their use.

Not many staffers mentioned the radio, such as listening to National Public Radio. NPR has, at times, come under attack from right wing pro-Israeli supporters, prompting one interviewee to assert that "It [NPR] is unfairly made to be a target—they don't deserve to be browbeaten as they have been in recent months." (And it is noteworthy that NPR came under attack in 2011 from the new Tea Party elements in Congress.) Radio news may be too time-consuming, it being much easier to scan news presented in print than to try to remain tuned in to a more laborious radio broadcast, or to go fishing for the print version of broadcasts. A very small number of staffers did note that they listened to BBC news on a regular basis.

As with their youthful counterparts, older staffers tuned in to the major US media sources, the *New York Times*, the *Washington Post*, the *Wall Street Journal*, and perhaps a major regional paper, such as the *Los Angeles Times*. However, a somewhat greater percentage of these veterans looked closely at regional publications, with *Ha'aretz* and the *Jerusalem Post* mentioned most often. A handful of people also referred to the *Daily Star* as an occasionally useful source.

Veteran staffers are typically able and willing to cite a long list of websites from which they derive relevant information. Sites that were mentioned included Middle East Media Research Institute (MEMRI), which is news compiled largely by strong right wing pro-Israelis and former Israeli intelligence agents, and Foreign Broadcast Information Service (FBIS), a US-government compilation of foreign news. But the aforementioned print media sources were in far greater use.

A smaller number of staffers have the luxury of interns whom they ask to compile articles on topics of particular interest. Those working for the majority party on the HIRC/HFAC foreign policy staff could have as many as six to eight interns collecting information for them, but they're operating in a distinct category.

Congressional Research Services: A "Go-To, Unbiased Source" to Most

Another commonly cited source of information is the in-house, Congressional Research Services (CRS). References to CRS held strong among interviewees in 2011–13. The CRS is divided along functional and geographical lines, and in 2005–2006 there were five individuals working on the Middle East, of whom I interviewed two. Most staffers see it as a source of solid, unbiased, nonpartisan information—especially straightforward, factual information—about Middle East issues. Here's a collection of brief comments on CRS by House staffers.

"Oh yeah, I've got them [CRS] on speed dial." "Reading CRS is invaluable; I don't know how the Hill would function without them." "CRS is a good starting point; it offers kind of a template for those who know nothing." "CRS does a fabulous job. I can call them and ask any question; they'll do research on any subject." "The media is slanted, so we like CRS." "I use CRS a lot. They have a history of what happens and how Congress reacted to it." [And] "CRS is always my first stop—they're fantastic because of the details they provide on specific questions, and they're non-partisan. They'll give all sides of the issue, then say our sense of the situation is this."

The less-experienced staffers were more likely to see the CRS as a valuable resource than were the older hands. One veteran found CRS "too sluggish" and "lacking in timeliness." Another noted, "I use CRS a little, but not on the A-I conflict because they don't come up with new stuff. I know or can find out most of the stuff on my own." And a third veteran stated: "CRS is more a resource for people who don't do this on a regular basis." Finally, a few staffers saw CRS as succumbing to domestic political pressures, as made clear in the following quote: "I use CRS somewhat, but they're under a lot of political pressure, too. The majority [Republicans at the time] wants more anodyne reports; CRS was critical of the NSA's wiretapping, and people there may have gotten their hands slapped."

For most staffers, however, one of the great appeals of CRS was perception of it as factual, unbiased, and nonpartisan; this warrants additional commentary. It speaks to many staffers' sense that they are so inundated with information they perceive as biased and/or generated by "special interest" groups and individuals that they prefer the measure of objectivity afforded by the CRS analysts. Of course, this, in turn, raises the question of who the CRS analysts are, and what information they are serving up.

The CRS staffers working on the Middle East in the early stages of this study included Alfred Prados, Kenneth Katzman, Carol Migdalovitz, Jeremy Sharp, and Christopher Blanchard. By 2006, Alfred Prados had been on the job for some 20 years. Sharp was a recent Princeton grad, but Katzman, Migdalovitz, and Blanchard all had considerable experience on the job. By 2013, Prados, Blanchard, and Migdalovitz were gone, Katzman and Sharp were still in place, and Jim Zanotti had been added to the Middle East staff. These are all highly knowledgeable individuals, with excellent credentials. I didn't have enough time to examine their own political orientations more carefully. Generally speaking, the reports "penned" by these staffers appear sound and heavily factual in nature, although often one senses when reading them that their authors are so wary of offending political sensibilities as to render the reports either anodyne or too biased by mainstream sources. It is tempting to characterize some CRS reports as providing staffers with a sort of Cliff's Notes coverage of issues and events, but given most staffers' own time constraints and needs, this is perhaps a virtue.

House Foreign Affairs Committee Staffers = Very Valuable Sources

Staffers often seek information and guidance from individuals working for HFAC. This committee's staff positions are filled along party lines, so there are two smallish groups of individuals working for the majority and minority parties, respectively. Titled professional staff members (PSMs), they work in special office suites allocated to them as is the case for other committees' PSMs. In general, the PSMs are slightly older and typically possess greater, at times even considerably so, area expertise. Therefore, many staffers regard PSMs as "go-to" persons for information in general or when they're prepping for briefings or hearings specifically. Of course, in Washington, D.C., everybody has his or her critics, and not all drink from every PSM's cup. Observed one staffer: "The standing committees are the best source of information, although they do have their own slants. I can get a wealth of information from the committee staffs. With regard to these slants, for example, from the majority party [R's], I'd hear positive information regarding military progress in Iraq, whereas the Democrats would concentrate more on what we need to do to get out. There wouldn't be much difference between majority and minority views with respect to the Arab-Israeli conflict."

Another staffer, interviewed in 2006, more pointedly asserted:

> I get a lot of emails from the Middle East subcommittee—there's a woman there [Yleme Poblete] who's very proactive; she's very hyperactive on this Middle East stuff. I don't read it as much because I find it one-sided. Gordon Prater in New Mexico writes for antiwar.

com; it's a counter-balance to [Rep.] Ros-Lehtinen's material. [Ros-Lehtinen was subcommittee chairwoman, and Poblete's boss] But I think most of the subcommittee people buy into the Ros-Lehtinen stuff hook, line, and sinker. There's very little brain wave activity up here. My colleagues at hearings are reading the *Congressional Daily* and *The Hill*; they're not digging for information from more reputable sources.

At the time of my initial research effort, the major figures on the committee staffs included Hillel Weinberg and Yleme Poblete, the principal staffers on the Republican side for the full HFAC and the Middle East subcommittee, respectively, and Alan Makovsky and David Adams, their Democratic counterparts. Due to majority privileges, Weinberg and Poblete benefited from a greater number of staff assistants. This situation changed in 2006 when the Democrats took control of Congress, and flip-flopped again after the 2010 elections when the Republicans regained majority control of the House. With the exception of Hillel Weinberg, the others lasted through this five- to six-year period of congressional instability, and through the duration of my study. By 2011–2012, Poblete was filling Weinberg's spot, as she was still working for Ros-Lehtinen, who had become the chair of HFAC. The subcommittee slot for the Republicans was then filled by chairman Steve Chabot, whose key staffer was Kevin Fitzpatrick. On the Democrat side, Makovsky still had Rep. Berman's back; and Adams had been replaced by Rep. Ackerman's longtime office staffer, Howard Diamond, who served Ackerman in the latter's capacity as the subcommittee's ranking member. (By mid-2013, both Poblete and Makovsky were gone.)

Again, the party in power and its associated chairpersons benefit from greater budget allocations, such that the majority staff on HIRC/HFAC or Appropriations is beefed up by comparison with the minority staff. The latter are doomed to complain about being outgunned by their counterparts and at a loss to compete more effectively with the majority's output. All of these individuals graciously granted me interviews at one point or another, and I was impressed by all of them in terms of their intellect and congressional skills. Weinberg, Makovsky, Diamond, and Adams all struck me as more familiar with the history of the Middle East through combinations of formal study, living experiences, and "on-the-Hill" work on related issues. All of these individuals espoused strongly pro-Israel positions, with the slight exceptions of Adams and Fitzpatrick, who struck me as more cautious and balanced. As will be discussed later, Poblete's views were such that she ran afoul of even right wing Israeli government officials for advancing policies even they deemed too extreme.

Taking Cues from the Party Conference or Party Caucus, and Other Caucuses

Staffers often mentioned the importance of the party conference or caucus, as well as various other caucuses as sources of information. The Republicans call their party caucus the "Republican Conference," the Democrats have the "Democratic Caucus." The party caucuses send out regular communiqués to their party's members informing them of the party's position vis-à-vis specific resolutions and bills. Both the Republican Conference and the Democratic Caucus receive funds to cover their costs—they each got about $1.6 million in 2012, for example—and this enhances their ability to communicate their policy preferences.

The parties, as national entities, work hard to gin up support for themselves and their candidates in many ways, and of course much of this activity is centered on fund-raising and winning elections as noted in chapters one and two. Again, this involves keeping the party attractive to major donors. One means is to present a party platform that resonates with particular special interests and, at times, this concern creates conflicts of interest and clashes over values and priorities between party leaderships and their own rank-and-file members. Such a clash was placed on full display before a national audience on September 5, 2012, during the Democratic National Convention (DNC) in Charlotte, North Carolina. During the DNC's nominating proceedings, and before a chamber that was roughly one-half to two-thirds full, the presiding chairman, Los Angeles Mayor Antonio Villaraigosa, called for and easily won by voice vote a suspension of the proceedings for the purpose of revising the party platform's language. He then called on Ohio Gov. Ted Strickland to introduce two amendments, to be voted on simultaneously. One called for reinstating references to God in the platform's text, and the second, more controversial revision called for reinstatement of a reference to Jerusalem as "Israel's indivisible capital." A two-thirds majority was required to pass Strickland's amendment. When Villaraigosa called for the voice vote, a moment captured for posterity on Internet sources, a loud shout of "Ayes" was followed by an equal if not louder chorus of "Nays" by party members on the convention hall floor. Caught off guard and visibly flustered—one really needs to watch the film clip—Villaraigosa ended up calling two additional voice votes, each of which yielded comparable results, albeit at an increasingly high pitch. Villaraigosa, with some onstage coaching by another party official, then declared what was clear for all to see and hear was not the case; that is, that the "Ayes" had it, and that the language in the platform would be amended. Nothing could have more obviously demonstrated the party leadership's disregard for its own delegates' sentiments.

Additional caucuses exist with distinct group identities and interests. For example, members of the Congressional Black Caucus (CBC) and Congressional Hispanic Caucus (CHC) will confer with one another's staffs to see how they are sizing up a particular letter, resolution, or bill relating to a range of issues, including the Middle East. Other, issue-focused caucuses provide references to House members, such as the Women's Caucus and the Blue Dogs Caucus, as will be seen below.

The Importance of Lobbyists as Sources of Information

For a whole host of reasons, most staffers rely heavily on information provided by various lobbying organizations. While much has already been said about lobbyists above, and much more will follow, I will limit myself to providing some important background information here. Most if not all the lobbying groups for this issue area may be divided along ethno-religious lines. Thus, there are predominantly Jewish American, Arab American, Iranian American, Arab nation-state, Christian Arab, and Muslim groups. But there are ideological, national, and/or partisan divisions within these ethno-religious camps. Especially important are the divisions among Jewish American groups, as discussed shortly. This also means that there exists an overlapping of objectives across the ethno-religious divide, such that some Jewish American groups can and do ally with other non–Jewish American groups. Finally, as the reader will see, there is a small, residual category of groups that does not fit this schema.

In his highly informative 2009 book *Transforming America's Israel Lobby*, Dan Fleshler presents an excellent chart of the "Organized" American Community and the Conventional Israel Lobby.[137] He classified Jewish American organizations into the following ideological camps: six "Far Left or Religious Anti-Zionist" groups, sixteen "Pro-Israel Left" groups, eleven "Center Left" groups, twenty-two "Center" groups, five "Center Right" groups, and fourteen "Far Right" groups.[138] Of these 74 groups, only 16 were mentioned by my interviewees. I will note here that the Conference of Presidents of Major American Jewish Organizations, the most important American Jewish umbrella organization, was hardly ever mentioned by my interviewees, perhaps not surprising because its efforts are focused on the executive branch.

The most mentioned lobby group in this issue area is, far and away, AIPAC. Over the years, AIPAC has been closely examined, and any uninformed reader would benefit from previous studies of it.[139] For years Washington cognoscenti have consistently ranked AIPAC among the top two or three most powerful and effective lobbies in Washington, D.C., usually second only to AARP.

AMERICAN ISRAEL PUBLIC AFFAIRS COMMITTEE (AIPAC): VITAL STATISTICS[140]

Year	Annual Operating Budget	Membership	Staff Size
2010	$67–70 million	c. 100,000	200
2004	$33.4 million	85,000	165
1992	c. $15 million	55,000	150
1989	$10 million	n.a.	100
1974	c. $20,000	n.a.; small	under 5

With a budget in recent years of c. $68 million, over 200 staffers, and 100,000 members nationwide, AIPAC's material and human resources exceed the resources focused on Middle East matters by all of its noteworthy competitors combined. As already shown, AIPAC provides a steady supply of information via email on a wide variety of Middle East developments, with particular emphasis, of course, on issues relating to Israel, the Arab-Israeli and Israeli-Palestinian conflicts, and Israel's concerns about Iran and other countries. The organization can, at a moment's notice, dispatch at least twenty lobbyists to the Hill to respond to queries or deliver messages, or mobilize supporters across the country to phone their congresspersons' offices.

On the basis of my interview experiences, most staffers seem to accept

AIPAC's assistance and information happily and uncritically. Faced as they are with a daily deluge of information, reports from AIPAC save them considerable time and effort in deciphering Mideast affairs. All but a small number of my interviewees, including even most of those working in offices known for greater sympathy for Arab and Palestinian perspectives, expressed admiration for the high level of professionalism exhibited by AIPAC representatives. All 106 of my first-round House staffer interviewees "mentioned" AIPAC at least once during the interview, and all but one, who was new to her job, said they had at least one contact per year by an AIPAC rep!

Other predominantly (if not completely) Jewish American, domestic-based lobbyists and external organizations similarly "mentioned"—that is, at least once—by staffers in 2005–2006 were, again in descending order based on my sample: Americans for Peace Now (39 staffers), the Zionist Organization of America (28), Israel Policy Forum (24), American Jewish Committee (15), Brit Tzedek v'Shalom (6), NORPAC (6), B'nai B'rith (4), the Anti-Defamation League (2), and Hadassah (2).

Americans for Peace Now (APN) was founded in 1981 by Mark Rosenblum as an American sister to Israel's Peace Now movement. It actively endorses a two-state solution agreeable to moderates on both sides of the I-P conflict. With its roughly $2 million annual budget and modest staff, it does perhaps as fine a job as any group in terms of data collection, analysis, and information dissemination concerning developments on the Hill. In essence, it packs a bigger punch because it has supremely knowledgeable staffers, like Lara Friedman, who is steeped in Hill information and highly skilled at sharing it with all interested parties via APN's website. An APN figure told me: "The bottom line is that IPF and Brit Tzedek uses all our information; and staffers at many of the other lobbies, including J Street, readily acknowledge that they rely heavily on APN information. APN bills itself as a pro-Israel organization, comprised of Jewish American staffers who love Israel, but fear that right wing Israel government policies are destroying Israel's chances for a prosperous, peaceful place in the Middle East. It's an orientation that has been largely shared by Israel Policy Forum (IPF), Churches for Middle East Peace (CMEP), Council on American-Islamic Relations (CAIR), Brit Tzedek v'Shalom, and the Arab American Institute (AAI), and does not vary greatly from the positions of groups like J Street, Telos, and Friends Committee on National Legislation (FCNL). APN views and activities regularly pit it against AIPAC and the Zionist Organization of America (ZOA). APN has tended to use its more limited resources wisely. As Lewis Roth, former APN director told me in the mid-2000s, "We concentrate on the core of the core of opinion makers: the subcommittee members, Jewish members' staffers, etc.; there are about 40-50 staffers on the House side; about 30-40 staffers on the Senate side."

ZOA is one of the oldest, official Zionist organizations in the United States, with roots going back to 1897, the year of the foundation of the World Zionist Organization. ZOA has long been headed by Morton Klein, the son of Holocaust victims. Klein was born in a displaced persons' camp in Germany. In adulthood, he worked as an economist in the Nixon, Ford, and Carter administrations. ZOA posted $2.49 million in revenues and $3.86 million in expenditures in 2012.[141] It has chapters in most major American cities, and a membership ranging from 30,000–50,000. Seen as more hard-line than AIPAC, the organization is placed on the far right end of the spectrum of lobbyists. ZOA opposed, for example, Israel's unilateral withdrawal from the Gaza Strip in 2005; supports retention of the annexed Golan Heights; supports continued settlement activities on the West Bank; and sees Israeli governments' major military responses to Palestinian and other national security threats as either appropriate or, on some occasions, not strong enough.

Israel Policy Forum was set up in 1993, and until 2009 had M.J. Rosenberg as its director of policy analysis. Rosenberg had previously worked at AIPAC, as well as for many years as a staffer for Sen. Carl Levin (D-Michigan). Several poignant, personal experiences, one of which is discussed later in the book, caused Rosenberg to change his views. While retaining his great love for Israel, Rosenberg underwent a nearly 180 degree change of orientations, becoming one of the strongest, most indefatigable advocates of peace based on a two-state formula. As noted below, his weekly commentaries and counsel appealed to many Hill staffers. Given his energy and the power of his pen, his 2009 departure from IPF left a serious vacuum, but IPF staffers soldier on, promoting the two-state formula. In terms of its approach, an APN veteran noted: "IPF goes after big machers, whereas Brit Tzedek is more grassroots."

The American Jewish Committee (AJC), founded in 1906, recognized Israel upon its creation in 1948. However, long fearing accusations of "dual loyalty" for the Jewish Americans whose welfare it sought to safeguard over the decades, it retained a "non-Zionist" position until the time of the 1967

Arab-Israeli war. In 1982, it opened a wing called the Institute on American-Jewish Israeli Relations. AJC has tended to adopt positions supporting the policies of whichever government holds power in Israel, including more conservative, right wing governments. With annual revenues of $47.89 million and expenditures of $43.33 million in 2012,[142] the AJC has roughly 50,000 members. It has been directed by David Harris since 1990. Although lobbying activities are not part of its official mandate, it behaves like a lobbying group both at home and abroad in mobilizing support for Israeli government policies. It publishes numerous materials, the best known of which is *Commentary*, a magazine for neoconservatives.

The strongly right wing, pro-Israel group Christians United for Israel did not exist at the onset of my study. Set up by Texas evangelical Christian preacher John Hagee in early 2002, it became more active only in 2006. It's annual, National Night to Honor Israel events in Washington, D.C., are attended by thousands of Christian evangelical supporters of Israel.

Most Arab or Muslim lobbying groups focus their time and energy on a much broader range of topics than the IME conflicts. They're concerned with addressing other, domestic challenges affecting their well-being in American society. But all do show concern for Middle East matters as well. Among Arab or Muslim lobbying groups mentioned in 2005–2006, again in descending order, the Center for American Islamic Relations (10 staffers), the Arab American Institute (6), and the Arab-American Anti-Discrimination Committee (5) were noted most often. Mentioned by a few staffers was the American Task Force on Palestine (3). As for groups without a more "organic" link to the conflict, Churches for Middle East Peace (CMEP), a pro–two state solution advocacy group supported by numerous mainline Protestant churches, tied CAIR for mentions by staffers at ten. Four staffers spoke of Bannerman & Associates as a source of information, an organization—owned and led by Graeme Bannerman—contracted to represent PLO/Palestinian Authority and other interests, and the Council for the National Interest (CNI) had two staffers mention it. CNI was founded in 1989 by former Reps. Paul Findley and Pete McCloskey; both saw themselves as victims of AIPAC and other "pro-Israel" pressure groups when they sought and lost reelection.

Teasing the "staffers' mentions" statistics in different directions, one finds that all the non-AIPAC groups together registered 165 mentions (61 percent), compared with AIPAC's 106 (39 percent) all by itself. Jewish American groups, combined, garnered 232 of 272 (85 percent) total mentions; Arab and Muslim groups, per se, had just 24 of 272 mentions (9 percent). Finally, right wing pro-Israel groups (AIPAC, NORPAC, ZOA, etc.) made up 165 of 272 mentions (61 percent), whereas pro–two state solution groups (APN, CMEP, AAI, etc.) accounted for 105 of the 272 mentions (39 percent). Once again, the numbers are misleading in the sense that AIPAC personnel make repeat visits to a great many offices in a way that the others do not. And finally, it should be noted that a "mention" here is not to be equated with a "like." As will be seen, AIPAC drops into offices where it is not well liked, or even despised, but on the other side of the ledger, a fair number of the "mentions" associated with groups like APN, CAIR, or AAI were granted because these groups had sent a memorable fax, email, or literature—not a person—and these "contacts" were seen by a good number of staffers as unhelpful or a waste of their time.

Of particular interest, and as might be deduced from the numbers given above, was the common inability of most staffers to even name any pro-Arab lobby or "two-state" advocacy group. This was as true in 2011–2013 as it was in the mid-2000s. On more occasions than not, in both research time frames, special prodding was required by me to see if the average staffer could think of any pro-Arab voices, and it was not at all uncommon for the respondents to draw a complete blank. Those who could remember a particular pro-Arab group would say things like "Yes, there was some Christian church group," by which they were most likely, but not necessarily, referring to CMEP. Although supported by 21 mainstream churches, at just under $300,000, CMEP's annual budget is a fraction of APN's budget, and less than one percent of AIPAC's. CMEP has just one person engaging in Hill liaison activity. Interestingly, CMEP executive director Warren Clark, a former US ambassador, told me: "The media exaggerates the role of the Christian Zionists without real intent. We find it very difficult to get the mainstream media to cover the mainstream churches."

Some staffers know of and explicitly refer to AAI, the American Task Force on Palestine (ATFP), and CAIR, as well as the ADC, but again, these references were not common in 2006, and matters had not changed much at all 5–6 years later. In fact, AAI, which in recent years has had an annual operating budget of roughly $1.4 million (2012), had largely withdrawn from Hill lobbying activities to focus on informing and mobilizing voters for elections.

Indeed Speaking in 2006, AAI's director, James Zogby, told me: "We do what we do, but we've decided to target a smaller number of congressmen: people of Arab descent, or those in districts with Arab constituencies. We don't consider ourselves a lobby, but congressmen, maybe some 45–50 members, have tried to engage us. We're a pre-lobby." AAI has made great strides in this regard and has experienced some success, one might note, as in Rep. Bill Pascrell's 2012 primary victory over Rep. Steve Rothman. Some staffers credited AAI and ATFP for sponsoring informational events on the Hill from time to time. ATFP had reported expenses of just less than $400,000 in 2012. Meanwhile, CAIR, which had an annual budget of roughly $2 million (2012), had become somewhat of a "third rail" by the 2010s because it was tagged as being linked to radical Islamist causes. ADC, for its part, has always focused more on human rights issues. It had slightly more than $1 million in expenditures in 2012. According to a leading figure at ADC in summer 2013, Raed Jarrar, "we spend less than 10 percent of our time on the Hill, but we do have plans to reactivate out work there." Still, it has scored some small victories on the Hill.[143]

As regards the frequency of lobbyists' visits to House members' offices, AIPAC far and away tops the list. In a very limited number of cases, staffers (along with his or her "boss") may be seen as either so firmly in the pro-Israeli camp or so strongly committed to an independent line that AIPAC personnel have decided either not to contact them as much or to do so sparingly. For staffers working for representatives with a strong interest in the A-I conflict, however, AIPAC visits are frequent and only decrease for representatives who have acquired a reputation as hopelessly hostile to AIPAC's perspective.

On balance, individuals in the veteran staffer group were far more likely to have developed their own routines for information gathering and to "make up their own minds" on IME issues. They might cite one or two colleagues as individuals they trust to provide useful information, but not much more than that. Included among the group of sound sources of information was usually, although not always, their parties' principal HIRC/HFAC. Once again, veteran staffers' views of others' usefulness appear to be heavily affected by their strong sense that they know the issues very well and therefore do not really need to turn to others to help them figure things out.

By 2011–12, in addition to the widely discussed J Street, two other new groups had acquired considerable recognition: the National Iranian American Council (NIAC) and a smaller group, known primarily by specialists, called Telos. In 2012, NIAC had a budget slightly over $1 million; Telos's 2010 expenses were under $800,000. J Street was not yet in action when I conducted my first round of interviews, but interviews conducted during 2011–13 confirmed sentiments that it had made inroads into AIPAC's dominance. The group is directed by Jeremy Ben-Ami. He's a former Clinton administration domestic policy adviser, son of Israeli parents, and descendant of grandparents who helped found Tel Aviv. Given J Street's ability to attract national mainstream media attention and provide campaign finance support, it rapidly acquired a reputation as a useful source of information to some Hill staffers, but in 2013 it still remained far less influential than AIPAC. J Street's total D.C. staff was roughly 50, less than one-quarter the size of AIPAC's, with just four people working the Hill from its "Government Affairs" department. One can find estimates of its annual budget running as high as $7.5 million, but Guidestar.org puts its 2012 expenditures at just over $2.5 million. In brief, J Street's budget has been tiny compared to AIPAC's.

NIAC was highly regarded as a source of valuable information, and was being turned to with greater frequency due to the shift of focus from Israel's Arab adversaries to Iran. It's handicapped by a very small operating budget and national membership. Telos is also a tiny group, designed to enlighten evangelical Christians to the Palestinians' legitimate grievances[144] and to act as a counter to most evangelicals' unswerving devotion to Israel. Telos sponsors trips to the region and hosts events to bring all parties into dialogue to engender peace. Both NIAC and Telos lent credence to the notion that even groups with very limited resources, and not even a handful of full-time workers, can make a difference.

In 2013, I also heard many references to the role played by an older, better-endowed organization, the Quakers' Friends Committee on National Legislation (FCNL), whose Mideast initiatives were primarily handled by Kate Gould. For fiscal 2012–13, FCNL had slightly over $1.5 million in expenses, but like many other organizations being discussed here, its efforts were focused on a much broader range of issues than the Middle East. Again, there will be more on these lobbyists' activities later.

If one aligns all of the "mentioned" lobbies spatially, on an American ideology-based liberal left to right spectrum, then most would do so as follows: clustered on the left would be APN, ADC, and AAI; in the middle would be

Telos, CMEP, FCNL, and NIAC; on the center-right would be J Street; and on the right would be AIPAC, with NORPAC and ZOA to the far right end of the spectrum. However, such a schematic is problematic for at least four reasons. First, although some organizations, like APN, unabashedly present themselves as on the left, the IME conflicts are not left-right issues. They are about competing nation-state claims, or national aspirational claims, and are seen by others as involving rival religious claims. Second, the left-right language comes into being and acquires a certain logic because there is a parallel with the policy positions held by parties in Israel, where parties from the far left to even the center right—ranging from Marxist parties, to the Labor party, and more recently to the center-right Kadima party—have been more likely to press for a two-state solution to the conflict. Meanwhile, the harder right wing (Likud) and far right wing parties (Avigdor Lieberman's Yisrael Beiteinu/Our Home is Israel; and Naftali Bennett's Bayit Yehudi/the Jewish Home) promote continued settlement activity on the West Bank Occupied Territories, or what their members, using the names from ancient Israel, call Judea and Samaria. They show no signs of any compromise over the fate of Jerusalem, and in the case of the far right wing parties advocate discriminatory policies against Arab citizens of Israel, including the "transfer" of Arab Israeli citizens outside of Israel proper. To understand these matters, this author cannot encourage the reader enough to acquire a stronger sense of the history of Israel's political parties and their full ideological and policy orientations, if this is not already the case. Third, the spectrum is also problematic because there are few differences in terms of stances on how to resolve the conflict among lobbies placed at the left end of the spectrum; that is, nearly all call for the same "two-state" solution to the conflict on terms acceptable to moderate, peace-minded Palestinians and Israelis alike. Fourth, groups like CMEP and Telos, which are anchored more in a religious orientation, or NIAC, with its Iran focus, do not fit neatly into a left-right schema.

Personal Contacts: Friends, Former Professors, and Others

For many staffers, personal contacts with "off-the-Hill" individuals yield valuable information. These contacts include former professors, friends working at think tanks, friends of their bosses, and people at the State Department, the White House, or the Pentagon. With variations on the contact's background, many staffers would make comments to me similar to the following one: "There's a professor at my alma mater who was an IDF [Israeli Defense Forces] officer for 20 years; I contact him on a regular basis, like once per month. Everything in D.C. seems jaded; I want outside the beltway perspectives."

Some staffers are pulled into their bosses' personal contacts and connections, of course. One should not lose sight of the fact that venerable House members have had opportunities in Washington, D.C., or on trips abroad to meet with monarchs, presidents, top military brass, and other key regional figures. In some cases, strong bonds of loyalty have been shaped as the result of shared historical experiences and close cooperation. Such relations are more common among American senators, but House members are "in the club."

Lastly, in keeping with a time-honored tradition, some House members have gone into the private sector to reap considerable personal benefit from their knowledge of Appropriations and contacts with their former colleagues therein. A relatively recent example is that provided by Rep. Bob Livingston (R), who set up a lobby shop called the Livingston Group. One of its top clients became the Egyptian government, which allegedly procured the Group's service for some $1.1 million annually. Livingston personally escorted Egyptian military delegations to Congress on over 100 visits. Such persons not only call in, but are also contacted by staffers seeking information.

What Staffers Learn Directly or Vicariously from Foreign Travel

Staffers often cited information obtained through their bosses' or their own travel to the region, which offered direct or indirect exposure to the region's citizens—from its elite members to its downtrodden ones. Congressional staffers are themselves beneficiaries of Congressional Delegation trips (CODELS), and here again, many staffers had taken advantage of trips to Israel sponsored by AIPAC's educational wing, AIEF. A few staffers had been on trips sponsored by other pro-Israel organizations, such as the American Jewish Committee. Overall, 57 percent of the staffers I interviewed had been on such trips, whether CODELS or interest group–sponsored trips, and most were strongly affected by the experience. To a person, staffers would say that such trips were of great value, even if some viewed the message delivered by their hosts as heavily biased and took it with a grain of salt. While staffers were quick to acknowledge that such trips represented a welcome break from their Washington routine, they also noted that the trips were usually rigorous, highly informative, and well worth the time and effort. "There's nothing like it to get better informed," said one staffer, who had been to Israel, Egypt, and Jordan. Another staffer testified:

> I was in Israel in the mid-2000s. I went with [American Jewish Committee's] AJC's Project Interchange for staffers. There were nine Democrat and three Republican staffers. We went for one week. We went to Tel Aviv, Jerusalem, the Golan Heights; we met with Palestinian teachers, too. We met victims of bombings, one of Sharon's advisers, and went swimming in the Dead Sea. We acquired a greater understanding of Israel's needs. It would be a great disservice if the travel is stopped. It would be too bad; people learn a lot on these trips. We go from 8 am to 8 pm every day on these trips. The lobbying turmoil [in 2006] plus the 80-hour work week have many colleagues thinking it may be time to leave. One of the perks for this hard work was getting to see the world, free trips. If there's a $20 lunch that can buy a vote, that's pitiful—that's not gonna happen. The boss has been on many CODELS, too.

Because much of the early research for this book was conducted during a period when interest group trips were being heavily scrutinized by Congress and its critics due to the Jack Abramoff scandal (2005–2006), I received many unsolicited comments from staffers, like the one above, to the effect that serious restrictions and/or the elimination of trips for staffers would be a hugely negative development. Here again the number of trips taken by staffers to Israel has by far exceeded the number taken to Arab countries, and the trips to Israel have made a difference in affecting the perceptions of most staffers who had this experience. As noted earlier, one strongly pro-Israeli staffer went so far as to say that if interest group reform resulted in a termination of pro-Israeli interest groups sponsoring of trips to Israel, "the result would be highly detrimental, perhaps even ruinous, to Israel's interests."

A commonly held view among seasoned staffers is that House members, as a group, have very unimpressive foreign travel résumés, and that this has important implications for their handling of foreign affairs. As one veteran staffer told me with an air of considerable confidence: "There are probably a great number of House members who do not even have a passport, and this undoubtedly constitutes a badge of pride for them in the eyes of most of their constituents in a kind of 'no foreign travel junkets for me' manner."

And another veteran staffer noted: "The majority of people on the House side, if they've traveled overseas, it's through military duty. Most people haven't traveled. Most are self-made businessmen; they didn't have time to travel abroad. My boss is going to Israel later this summer for the first time through AIPAC. My boss is looking forward to going to Israel; he's never been. It's hard to legislate when you don't have that firsthand experience."

The two critical observations prompted me to ask subsequent interviewees what they thought about the statements, and on balance responses suggested that the claims were perhaps a little exaggerated. Interestingly, one seasoned staffer opined that these observations were probably more accurate for the years following the 1994 Republican revolution due to the influx of Republican freshmen. It seems the most accurate view is that, as one interviewee noted, "The vast majority of members have traveled outside the US, especially after they came to Congress and could take advantage of trips."

I did devote some time looking into how many House members had traveled to the Middle East, and I would be surprised if it isn't true that more members of Congress have traveled to Israel than any other single country on the planet, perhaps even including Canada and Mexico. Through my interviews, I learned that at least 47 percent of the House members in my sample had visited Israel, and many had been there on numerous occasions. Some House members, like (the late) Tom Lantos and Steny Hoyer, had/have visited Israel with great frequency, and this is true of many others.

AIPAC's "educational wing, the AIEF, by 2006 had already "planned and paid for almost 220 trips to Israel for lawmakers and their staffers" and "only two other groups spent more than the foundation's $1.5 million."[145] Between 2000 and 2006, "[AIPAC's] nonprofit arm . . . financed more than half of all congressional visits to Israel; the next largest sponsor was the American Jewish Committee with about $133,000 worth of trips."[146] As a current House member observed in 2014, "Steny Hoyer is in charge of leading the AIPAC delegations on ten day trips to Israel. Ten days is a long time to devote to something like this. There's always a lot of pressure to go from his office, and he's in a position of power, so many members are intimidated."

Tours of Israel are obviously designed to imbed in the conscience a deep appreciation for Israel's small size and vulnerability. And the trips do bear fruit. As yet another staffer noted, "The Congresswoman is very supportive of Israel. Part of her connection to Israel comes through many good, strong friends back home who support Israel and she trusts their views, but she and her husband also went on a trip to Israel long ago at the urging of her close friends. I don't think she's been to any other countries in the area."

It's germane to mention the members' travel here because their experiences often have had a strong, indirect impact on their staffers. For House members who have traveled to the region, most to Israel, their staffers often describe the impact of these trips on their bosses as life changing. Here are examples given by two staffers.

"She made up her mind a long time ago on the Arab-Israeli conflict. She made a trip to Israel in the early 2000s . . . She went to the Golan Heights. She's a very intuitive thinker. This is a conflict with no gray area. She looked at the Sea of Galilee from the Golan Heights and said, 'I don't see how you can consider giving this up.'"

"My boss was in Israel this past summer 2005 on an AIPAC tour. They met with Abbas and Sharon. It would be one of the most devastating things if they cut out trips and going out to see the world."

Of course, some people have reservations about the value of these trips, or at least try to keep the experience in perspective. Remember the earlier staffer's quote that "Many junkets are put on by foreign governments or organizations enabling them to skirt the laws against it. They then see what the foreign government wants them to see. I've been on these before; you get a very skewed view. I personally know this is bullshit, but what does a former city councilman know?"

As several staffers noted, no US president or secretary of state has ever traveled to the Gaza Strip, nor have many members of Congress. But some House members have traveled to the Occupied Territories and seen the "other side," or been to Arab countries, and come away with powerful impressions and positive outcomes. One staffer said, "Sometimes the representatives meet with foreign heads of state and come away feeling as though the experience made an impact on [the representatives'] thinking. We also went to a Palestinian refugee camp of 100,000 north of Amman. There was great hatred of Israel. On this tour, we saw homes with eight kids in one room; a little outhouse; one meeting was very hostile."

Because trips to the area can make lasting impressions on congresspersons and their staffers, groups like J Street and the Telos Group have recently increased tours to Israel and the Occupied Territories. Such trips, too, are influencing congresspersons' perceptions and affecting their policymaking. As Linda Gradstein of NPR wrote in an article about a J Street Education Fund–sponsored trip for a group of US congresspersons to Israel and the West Bank:

> The congresswomen clearly are moved by their experience at the checkpoint, and that's the point. J Street, the "pro-Israel, pro-peace" lobbying group that heralds itself as a left-wing alternative to the American Israel Public Affairs Committee, is trying to present an alternative to the usual pro-Israel fare on congressional missions to Israel. The trip last week included six US congresswomen and a group of women from the Women Donors Network, a coalition of Women involved in progressive and social causes. . . . "Our hope is that this and future delegations will help to open up and deepen the conversation in Congress about American policy in the Middle East," Rosenblum told JTA. "The congresswomen are so brave to be here, especially in an election year."

The same trip included visits with Jewish women from several West Bank settlements. One of the congresspersons' Jewish interlocutors said they had no intention to leave their homes. As Gradstein added, one of these women asserted:

> "I'm holding the Bible; Shiloh was our first capital before Jerusalem and it has layers and layers of history," Tzofiah Dorot, the director of Ancient Shiloh, told the women. "This is the heart of Israel and I don't see a future for the state if you take the heart out."

When some of the settler women said they could envision allowing Palestinians to remain in their homes but not receive national or voting rights, this produced "a sharp reply from the congresswomen, five of whom [were] African Americans. 'Some people would call that apartheid,' said Rep. Jackie Speier (D-Calif.), the only white congresswoman on the trip.'"[147]

The congresspersons' reactions to this trip suggest that if more members of Congress took comparable tours, different impressions of the "facts on the ground" might add a new dimension to policymakers' views of the conflict. Of course, trips don't always yield their desired fruit. A pro-peace advocate told me of a House member who visited Palestinian sites, and was "moved," but still ended up cosponsoring a right wing pro-Israel resolution because he felt pressured by other factors to do so.

Cues from Congressional Colleagues and Party Leadership

Another oft-used source of information by staffers is congressional colleagues or those in leadership positions. Because the congressional "campus" is large, staffers establish relations with peers working in nearby offices, sometimes finding it easier to run "next door" to a neighboring congressional office to pick the brains of their peers. On a slightly different path, staffers will head to nearby offices of more seasoned members to obtain information. As one staffer put it: "Rep. [Frank] Wolf's office is nearby; he's been around forever. He's a cardinal [explained below], so he knows his stuff; so if his staffers tell us he's a cosponsor on a bill, it's a good sign. He upholds the values we do."

Because I found this form of interoffice or intercongresspersons communication potentially powerful and significant, I invested some time conducting an informal network analysis, trying to establish which figures and/or whose offices were deemed most important. This effort was prompted by the strong, acquired sense that most members do not know this issue area very well, and therefore are all the more likely to depend upon colleagues they perceive to be best informed or politically safe sources of information. Thus, while conducting my interviews, I would ask my interviewees from whom they and their bosses took their cues, if anyone. Here is what I established in 2005–2006 for the House in terms of a rank ordering of House members as reference points on the Middle East. (Most, if not all, of these same actors remained in place in 2010–2012.)

Gary Ackerman, D-NY: RM of HIRC Middle East subcommittee
Tom Lantos, D-CA: RM of HIRC full committee
Ileana Ros-Lehtinen, R-FL: Chair of HIRC subcommittee
Howard Berman, D-CA: Member, Middle East subcommittee
Henry Waxman, D-CA: RM of Government Reform full committee

Chris Smith, R-NJ: Vice Chair of HIRC full committee
Eric Cantor, R-VA: Ways and Means committee member
Charles Rangel, D-NY: RM, Ways and Means
Tom DeLay, R-TX: R-Majority Leader
Henry Hyde, R-IL: Chair of HIRC full committee
Lois Capps, D-CA: Member of Budget; Energy and Commerce[148]

As one can deduce from a perusal of this list, committee positions, and the experience attributed to the members of those committees—party leadership, length of time in office, and a reputation for knowledge of the Middle East— all contribute to make certain members most likely to be used as cues and reference points by House members in general. The only members meriting some additional commentary here are Henry Waxman, Charles Rangel, and Lois Capps. Waxman was (and remains) widely recognized as the "dean" of Jewish House members; and his staffer Zahava Goldman was considered an invaluable source of information. Rangel is a touchstone for many African American House members given his many years of Hill experience. Capps had become a reference because, following in her husband's footsteps, she took a strong interest in IME issues, played a strong role among progressives, and was very ably assisted by her staffer Jeremy Rabinowitz. A quick review of the list also adds weight to staffers' and off-the-Hill players' 2013 comments, presented later, regarding the loss of influence and gravitas brought about by Rep. Lantos's death in 2008 and by Representatives Ackerman and Berman leaving the House in 2013.

Staffers also often call their peers working in the offices of other con- gresspersons from their home state. They are often more familiar with these individuals, know which people from their state delegation have greater expertise in a given area, and feel that kindred state staffers would have a better feel for how positions would play with constituents back home. All of the aforementioned types of references provide a time-saving means for arriving at a relatively safe decision on a particular letter, resolution, or bill.

Finally, I found it intriguing that veteran House staffers, like the less-ex- perienced and younger staffers, do not communicate much at all with their Senate counterparts. One would think that, given their geographic proximity—just the other side of Capitol Hill—and shared "same-state" interests, such communication would occur. That is rarely the case, however. Indeed, many veteran staffers noted that their Senate counterparts left them feeling unworthy of their attention, and this sense of disdain is often reciprocated. In this regard, staffers' behavior matches that of many of their bosses. When I quizzed a multi-term House member about relations between House and Senate members, she responded: "What you've heard is absolutely right, there is considerable disdain as regards the way Senators and House members look at one another. My constituents often ask me, 'Do you see our Senators often in DC?' I'll say, 'Almost never. I rarely go to the other side, and they rarely come here.'"

Think Tanks as Sources of Expert Opinion

Some House staffers tune in to think tanks for information. Think tanks bring their own ideological bias, generally speaking. The Washington Institute for Near East Policy (WINEP), the Brookings Institution (Saban Center), and the Council on Foreign Relations (CFR) were the three think tanks most commonly cited, followed by the Center for Strategic and International Studies (CSIS), the Jewish Institute for National Security Affairs (JINSA), the Heritage Foundation, Project for a New American Century (PNAC), and the CATO Institute. Lobbying groups such as AIPAC, APN, IPF, and Brit Tzedek were named by many staffers in response to this question as well.

The Brookings Institution was long a bastion of more liberal thought, but acquired a stronger mix of liberal and conservative analysts well before the time frame of this study. Its Saban Center for Middle East Policy was itself created by a $13 million gift in 2002 by Haim Saban, an American-Israeli TV and film producer and a strong supporter of Israel. Once more moderate in his views, Saban described himself as deeply affected by the 2000 "failed" Camp David summit, noting specifically: "History proved that [Ariel] Sharon was right and I was wrong. In matters relating to [Israel's] security, that moved me to the right. Very far to the right."[149] Although it has provided a home for scholars sympathetic to Palestinians and Arabs, like Shibley Telhami, its overall thrust has been largely pro-Israeli. Its now longtime director, Martin Indyk, was born to a Jewish family in England, raised and educated in Australia, then came to the US and worked for AIPAC. He left AIPAC to help establish WINEP, which has served as AIPAC's think tank, before going on to serve as the US ambassador to Israel and occupying other high-level

US foreign policymaking positions. The major Middle East figure at CSIS has been Jon Alterman, a Harvard Ph.D.; he also came out of the WINEP stable, but delivers balanced analyses of Mideast affairs and has helped greatly boost CSIS's overall prestige. Heritage is well known as a bastion of conservative thought, and its reports are typically unquestioning of Israeli government policies. PNAC—created in 1997; extinct by 2006—was a neoconservative think tank in lockstep with right wing Israeli governments, and was a major proponent of the US invasion of Iraq. JINSA is of a far right, neoconservative orientation, and draws assistance from former Israeli intelligence officers. In essence, all of the most important and active "think tanks" doing work on the Middle East in Washington, D.C., are either very favorably predisposed to or unquestioningly supportive of Israel, with some variations in support for its right wing governments. Indyk, for example, can be critical.

Elsewhere, CATO is home to libertarians, and libertarians like Ron Paul espouse a noninterventionist foreign policy and reduced foreign aid, both of which are unattractive to most Israeli governments. But CATO is among the least influential of the "think tanks" on this list.

The only other organization doing "think tank"–like publications that was mentioned by staffers is the tiny Foundation for Middle East Peace, headed by former US Amb. Philip Wilcox, and strongly assisted by Geoffrey Aronson. It is pro–"two-states" and offers a perspective reflecting greater understanding of Palestinian and Arab concerns. It also publishes very useful information on developments relating to West Bank settlements and other matters.

Staffers hold mixed views of the think tanks. Said one staffer, "I rely on people I think I can trust. I put less credence in the think tanks. You can get screwed by the think tanks. Everyone has a vested interest." A commonly cited problem associated with think tank–based information is that much of it is too "heavy." Much information supplied by think tanks doesn't meet the staffers' need to be provided with faster or more readily digested forms of communication. As one staffer said: "I'll get 20–100-page reports all the time from think tanks. They're all a waste of time; I can never read them. What's smarter are the two- to three-page reports sent by various organizations—Project for a New American Century, Council on Foreign Relations, Brookings, Carnegie. I have time to read these." "You do get the same old people from think tanks because we shop locally, for the most part, because of simplicity; WINEP and Brookings are the two main ones."

Foreign Embassies as Lobbyists

Foreign embassies provide information to congressional offices through direct meetings or via indirect forms of communication. The embassies most frequently mentioned by interviewees were those of Egypt, Jordan, and Israel. On the basis of my research, the Egyptian embassy was the most active on Capitol Hill, especially on the House side. Out of my sample, more than one-fifth of the interviewees had been contacted, often repeatedly, either by the Egyptian ambassador or by other Egyptian representatives, including military generals. Long the second largest recipient of US aid, after Israel, at $2.2 billion (in more recent years, $1.55 billion) per annum, the Egyptians have gone to considerable lengths to safeguard continuation of this assistance. As the Egyptian ambassador told me in summer 2013:

> We see Egypt conducting its foreign policy based on its interests, not ideological predispositions. There is great complexity to congresspersons' decision making. Many states, even in the Midwest, have grain and beef exports, etc. There are military assistance programs, the export of arms to Egypt, and the production of weapons in Egypt. All of these factors make it easy to explain to Americans that they have a personal interest in good relations with Egypt. Add to this the importance for the US of having stable and dependable allies in the region; and that this means fewer US troops having to be sent to the region. It's pretty easy to convince people that war-like situations cost more than peace-like situations. Part of my work is to present these arguments to the congresspersons.

The ambassador added, "With regards to Egypt, the US, and Israel, it's not a zero sum game. Many pro-Israel types in Congress also support Egypt. Also, being not such a great supporter of Israel does not translate into being a strong supporter of Egypt."

The Jordanian embassy maintains excellent contacts with congressional members and staffers. They also arrange Mutual Educational and Cultural Affairs (MECA) trips to Jordan for congressional figures to good advantage.

Israel, the number one recipient of US aid at $3.2 billion per annum for many years, reduced to a range of $2.5 billion to $2.8 billion from 2006 to 2010, also has the greatest amount of assistance to protect, but it would appear that it relies more heavily on other mechanisms to sustain influence. Although a few staffers mentioned contacts made by Israeli embassy officials, significantly, contact with Israeli embassy personnel was less frequently noted than that with Egypt. My research recorded just eleven references to direct Israeli embassy contacts, roughly half that with Egyptian contacts, and equal to the number recorded for Jordanian ones. Remember, this is based on a random sample. One is left to engage in important speculation as to why this is the case, with the most likely answer being that domestic lobbying groups are so effectively doing the Israelis' bidding that less direct engagement is necessary by the Israelis. They may prefer, in many instances, to have American domestic interest groups serve as Israel's advocates. It is also entirely possible that Israeli embassy officials are contacting House members directly, leaving some staffers ignorant of these communications.

On the basis of my survey, no other country in the area was competitive with the aforementioned three. Others noted included Saudi Arabia (4 mentions), Syria (3), Lebanon (3), Bahrain (1), UAE (1), and Qatar (1). And usually these were "one-off" meetings relating to some specific issue. By 2012, prima facie evidence suggested that the Bahrainis were making a greater effort than they had a half a decade earlier.

House Staffers' Attention to Constituents' Concerns

Last but far from least, most House staffers feel compelled to listen to their constituents' expressions of interest and opinions. Indeed, one of the major tasks dealt with by staffers is constituents' concerns. The constituents are, after all, the "bosses" of the congressional members. As such, they are the people whose satisfaction must be kept in mind by all those keen to keep their jobs. "He's here to be the voice for his (or her) constituents" is a common refrain among staffers. There are alternative attitudes: "He's not constituent driven," or "he doesn't really rely on his constituents; he does pretty much what he feels is right." Still, when one looks behind these cases, one usually finds that either the congressperson comes from a district where there is minimal to no concern about these issues, or there are competing constituencies balancing out one another.

The range of constituents' concern for foreign affairs in general varies enormously across the country's electoral districts. Many citizens simply do not care, and this is reflected in attitudes held by their representatives. Interest in foreign affairs is of secondary importance to most House members, as articulated by many staffers.

> "Our constituents are far more concerned about agriculture, so there's no heavy traffic, no keen interest in foreign affairs."

> "We have to focus on the constituents' issues, not foreign policy. We only won with 52 percent of the vote."

> "I spend very little of the 15 percent time spent on foreign policy issues on the Arab-Israeli conflict. There is little to no constituent concern, so it's difficult to justify spending time on the conflict . . . we're mostly concerned with domestic energy issues."

> "This is a heavily rural area, one that is economically depressed. It's one of the poorest districts in the country. We get calls from people because the neighbor's dog won't stop barking, or to get a high school transcript. They're not concerned with what's happening around the world. People might get concerned about whether we're gonna start a war or not, which they don't want to have."

Unsurprisingly, given the size of the country and its tremendous demographic diversity, constituent interest in the IME conflicts runs the gamut from apathy to xenophobia, with any putative graph heavily skewed in the direction of apathy. In most cases, the absence of constituents' concern leaves House members in a position to behave as they see fit on Mideast issues, other factors notwithstanding. So for example, as one staffer said about a congressperson known for his empathy for Palestinians and Arabs: "We have no big Jewish or Arab populations in our district. They don't care about the Middle East, so he acts as he sees fit. Some people respect him for his seriousness [on these issues] and the media attention he garners." Or as another staffer coming from a comparable, low-IME-interest constituency responded when asked if his boss felt pressured by constituents: "No, not really. There are a few zealots on both sides. Politics is the manipulation of the ignorant. We represent a rock-hard Republican district. This issue is not of concern to our constituents. There are some Lebanese Americans in the northeast part, but very few of them. There are so few people that there is little pressure on the congressman."

Some members of Congress can get away with bucking the tide of constituent sentiment. As a veteran staffer told me about a congressperson who espoused an ardently pro–right wing Israeli position: "He has virtually no Jews in his constituency; it's a very liberal constituency. Staff warn him some positions might hurt him and he'll say, 'I don't give a shit; that's my view.' I find this impressive." However, in most cases where constituents have strong views running in favor of one Middle East protagonist, the congresspersons cannot ignore them. Even in districts where the size of a "concerned" community is very small, a few voices can make a big difference. Emblematic of what many staffers told me, one said, "There's a wealthy Jewish businessman [name deleted]; he's an [Ivy League] grad who started [two very successful companies]. He doesn't call me personally; he works through other organizations. Mainly individuals call up and drop his name. They'll say, 'He's concerned about ensuring that this bill passes.' [Name deleted] is another very powerful Jewish family that lives in our district; they do call in themselves." And yet another staffer observed: "He [the congressman] has one friend who's a founder of JINSA who's from back home. He always looked to this man as a mentor—he's a successful businessman who has traveled to the area a lot and has contacts there."

Out of the rather miscellaneous set of persons who established contact with congressional offices, the most common references were to concerned constituents. Staffers would cite the names of one or two individuals, almost always Jewish Americans who resided in their boss's electoral district. In some offices, these people call so regularly that the staffers converse with them on a first name basis; and these callers almost always voice staunchly pro-Israeli positions. The common lack of constituent concern in most districts can be altered in many congressional offices with the advent of an eye-catching, foreign policy crisis. One staffer said, "Calls depend on events on the ground. A suicide bombing will produce calls." To this point, during my 2005–2006 round of interviews, constituents' foreign affairs concerns focused more on other issues, especially the Iraq War, than the A-I and I-P conflicts, but the 2006 election of Hamas elicited its own very strong response. When the Dubai Ports crisis broke in February 2006, American citizens, in full post–

9/11 mode, were concerned that the "Arab" [UAE-based] firm's acquisition of control and management of port activities in numerous US cities might facilitate malevolent acts by Islamist terrorists. Phones were ringing off the hook in just about every congressional office I entered. As one younger staffer noted, "Constituent interests drive a lot of our agenda here. They're calling in, saying 'I don't want us selling our ports to Dubai, a country that supports terrorists.'" Meanwhile, in another office, a staffer noted: "I've actually been to the UAE. They were really wonderful people; I was so impressed. So it's disturbing to hear what a lot of the callers are saying."

Another staffer, commenting on calls about US involvement in the war in Iraq, noted: "We hear loud and often from our constituents about the [Iraq] war; they want an immediate withdrawal. We have a diverse constituency, but folks back home are mostly European and Latino immigrants. They're all very vocal about the war; it's dominating everything."

In late 2011 and early 2012, with the drumbeat for a war against a recalcitrant Iran resounding loudly, calls to offices where concern for IME conflicts is typically lower focused heavily on the Iranian issue. Staffers in most offices indicated that most callers did not want to see the US involved in yet another Mideast imbroglio. This is significant because AIPAC and right wing pro-Israel groups were calling for the US to take a harder line against Iran, and most congresspersons were falling in line even though polls showed the majority of Jewish Americans disapproved.

In mixed electoral constituencies, ones in which there are vocal groups with opposing views with something akin to a balance between the size and activism, members may be relatively free to deal with issues as they see fit. Ergo, I heard comments from a range of staffers like the following two:

> "There's an established Jewish community; there's also an immigrant population of Palestinians and Arabs. He does pretty much what he believes is right. He sometimes angers Jewish constituents; other times he angers the Arabs."

> "Earlier this year, some of our Jewish constituents were very pleased to see the boss condemning Iran on human rights because they hadn't even asked him to do this. They don't seem to know that we have Iranian constituents; that there are two bases in the district. They're

not together, and they may endorse the same resolutions at times and they don't even know it. For example, the Iranians are wanting us to condemn Iran's nuclear power drive—they asked us to sign on to a Ros-Lehtinen bill even before the Jewish constituents did. I find this funny. The staff asked me if we'd be in trouble for backing the Iranian constituents—I had to explain to them why I thought we'd be okay."

To have success on the Hill, any particular community needs to get its act together, and Arab Americans in general have been far less successful to date than pro-Israel Americans in general, and AIPAC's legions in particular. One staffer said, "We do have a lot of Arabs and Middle East types in our district, but they don't speak with one voice." Another staffer observed, "We have a constituent who is on the board of the ADC [Arab American Anti-Discrimination Committee]. She called me and we had a very heated discussion; she opposed the Hamas bill. I've only heard from one person on this side of the issue. She said the Arab community is nervous about voicing their concerns because 'we don't want to draw attention to ourselves.'" No voice, or greater reticence, means less attention.

Where an ethno-religious community enjoys a high per capita percentage of the population, constituent concerns are far more likely to be considered by congressional representatives. Because there are many more congressional districts across the country with large and politically active Jewish populations than there are with large and politically active Arab, Iranian, or Muslim populations, a greater number of representatives' views are shaped by their Jewish American constituents. It is no secret that in those rare districts where the opposite is the case, one finds representatives—such as Charles Dingell in Dearborn, Michigan, and Jim Moran in Virginia—whose views on Mideast issues reflect the need to demonstrate a more sympathetic view of the Palestinians and Arabs in the conflict.

Meanwhile, there is indeed a far greater number of districts with either a moderate to large or small, but highly active, Jewish constituency, of which many of the members are ardent Zionists. Staffers for bosses from these districts remarked:

"Our district had one of the biggest number of Jewish constituents in the country. We reach out to the rabbis and the synagogues. We do hear from our constituents. The Jewish community in our district is very well organized. We have ZOA, AIPAC, and others further to the Left—we have the full spectrum [of Jewish American groups] in our district."

"We have one of the largest Holocaust survivor communities in the United States; and yes, we do hear from them."

"We have strong pro-Israel constituents in our district—some AIPAC, some independent. We have good contacts with AIPAC; and we get lots of Jewish groups, like Hillel. Congressman Reynolds sponsored a bill calling for Jerusalem to be recognized as the capital of Israel. We've been happy to sign on to this. Our folks [back home] love it that we do this. This bill gets introduced every two years."

"Our constituency is one of the few in the country where foreign policy is domestic policy. We have a large Jewish community, but now also have people from many other [predominantly Muslim] countries. The Jewish community is very mature politically. The [another national community] is getting there. Many still don't believe that Congress is theirs. Even the Latino community has little sense of ownership."

In some places, of course, one's constituents hold rather extreme positions, and it is interesting to see how even an otherwise liberal politician may don far more hawkish garb to play to the home crowd. A perfect example here was the behavior of Anthony Weiner (D) of Brooklyn, New York. As noted by Jo-Ann Mort: "Rep. Anthony Weiner (D-Brooklyn) ran as a new type of liberal in last year's NYC mayor's race. Yet, in his Brooklyn district, he's been playing old-time politics, posturing on Israel in the worst way, from the minute he was elected. He is consistently the most conservative voice in Congress regarding Israel and the Palestinians, siding with the most extreme elements among the Israeli settler population (for whom there is strong support in his district and some West Bank settlers probably even hail from there). His politics on this issue are way out of sync with his cultivated image as a liberal."[150]

And sticking with the "extreme theme," one staffer contributed the following characterization of input from his boss's congressional district: "One representative has a really active ZOA chapter in his district. They're very tough. Their attitude about Arabs and Muslims is: 'Just kill the fuckers.'"

A Note on Lobbyists' Mobilization of Constituents

How AIPAC Mobilizes Constituents:

> "Five to six AIPAC members came into the office last month and the Congressman went to dinner with them that night. We take time out to meet with them; the people from the district."—a mid-level staffer

> "We have a huge Jewish population in our district. They have day jobs, but their second thing is being AIPAC people. It's not the national level people; it's the local/district reps; it's the constituents who know your boss back home who call me. AIPAC is the only lobbying group I can think of on the Middle East stuff."—a young, less experienced staffer

Perhaps one of the most effective approaches with regard to constituents is that deployed by AIPAC. The AIPAC representatives come knocking on the door of most new staffers early and often. "I've been on the job for one and a half months; AIPAC has been by to see me several times already." Another new staffer said: "I've been on the job six and a half weeks; I've heard from AIPAC already."

Nearly all representatives and their relevant staffers are familiar with AIPAC representatives, not necessarily at the national level but, more importantly, from their home district. Any number of staffer interviewees indicated to me their strong preference and need to listen to people from back home, and this penchant has not been lost on AIPAC officials. AIPAC has made a point of assigning members who are constituents to maintain active contact with a great number of congresspersons, thereby "individualizing" and "personalizing" its approach to disseminating information and opinions. In many cases, constituent AIPAC representatives become personal friends or acquaintances of House members and/or their staffers;

numerous staffer interviewees referred to home-based AIPAC members by their first names. As one young staffer noted, "Yeah, [Dan and Gary] from the home district are AIPAC members. They're my go-to guys on Mideast stuff. I'll call them or they'll shoot me an email. [Dan] gets the AIPAC action letter and he'll forward it to me." As revealed in the preceding quote, some staffers not only know home-based AIPAC activists on a first-name basis, but also often regard them as people whose views deserve a special place in their deliberations.

Even in those very numerous districts where constituents' interest in the conflict may be characterized as low to nonexistent, it was still common for staffers to note frequent contact with Jewish American groups in general, compared to Arab American groups. Here's one staffer's assessment:

"We have some Arab Americans in the district. Many of them are Christians, and this does affect their views. We hear from Arabs of numerous national backgrounds, but we definitely hear from the Jewish population as well. The Jewish American population is far and away the most effectively organized—the most and best organized as far as any ethnic group is concerned. They send you 'Thank you' notes for 'positive signatures' on House letters, resolutions, and bills, etc. They have phone call trees and email distribution lists. On the Arab side, there's no structure, no organization. They don't have the email lists, etc. They [Arab leaders] don't know how many voters they have in their community. The Arab community is very fragmented into different tribes and extended families. There is no leader of the Chaldean community, for example. Jewish American organizations bring kids to D.C. for a weeklong learning experience on how to influence Congress and then they'll set up meetings with renowned Jewish leaders. They tell them, 'Always start the meeting with "Thank you."' This is an unmatched, sustained effort. It stands in stark contrast to the Arab American organizations."

And as is known to all, AIPAC is head and shoulders above all other Jewish American groups in the frequency of Hill contacts by its activists. Here is one additional staffer testimonial to AIPAC's comparative advantage:

"AIPAC is far and away the most effective. Interest groups need to see things in their own complexity, to be able to describe that complexity; who benefits and who loses. AIPAC does this and almost no one else does; no other groups have the same effectiveness."

AIPAC's approach involves keeping its members well informed of congressional activity and their policy preferences via electronic communications and phone calls. But this activity is supplemented in a very important way. All across the country, AIPAC holds regional or home district meetings, luncheons, or dinner events—with members invited by the hundreds—that feature local congresspersons and other political dignitaries. Additional, well-known, nondistrict congressional actors may be invited to speak to ensure larger turnouts. These events raise lots of loot.

While regional or local events are significant, they pale in scale to the mobilization effort undertaken by AIPAC for its annual conferences in Washington, D.C. This annual event, almost always held in the spring, is attended by 5,000–7,000 members from across the country. The conference is also usually attended by a greater number of members of Congress than any event other than the president's annual State of the Union address. Major speakers at the conference include the leading elements of both parties, with high-ranking executive branch officials—the president, the vice president, and the secretary of state—also often invited to speak. If Israel's president or prime minister does not attend the event to speak in person, they deliver "live-feed" speeches projected on an enormous screen to the attentive crowd. With seemingly no expenses spared on staging, sound, and lighting, and with the glitterati of American politics following one another to speak in steady succession, these annual conferences take on the aura of an incredible, Hollywood-type spectacle, something akin to the Oscars near the Potomac.

Spread out over a number of days, these annual conferences enable AIPAC's leaders to get members on the same page in terms of the issues they consider of greatest importance to Israel's welfare. The members and citizens in attendance are then released to fan out across Capitol Hill, making their way to their representatives' and/or senator(s)' offices to inform the lawmakers of their concerns. In recent years, greater care has been taken to bring a very large number of college-age individuals to the conference from across the country; this brings a more youthful exuberance to the meeting and creates a strong political socialization experience for the younger generation of AIPAC members.

Numerous staffers told me it's often difficult to find rooms large enough to accommodate their AIPAC visitors during this annual conference invasion. They also note—and I've heard this from AIPAC attendees as well—that although the groups are mostly made up of regular constituents, AIPAC "experts" are often planted in the groups to make sure issues are discussed as desired by AIPAC's leadership. Indeed, many staffers take objection to this practice. Finally, as discussed later, staffers also point out that the conference is scheduled in the spring to mesh with the legislative cycle and the advancing of Israel-related resolutions or bills in order to maximize the application of pressure at the most opportune time. For example, the spring 2012 annual conference coincided with heavy pushes on Capitol Hill against Iran and with efforts to maximize pressure on Pres. Obama to take a more forceful stance with the Israeli government against Iran.

AIPAC's behavior has been emulated by many, but among other Jewish American groups, NORPAC's behavior is noteworthy. Hailing predominantly from the Northeast, NORPAC also sponsors its own day on the Hill, and similarly dispatches a large number of followers to meet with congresspersons in their offices. Although NORPAC is perceived as slightly to the right of AIPAC by most observers, the overall thrust of its activities must be seen as complementing rather than countering those of AIPAC. I have already noted the contributions of APN, and will have more to say about that group, as well as J Street, later in the book.

MOBILIZATION BY OTHER GROUPS: EVANGELICAL CHRISTIANS, ARAB AMERICANS, MUSLIM AMERICANS, IRANIAN AMERICANS, AFRICAN AMERICANS AND HISPANICS, AND PRO-PEACE ACTIVISTS

Other groups that emulate AIPAC's behavior, and do so largely with AIPAC's blessing, include the Conservative Political Action Conference (CPAC), hosted by the American Conservative Union, and Christians United for Israel (CUFI). CUFI is led by the evangelical Texas pastor John Hagee. The February 2011 CPAC meeting attracted over 11,000 conservative leaders and activists from across the country, and its keynote address was delivered by

Rep. Allen West. Here are a few excerpts reflecting Rep. West's views on Pres. Obama's approach to the conflict.

> "I believe President Barack Obama is completely incorrect when it comes to his Middle East foreign policy. I was hoping that the President would clarify the statement at his AIPAC speech. However, the President did not rectify the unconscionable policy faux pas statement on 'pre-1967 borders' to resolve the Middle East peace process. He did not seek an honorable way to publicly apologize; in turn I have come to one concluding assessment: America has a President who lacks moral courage and integrity when it comes to America's long standing relationship with Israel. . . . I cannot attribute this incompetent statement to naïveté, but rather to conscious, nefarious, and malicious intent. Yes, I am very aware these words and the statement I released will be carried forward all across America, and possibly beyond—and yes they are strong words. However, it is time that someone rose up to speak the truth. The statement President Obama made, one without sharing with Prime Minister Netanyahu, is one of the most insidious and heinous policy statements ever made by any United States President, and completely unacceptable. I will not sit back idly and watch us saunter down the road to perdition!"[151]

At the Fifth Annual CUFI meeting in Washington, D.C., in 2010, roughly 4,500 Christians, mostly evangelicals, were in attendance. On the CUFI website for that event, the following message was posted:

> "We opened our meeting Tuesday morning with one session after another providing education to those in attendance of the biblical reasons Christians should support Israel and up to the minute information of the current conditions in Israel and the Middle East. The Prime Minister [Netanyahu], via lie feed during the Middle East Briefing, brought greetings and thanks for CUFI's support. The last event at the convention center was the finest Night to Honor Israel that we have ever had in Washington, D.C. . . .The next day CUFI delegates from 477 Congressional districts met with their Senators and Congressman on the Hill and voiced their support of Israel and

Jewish people. Once again you could sense the Lord's guidance as Isaiah 62:1 was fulfilled,

> For Zion's sake I will not keep silent,
> And for Jerusalem's sake I will not keep quiet . . ."[152]

One year later, at the July 2011 CUFI annual event, over 5,000 individuals were in attendance. They listened to speeches by Israel's ambassador the United States, Michael Oren, Glenn Beck, and saw a satellite speech by Prime Minister Netanyahu, before again deploying across Capitol Hill to congresspersons' offices.

What did my House staffer interviewees say about the Christian Zionist activists? Surprisingly, not all that much. Here are some representative samples.

> "Yes, there is a good amount of Christian fundamentalists and people with strong pro-Israel backing. We definitely hear from them, but they're gonna contact him about abortion and immigration, not on Israel. His position on Israel [solidly pro] is clearly enough known."

> "Not many of our constituents are interested in the Middle East, but this is the Bible belt. It's a very evangelical district. We hear from a lot of church groups—petitions signed by congregants—but not so much about Mideast regional politics as issues like religious persecution, religious freedom, etc. Eight out of ten contacts are about Sudan, Darfur, Southeast Asia, China, etc."

> "We get constituents calling in saying, 'The White House is forcing Israel to give up land.' It's more of an evangelical perspective. There is a small number of people who are very vocal. On balance, we don't hear from constituents on Israel so much because these issues are too complex for [our state's] constituents. Those who do call will argue, 'Why should we provide any aid to Palestinians or support any Palestinian state?'"

> "The evangelicals are more on morality issues. On the evangelical stuff, Mr. Pence [R-Indiana] is number one, but there are so many of them now."

In sum, although a fairly large amount of ink has been spilled over the Christian-Zionist connection, staffers do not see or hear Christian evangelicals concerning themselves as much with Arab-Israeli conflict related issues as they do with issues disturbing their social morality compasses. And most staffers did not give me the impression they were taking these evangelical voices very seriously on Middle East matters.

While groups such as AAI, ADC, CAIR, NIAC, and others have sought to mobilize American citizens to engage in greater grassroots activity and to contact their congresspersons, there is still much work to be done. With the exception of CAIR, which seems to have been blackballed, AAI, ADC, and NIAC were all making progress, but still lagged far behind the competition midway through 2013. I have already presented some references to factors impeding their progress in the preceding material. Remember, most staffers didn't even mention such groups during my interviews; I had to ask if they had heard of them. More references to these groups will appear later on, but here are just a few, additional observations from staffers about these groups and related communities.

"We have some Muslim Americans in our district. We get some calls from Muslim constituents, but it must be a small minority."

"I don't hear much from our Arab/Muslim constituents about the Arab-Israeli conflict. We're trying to reach out and mobilize that part of our base. We're working with CAIR and ADC."

"Yes, the African American community has empathy for the Palestinians; yes, there is concern on occasion. If there's an issue or incident in the news, I think there is real concern; a sense of oppression of the Palestinians. [The boss, who is African American] has always supported keeping the PLO office open in the US and his African American base supports that. But any member of Congress is not going to support his base 100 percent of the time."

As we'll see later, there is greater support in some Hispanic communities for Palestinian and Arab concerns, as well. But it's not rocket science to understand that a very long list of issues take precedence over Middle East affairs for constituents with African American or Hispanic backgrounds.

In recent years, J Street and FCNL, with support from APN, Telos, and other groups, have engaged in more concerted efforts to mobilize a mass base of support for a "two-state" solution. This is done primarily via email. Brit Tzedek v'Shalom (the Jewish Alliance for Peace and Justice), which has been very active through mass mailings, brought its support to J Street in January 2010 via an agreement over "strategic coordination," not a full merger. This was significant in that Brit Tzedek billed itself, not inaccurately, as the largest grassroots pro–"two state" solution organization in the country.

STAFFERS' PERCEPTIONS OF THE LOBBIES

For many of the new kids on the block, contact with professional lobbyists represents a way to get a quick fix on issues, facilitating their incredibly hectic daily work. Lobbyists presenting information in the most professional, coherent, and persuasive manner rise to the top, and it is for this reason, although not this reason alone, that AIPAC is commonly cited as a model for influence and success. Staffers believe they can get excellent feedback from AIPAC on any Mideast issue with the ease of a phone call, and that AIPAC will happily send a representative to meet with them in their office in an expeditious manner. No other group is seen as able to compete with AIPAC in this regard insofar as Middle East issues are concerned.

Veterans are likely to be in contact with the usual cast of lobbyist characters, with AIPAC again topping the list. Once again, in a very limited number of cases, however, the staffer (along with his or her boss) may be seen as either so firmly in the pro-Israeli camp, or so strongly committed to an independent line, that AIPAC personnel have decided there is no need to contact them at all or do so sparingly. For staffers working for reps with a strong interest in the IME conflicts, however, AIPAC visits are likely to be frequent, in some cases even where the House member has established a reputation as a consistently less cooperative or hostile actor from AIPAC's perspective. The reader should also recall that veterans' views of others' usefulness appear to be heavily affected by their own strong sense that they know the issues very well, and therefore they do not really need to turn to others like lobbyists to help them figure things out.

What follows is a brief categorization of staffers' responses to AIPAC's outreach to House members' offices, followed by a look at their appraisals of other noteworthy lobby shops' efforts.

HIGHLIGHT ON AIPAC: HOW IT WINS FRIENDS AND INFLUENCES PEOPLE, OR NOT

Here are a few quotes about AIPAC from the staffers' mouths, categorized by their degree of fondness for AIPAC.

Very Favorable Views of AIPAC

"The most effective group is AIPAC. AIPAC is the king of the lobbying organizations. It's very good at providing information, but also because of their grassroots base and campaign support—their money. AIPAC maintains very close relations with us."

"We get weekly visits, at least, from AIPAC. AIPAC also has briefings every other week. AIPAC does the best job."

"AIPAC is tops on the list. I meet with an AIPAC rep every one month to six weeks. This is initiated by them unless there's a hot button issue. The AIPAC reps are mostly from the state level—they'll fly up for about 80 percent of these meetings. The national people will be introduced to us by the local AIPAC folks. They're always very professional. There's not a lot of turnover, so I'll get to see Michael five times per year. It's never a worthless visit. He brings letters from constituents."

"AIPAC is by far the most important; they come two times per week officially, plus I am personal friends with AIPAC people. They're now getting better at reaching out to the non-usual East and West coast suspects. They just created a new liaison person to do this outreach work. I also hear from ZOA. Most members from rural districts will follow the leaders on foreign affairs issues—and they almost only hear from pro-Israel groups. Pro-Palestinian groups are only one one-hundredth as well organized."

"AIPAC is our number one contact and concern. I rely on people I think I can trust. I can call Deb at AIPAC and say, 'Cut the b.s.;

here's what I need to know.' There are not really other groups that I hear from. I've never heard of ZOA. We'll get blast faxes from other groups and I'll scan through them quickly to see if there's a pertinent, sound argument."

"[The Representatives] had a decades-long relationship with AIPAC. He has close, trusting relationships with AIPAC. Few members of Congress have direct conversations with people from AIPAC the way he does at his level. Most AIPAC contacts are at/with the level of the staffers. Others include ADL, Jewish Federation, the Republican Jewish Coalition, the Israeli embassy, and the Israeli consulate in our home city. There's limited contact with Peace Now; they don't reach out because he's so close to AIPAC. ZOA will reach out, but we don't always go with what they have to say. There's contact with the PA because of the boss's [committee] work."

"AIPAC is in all the time. We also hear from APN, and ZOA is pushing for greater accountability for Palestinians, but the boss has really close relations with AIPAC. We travel around the US with AIPAC and do work with them. AIPAC is a huge force in the House. They do a Republican trip and a Democratic trip to Israel. Our boss and another D led the Democratic trip a few years ago. They took 10 to 20 members with them. Every August AIPAC does these trips. And the Jewish Community Center in New York City does a staff trip."

"Our Jewish constituents are very active and vocal; AIPAC is tops on that list. The disengagement this past summer [August-September 2005] affected our office the most due to relations with the Jewish constituents in [major city]. They wanted to know exactly how [the congressman] felt. He had never been there before [to Israel] which put the onus on me to provide information to him. He felt the Israeli settlers should have the right to something. It took constituents, AIPAC, and myself to convince him that disengagement was good to jumpstart peace."

"The Israeli lobby makes it easy. We have strong pro-Israel constituents in [our district], some AIPAC, some independent. We get lots of Jewish youth groups, like Hillel. ZOA does not come to see us. We are on the spam list for APN—this is a turnoff. We've had numerous contacts with AIPAC over the Iran issue. This is pretty clear cut for us."

Neutral and "Matter of Fact" Perceptions

"AIPAC comes first to mind. We meet with them every six months. There's no other group that comes to mind at the moment."

"AIPAC organizes a lot of events. I don't know if there's a Palestinian caucus."

"We have a strong Jewish lobby in our area [even though the area is mostly African American and Latino, with some more affluent suburbs]. The Jewish lobby is often in communication with the congressman; they play a big role in his policymaking. There's a strong group of women from Hadassah. They could be from AIPAC, but if so they're not identifying themselves as such. There are also concerned citizens from a synagogue. Naturally, it's AIPAC that talks to us the most. My predecessor went to Israel with AIPAC. Votes tend to be no-brainers. You always vote fully to fund Israel because that's the makeup of the people he represents. It's all a no-brainer for us to support Israel."

"There are two or three types of contact with AIPAC. (1) Policy briefings via email once per week. (2) Direct talks with AIPAC; their representatives came in last week, for example, at the time of their big annual conference. (3) They get out front encouraging us with particular pieces of legislation and ask us if they can provide assistance."

"In contrast to Arab groups, AIPAC comes in and they all say the same thing. When they have their annual convention, 7,000 people hit Capitol Hill; 7,500 people are at the dinner—everybody in Congress is there. There was a big pro-Israel rally recently and 10,000 people showed up. They're so good at choreography, with everyone doing their role. The Arabs all want to do their own thing. AIPAC has a good understanding of when to play hardball and when not to do so. AIPAC is not pushy; they're polite; they don't usually play hardball. Arabs do play hardball."

"You need institutional backing to get people's attention. This is one reason AIPAC and AJC do so well, and this applies to more than just the Israel issue—the need for institutional backing. There isn't the same presence for any other group or cause. It's not power AIPAC has so much as influence. There's a lot of social capital that is lacking on the other side—there's no countervailing influence. You could see how someone would speak of a Jewish conspiracy."

"The number one factor is domestic political considerations and the influence of AIPAC and other pro-Israeli actors; the Israel lobby. The Armenian, Greek, and Cuban lobbies are much less important. Most members look at how this is going to play with their district. AIPAC is far and away the most influential. Two to three times per year they have major conventions or activities."

"In the House, the factor of greatest importance is access. AIPAC is number one; they provide information, sponsor trips to Israel, put on events and speaking engagements. Compared to other pro-Israel groups, none is as effective as AIPAC. For example, ZOA does not even have a cover of objectivity. ZOA will just talk about 'How badly the Palestinians are making it for Israel.' AIPAC comes with an air of objectivity. I can't think of others who do the same. There are not really any groups on the other side that stick out. You're either pro-Palestinian or pro-Israel here; there's very little to no middle ground. Any criticism aimed at Israel is taken as anti-Israel or even anti-Semitic."

Mixed to Negative Views of AIPAC

For a small number of staffers, AIPAC's methods are viewed negatively, even if its mission is seen as laudable. The following staffer's comment is emblematic:

"I tend to agree with a lot of their [AIPAC's] positions, if not their methods."

On balance, a number of staffers are wowed by AIPAC's professionalism, efficiency, ability to reach out to all offices they consider worthwhile, and overall lobbying effort, but are clearly left wary, lukewarm, or negative with regard to AIPAC's mission. Notice one staffer's reference to the perception that other groups, like APN, may be disseminating important, alternative views, but that there's not enough time to digest the material. Also observe the discrepancy in contact rates by AIPAC versus other lobbyists, as well as how and why staffers feel obliged to pay heed to AIPAC's overtures. Here are quotes from nine staffers in this cluster.

"We have contact with AIPAC's Deb Stern, who is at the national level. Our contact is mostly with AIPAC. There is contact with APN, but there's no real time to read all their stuff. I also know Bannerman and Associates. On sensitive issues, I know AIPAC has their perspective, so you need to be very careful."

"AIPAC is the first one. They come by a few times per year. My boss traveled to Israel once on an AIPAC junket. AIPAC is more hard core than the hard core. They don't seem to realize that at the end of the day, people are dying. There's nobody more strident than these groups. It makes you somewhat distrustful of them. Unless you're on HIRC and HASC [House Armed Services Committee], the only people who show up routinely in other offices are the ones from AIPAC. If they're the only ones you're hearing from, then, you know . . ."

"AIPAC is very good about being clear on their priorities. They have an annual legislative conference. They also hold a staff retreat at the beginning of every year that's held at a local hotel; it's a daylong thing during a recess day, and they'll have workshops on foreign aid, Iran, and other issues. There will usually be 30 to 40 Hill staffers there. AIPAC trips are also very popular among staffers. What do I think about this? I have my marching orders: [the boss] agrees with AIPAC and Israel. If AIPAC is pushing it, she'll sign on quickly. She doesn't spend a lot of time on it. She's slower to sign on to resolutions. There's no big vetting process here; it's a no-brainer. I just check to see if AIPAC folks approved it. The main arguments made are that Israel is a democracy; that they're under constant attack. I've become more open to this over time, but I still don't buy all the pro-Israel line. You should take a look at the three spies case. [The 2004–2005 case involved two high-ranking officials, Steve J. Rosen and Keith Weissman, and a Pentagon employee, Larry Franklin.] They got thrown over the side quickly [by AIPAC] and nothing was mentioned afterwards. So are members of AIPAC blindly supportive? It's interesting that there was nothing even remotely negative in the press."

"It's all driven by AIPAC—we're tracking the phone calls on this. They're so good at mobilizing the grassroots. It's not a help to Israel. AIPAC is so focused on the two to three week timeline that they can't see the forest for the trees. We have very few Jewish constituents. A local AIPAC person makes the phone calls to our congressman—they're very good at mobilizing the grassroots. AIPAC promotes a constant one-upmanship [among the congresspersons]. They throw the red meat out there and let people, let the lions fight over it. This week's resolution is on congratulating Israel on its UN General Assembly slot."

"AIPAC is not as powerful as people give them credit for. There are others who believe the neocons control all, and that AIPAC approved this or that nomination. They are masters of the English language, and they position themselves to influence people. They are very active in the world of op-eds, on Fox News, etc. They're just really good at making their arguments; really good at knowing when to push or pull back. I'm sure they hate [Bush's 2002] Road Map, but they know they can't say 'No,' so they bite their tongue and seem supportive but will always seek ways to undermine it. And there's always the possibility they'll use the accusation of anti-Semitism, so people will say, 'Screw it, I won't go against them.' If you compare AIPAC with AARP, the former just represents a few people; the latter has real power, and will even become more powerful."

"With regard to influence, I attended the AIPAC March conference. There were more members of Congress there than at anything except a State of the Union address. There was over one-half of the Senate and one-third of the House members at the dinner. There were 5,000 attendees at the conference; all constituents. It was overwhelming. AIPAC is so powerful and effective—I don't want to use the word monopoly, but . . ."

"We did get pressure from pro-Israel groups to sign Lantos's letter about the Road Map. The congressman said, 'Listen, we can't have 435 secretaries of state.' Rep. Capps [ardently pro–"two states"] had a counterletter. We didn't get pressure from any groups to sign her letter. Lantos got 330 to 340 signatures; Capps got perhaps a dozen signatures."

"People contact me a lot; I get unsolicited emails from lots of groups. If AIPAC sent me something, I'd mark it as something I have to read; I'll make a special note. [Why make this special response to AIPAC?] They're a very conscientious, deliberate, organized group. If I get something in writing from them, I know it's not just a casual, relationship-forming group. This attitude came from my own political experience. AIPAC has much more clout; you realize this early on. AIPAC lobbies us over the Ros-Lehtinen bill on Hamas. Also, two college-aged people from AIPAC came in and lobbied me on Iran about one month ago, at the time of their big spring convention. They're so organized; that's what I mean. It's the way they lobby—they're just so well informed. Others have a conference and fan out, too, but they can't do the details the way the AIPAC folks do. I know the congressman is a supporter of AIPAC, but he's also a serious legislator and likes to hear both sides of an issue. Our LD and the boss go to dinners, receptions, etc., put on by AIPAC. AIPAC is so well organized that every congressperson probably has someone assigned to deal with them. The Hellenic Council, and the Armenians are well organized, too, but neither is as well organized as AIPAC."

Negative to Hostile Perceptions of AIPAC

Here is a series of quotes, all taken from interviews with veteran House staffers.

"AIPAC is head and shoulders above the other lobbying groups, but there's virtually no dialogue between AIPAC and our office because we regularly disagree. They don't want to waste their time with us."

"So many members are given an agenda from AIPAC, etc. On the Republican side, they tolerate no dissent at all. The situation is not great for Democrats either. There's a huge lack of information brought [to this issue area] by most congresspersons and then they're given an agenda."

"You can be very pro-Israel and still espouse positions that are not in line with AIPAC or others that say they are pro-Israel. The Likudization and Republicanization of AIPAC are true. Ask [Rep.] Dave Obey about [Israel's Prime Minister] Rabin telling Obey to keep AIPAC off his back. Rabin told AIPAC to back off, and the creation of the Israel Policy Forum was perhaps a reaction to this. Rabin reached out to the 'machers' to help him. AIPAC is not comfortable in the realm of peacemaking. They want to fight off Israel's enemies in Washington. If a liberal government came in, AIPAC would have a hard time changing course."

Shifting gears, the staffer quoted directly above added:

"AIPAC is really shorthand for the whole network. They have their rote answer regarding noninvolvement in politics, but they do help candidates get money. I know—I used to work for them. But AIPAC also plays or makes a 'pain in the butt calculus.' The national level lobbyists will come in, five to six of my big Jewish donors back home will call in and threaten to cancel events, or the rabbi calls, or 40 to 50 constituents will call—so is it worth it to buck this group? It's a pain in the butt. That's their strength on the bill, versus 'if I vote with them, I can make points and get money. So AIPAC can make your life easier or be a pain in the butt, and since most people's constituents don't care anyway . . . [Other congresspersons] may say 'AIPAC can defeat me if I vote with [your boss].' They'll say, 'I've got this big event scheduled in [big city] and if I vote with your boss . . .' But I think we're beginning to chip away at this line of thinking. AIPAC no longer dominates the Hill—there are other Jewish organizations, and even some money going to other candidates."

"We get requests for meetings with AIPAC. Whoever asks, we meet with them. NORPAC came to the Hill with some 500 constituents, none of whom came from our district—we should have told them 'No.' Six people came in to talk about 4681, the Israeli Energy Bill, a Saudi Arabia Accountability Act, and Iran. AIPAC people also came in to meet with the congressman to lobby 4681. There were six of them, two from the district. The youngest was a high school student. The congressman was clear he wouldn't change his mind—he opposed their recommendations—he just told them, 'Thank you for your time.' It seems as if more junior people had been sent. The high school student spoke to the congressman in a condescending tone."

"We don't get any visits from AIPAC. We got one visit from NORPAC last year. Ours is not an anti-Israel position; it's rather a noninterventionist stance. We think it's better for Israel to be free of our aid. Israeli papers and opinions are much more diverse than here. There are many Israelis who don't approve of what AIPAC does here."

One staffer, who described herself and her boss as totally pro-Israel, in her case for religious reasons, noted: "I read very little material from AIPAC because it's so biased."

And to conclude, here are some staffers more vituperative comments about AIPAC.

"AIPAC is more hard core than the hard core. [The congressman] is well aware of Congress's role in foreign policy; he always wants us to check with State [Department]. The administration is always saying, 'Why do you want to know?' Every outside group wants to come in and vent. He becomes a bit taciturn; he rocks in his chair, says thank you, keeps the room ten degrees cooler than it is now so the people want to leave early. The Egyptians are more reasonable."

"AIPAC does operate with a certain arrogance. They're so unused to people defying them that when it happens they try to create so much pain for your office that it's not worth the effort."

"It's almost impossible to think about these issues without thinking about politics on the Hill. There are very powerful forces on the Hill that demand you think one thing and one way only. [Who are you thinking about?] AIPAC. As regards their professionalism: They're not always friendly. They don't see staffers as important; they slight staffers at their peril. They are exceedingly demanding; black and white. If you talk favorably of the Palestinians at all . . . you just don't. The peace and justice community leans more towards the Palestinians; they do it more on an individual basis. AIPAC sends emails and blast faxes, but regarding individual contacts, they don't mess around with lower level staffers; they call [the congressman]. I feel a lot of bitterness; I really don't like their approach. What's professional about them—that they show up on time? I had a particularly bad experience with the boss at an AIPAC dinner. They packed me and the staffers off to the corner. There was a big screen with Ariel Sharon on it; the whole thing was cult-like. I lose respect for politicians. No one can love AIPAC enough. All the D's and R's are going to say more than the next person. It's just gross. The whole thing is repugnant. If I/we had our druthers, we'd be with Lois Capps on a lot more issues, but we don't dare."

PERCEPTIONS OF ARAB, PALESTINIAN, AND
IRANIAN AMERICAN LOBBIES

As noted earlier, the great majority of staffers I interviewed were unlikely to have even seen any pro-Arab or pro-Palestinian representatives. More often than not, staffers voiced puzzlement, but usually not any embarrassment, over the inability to name pro-Palestinian or pro-Arab groups. In the 2005–2006 time frame, a fair number noted that it was unfortunate that these interests did not enjoy more and better representation, assuring me that they and their boss would be ready and willing to listen to all sides if provided the opportunity. For those who had experienced contact with Arab lobbyists, many found the experience a negative one. In stark contrast to most staffers' characterizations of AIPAC's representatives, interventions by Arab American lobbyists were typically described to me by staffers as unfocused, overly aggressive, and lacking in professionalism. Many staffers left me with the distinct impression that these "pro-Arab" interlocutors were, sadly, just shooting themselves in the foot. Add a not infrequent "they suck at lobbying" and one gets the general picture. More sympathetic staffers, recognizing these shortcomings, said they have even tried to coach these lobbyists to enhance their effectiveness, and they saw some as improving their lobbying skills, but they readily acknowledged that most had a great distance to travel before they were on a par with AIPAC. So I often heard assessments akin to what one staffer observed: "Yes, I've heard from pro-Palestinian and pro-Arab groups; I've dealt with some, but I can't remember names at all. One large group came in early to talk to the congressman, but I recognized right away how poorly organized they were. AIPAC is beautifully organized; a beautiful organization. The Chinese government, too, could learn a lot from the Israeli government on how to lobby."

One caveat is in order. Because so many staffers were unlikely to know the names of "pro-Arab" and/or "pro-Palestinian" groups, or because their knowledge of them was thinner, I have left references to those groups embedded in the context of their comparison to pro-Israel groups. Here, then, are some of the more memorable quotes from the 2005–2006 time frame. I have arranged the staffers' quotes in the following categories: (1) Staffers with very little to no knowledge or contact with such lobbies; (2) staffers with contact from these lobbies with negative perceptions; (3) staffers with contact with mixed, hopeful, and/or positive views.

Little to No Knowledge or Contact

"I've never gotten a call from any Palestinian interest group. We get visits from AIPAC, of course, two to three times per year."

"NORPAC is our touchstone. AIPAC asks us to look at stuff that concerns them, like Iran. I don't think I've ever even seen a letter that is supportive of Arabs."

"As regards pro-Palestinian and pro-Arab groups, I don't even know who they would be, but we do hear from human rights people and activists."

"It's like apples to oranges—the Israeli side compared to the Arab side. There is no organization to the Arab side. [Are there any note-worthy Arab groups? He shook his head to indicate no.] It's either individualized, or people talking about discrimination."

"We still get AIPAC once or twice per year, and ZOA types, too. But we don't see them every day like Ros-Lehtinen and others get visits. The ADC, an Arab group, came here once four years ago."

"Interest groups tend to cluster with their friends. Jewish groups tend to call me. Arab American groups don't really call me because they know where my boss is. I think this is a mistake on their part. It's really a mistake that Arab ambassadors don't make more of an effort to see my boss."

Some Contact; Generally Negative Views

"I get the Palestinian perspective sometimes, but it's not well organized. I don't know that I've ever had a formal organization advocating for Palestinians ever contact me. People in our district are very active with AIPAC. I rarely hear from AIPAC in Washington; I hear from AIPAC people back home. Another guy contacts me regularly, too; he's extremely interested, but he's closer to ZOA, to the right of AIPAC. ZOA does contact us two to three times per year. The Republican Jewish Coalition also sends us blast emails. I hear from the American Jewish Committee, too."

"AIPAC is most in touch with us. ZOA is in contact, but with no regularity, and there are no personal relations. We get some letters from Palestinians and Arabs. We hear from some Iranian people, but not about Arab-Israeli or Israeli-Palestinian matters."

"Pro-Palestinian groups are only one one-hundredth as well organized. The difference between pro-Palestinian and pro-Israeli groups is remarkable. I could call right now and get briefings from AIPAC types. Unfortunately, the other side can't do this. The pro-Israel interests 'have it down.'"

Some say AIPAC or the Jews are running Congress—this is a mantra. I say this is bullshit. It's truthful to the extent that it [AIPAC] does its homework. It's a person from our district; they have their issues, and come to see the boss. By contrast, the Arabs suck at lobbying."

Contact, with Mixed, Hopeful, and/or Positive Views

"We hear from American Task Force for Lebanon. And he meets informally or contacts Jim Zogby. There's no question that the Israeli lobby sets the debate on these issues. The terms of the debate very rarely discuss our relations with other Middle East countries, with the rest of the world, and so forth. My boss says 'We get criticized here in the US for arguments that are commonplace in Israel.'"

"Look at the pro-Arab groups: (1) American Task Force for Lebanon: very targeted missions; no mission creep; good, strong constituency; have money and money is well spent; monitor Hill activity; Lebanon gets $35 million in Appropriations—more than they should get; got the travel ban to Lebanon lifted; stopped SAA; have good relations with the White House; (2) Arab American Institute: good grassroots following in Michigan; not so politically effective; (3) ADC: marginally powerful; there are some whackos in the group; Ziyad Asali is a great guy—gentle and polite; (4) CAIR—not very effective yet; (5) there's a Maronite Christian group—they're whackos. Many Arab Americans just don't get American politics; they're too aggressive."

"AIPAC is the 800-pound gorilla in Congress. National publications cite them as one of the strongest groups—clearly they have the ability to affect policy in Congress. All others pale in comparison. AIPAC organizes personal visits by district members; engages in 'grassroots' and 'grasstops' lobbying; provides information to members of Congress by issuing papers, faxes, statements on particular issues; and by having individuals, through constituents, drop in to offices. The two biggest Arab groups are the Arab American Anti-Discrimination Committee and the Arab American Institute, Jim Zogby's group. We work with them. They're learning to navigate D.C. and should get better. APN shares the congressman's views; we dialogue with them and many others. We get buried in so much paper here."

"On every issue we meet with reps from both sides. On the conflict, we meet with Churches for Middle East Peace, AIPAC, AJC, ADL; I haven't met with ZOA in quite some time. Within one week, I'll get 20 phone calls saying thank you from AIPAC, AJC, and ADL members. Regarding MPAC—Muslim Public Affairs Council—the Muslim voice in America is their focus. We haven't used American Muslims enough. MPAC has done a lot to bring greater transparency with regard to mosque finances. Many Arab groups are much more concerned about the Patriot Act, etc., than about US foreign policy."

"I'd go to IPF before I went to AIPAC. IPF has a better perspective on where people should be going. AIPAC seems to be more a reflection of Likud, whereas IPF has understood the significance of the demographic explosion in Palestine, etc. There's not a huge

Palestinian lobby. I speak with Bannerman's people semi-regularly. Very few people here back ideas out of a sense of righteousness and belief. What AIPAC says, goes. AIPAC is very good at organizing. Sarah Enman was with AIPAC in the 1960s and 1970s; they decided to cherry-pick members who have no Jewish constituents; people [constituents] like Jerry Nadler has. They go to [districts] with no Jewish constituents and introduce them to donors. They get people who couldn't care less. I think there's no countermobilization by Arab groups because the undertaking would be so huge, so extravagant. Only Israel and the Israeli public can counterbalance AIPAC. In 1991 and 1992, Rabin told AIPAC to back off. When Netanyahu beat Peres, there was a huge purge of Labor folks in AIPAC, and the people who formed the IPF were busted, too. AIPAC people have consistently been Netanyahu people. I worked at AIPAC for Ken Weissman—he was a peacenik; it's a strange aspect of the scandal that he's gone. There's not an AIPAC for Palestinians. Probably APN is best, and that is a Jewish group."

A FEW PERCEPTIONS OF OTHER NOTEWORTHY MIDDLE EAST INTEREST GROUPS

Beyond the comments that can be gleaned from the preceding quotes, here is a series of staffers' comments about other Middle East interest groups that I recorded in the mid-2000s. I think they're helpful in terms of providing color, flavor, and context to earlier and later commentary. I'll begin by looking at several staffers' views of NORPAC and ZOA.

"Many of the [lobbyist groups] are on a cyclical schedule. For example, the NORPAC reps and family members came to see me last year, and I'm scheduled to see one of their reps in two months. NORPAC claims to be the largest pro-Israel lobby in the US [sic]. On amendments for Appropriations on Israel-Arab stuff, the bottom line—I call NORPAC and they offer advice on these issues."

"Yes, I hear from ZOA sometimes. You don't want to get on their 'crap' list because they're very vocal against their enemies. I think

ZOA has their favorites and they go with them—people like Eric Cantor, Butch Otto, and Anthony Weiner—on efforts like cutting aid to the Palestinians. At times ZOA is popular; for example, they had a feasting time when the intifada was on; or now with Hamas getting elected, they do better."

"I used some of ZOA's paper resources, but I didn't call them in. You don't want to stoke the boss's fire." [In other words, this staffer was playing gatekeeper to lessen the chance that his boss would take an even more aggressive, right wing position.]

"Other organizations [after AIPAC] that weigh in include ZOA, but sometimes I wonder if they're paid for by AIPAC because they're so over-the-top outrageous."

"With the emergence of Ahmadinejad [president of Iran, 2005–2013], there's been a new focus by AIPAC on Iran for some time now. We get faxes regularly from some groups that I don't even read—negative faxes—people saying things like [Israeli PM] Ehud Olmert is as much of a butcher as [PM Ariel] Sharon; I think the faxes are from Women in Green. Americans for Peace Now, they're primarily American Jews as best as I can tell. They were considered pretty extreme left, now they speak in more general terms about peace. But I'm skeptical of their toned-down rhetoric. [Do you hear from ZOA?] No. UJC [United Jewish Council] sends us faxes, but more about domestic issues. [Arab lobbies?] No, not really; perhaps because the congressman's position is so well defined on this."

I've already registered numerous comments by staffers about APN, IPF, and CMEP here and elsewhere, so I will make a conscious effort not to add on here. Of these three, APN was most valued for its informational input, but its self-proclaimed "leftist" orientation damaged its appeal in many circles. There have been efforts by smaller, dovish elements to promote peace, as indicated in the following, veteran staffer's reference. I have also provided quotes about newer pro-peace groups, such as J Street, Telos, and a rejuvenated FCNL earlier in the book, and will have more to say about them later.

Most of the quotes presented here were harvested during my first round of interviews in the mid-2000s and relate to efforts by small pro-peace groups and individuals.

"I have a friend who works for the Council for the National Interest—Paul Findley's group. Many people won't meet with him."

"Yeah, I hear from some Christian group, but I can't think of their name."

"The Religious Action Center [RAC], the political office of the Reform Judaism movement, is making some positive forays—Rabbi Saperstein is doing interfaith dialogue, addressing hunger and civil rights issues. Churches for Middle East Peace also plays an important role. They help offset the evangelicals; they introduce new programs on Israel and Palestine. I try to tell these groups to not come across as being anti-Semitic and don't just talk about the oppression of Palestinians. They just need to reorient their message a little. For example, look at the IPF Friday newsletters by M.J. Rosenberg— 'we're pro-Israel and this is why peace is in America's best interest.'"

In the mid-2000s, most pro-peace groups were not making any heavy mark in the IME conflicts debate. But by the time I undertook my second wave of interviews, new pro-peace groups and lobbyists had entered the picture. As regards new groups, J Street topped the list, but NIAC and the Telos Group were now present as well. For the most part, these new groups were working for the same "two-state" goal sought by existing groups like APN, IPF, CMEP, the Middle East Peace Initiative, and a now more active FCNL. When I spoke about J Street with staffers in early 2011, some observers were optimistic about its long-run potential, but they did not feel it had yet done enough to diminish the powerful grip of AIPAC. By 2012–13, as noted elsewhere, several more attentive staffers agreed with one staffer's assessment that J Street had succeeded in "opening up a new space, a critical new space for discussion and the ability to challenge Israeli government policy,"

As if reading from the same script, a second House staffer said: "The big difference is that J Street really has opened up some more space and breathing room for criticism. Before, AIPAC pretty much dominated all the discussion. The presence of J Street gives [the boss] some cover; it makes it easier for him to adopt a more critical position." And as a third staffer intoned: "J Street is good. They're a welcome addition because they provide cover for my boss and others who don't want to march with AIPAC hook, line, and sinker."

So J Street was gaining traction. In addition to the 50 staffers at its Washington, D.C., office, it had taken its viewpoint to the rest of the country, opening offices in New York City, Boston, Miami, Chicago, Seattle, San Francisco, and Los Angeles. Initially heavily backed by liberal billionaire George Soros, the group survived the embarrassment of lying about his support. This matter aside, from some 30 endorsers back in 2008, J Street's popularity had grown to the point that, as J Street staffer asserted, "People are coming to us; we no longer have to solicit support."

Efforts by J Street, APN, and others may augur well for the development of a mass base among citizens, with more people calling their congresspersons in support of a "two-state" solution acceptable to moderate Israelis and Palestinians, and for the use of diplomacy to abate conflict with Iran. As a key figure at FCNL told me in summer 2013: "These Middle East issues are very much driven by constituents or made in accordance with a very vocal grassroots constituency. A more vocal minority advocates for more sanctions on Iran and preparing for war, instead of using diplomacy, but from 2007–2009 to 2011–13 there has been remarkable growth in the number of constituents pushing for and advocating for peace."

SOME CONCLUDING COMMENTS ON HOUSE STAFFERS

Most House staffers are holding foreign policy portfolios as just one of five if not fourteen other portfolios. In general, they are bright, industrious, and eager to learn, but most are also young, inexperienced, not knowledgeable about the Middle East, less interested in it as an issue area, and so pressed for time that they need to look for quick answers to pressing, complex issues. This combination of factors leaves them all the more likely and willing to depend upon other individuals and interest groups, and as regards the latter, they become quickly attuned to the reality that what some "special interest" groups proffer can only be ignored at their boss's own peril.

It's important to note that staffers' views are often consonant with those of their bosses, but this is far from always being the case, as reflected in many of the quotes above. On a few occasions, I came across staffers holding views that were more hawkish and right wing pro-Israel than those of their bosses, but where there were disparities and disagreements, it was far more likely to be the case that staffers felt their bosses as too hawkish or too slavishly pro-Israeli. As one staffer asked me: "Have you asked whether staffers agree with their bosses? If you took a survey, you'd find differences. Democratic staff are probably less hawkish than their bosses are. I don't think being hawkish is the best thing for Israel. I wouldn't sign on to or vote for all the things she [the staffer's boss] does."

Among my Jewish staffer interviewees, there was great diversity of views. Of those I initially interviewed, all but one were very knowledgeable on the subject matter, and many had impressive track records on the Hill. The least knowledgeable person held even more hawkish views than her already conservative, hawkish boss. Among the others, again all knowledgeable, one shared the hawkish views of his boss; two criticized the hawkish views of their bosses; two were in lockstep with their bosses' strong but not slavish commitment to Israel; and the remaining four had more dovish views than their bosses' moderate-to-strong commitment to Israel positions. Worded differently, seven of the Jewish staffer interviewees disapproved of the power wielded by AIPAC. As Jewish Americans, they found AIPAC's power and influence both embarrassing and unhelpful with regard to Israel's long-term welfare. While some of these staffers spoke quite openly of their disapproval, a few took a more sotto voce approach because they were afraid. One woman called me back, despite my having stated to her my standard, sincere reassurances about respecting everyone's anonymity, and said: "Please be careful with how you use the quotes; I'm really afraid of the consequences of what I said being traced back to me and the office."

Again, criticism by Jewish American staffers could be found among staffers working for House members with passionate commitments to a right wing pro-Israel position. For example, one such staffer, a young Jewish American who had studied at a predominantly Jewish American university, resided in Israel, and studied Middle East affairs, noted: "Certain liberal Democrats are taking a very harsh, right wing, automatic response to Middle East issues. Your logic should be universal; so it seems bizarre to me that if you're criticizing the war in Iraq, why not criticize Israel's war on the West Bank. I've been there in recent years and seen the Palestinian cities, and it's really unpleasant stuff. You drive ten miles and go from a very progressive place in Israel to third world shit."

I am constrained from commenting on the relationships between staffer interviewees of Arab or Muslim background. Their presence in the House, as is also true in the Senate, was and is so limited that to identify them by background would make it far too easy to identify them as individuals. I do not think it unfair on my part to divulge that none of these individuals—who were both knowledgeable on the issues and experienced on the Hill—approved of the way the House dealt with matters relating to the Arab-Israeli and Israeli-Palestinian conflicts.

To sum up, AIPAC's domination of the congressional arena was nearly total in the mid-2000s, as reflected in staffers' quotes from that time frame. By 2011 to early 2013, the entry of J Street onto the scene had affected House discussion of Mideast matters to some degree, as had the heavier push from FCNL. So J Street, APN, FCNL, IPF, the Telos Group, and others were making a difference just past the turn of the decade. And one other noteworthy change between 2006 and 2013 was the appearance of NIAC. This small group was making a relatively big impact on matters relating to Iran because its D.C. members were seen as "dispassionate, logical providers of information" on US-Iranian and Iranian-Israeli relations. As a handful of actors on the Hill sought arguments to counter those presented by right wing forces pressing for greater US sanctions against Iran and/or war, NIAC was widely credited for its astute responses to those calls.

Chapter Four

SENATE STAFFERS ON THE JOB

SOME USEFUL BACKGROUND ON THE SENATE OFFICES' SIDE

If the House office buildings generate more of a collegiate atmosphere among staffers, in crossing the Hill to the Senate office buildings, one moves into much more of a sober, somber, advanced graduate or law school environment. Senate staffers are, on average, older, more experienced, and more likely to be bearers of degrees from prestigious universities. The mood is more sedate, the corridors less bustling, and the offices more spacious. The most noteworthy dining venue, frequented by senators and visitors, features a hostess who orchestrates seating at linen covered tables. Diners make their way through a fine buffet, and the experience differs greatly from that provided by the bustling, mass food court on the House side, erstwhile home to the "Freedom Fries." A longtime staple of the Senate buffet was the "Washington 'pork' and bean soup."

Lest one think the Senate staffers are totally removed from the younger, House-side mind-set, I offer the following, refreshing comment by one of my Senate interviewees: "There are two Washingtons, the days you wear socks to work and the days you don't wear socks to work." But a former Senate staffer who reviewed this text penned a quick rejoinder that: "in my office jeans were never allowed . . . the only time we could wear them was when our executive assistant, who was the one that truly ruled the office, was on vacation, and that was only once a year."

That Senate staffers as a group are, on average, older and more highly educated than their House counterparts is reflected in the data I collected. Of the Senate staffers I interviewed, the average age was 34, the median age 35.5, and the mode 36; that is respectively 3.7, 8.5, and 13 years older than the interviewees in my House sample. There was a much higher percentage of Senate staffers holding master's degrees: 61 percent, versus 29 percent in the House. Moreover, nearly all held their degrees from prestigious universities such as Harvard, Georgetown, George Washington University, Columbia, UC Berkeley, Michigan, Johns Hopkins School of Advanced International Studies, Tufts Fletcher School, Brown, UCLA, Texas, and North Carolina. Exactly ten times as many—66 percent—were recipients of degrees from Ivy League universities compared to the House counterparts in my sample. And a greater number had earned degrees in politics or public policy—86 percent (versus 71 percent in the House). Once again, formal study of the Middle East was low—just 36 percent had taken at least one course on the region—although this was still higher than the 29 percent score of House staffers. It seems safe to assume that, on average, the Senate staffers' higher level of political studies has equipped them with more robust conceptual frameworks than their House counterparts, enabling them to more effectively assimilate and process information about the Middle East. In addition, my prima facie evidence suggests that a greater number of Senate staffers had already worked for several years at the State Department, the Pentagon, or another government agency. Finally, compared to most House staffers, Senate staffers benefit from sitting in more prestigious seats. As one noted: "Staff for Foreign Relations are better placed [than House staffers]; we get memos before briefings by the White House, State, etc. The staffers are much more important here, more influential, than in the House. There, no one cares what 330 of the 435 members think. Junior congresspersons are not listened to. Here, in my case, I don't steer my senator at all. He's been in the Senate for 20 years. Most senators are older men, not born yesterday. Biden and Lugar have seen and done it all. They have incredible perspective and judgment based in years of experience." I'll just quickly note that there are obviously many veteran women senators as well.

Average years spent working on the Hill by Senate staffers was 5.59, with 4.50 the median and 9 the mode; compared to 5.47 years, 3.13 median, 3.00 mode on the House side. While the modal figure, and its disparity with the House, is perhaps the most telling of these statistics, the greater proximity of the mean and median scores indicates that high rates of burnout, bailout, and turnover in the Senate are not so different from those seen in the House.

Senators receive considerably larger MRAs than House members, and can afford to hire much larger, better-paid staffs. For FY 2012, Senate office and personnel allocations ranged between $2.96 and $4.67 million, with an average of $3.21 million. Of course, senators have experienced the same 11 percent cutbacks and then the sequester that affected the House over the past three years.

In the 30-plus Senate offices in which I conducted interviews, the number of staffers ranged from 15–17 on the low end, to nearly 30 on the high end; that is, from 50 percent to 300 percent bigger than House office staffs. A typical senator will have a staff comprised of one chief of staff; one or two legislative directors; and five or more legislative assistants, each of whom will have at least one legislative correspondent assisting them. Both the chiefs of staff and LDs are "big picture" people. One staffer noted, "The LD has to see the bigger picture; he has to worry about the home state voters." LAs do heavy lifting, but can concentrate on a narrower set of portfolios than their House counterparts.

Because I was interviewing staffers who focused on foreign affairs, their portfolios typically included foreign affairs, defense, intelligence, veterans' affairs, and homeland security. Again, each office might be slightly different, so subtract one of these portfolios, or subtract one and add another, like trade, and the reader has a pretty good idea of what's on a Senate staffer's plate. In brief, it's a great deal, for sure, but far fewer portfolios—roughly half as many—than held by the average House staffer. Unless a senator is more heavily involved in international affairs, he or she will have just one foreign policy person, and just one working on defense, out of roughly 25 total staffers, an obvious reflection of the low priority assigned to such matters.

The pay scale for staffers varies significantly from one side of Capitol Hill to the other. There is greater funding for staffing in the Senate than in the House, and senators can pay mid- to lower-level staffers more; Senate staffers at these grades can top $50,000–$60,000 versus an average of $30,000 in the House. And as a Senate staffer remarked: "There's a much higher turnover rate with House staffers as a result of the low pay. There, you can have a 50 percent changeover in one year or less. So there's a huge loss of knowledge there." However, Senate staffers are just as aware as their House counterparts of private sector pay scales, including those of lobbyists. And the "early departure" of Senate staffers carries its own implications for how staffers manage their assignments. Talking about money and their jobs, Senate staffers in 2005–2006 made the following comments.

> "LAs make in the upper $40,000 and it doesn't get much higher than that, so that caps the experience. D.C. is a very expensive area to live in, too. People working at think tanks, defense contractors, make much more. So the salary level keeps the staffer corps relatively green."

> "The career path or progression is not a good one—intern to LC to LA. The pay is weak and leads to [Jack] Abramoff mischief; there is much potential for abuse. You're not getting 35 to 40 year olds with big political or military savvy because it's too much of a hit paywise; and this promotes rotation to lobbies for work and for information."

Still, competition for Senate staff jobs remains intense. Said one staffer, "I got in this office because [my previous, lobbyist boss] knew of an opening. There can be as many as 500 applications for an LA opening here in the Senate." This situation had only perhaps worsened by 2010–2013.

The specific pathways to staffing positions are incredibly diverse. But because most of these staffers are somewhat older, not directly out of university like so many House counterparts, their curriculum vitae and personal networks are usually more impressive. Here are two examples that demonstrate this point.

> "I worked on the House side. I did [national presidential] campaign work in [a southern state], but really got the job through a [DC-area university] alum who had worked in this office. There's no clearinghouse, so networking and being seen is most important."

> "I knew my predecessor, who got a plum job working for the State Department, and knew that there wasn't anyone lined up to replace him yet. I'm a Republican, was getting a little older, and just thought it would be an interesting position to be in. Some senators are more willing than others to invest in a top staff. [My boss] is on many committees: we have a senior person for international financial

matters, a senior defense and national security person—a retired [military officer]. So we're pretty loaded with senior people; I think it's probably atypical."

In brief, while there are very intelligent, energetic, highly educated, extremely competent, and engaging staffers in the House, one finds more uniformly talented, highly educated, and experienced staffers on the Senate side.

Because Senate staffers carry a smaller number of portfolios (3–5), they can and do devote more time to foreign affairs than their House counterparts, as well as to examining the Arab-Israeli and other Middle East conflicts.

PERCENT OF TOTAL TIME SPENT ON FOREIGN AFFAIRS— ON IME CONFLICTS OF FOREIGN AFFAIRS—ON IME/TOTAL TIME

Senate Staffers			
Mean (average)	48.5	27.2	13.2
Median (midpoint)	45.0	25.0	11.3
Mode (most common)	30.0	30.0	9.0
House Staffers			
Mean	36.3	35.9	13.0
Median	30.0	30.0	9.0
Mode	10.0	20.0	2.0

Again, the modal scores are probably most indicative, and clearly depict the Senate vs. House "time" disparity, while still demonstrating that even the average Senate staffer does not devote much of her/his time to working on the IME conflicts. For many Senate staffers, like in the House, the amount of time spent dealing with Middle East issues is dictated by events. One staffer in summer 2013 said, "I could spend an entire week working on Syria, then do nothing on foreign affairs for two whole weeks."

SENATE STAFFERS' PREFERRED INFORMATION SOURCES

As I did with my House interviewees, I asked very open-ended questions about the sources of information that Senate staffers found important. Only after I had given them more than ample opportunity to cover as many bases as they found relevant did I quiz them about sources they might have forgotten. Again, my assumption is that staffers' references to preferred sources of information offered insight on inputs to their and their bosses' decision making. With that in mind, here is what Senate staffers told me in 2005–2006 and 2011–13 about those sources.

What Are Their Favorite Media Sources?

Like the House staffers, Senate staffers usually began their response to the question about sources of information with a litany of media staples. With regard to print media, the list is quite comparable to that noted on the House side, as one might well surmise. The *New York Times* and the *Washington Post* led the list, followed by many references to the *Financial Times*, the *Wall Street Journal*, and even more references to the Pentagon's "Early Bird" press clippings than in the House. The *Economist*, *Congressional Quarterly*, and *Congressional Daily*, as well as *Roll Call*, *The Hill*, and *Politico* were also noted by some staffers. In more recent times, some staffers have been reading *Foreign Policy*'s "Daily Brief." Interestingly, among my set of Senate interviewees, only a small number read foreign publications, with Israel's *Ha'aretz* and the *Jerusalem Post* mentioned more than any other Middle East publications. As in the House, staffers noted that the flow of information was overwhelming. One staffer said, "There's no lack of info, just lack of time and resources to read and manage the information."

In addition to reading the newspapers, Senate staffers are also deluged on a daily basis with printed materials, faxes, and email communications. One staffer said, "A ton of stuff gets delivered to the office. I have two stacks of reading by my desk." Another remarked, "I'll get 120 emails total per day, all mixed. With everything else going on, it's impossible to digest." Senate staffers thus have the same need as House staffers to cut through the piles and establish what's most important to digest, a situation that has only worsened over time.

In 2006, one staffer said, "The flow of info is a mile wide and an inch deep. I try to stay enough on top of current events to speak intelligently on issues, but if something big comes up and I have to dig, I'll go to the *New York Times*, the *Washington Post*, or the BBC website for current events. I'll look at Israeli newspapers like *Ha'aretz* and the *Jerusalem Post* for analysis, depending on the issue."

In 2013 one said, "I am flooded with information. It's like a fire hose of emails coming into my inbox. The human eye cannot keep up with the stream, so I scan for recognizable names."

As is true in House offices, the deluge of information overwhelms Senate staffers. Thus, Senate staffers are forced to go into triage mode as well, which means that information coming from more "recognizable" names and sources—read more influential and powerful sources—are paid more attention to than others.

Do They Use Congressional Research Services (CRS)?

Numerous Senate staffers turn to CRS for information, just as many House staffers do. This was true in 2005–2006 and 2011–13. Here are two representative, Senate staffers' comments about CRS. "CRS is a great [source of information], one of the few places offering non-partisan writing on the Middle East." "When I engage on an issue and have to delve deeper, I use CRS—they're incredibly important."

Here, too, it is significant that CRS is perceived as "apolitical" in nature, and that this perception contributes to making it a "go-to" source for many Senate staffers. Indeed, many staffers stated explicitly that they are wary of information fed to them by lobbyists, interest groups, and think tanks because it carries an inherent bias.

Some staffers are so overwhelmed by their workload that they have a hard time simply staying on top of media news and CRS material. This, in turn, causes them to question how reliable or accurate their perspective is given the limitations on their acquisition of information. Here are several staffers' observations: "We can't be in all places [hearings, etc.] at the same time; we can't read all the manuscripts, so this makes people dependent on the *Washington Post* or the *New York Times*, etc., so you get legislation as a reaction to journalism." "I take care to give the senator a balanced viewpoint, including what Arab moderates are saying. I get info from the press, from CRS, but there's always that question of how biased our information is."

Foreign Relations Committee Staffers and Committee Hearings as an Important Source?

Foreign Relations committee staffers, the Senate Professional Staff Members (PSMs), represent a valuable source of information for staffers in general. Most PSMs have years of experience, have traveled extensively, met the major regional "players," and are very knowledgeable about Middle East affairs. But there are still structural difficulties in the way the Senate operates, and Senate leaders may choose to block, obfuscate, or omit communications and hearings that would otherwise prove of value to open-minded decision makers. So all things considered, as one Senate staffer observed, "We do live in a bit of a bubble up here. There's a certain viewpoint we get over and over. You're always thinking of things in a political context here. There was a great session with Bernard Lewis [the well-known Middle East historian from Princeton] organized by [Sen.] Santorum."

The latter comment suggests that even when staffers think they are receiving unbiased input, they might need to remain more circumspect. Prof. Lewis provided his intellectual firepower to back the neoconservative policies that led to the Iraq War. At any rate, these observations reflect staffers' (and other observers') fears that they may be getting a biased image of events.

As has become well known to anyone attentive to such matters, the number of Senate hearings on Iraq during the war was abysmally low. I, myself, made my way to a room designated for a hearing on Iraq in the mid-2000s, only to find a placard announcing its cancellation. The Republicans controlled the Senate chamber then and, by all appearances, preferred to diminish opportunities for criticism of Republican President Bush's handling of the Iraqi war rather than maintain a keener oversight role via the potentially feisty but informative hearings. Of course, congressional oversight is supposed to be one of the more important roles Congress is designed to play.

How Much Do They Depend on Think Tanks?

Think tanks represent another important source of information for many Senate staffers, seemingly more so than for their House counterparts. Senate staffers repeated the names of think tanks thought by House staffers to be most influential. One veteran staffer said, "There are a lot of think tanks here in town, but the most influential think tanks for foreign affairs in general are CFR, CSIS, Brookings, Rand, Heritage, and WINEP."

But Senate staffers were more likely to make references to a broader range of well-known organizations: the CATO Institute, National Democratic Institute (NDI), International Republican Institute (IRI), American Enterprise Institute (AEI), the International Crisis Group (ICG), and various NGOs. New organizations mentioned in 2013 included the Center for New American Security (CNAS), and the Project on Middle East Democracy (POMED). When it comes to Middle East affairs the think tanks that mattered most to Senate staffers in the time frame of this study were WINEP, Brookings' Saban Center, CSIS, and CFR. It should go without saying that the think tanks are often counted upon to provide expert witness testimony for hearings and briefings, and that experts from the "most relied upon think tanks" frequently push "a certain viewpoint we [staffers] get over and over."

Senate staffers echoed House staffers' complaints about the length of think tanks' written reports. One staffer said, "They're too wordy—too deep in their words for what I need. I don't have half a day [to digest their material]. Folks who bridge the gap between the think tanks and normal press coverage are the ones who get my attention."

Think tanks are valued, but there is again a belief among many Senate staffers that they need be wary of bias, and that bias runs fairly consistently in a moderate to right wing pro-Israel direction in the dominant institutions.

Access to, and the Influence of, Other Government Departments and Agencies

The average Senate staffer is well placed to draw upon a broad range of informational sources, and benefits from easier access to more highly placed political actors than their House counterparts. In general, they are also more often on the receiving end of information and entreaties by knowledgeable and influential players. As one staffer noted, "With respect to groups—I have to turn the phone off. I'll get 20 to 30 calls per day from think tanks, academics, etc. I turn to ICG on Africa, the Asia Foundation on Asia, the Agency for International Development (AID), the State Department, and the CIA; and I call reporters. NDI has people on the ground. I'll call ambassadors at any time of the day. I'll also contact NGOs." According to another staffer, "We talk to former officials with Clinton and Bush; I can call up [Dennis]

Ross and ask him. I talk directly to the experts. We have more time to process information on the Senate side than they do in the House. We can and do find people who have expertise, as opposed to depending on someone who was answering the phone six months ago. I don't talk to academics, although your goal as a staffer is to get the best information, so this might make sense. I do read Juan Cole and Shibley Telhami [two well-known Middle East specialists, both known for their greater empathy for Palestinians]. We reach out to those guys, but we're most likely to call the think tank guys."

Senate staffers are also more likely to have friends working at State and/or initiate inquiries with relevant State Department officials on a need to know basis. One staffer said, "The State Department and its country desks serve as an important source to many staffers." The State Department also has a Senate liaison assisting in the flow of communications. But generally speaking, this contact is more limited than the external observer might think would be the case. For me, a commonly heard refrain was: "The only time I hear from State is when I call to get their position on something." Contacts with State are made, and in addition there are almost always a handful of Senate aides who have been seconded to Senate offices as the reader saw on the House side. But there is not any heavy, continuous contact between most Senate offices and the State Department.

Personal Cues and References

Some senators are "lone wolves"; they trust their own instincts and/or depend more heavily on their own staffs to provide information relevant to their making an informed decision. For example, many described Sen. James Inhofe as acting on his own in this issue area. Other "lone wolves" include senators who are not very active on Middle East issues. According to one staffer, "The senator's chief of staff is very well informed. She listens to him and me on these issues, but we don't have the time or resources to take a more in-depth look at these issues." But the "lone wolves" category includes others who are heavily involved: "[The senator] has been in Congress [for a long time]. On Israel, I don't think [the senator] feels the need to consult people; on national security, yes, but not on the Arab-Israeli stuff. [The senator] does seek the counsel of a few people [the senator has] known for a long time; e.g., Former Secretary of State Albright. The senator has known [name deleted], the outgoing AIPAC president, for a long time." And yet another staffer noted, "My senator will make suggestions to Secretary of State Rice. He meets often with Nick Burns" (a high-ranking, Middle East–focused, State Department official).

However, most senators, I found, do engage in a greater measure of communication with other offices in this issue area; many take their cues from colleagues they view as particularly well informed and/or as having an important opinion. Some senators clearly distinguish themselves through their efforts to get "out front" or assume a higher profile on the IME conflicts, with one means being authorship and circulation of "Dear Colleague" letters. I will discuss these factors more fully in a later chapter but will register a few points here.

Based on my interview research in the mid-2000s, there was a strong proclivity for Jewish members to consult with one another. Staffers indicated that fellow Democrats Herb Kohl, Russ Feingold, Dianne Feinstein, and Carl Levin, all senators with strong, but not blind, commitments to Israel, liked to test each other's positions on IME-related issues. Feinstein's people would also reach out to her fellow Californian Sen. Boxer—who is commonly perceived as more hard-line on these issues—and would contact Sen. Clinton's office. Yet another informal bloc involved contacts between more diehard defenders of right wing Israeli policies, like Senators Susan Collins, Rick Santorum, Jon Kyl, Jim Talent, and Joe Lieberman—the latter three of whom were/are motivated by strong religious beliefs. A third mini-bloc was comprised of senators with greater understanding for Arab countries and causes, like Senators Jim Jeffords, Patrick Leahy, and Lincoln Chafee (all New Englanders). Both Chafee and Jeffords had a solid rapport with Senate Foreign Relations Chairman Sen. Dick Lugar, as well.

Because senators serve longer terms, they are more likely to acquire greater familiarity and depth of experience on many issues. Therefore, they may also be more likely to arrive at their own conclusions on these issues and depend less upon information obtained from Senate colleagues. Senate staffers themselves, with their higher educational pedigrees, are also more inclined to depend upon their own resources, contacts, and sense of matters than to call fellow staffers. That said, high on the list of those they would turn to would be staffers serving for members on the Committee on Foreign Relations; during the mid-2000s, staffers contacted people like the PSMs for Senators

Biden and Lugar, and this phenomenon held true for many staffers, albeit to a slightly smaller degree, five to seven years later.

Other Senate-side sources of information seen as useful to some staffers include the policy committees of the Democrat and Republican parties. As two staffers noted: "They provide a good flow of information to interested staffers." "On Tuesdays and Thursdays there are policy lunches—the senators eat with their party members, and there are experts speaking, or a Condi Rice."

Do Senate Staffers Listen to and Care as Much About Constituents?

Constituents' calls are taken and usually dutifully listened to in senators' offices, and letters do elicit responses, like in the House. Again, on a great number of occasions I observed and heard staffers engaged in these phone conversations while sitting in Senate office lobbies waiting to meet my interviewees. And as a Senate staffer told me, "Every letter we receive gets answered within a two-week period."

In some states, the size of communities with either pro-Arab or pro-Israel leanings is too small to appear on the senators' radar screens. Or as one staffer put it, jokingly, "Yes, we hear from all eight people in [the home state] who are Jewish. There's no real Jewish community there; or the one that's there is very small." And the same holds true of other states and the absence of an Arab or Muslim American community of any size. As another Senate staffer commented: "We have a Peace Now constituency in [our home state] among our Jewish [constituents], but really, there are no constituent constraints for Vermont, New Hampshire, West Virginia, etc."

If one takes as a point of departure the fact that Arab and Jewish Americans are clustered primarily in about ten states, that leaves a great majority of states in which citizens are less likely to be keenly interested in Middle East affairs. One staffer noted how constituent makeup determined that staffer's low priority on foreign affairs: "Our constituents are more interested in interior, energy, agriculture issues. This means that in our office I cover military affairs, veterans' affairs, intelligence, and foreign affairs by myself. This happens in other offices where there are similar emphases on agriculture, etc."

Other staffers made reference to their constituents' ignorance or lack of concern about the issues. "I think most people in [the home state] don't know the difference between Islamist terrorists and Arabs." In many senators' offices, these factors can lower foreign policy staffers' levels of concern about constituents' views on the Middle East. One staffer said, "Unless I personally get a letter or email, I don't have much contact. We've had deployments by [home state] National Guard to Iraq, so this generates constituent interest. What's on television, C-SPAN, Fox news, etc., may prompt calls by constituents as well as people's long-standing views, but I don't talk to them."

Alternatively, some states are so big and diverse that there's a mix of levels of concern. One staffer said, "We have a large Jewish and growing Middle East demographic. The senator hears from people directly a lot; and he hears from groups across the whole spectrum: AIPAC provides lots of info; CAIR is a large group, one of about half a dozen Muslim groups; Hadassah [the world's largest women's organization]. All are pretty good at providing information, but it's rare that you see poor lobbying efforts that last long." Another Senate staffer struck a comparable chord, noting: "For our senator, constituent concerns constitute a primary reason for him to latch on to a particular issue. [Our state] has people with Middle East connections and concerns. There's a heavy flow of information from constituents; it's very mixed. There was a mixed response to the [September 2005 Israeli] Gaza disengagement. Most wrote in saying they didn't support disengagement because the Bible gives the land to the Israelis. Others say we shouldn't be giving money to the Israelis in these times." In such states, concerns may balance out one another to give senators a freer hand.

In a few states, staffers indicated that they heard more from people troubled by Israel's actions. For example, in response to Israel's summer 2006 invasion of Lebanon to pursue Hizballah fighters, a campaign which included heavy bombing of Lebanese infrastructure, many Lebanese Americans were irate. So as a Senate staffer noted: "We heard from Americans with family in Lebanon who know people in Beirut; there are also typical calls from constituents with strong opinions. [Our home state] is pretty left-leaning; they saw Israel's response to the Hizballah threat in 2006 as disproportionate." With regard to these same events, another staffer remarked that "The senator is very pro-Israeli, but our constituents are more circumspect with regard to Israel."

Many more staffers, however, are contacted by a variety of "pro-Israel" constituents whenever any big IME-related event occurs, or IME-related legislation is pending. And they were keen to point out which individuals and interests groups were most commonly behind these calls, as seen in these quotes.

"The conflict is a very important issue for many constituents. Much of the office's interest is driven by constituent concern; there's also empathy for Israel along philosophical lines and it's a bipartisan approach on these issues. The constituents who are concerned—these are important folks. Some require more attention than others; for example, prominent businesspersons with long-standing connections with the Senator. So the senator meets with them. One month ago we met with a 100-member AIPAC delegation from [the home state]—during their annual convention—there were so many people that we got a hearing room. We discussed Iran, the Hamas election, etc., and they asked for cosponsorship on bills addressing these issues. . . . We have overwhelmingly one-sided, pro-Israel constituents. Sometimes there are people who call who are more liberal, like more educated people in [one major city], or the small Arab community in [another major city of the home state], but this is very very small."

"We get a fair amount of letters about the Middle East stuff. There's a steady stream of letters to provide aid to Israel or not pressure Israel to withdraw from territories. There's a much smaller number of letters from people about human rights abuses by the Israeli military or regarding Israeli espionage in the US. A lot of pro-Israeli policies are driven by your state's demographics: New York, New Jersey, Florida, California. Look at the past Senate elections in Florida—people need to say the right thing."

"If he latches on to an issue, it's because it comes from a colleague [via a 'Dear Colleague' letter, etc.] or constituents. He doesn't like to sign on to things unless he wants to assume a leadership position. Most constituents don't care about foreign affairs issues; there's no money for home communities; but [our home state] is different because of the [size of numerous immigrant communities], and he does care about constituents with Middle East connections and concerns. He has strong concern about Middle East issues; there's also a very large Jewish population in [the home state] that keep him very interested. All senators are interested in the Middle East for strategic, moral, and democratic political reasons."

"Our decisions are all much more driven by policy than by constituents. But you can commit political suicide by constantly attacking Israel. People are afraid of AIPAC because it takes on a myth all by itself. They [AIPAC] try to get the senator's people back home to weigh in but they [back home] get it. They understand where [the senator] is coming from."

In a fair number of states, the pro-Israel voices of evangelicals are also heard from loudly and clearly; but as the reader will also see, many Senate staffers and their bosses seem to take these concerns with a grain of salt and a dash of contempt.

"With regard to constituents, the [deleted—Jewish] family in [major city] is very important. But we have a strong evangelical community in [the home state], too. They're very strong supporters of Israel. The three monotheistic faiths have a great deal in common, but it will be very hard to reconcile matters if people allow religion to dictate matters. I try to look at things in an evenhanded manner. The way Congress has operated it's like 'either you're with us or you're against us. If you're for the Palestinians a little, you must be for torture.' An evenhanded position is essential; not a European perspective, which posits that Israel wants to run the world; nor an evangelical position. We must sit down at a table and talk to people."

"People think we're in a clash of civilizations. They saw the Dubai Ports—the phones were ringing off the hooks here—as an 'us' against 'them' issue . . . but there is no monolith—look at Iran vs. Saudi Arabia."

"Evangelicals write in. They may even be anti-Semitic, but they believe God said this should be Israel's land; it's written in the scriptures. God wouldn't let it happen—don't give up one inch of that land. And they tell us to write or tell the president this. Again, all of this connotes that they believe we have a lever over Israel. And [the senator] reads every letter that comes in. [Prominent Jewish businessman], [prominent Jewish family, who owns a major corporation], and [prominent Jewish businessman]—they all contact us. There's a huge interest in Israel in NYC, Boston, Philly, and among evangelicals who are spread out pretty much throughout the South."

"[My boss] reads every letter that comes in. We hear from [a professor at an evangelical university]; he's ardently pro-Israeli—he thinks we're in a 'clash of civilizations.' From 1995 on, the evangelicals' compassion was unleashed. They think we're being attacked by terrorists. But my boss is a genuine Christian thinker; it guides his thinking. He wants to put people at the same table to talk about the issues. The need for dialogue and compassion is Christ-like behavior. We need to concentrate our fight against the [Islamist extremist] takfiri types and Wahhabi types, not 'Muslims' as the people who write in say. I think most [folks in our region] don't know the difference between Islamist terrorists and Arabs. They say, 'Get the president to stop telling Israel to give away their land.' I can't tell you how many people I've had to write to tell them that the Israelis themselves are doing this [reference to the Israeli decision to withdraw from the Gaza Strip]. [The senator] wants to be and is tough against terrorism, but he still wants to be compassionate and evenhanded."

A "Deep South" senator's aide made it clear that they heard from evangelical constituents too, but not so much on the Arab-Israeli conflict as on other social and moral issues, as was seen in the House.

On the Senate side, I got the distinct impression that the constituents are not, in general, as important to senators as they are to House members. One gets the distinct impression that individuals with financial clout are far more likely to get senators' attention than others. As one staffer put it, "If you're talking to me, you're talking about money. People are not coming to these issues for the first time. But for us, where our constituents are is very marginal." That said, a small number of well-heeled individuals can get senators' attention in many but certainly not all cases. The bias here runs distinctly in favor of putative supporters of Israel. While other religious or ethno-religious factors are in play, like the size and strength of a senator's evangelical community, senators appear to be less concerned about these voices, unless of course the senator either shares or sees utility in that perspective. This parallels views held by House staffers, leaving one to think that evangelical senators' commitment to Israel exceeds the level of pro-Israel concern by the evangelical masses.

How Important are the Lobbyists to Senate Staffers?

Lobbyists, by contrast, usually do get the senators' attention, and as was demonstrated on the House side, pro-Israeli groups—especially right wing ones—have been much more successful at playing the game. Part of the problem with the Arab camp in the mid-2000s, one that largely persisted into 2011–13, was caused by a failure to show up. This was reflected in comments like the following, which came from four different senators' staffers.

> "We've never had a visit by an Arab-American group here; and any [state resident] who requests a visit, she'll meet with them"; "There are 4 or 5 interest groups that come in and talk—all from an Israeli perspective; never from the Palestinian side"; "I've heard almost nothing pro-Palestinian"; "We don't get a lot of lobbying from Palestinian lobbies or from Arab lobbies at all."

As with my House staffer interviewees, there were many Senate staffers whom I had to ask if they had had any contact with these groups. When I did, they responded by saying things like the following three staffers did.

> "Not much at all. [Do you hear from the ADC, for example?] They send faxes; they're more influential with the Michigan delegation. They're not so influential in general; they're not here in the same numbers."

> "Pro-Arab groups rarely come in. You know the ADC may come in, but . . . [Do they come in the same numbers?] No, not even close." "There is no pro-Arab organization with that kind of contact —[comparable to that of pro-Israel groups]."

"As regards Palestinian voices and points of view: it's a void; a huge void. The most that you hear is from Peace Now, which is American Jews." [Do you hear from Arab or Palestinian groups?] "No. Iranian groups a couple of times, but they're very secretive. Also, Iranian women's groups come in; they're very aggressive."

Some staffers and their bosses even rue the absence of representation of Palestinian or Arab interests. Noted one: "My senator has a strong pro-Israeli position, that's true. But there has been no counterpoint to the AIPAC or Israeli embassy point of view regarding aid to the Palestinian community. It's not that we wouldn't listen. We would sit down with Palestinians or Jordanians or others advocating for the Palestinians if they presented themselves."

Groups with Arab or Iranian interests at heart are not totally missing in action. But even here the prima facie evidence shows that those involved were either independent actors or others who were not connected to the Palestinian or Arab community and its experience by family history. In other words, more staffers were likely to have been contacted by those in favor of peace and a "two-state" solution. One staffer said, "We heard from both sides both before and after the [2006 Palestinian] elections. AIPAC had their big conference two weeks ago. We heard from Palestinian businessmen and church groups." Another said, "Yes, we've heard from lots of church groups, lots of Christian groups. The bishops' group was here 5 or 6 weeks ago; also synagogue groups. The bishops' group asked us to not cut off aid to Palestinians, adding 'We don't like Hamas either.' The Quakers [FCNL] come, too." But others had never even heard of CMEP, for example.

In the mid-2000s, some staffers had met with representatives from CAIR. However, CAIR representatives were more interested in discussing issues of discrimination against Muslims than the A-I conflict. A few staffers were also lobbied by Iranian regime opponents, as alluded to above, or by other, equally less known groups, such as the US Campaign to End the Israeli Occupation. But references to more obscure or less-known groups were often quickly followed up by statements to the effect that the "boss" just didn't have the time to respond to their concerns.

But by the end of the decade, J Street, NIAC, and FCNL were making a positive impression upon some Senate staffers, just as they were among House staffers. Nonetheless, AIPAC retained its dominance.

The broad array of Jewish American and pro-Israel groups is well deployed on the Senate side of the Hill. The most effective of these groups owe their relative success in the Senate to the same factors displayed in the House: greater earned access due to campaign finance–related concerns, a high level of professionalism, the efficient and timely provision of information, and the skillful use of lobbying tactics, such as the use of constituents from senators' home states. As one staffer said, "The most articulate groups are the Jewish groups. The Washington lobbies recruit local, state-based individuals to approach the members of Congress. Constituent meetings get bumped to the top of the list."

In the mid-2000s, in a small number of Senate offices, staffers indicated that they had actually heard more from other Jewish American organizations than from AIPAC. One staffer noted, "We don't have that much contact with AIPAC; we seem to hear a lot from B'nai B'rith's people. I don't know how much others are lobbied by B'nai B'rith—they called a few days ago to cosign some letter that already had 90-plus senators on it. [Our senator] has been a strong enough supporter of Israel for such a long time; there's no real need to prove himself." But if anything, these "cases" seemed to be nothing more than an aberration, or because no effort by AIPAC was even necessary.

The greater presence of other Jewish American groups did not always translate into successful impressions and influence. APN, for example, had, and still has, a tendency to be pegged negatively as "to the left," whereas ZOA people are seen by many as too far to the right. This is not surprising in light of its own representatives' propensity to present themselves that way. Such ideological identifications can be off-putting, depending on one's perspective. As a staffer said, "ZOA is a little too extreme; too right wing. [Have you heard from ZOA?] No. [IPF?] No. [Americans for Peace Now?] No. I try to get rid of the email blasts from those organizations—they're not helpful."

Such perceptions may help place AIPAC enviably in a Goldilocks' porridge "just right" position. With many senators, of course, AIPAC has already set the stage for success through preelection screening, as noted in chapter one. Once a senator is elected, AIPAC hits the ground running. Its "postelection" access and influence are unparalleled, whether through direct meetings or calls to senators, or a steady flow of messages, or requested meetings that most staffers either appreciate or feel they cannot afford to ignore. Thus, a host of Senate staffers made comments like this: "Within the first three days

I was in this office AIPAC came in, and on the second day in my office the Israeli embassy set up a meeting with the Israeli military guy. My senator has a strong pro-Israeli position."

Here are some additional comments by staffers. I think they provide a helpful look at how these staffers sized up AIPAC, and how AIPAC was seen compared to its competitors in both the mid-2000s and 2011–13 time frames. It's important to note that nearly all offices seem open to receiving all concerned parties, but the frequency of visits by AIPAC representatives, perhaps due to its greater resources, gives it a potential advantage over its competitors. Arab, Iranian, and strong "two-state solution" groups, by comparison, are not visible to some staffers.

> "I see folks from AIPAC pretty regularly. We have an open door policy. I've met with reps from CAIR, AIPAC, and the ZOA. AIPAC has its annual lobby day on the Hill. I've met with APN from time to time; it's a left-leaning Jewish group. I met with a group of Arab high school kids last summer, 20 to 30 kids—'Seeds for Peace' kids. I see folks from AIPAC pretty regularly."

> "There are several interest groups that come in to see us; they all represent an Israeli point of view. We never hear the Palestinian side. We talk with AIPAC and NORPAC. AIPAC is not necessarily at the top of the list, but they do come in once per month."

AIPAC's greater frequency of contact does not guarantee a positive reception, however, as at a minimum staffers and their bosses want to examine diverse perspectives. One staffer said,

> "I'll read AIPAC's material because I feel obligated to do so to know where they are coming from. Otherwise I wouldn't read it because it's very partisan. They're one of the strongest lobbies on these issues. I also read [IPF's] M.J. Rosenberg's stuff a lot. I like his views; he doesn't get everything right, but it's in a readable format. I'll look at APN to see the exact opposite of the other [AIPAC] folks. I google stuff; go to CRS. I may turn to peers to get some information, but not too much."

As the above quotes demonstrate, AIPAC outpaces all other groups in terms of its contacts with Senate staffers. Many offices keep their eyes and ears open to alternative views, and some lament the absence of a broader range of perspectives. For most offices, input from lobbyists is of great importance, but there are always exceptions to the norm, as made clear by the following Senate staffer: "I get a stack of material from Arab-Israeli conflict interested groups every day. I have yet to find the reasons to reach out and dig beyond turning to organizations beyond CRS, State, and AID, and some journalists and faculty at Harvard, Berkeley, and Hopkins. I still have difficulty gauging the slant of various organizations."

What Is the Congruence of Staffers' Views with AIPAC's?

Among my 2005–2006 interviews with 28 Senate staffers, 11 identified their bosses as strong supporters of Israel, of which 5 asserted that their boss was a very strong supporter. No one voluntarily made a comparable assertion with regard to any Arab country or the Palestinians, although everyone knew Sen. Chafee to be highly empathetic and helpful to the Palestinians.

For senators described as very strong supporters of Israel, the consonance of views with AIPAC is nearly or always total, as the below quotes demonstrate.

"[The senator] is a strong supporter of Israel. His view is 'Whatever Israel needs for its defense!' AIPAC can get straight to the senator—this is not true of most groups"

"Senator [X]—she has many friends back home who are very active in AIPAC. She always supports Israel."

"AIPAC and Jewish groups in general are most influential. She has done a lot of fund-raising events for AIPAC; keynote speeches at fund-raisers for AIPAC [in numerous, major American cities]. She has close personal relationships with AIPAC people. She also gave an address to a group of people at a recent AIPAC convention in D.C. When AIPAC makes recommendations to us we take them very seriously. They send us email alerts, memos, occasionally they come see us personally. They're very professional; they know when to harass you and when to leave you alone. They're succinct, professional, and to the point. I pay attention more quickly because I'm so busy."

"I read the emails from AIPAC. I have a good relationship with AIPAC. ZOA is a little bit too extreme. AIPAC doesn't come in too much. [The senator] is a strong supporter of Israel; he has personal relations with leaders of these groups. NORPAC comes in about once per year on lobby day. But the 'go-to' people for me are AIPAC. I have a lengthy, very good relationship with them personally, plus the senator has good relations as well. If you need information, they can get it."

Even among staffers who did not describe their boss as a very strong supporter of Israel, their offices' position remained largely congruent with AIPAC's. For example, one new staffer noted, "I don't really know what AIPAC's agenda is right now. I've only been on the job one month. But we've never been asked to do something by those guys that wasn't already in keeping with our thinking."

Another new staffer made a comparable statement, but I detected a desire for greater independence in his ruminations.

"She has always supported Israel. I don't know if people have talked to you about AIPAC, but they're very important. She recently met with AIPAC to hear their concerns about Hamas. [The senator] said she wants to explore the issue—not set the bar so high that the Palestinians can't achieve their goal. She probably hadn't thought much about this because she was involved [recently in a tough budgetary vote]. AIPAC people were convinced that [the senator] didn't understand the Hamas issue well enough. They told us: 'People have been murdered'; 'we can't trust Hamas.' They called to ask if it made sense to brief her again on this issue—I said I think she understands the issue perfectly well. She thinks we need to go slowly and respect the democratic process of the Palestinians. She has some very close friends personal friends from her home state who are with AIPAC. They call her, and they call me directly, too."

But even in offices where AIPAC's policies are regularly endorsed, its positions and activities do not leave everyone feeling good about them. Some staffers' qualms are relatively muted: "The pro-Israel lobby has made it harder than anything else to be evenhanded. You have Democratic senators from New York, conservative Republicans from Tennessee, liberal senators from California—all are beholden to different interests to keep Israel strong." Meanwhile, some staffers are less restrained or reticent in their criticism of AIPAC, as clearly reflected in the quotes below.

"AIPAC is just brutal. Staffers here see both sides, but they know how the deck is stacked. There's nothing to be gained nationally by being perceived as pro-Arab, so you keep your pro-Israel position. Foreign ministries go ignored while deference is done to the UJA [United Jewish Appeal] of Westchester County [New York]. AIPAC's core outreach is pretty strident. AIPAC made a decision two years ago [circa 2002] that war in Iraq would be beneficial for Israel's situation. Then they pushed the [2003] SAA and comparable efforts against Iran and Saudi Arabia. AIPAC delivers messages with a small phalanx of people."

"My predecessor told me AIPAC was sometimes pissed [at the senator]. AIPAC activated its membership in the home state to call his sister, calling him a self-hating Jew. Hey, listen, AIPAC has a great website. AIPAC has been in twice to see me; they have me on speed dial. But I think they get the hint that we're not totally on board. They send emails, letters; they're very intense folks."

"I'll read AIPAC's material because I feel obligated to do so to know where they are coming from. Otherwise I wouldn't read it because it's very partisan. They're one of the strongest lobbies on these issues. I'll look at APN to see the exact opposite of the other [AIPAC] folks."

"AIPAC used to give us flack, but [our senator] is now on the hopeless list. It used to be that the head of AIPAC would call, but after ten years it was clear it wouldn't make any difference. The national-level AIPAC guy used to invite us to lunch before every important vote.

[Former Sen.] John Chafee was also written off [by AIPAC] a long time ago."

To sum up, during my first round of interviews in 2005–2006, a significant number of Senate staffers made strongly negative comments about AIPAC. They added up to at least 8 of my 28 initial interviewees, with a few others on the more muted, negative list; that constitutes a very strong percentage of the total that were interviewed. But don't misinterpret these data, AIPAC was still ruling the roost.

By 2011–13, the state of play had changed somewhat due to J Street and its election PAC's entry onto the scene. An off-the-Hill person, highly knowledgeable about J Street's work among congresspersons, stated in summer 2013:

"Over the past three years, a big shift has occurred. Now we're starting to get bipartisan support. I've felt the change. Sure, AIPAC is still very powerful, but they do a lot of boilerplate stuff: letters, resolutions, bills. But a lot of this stuff is of little substance. We like to pick our battles. You can see how J Street is gaining ground. Take a look at the letter presented by Sen. Feinstein before Pres. Obama's trip to Israel, urging a more balanced approach. We went toe-to-toe with AIPAC in the Senate over this and got 28 or 29 senators to sign our letter, and 46 senators signed AIPAC's letter. Many senators did not sign either, and told us that 'they weren't picking sides.' This was a big victory for J Street. Sen. Durbin is the second most powerful Democrat in the Senate, and he's become a powerful ally of J Street. Sen. Feinstein has accepted J Street's endorsement as well. It's now very easy for J Street to pick up support from ten senators, whereas three years ago they got no one to sign on. So you can see the change. Other groups, like AIPAC, are having to change their approach to counter J Street's efforts and newfound success."

So on the Senate side of the Hill, as in the House, there were a good number of staffers pleased by J Street's entry on the scene. These staffers concurred that J Street offered greater "cover" and "breathing room" to adopt positions different from those advocated by the folks at AIPAC.

Foreign Travel as an Influence on Senate Staffers?

Numerous senators have visited one or even many Middle East countries and thereby have acquired greater familiarity with their people and politics. Sen. McCain comes most readily to mind. Many Senate staffers have had comparable experiences, or have studied the area formally. Visits to Israel, once again, lead the way. Of the Senate staffers I interviewed in 2005–2006, 18 of 28 indicated that their bosses had visited Israel, and 15 of the 28 staffers had done so as well. It is easy to guess that Israel is at or near the very top of the list of "most visited" foreign countries by US senators, as well as Senate staffers. The impact of these trips can be enormous. Here is the "testimony" of Sen. Pat Toomey of Pennsylvania, which appeared on his campaign website.

> I had the great pleasure of visiting Israel in 1999 on an AIPAC-sponsored trip. On a policy level, this was an incredibly informative experience. Not only were our official meetings with governmental and military leaders insightful, but directly seeing the physical terrain and challenges Israel faces was eye-opening. My Israel trip was also moving on a personal and spiritual level. No one who takes their faith seriously, as I do, can leave Israel without a profound sense of the historical and biblical importance of the land, and without a profound respect for the manner in which the Israeli government and people treat the holy sites. Israel is without question the United States' greatest ally and friend in the Middle East, and among its best allies in the entire world. Israel is a beacon of democracy and freedom in an area of the world dominated by dictatorships and political persecution. US cooperation with Israel strengthens both countries in the continuing fight against global terrorism.[153]

Toomey's reaction is more likely to represent the norm than an aberration among senators and staffers alike. Of course, because Senate staffers are likely to be more seasoned than many of their Hill counterparts, several intimated that they viewed these trips from a less impressionistic vantage point, akin to the one espoused by House skeptics. Still, Israel's specific geostrategic situation is bound to leave a powerful impression upon most visitors. As one staffer remarked:

"I was selected for an AJC [American Jewish Committee] trip to Israel when I was [in graduate school]. We had access to all the leadership in Israel. On the AJC trip, people sold me on the true passion of the place."

Given heavy US military engagement in Iraq during the 2000s, in addition to close ties with Egypt, Jordan, and various Gulf Arab states, these countries have also been heavily visited by senators and Senate delegations. One youngish staffer had just returned from a trip to Jordan prior to my interview with her. Jordan was, of course, the second Arab nation to make peace with Israel. This staffer felt that:

"The king was very forward-looking. We're pushing them to make democratic reforms, but our embassy sees the Muslim Brotherhood as the only organized party in the country, with about 30 to 40 percent support. According to an embassy survey, only 1.4 percent of the population in Jordan is interested in belonging to a political party. As regards democratization in Jordan and its large Palestinian population, they [the Jordanians] tried to ignore it completely. They don't talk about it. There's a big fear among Jordan's political elite. Owners of the banks, etc., are Palestinians; their potential influence in politics is great."

In brief, foreign travel matters. More senators are likely to visit Israel than other countries in the area, and this appears to redound to Israel's benefit.

What of the Evangelical Dimension, and Christians United for Israel?

In 2005–2006, Senators Sam Brownback (Kansas), James Inhofe (Oklahoma), and Rick Santorum (Pennsylvania) were the figures most sympathetic to evangelical concerns. Only Inhofe remained when I returned for interviews in 2011–2012. Senators representing states with strong evangelical bases, like the one in Kansas, are more likely to hear from CUFI. A Senate staffer from such a state noted: "CUFI contacted me today. They act like the White House has a lever and can pressure Israel to give away God's chosen land. They distrust the neocons on the social/moral side and think neocons may be hijacking the process to bring about the war in Iraq—they're against it. You could look at denominations and denominations within denominations [among evangelicals] who are split on this. They have a very conspiratorial mind-set. If there's anything that goes wrong with Israel as regards US policy, there must be a conspiracy within the Bush administration."

But CUFI's impact in most offices is less strong than that of right wing pro-Israel groups, unless again the concerned senator has a shared worldview.

The Oil Lobby: A Powerful Influence, or a Mirage?

As to the question of a putative oil lobby, my Senate-side interviews replicated what I'd experienced on the House side of the Hill. Senate staffers were highly unlikely to even think of an "oil lobby" or oil interests as weighing in on debates over the Arab-Israeli and Israel-Palestine conflicts. In fact, in every interview, I had to ask whether or not the "oil lobby" played any role in this issue area, and every time I received blank looks and/or negative responses. The few staffers who waxed somewhat more expansive attested to the absence of any activity from such interests in this issue area. Emblematically, one said, "No, they don't play a role. We have [major oil companies in our state]. They're worried about ANWAR, etc., and building more refineries, etc. Many see the Arab-Israeli conflict as a burr under their saddle, but they don't weigh in on the Arab-Israeli conflict stuff . . . . Oil men just want to have stable prices of oil." Another staffer responded, "No. They [the oil companies] want to get into Africa or drill off Florida. They don't talk to us about these issues."

The reader should not misinterpret the paucity of data here. The dearth has everything to do with the absence of any significant input from a putative "oil lobby" in this issue area.

Embassies as Lobbyists and Sources of Information

From the information gathered from staffers with regard to contacts with foreign embassies, I also acquired further confirmation of a pattern observed in the House, with one slight variation. My data here suggest a slightly greater level of activity by the Israeli embassy among US senators, closely followed by that of Egyptian and Jordanian personnel. (The reader will recall that the Israeli embassy was less active in contacting people on the House side than other embassies.) All told, for 2005–2006, I recorded references to contacts with Israeli embassy officials by 9 of my 28 Senate first-round interviewees, with 7 references each to Egypt and Jordan. Tunisia and Saudi Arabia came in fourth place with two references each, followed by Bahrain with one. There was also one reference to the Palestinian Authority, and two references to private citizens from Lebanon. Here are a few examples of what Senate staffers had to say about these contacts during the 2005–2006 time frame.

> "Egypt and Jordan are good at lobbying in the Appropriations Committee. There is some lobbying in Defense. The Israelis care most about Foreign Military Finances."

> "There is much good feeling toward the Jordanians these days; for example, there was a hearing on the Middle East initiative earlier this week and they offered a Jordanian the opportunity to testify—this is very rare. I was invited to visit Israel. I went to Jordan on a trip. Staffers get invited on many trips."

> "[I meet with] Jordan, Israel, Egypt—the military types—, some Lebanese folks. Bannerman and Associates: they're nice people. Ed Abington is a good guy." (Abington represented Palestinian Authority interests while working for Bannerman.)

> "We had Knesset members here in September 2005; they represented the whole spectrum of Israeli politics. There were five people with ten opinions; there's clearly a much bigger range of views there than there is here."

> "The Saudis are coming in next week to talk about clamping down on Islamic terrorists."

> "The Israeli embassy people come; yes, at the staff level. Occasionally there were PA people, but that was before the Hamas election, of course. I have not seen Palestinians for a long time."

> "I sit regularly with the political attaché from the Egyptian embassy. No others. Not from the Israeli embassy, either; they're not big into lobbying."

"With the Israeli embassy? Not the government, but more organized groups like AIPAC."

"There is room for the Egyptians, Turks, and others to serve as conduits, but legislation now requires reports on progress by the administration in convincing everyone else in the world to not deal with Hamas."

Some staffers were disgruntled due to the relative absence of contact with formal foreign representatives: As noted above, "Foreign ministries go ignored while deference is made to the UJA [United Jewish Appeal] of Westchester County," commented one staffer, sarcastically. Other staffers noted they were content with information provided by domestic groups.

"The Israeli lobby makes it easy. We have strong pro-Israel constituents in [our district], some AIPAC, some independent. We get lots of Jewish youth groups, like Hillel. ZOA does not come to see us. We are on the spam list for Americans for Peace Now—this is a turnoff. We've had numerous contacts with AIPAC over the Iran issue. This is pretty clear cut for us."

The Arab Spring of 2011, and ensuing turmoil in the area, created serious issues for the representatives of certain traditional allies. The Egyptian ambassador, in particular, was taxed to navigate the fallout from the revolutionary upheaval election of the Muslim Brothers, and the "revocouption" that removed Pres. Mohamed Morsy from power. But quintessential diplomat that the ambassador is, he managed to land on his feet and carry on in Washington, D.C., now representing the new military government. It was the third he'd served in a span of just three years. As noted earlier, the Egyptian ambassador impressed upon me the importance of maintaining active ties with congresspersons via his and his staffers' frequent visits to the Hill, with senators being more heavily courted than House reps.[154]

The time and money spent by foreign countries to curry favor with senators again served as testimony to their view of the importance of Congress in US foreign policymaking.

Chapter Five

EXPLAINING CONGRESS-PERSONS' BEHAVIOR ON MIDEAST AFFAIRS

UNDERSTANDING HOUSE MEMBERS' BEHAVIOR

"It seems like there are 300 members who look at the Middle East and say, I don't care at all except for the Jewish organizations in my district, like AIPAC, or if they have Lebanese constituents . . . Another 50 to 70 members in the House have strong ideological positions—whether they're Christian fundamentalist types awaiting Armageddon, or Jewish types. But we just worry about our constituents."

—a veteran staffer

For most House members, a long list of issues takes precedence over the Israel-centered, Middle East conflicts. They're preoccupied perhaps foremost, sadly, by campaign fund-raising, then by the issues of greatest concern to constituents and themselves like jobs, health care, housing, immigration, economic policy, education, family and lifestyle issues, agriculture, and taxes—not the Middle East. In one of my earliest interviews, a former staffer, heavily involved in Middle East matters, proffered an unsolicited guesstimate of how many House members really care about these conflicts. The staffer said, "It seems like there are a little under 300 members who look at the Middle East and say, 'I don't care at all except for the Jewish organizations in my district, like AIPAC'; or others might care if they have Lebanese constituents. Maybe 50 to 70 members in the House have strong ideological positions—they're mostly Christian fundamentalist types awaiting Armageddon, or Jewish types. Otherwise, they [the members in general] really don't care."

This observation stuck in my head and prompted me subsequently to ask all of my staffer interviewees, and many others off the Hill, a few simple, straightforward questions: (1) How many members really know much about the Arab-Israeli, Israeli-Palestinian, or Iranian-Israeli conflicts? (2) How many of them really care much about those conflicts? And (3) What factors motivate their behavior in this issue area?

When I put the first question to former Rep. David Obey (D-Wisconsin), who served 21 terms in the House from 1969–2011, he answered in a guarded yet informative fashion. "I don't know," he said. "I have no way of measuring this. But I do think it's gotten where the work schedule in Congress almost guarantees that members don't know much about the substance of the issues. The workweek used to start on Monday at 2 or 3 pm, or Tuesday morning, then go until late Thursday or 3 pm on Friday. Now the first votes are usually at 6:30 Tuesday evening. By Thursday morning they're leaving for their home districts. There's no time to learn the substance of many issues, so they fall back on the politics of the issues. Even when they're back in D.C., they'll spend 50 percent of their time dialing for dollars."

In late 2014, a current House member concurred with Rep. Obey's depressing assessment, telling me: "Without a doubt, a very small percentage of my time is devoted to this issue. And fundraising and commuting back and forth to one's district is extremely time-consuming for most people. Most members only have the time to check in to their committee hearings or go to call time. You can't really take the time to go to committee hearings and learn about issues as is designed."

The statements by Mr. Obey and a current House member form a useful backdrop to the responses I harvested from my interviewees, which all point to the revelation that the brutally honest answers to the first two questions are one and the same; that is, not very many either know or care that much.

Beyond House members' preoccupation with fund-raising and the primarily domestic concerns listed above, House members' committee assignments—whether those assignments match their most ardent interests or are thrust upon them—cause most members to focus their energy on issues far removed from foreign policy in general, not to mention Middle East matters. But many members simply do not care about foreign affairs to any significant degree. Again, "foreign policy is not his (or her) cup of tea" was a common refrain among staffers. As a current House member told me, "This is not a big issue to most members. Most members wouldn't want to have to speak on Middle East issues because they really don't know much about them." For members who do care about foreign affairs, it was often because, as staffers said, "Cuba and Latin America is his thing"; or because "she's more interested in sub-Saharan Africa."

Prima facie evidence shows that representatives from districts with generally low constituent concern for foreign policy issues are likely to be less interested in foreign affairs themselves. There is no causal relationship at work along these lines and there clearly are exceptions; congresspersons are, after all, members of the political elite—they're wealthier and better educated than their constituents in general—so one might expect a greater number of them to be more cosmopolitan and more likely to take a stronger interest in foreign affairs. Indeed, some congresspersons take an interest in foreign policy issues that far exceeds that of the great majority of their constituents; or as one staffer said, "He has stronger personal interest in decision making on international relations than on agriculture. Our constituents are more interested in agriculture." But from my experience, it was far more common for staffers to say that their constituents and bosses alike were not greatly concerned about foreign policy issues in general, including those of the Middle East. For redundancy's sake, some congresspersons take their lack of foreign travel and non–passport holding status as a badge of pride, as staffers noted, in a "Look at me, I'm not wasting the taxpayers money traveling to foreign lands" fashion. This characterization, attributed to many new Republican members when the R's took control of the House in 1995, has also been attached to many recent Tea Party arrivals, whose penchant for "isolationism" runs deep.

Staffers' guesstimates varied as to how many congresspersons really do care and/or are knowledgeable about the Arab-Israeli conflict, but they were uniformly shockingly low. One astute former staffer, an individual who worked on the Hill and on Middle East affairs for decades, estimated that there were only twelve persons in the House who "really follow the issue" and fit the description of "knowing and caring." By way of a quick comparison, I also had highly knowledgeable veteran staffers guesstimate the number for the Senate at "five or six," or even "two." The devil in the details of these figures could be in how one translates the "highly knowledgeable" line, and both guesstimates are somewhat low based on my research, but I offer them here as stunning responses made by sober, veteran Hill staffers.

For the purposes of this study, I decided to establish my own categories of House members, and did the same for the senators. I divided members who do care about and follow the conflict into groups or clusters, running from those pre-disposed to behave sympathetically toward moderate Palestinians and Arabs and who have more aggressively sought a two-state solution to those widely regarded as unquestioning supporters of Israeli government policies. The creation of these categories and members' placement in them is based on a combination of the lengthy interviews I conducted as well as the members' observable behavior in response to "Dear Colleague" letters and their votes on bills and resolutions.

What motivates any individual congressperson to espouse his or her policy choices is usually a function of a set of factors shaping one's political social-ization: political ideology and political system preferences; education and/or knowledge base; religious background or identity; ethnic identity; friends; peers; the media; generation; history; constituent concerns and interests; party concerns and interests; and input and pressure from congressional colleagues, the executive branch, other governmental actors, lobbyists, and foreign embas-sies. That being the case, it is impossible to explain congresspersons' behavior in any simplistic manner. However, I think one can gain a better understanding of the lay of the behavioral land by a classification of congresspersons into these clusters, followed by an examination of what factors most strongly motivate behavior within each cluster or group. Inspired by organizational purposes and a small attempt at humor, I will move alphabetically from "A" (sympathetic to Arab interests) to "Z" (sympathetic to Zionist interests), with full appreciation for the diversity that exists across that spectrum.

A simple caveat to the reader: Remember, I am looking here at members described by their staffers as having a greater measure of concern and knowl-edge about the Middle East matters that are the focus of this book. I will get back to discussing the behavior of the large number who are not described as such later in the chapter.

ARAB SYMPATHIZERS AND EMPATHIZERS
Arab Americans and Muslim Americans in the House

There are only a small number of House members whose level of commitment to Arab, Palestinian, Muslim, or Iranian issues matches that of their colleagues who are passionate about Israel. One may present at least two easy explanations for this. First, at the time of my research in 2005–2006—and holding true during 2011–13—only a very small group of individuals had family links to the "Arab world", i.e., had ancestors who spoke some form of Arabic as their maternal tongue. These include(d) Nick Rahall, Darrel Issa, Ray LaHood, Charles Boustany, and Justin Amash. Second, all of these individuals are Christians. (Keith Ellison was the first Muslim American elected to Congress, in 2008. After the 2010 elections, this number doubled to two with the arrival of Andre Carson.)

Christian Arab Americans can have as passionate an attachment to the Middle East as is humanly possible. For the most part, however, they are related to minority communities in the Middle East and North Africa (MENA); that is, communities that have regularly been discriminated against by Muslim-dominated authoritarian governments in the region, and/or communities marked by religious-political strife, in countries such as Lebanon, Iraq, Syria, and Egypt. This has left many of them less than fully committed to the welfare of Arab Middle East governments. (Only in Lebanon did Christians once enjoy a dominant position.) These qualifiers aside, Christian Arab American and Muslim Americans alike have demonstrated strong concern for citizens of the Middle East due to their shared Middle East–based families, friendships, ethnic ties, and/or cultural ties; and at the top of the list of Middle East regional concerns are issues deriving from the A-I conflict, broadly defined.

Congressman Rahall and former Congressman LaHood are Lebanese Americans of Christian roots. Rahall is a Democrat from West Virginia; LaHood a Republican from Illinois. Rahall's family hailed from southern Lebanon, a region more heavily populated by Shi'ite Muslims. He was first elected to Congress in 1976, and has demonstrated a strong interest in finding a just solution to the A-I and I-P conflicts. LaHood shares Rahall's sentiments on the A-I and I-P conflicts. LaHood, first elected to Congress in 1994, is one of only three Republicans elected in that "revolution" that did not sign on to Newt Gingrich's "Contract With America." He served there until 2011 when he was appointed by fellow Illinoisan Barack Obama to be secretary of transportation.

Congressman Darrel Issa, a Republican from California, is also of Lebanese American ancestry and a Christian. A self-made millionaire—he invented an anti-theft device for automobiles—Issa is a self-described hawk in the Republican Party. As one staffer characterized Issa in 2006, "He supported going to war against Iraq, thinks very negatively of theocratic Iran, and sees Iran as the source of many problems. But he's very supportive of resolving the Arab-Israeli conflict; he sees it as a people to people conflict. He sees the importance of engaging Syria; and he opposed the SAA [the AIPAC-backed,

2003 Syrian Accountability Act]. He sees Syria's actions as directed at Israel, not the US."

Charles Boustany, also a Republican (from Louisiana) of Christian Lebanese stock, had just been elected to Congress when I was conducting my early interviews for this book. After getting his feet more firmly set on Washington ground, he has followed in the path of fellow Arab American congresspersons to become a strong, moderate voice advocating resolution of the A-I and I-P conflicts. But both Boustany and Issa are very conservative, and their voting records show that they are not as likely to exhibit sympathy for Arab and Palestinian matters as consistently and passionately as a number of their House colleagues.

Justin Amash, a shining light among the 2010 Tea Party winners, is of Palestinian heritage and appears to be following Boustany's path in this issue area. As of summer 2013, Andre Carson had not followed in the more activist footsteps of his fellow Muslim Keith Ellison, but was showing signs of some movement in that direction.

The behavior of these House members suggests that ethno-religious ties can make a difference, although their orientations could just as readily derive from their own definition of what policies best serve US interests and/or their own sense of what's best for the people of the Middle East. And it's important to note that none of these individuals shows any affection whatsoever for Hamas, Hizballah, or the mullahs in Tehran.

STRONG SUPPORTERS OF THE INTERNATIONAL CONSENSUS, TWO-STATE SOLUTION

Individuals with personal, family connections to the region do not stand alone in the House in their more sympathetic view of Palestinian, Arab, and Iranian moderates. Although again the number of House members in this camp is small relative to that of the strong supporters of Israel, these members demonstrate keen concern for the welfare of Middle Easterners in general and believe that US policy is too heavily biased in a "right wing pro-Israel" direction. Those whose positions are most readily identifiable and understandable are congresspersons with constituents who are heavily biased in a pro-Arab or pro-Palestinian direction due to ethno-religious factors and greater exposure to the area's politics. For example, Democrat Congressman John Dingell's congressional district includes Dearborn, Michigan, which includes the largest collection of Arab Americans in the United

States. Dingell—as of summer 2013 the longest-serving congressperson in US history—had so often sided with LaHood, Rahall, and Issa in Middle East policy battles that by the mid-2000s they had come to be referred to by many on the Hill as the "Gang of Four." This was an appellation they gladly embraced and wore as a badge of honor, but certainly one that also indicated their sense of isolation—their "gang" represented less than one percent of the House's total membership.

But in fact a larger support group of several dozen individuals exists, and it includes interesting figures from all corners of the country—House members Jim Moran of Virginia, former Congressman Brian Baird of Washington, Lois Capps, Barbara Lee and Jackie Speier of California, David Price of North Carolina, Earl Blumenauer and Peter DeFazio of Oregon, Donna Edwards of Maryland, and (again) Keith Ellison and Betty McCollum of Minnesota—to name some of its more prominent "members." The factors that led these individuals to embrace positions more sympathetic to Arabs and Muslims make for interesting narratives.

Congressman Jim Moran's (D-Virginia) district includes a rapidly growing Muslim and Arab community. These constituents' concerns combined with his own powerful personal experiences during visits to Israel and Palestine, where he witnessed the humiliating and abusive treatment of Palestinians at checkpoints. Additional, edifying interactions with Jewish, Arab, and Muslim constituents prompted Moran to examine more closely his position on Middle East issues and arrive at a position more sympathetic to that of the Palestinians. A former staffer said, "Moran is extremely interested in the Arab-Israeli conflict. The Center for Middle East Peace, with Danny Abraham, was very close to his heart. Also, he loved M.J. Rosenberg [formerly] at IPF. The office worked less with APN, although we never disagreed with what they put out, but they were more associated with the left. APN does put out great, useful talking points."

Here's a lengthier look at Moran's past, including how he became interested in the conflict. Moran became interested in politics in the 1970s; he was the vice mayor of Alexandria, Virginia. That city set up a sister city program with a city in Israel, so he traveled there many times. "During one of these trips he was traveling to Israel and came to a checkpoint and saw unarmed Palestinian civilians being harassed by armed IDF [Israel Defense Forces] soldiers," according to the staffer. "They had drawn their guns and were threatening the Palestinians. Moran has always rooted for the underdog, so this became a piercing image for him that affects the way he looks at the conflict to this day. Ever since he has been very interested in the conflict. Mr. Moran is a very quick study. He soaks up information like a sponge; he just devours books."

There was an important, personal dimension to Moran's interest in the region, as well. "Moran had developed a strong personal relationship with a rabbi in Alexandria. The rabbi had not only helped establish the sister city program, he also counseled Moran when Moran's daughter was diagnosed with cancer. The rabbi would also speak with Moran's foreign policy staff very frequently during some time periods. But over time, the rabbi and Moran's views became very divergent. The rabbi knew all along that Moran didn't take the spoon-feeding by AIPAC, but now he and Moran parted ways. The rabbi got more active in politics and got to the point where he backed Moran's primary opponent in 2004, Andrew Rosenberg—a 30-something lawyer from Patton Boggs with staunch, pro-Israel views. Rosenberg ran as a strong supporter of Israel and on labeling Moran an anti-Semite."

According to the same former staffer, at a March 2003 peace vigil held in Reston, Virginia, as the drumbeat for war against Iraq was reverberating, a woman asked Moran what she, as a Jewish woman, could do to stop the rush to war. Moran responded: "'If it were not for the support of the Jewish community, we would not be going to war in Iraq.' He was trying to urge this Jewish woman to work through her community to change things. His intent was not conspiratorial, etc., regarding American Jews, but that [Douglas] Feith and the neocons were behind this."

The role of Feith and his neocon colleagues has been firmly documented, as is well known. But back in that time frame, staffers warned Moran that his "independent streak on Middle East matters" might come back to bite him, especially fearing his "plum" role as an Appropriator could be affected because "pro-Israel" forces might fear he would oppose the billions of dollars in annual allocations to Israel. In fact, Moran did question this aid in a quiet way, asking his staffers: "Why are we giving all this money to Israel when just this week we've heard about extra-judicial killings by helicopter gunships or settlement growth?" As the narrator continued, "In general, the falling-out with the rabbi came due to Moran's opposition to the constant parade of completely one-sided, unhelpful, not productive in any way resolutions against Palestinians or supporting Israel. Moran thought the sponsors of these resolutions were just introducing them to show them to their constituents. But the downfall of Moran's relationship with the rabbi, its real downfall, started at the time of the second intifada. He would speak out about all of this [the parade of pro-Israel House activity] on the House floor. On the day [September 28, 2000, that Ariel] Sharon took his hike on the Temple Mount, which helped trigger the violence, that day there was a resolution being presented. Moran referred to the Temple Mount by its Arab name—Haram al-Sherif—and that lit a firestorm within our constituency. The rabbi sent a letter condemning Moran's words."

To date, Moran has remained steadfast in his positions on the A-I and I-P conflicts.

Asked what prompted another House member in this category to espouse a more Palestinian-sympathetic position, his staffer presented a rank ordering of factors: "Factors that are most important to the congressman include: (1) our constituents; (2) political interest groups; (3) think tanks; (4) the media; (5) political contributions; (6) personal interest in the region, some from life experiences. For [the congressman], his constituency includes a large number of Arab and Muslim Americans from Lebanese, Iranian, Iraqi, Qatari, Egyptian, and almost all Arab country backgrounds. Campaign contributions are not so important with respect to our votes in Congress. We have [important corporations] and get money from them, just as we do from [other sources]. So for us, constituents are more important."

A staffer for a third House member of this "group" stated, "[The congressman's] views are well known and he's not a man intimidated by anyone. We get less traffic from pro-Israel groups because he's a leader on Arab American issues. He approaches these issues with absolute certainty; he has sincere convictions on his Middle East position."

Many members arrived in this "cluster" due to their own practical experiences dealing with and debating Middle East issues. Like Rep. Moran, they have constituents whose concerns raised their level of consciousness about what was happening in the Middle East, causing them to listen attentively to accounts from the region, or they traveled there to see firsthand the conditions in which Palestinians and others were living. For example, Rep. Brian Baird (D-Washington) became more interested as the result of a young constituent, Rachel Corrie, being crushed by an Israeli bulldozer while protesting Israeli settlement construction in the Israeli Occupied Territories. Ironically, other congresspersons, according to their staffers, were actually pushed to adopt their positions by overly aggressive, "pro-Israel" constituents and Capitol Hill lobbyists because the latter sought to punish them for taking a more critical view of Israeli policies.

Rep. David Price (D-North Carolina) is another prominent member of this "group." A former political science professor at Duke University, Price traveled to the Middle East on CODELS led by Rep. Wayne Owens (D-New York) and Danny Abraham of the Center for Middle East Peace during the optimistic post–Oslo Peace Accords (1993) atmosphere of the early 1990s. Rep. Price met repeatedly with Israeli leaders, Yasser Arafat, and other dignitaries. These trips and encounters made a huge impact on the congressman's views, creating "an enduring optimism for a two-state solution to the Arab-Israeli conflict." Yet another staffer said of Rep. Price: "He knows a lot on this issue and has been on several trips and projects to the region. He has great concerns regarding specific projects in the occupied territories, like some that were going to be negatively affected by Israel's security barrier. Two to three months ago he sent a letter to State to support funding and training to expand the idea of teaching peace and a nonviolence curriculum."

Numerous staffers pointed to the efforts of Congresswoman Lois Capps (D-California) as yet another key figure in this informal group. Capps's interest was inspired by her late husband's focus on the A-I conflict. Staffers were also quick to note the respect they held for Capps's (former) foreign policy staffer Jeremy Rabinowitz, whom many saw as a font of information and wisdom. In recent years, Rep. Capps's fellow Californian Barbara Lee (D) has also become a leading figure in this camp. A highly informed staffer described her as driven by her "universal concern for human rights."

Individuals in this group number around 8–9 activists, with another 40 members who are solid supporters. They do not espouse radical views; only former Rep. Cynthia McKinney might have merited such a label. Rather, they agree readily and work closely with dovish Jewish American groups like APN, IPF, and J Street, or the Quakers' FCNL; that is, groups pushing more actively for a two-state solution. (Again, members of these Jewish American lobbies are motivated by their great love for Israel and their belief that failure to achieve a mutually agreeable two-state solution might culminate in Israel's destruction as a Jewish entity.) One staffer seemed to sum up how many House members arrived in this cluster, stating succinctly, "[The congressman's] views are more pro-IPF, not AIPAC, etc. His views came more into line because of the large Arab community. He used to be more pro-Israel, but his views have been tempered by many changes. I think I'm on the same wavelength with the congressman; I'm not sure AIPAC has the best views on this."

Most individuals in this group have been heartened by J Street's appearance in the late 2000s because, as many staffers told me, J Street provides dovish House members with "political cover" and makes it a lot easier to be critical of right wing Israeli policies. All members in this cluster are open to meeting any pro-Israel group, but at times they get pegged as "hostile" members and are written off by more right wing pro-Israel groups, such as ZOA, or at times even AIPAC. For some staffers in this informal group, their office's open door policy makes them feel they sometimes go too far to accommodate hard-line groups. "We get requests for meetings with AIPAC," one staffer said. "Whoever asks, we meet with them. NORPAC had 500 constituents, but none from out district. We should say no to these requests."

All members in this informal group are attentive to Palestinians' grievances and support policies designed to push the peace envelope. Most are Democrats, but there are a few Republicans; all are willing to buck the pressure to march in lockstep with AIPAC-proposed and party leadership–backed policies. Most are motivated by a strongly felt need to defend the underdog; they're inspired by principles of human rights and basic justice for all human beings. Thus, most progressive African American and Hispanic House members' staffers see this predisposition as the major factor affecting their bosses' behavior. Many representatives in this group are minorities, especially those also counted among members of the Progressive Caucus. Many progressive representatives, albeit not all, are likely to articulate positions that show a greater understanding of and higher level of sympathy for the Palestinians and other Arabs in the conflicts. This is especially true of minorities of a greater secular orientation; that is, those who are not religious conservatives. So, for example, Barbara Lee has been a strong actor on these issues, backed by Gwen Moore (D-Wisconsin), John Conyers (D-Michigan), Keith Ellison, Donna Edwards (D-Maryland), and others. Staffers working for progressive minority House members shared with me the following views, some of which reflect "boss vs. staffer" tension when bosses abandon their principled positions to cave to pressure and political realities.

(Staffer A) "House resolutions in this issue area are usually one-sided. The congressman eschews most of these votes. He is much more for trying to work for peace. He didn't sign [Rep.] Lantos's pro-Israel letter (2003); he saw it as unhelpful at least or even too partisan at worst. With the lobbying effort on SAA, the congressman refused to sign on. He doesn't see SAA as furthering the peace process. He has signed some antiterror things—on a political level; he has to do this or his constituents will call. [Is he apt to follow the party line?] Not so much, but the party doesn't advocate strongly on every issue. [The boss] examines what could be done to get the parties rolling along. He had the idea of a peace-keeping force. APN liked the idea. AIPAC let us know they didn't like the idea. He dropped the idea. He maintains an interest in the Middle East. The most influential factors for the congressman are as follows: (1) Access; and AIPAC is number one. (2) Conservative and libertarian think tanks—like the CATO institute—they provide a lot of information. (3) The White House, which is pretty good at getting out their messages via the press. And (4) we get messages from Sen. Daschle's office with respect to what the Bush administration will be pushing for—a big heads up."

(Staffer B) "US AID was provided before the Hamas election. Now what? I believed Hamas might win because they provide the social services. We get AIPAC visits; phone calls regarding Hamas. I have to talk to the boss about our position. I pointed out that this [AIPAC's] position is antithetical to Bush's position. Yes, we're not too happy with Bush's position overall, but there's a need for humanitarian aid. They [AIPAC] said, you can't legitimize a government that calls for 'our death and destruction.' I told them, but you need to talk, like a 'Talk with the IRA' type approach. We have a different perspective than [Israel's unquestioning allies like] Mr. Lantos. I use Lantos as a counterbalance, and work back from there. As regards Hispanics' positions on the conflict: I do think it's easier for some minority members to see it as a top-dog underdog thing. I do see Palestinians as the underdog. But the Progressive Caucus, which has about 50 members, is more important than the CHC [Congressional Hispanic Caucus] on this issue."

(Staffer C) "Elie Wiesel has written that he would/could never criticize Israel. I see this in a lot of others. I can understand this from a personal perspective, but if you're going to be a human rights leader, you must put aside your personal leanings and apply the same ethical standards to yourself as you do to others. I try to point this out to the boss."

(Staffer D) "There's no fundamental anti-Israel position here, but people can and do make this difficult on purpose by playing the anti-Semite card, like [Alan] Dershowitz's position versus [Noam] Chomsky's. People have been hit with that mud, and it's mud that sticks. [Can you provide any specific example?] Two weeks ago, there was an event sponsored by Mr. Lantos, organized by his office. Mr. Lantos was there at the beginning. It was UN Watch—the group was trying to show that the UN is anti-Semitic. I found this pretty offensive. They were harping on the case of Jean Ziegler, who said [Noam] Chomsky says the US is responsible for all the world's ills and he's like Chomsky. This isn't accurate with regard to Chomsky; it's not fair. So [there was a debate] and the guy stuck to his characterizations. [Someone] came with a list of UN resolutions condemning Israel from 1955–1995, some 200 resolutions. This person asked, 'If some are valid, which ones are fair and which are expressions of anti-Semitism. [He persisted.] I'll ask you for a third time the same question.' He [the UN Watch man] said, 'I'm not an expert on the resolutions.' 'Well, shouldn't you be?' [his interlocutor] asked. The UN Watch man would come back to [Iran's Pres.] Ahmadinejad as citing these things."

Picking up on the same theme articulated by Staffer C, Staffer D said,

"I've read the Mearsheimer and Walt piece—I think you can learn something by looking at the reaction to it. I read Chomsky and [Jonathan] Alterman's reactions to it. This tells you something about the sensitivity of this issue. I don't have any grudge against Israel, but I think there's a privilege that the US reserves for itself and this gets exercised to ignore Israel's transgressions of human rights and international law, which is clearly illegal. The World Court said so, and yet we condemned the World Court; around 2004, Congress condemned the World Court for having the temerity to apply international law to our ally Israel. This was somewhat like the World Court on the US versus Nicaragua—a $16 billion judgment against the US. If there were a World Court judgment against Iran, this would get a different reaction. I find all of this unacceptable. Sometimes the bias goes way too far. For example, another staffer penned a statement saying: 'Arafat was a cancer that had to be removed.' His congressman said this went too far and the staffer was removed."

The voices of staffers working for minority representatives quite consistently articulate concern for an equal application of humanitarian values. They create a chorus with other members of the Progressive Caucus, especially progressives whose humanitarian values do not stop at the borders of Israeli occupied territory. It's important to note that Jewish American staffers, usually working for progressives, voiced some of the most critical commentaries against AIPAC's power and Congress's "pro-Israel" bias that I heard on the Hill. As one of the most respected of these staffers stated in 2006:

> "I think there's a strong and growing view in the American Jewish community and thus perhaps in Congress that 'pro-Israel' behavior needs to be reviewed: 'vote for the Israel aid package; against any arms sales to Arabs; vote against anything for Palestinians'—this is the old 'pro-Israel' view. That old view isn't the case anymore. It's no longer a zero sum game. Israel's long-run best interest is wrapped up 100 percent in solving the Israel-Palestinian dispute and establishing a stable Palestinian state. That's what being pro-Israel means today to me and my boss. So all votes, resolutions, etc., that come to a vote, the standard rhetoric is 'It's pro-Israel to vote this way' and we say, 'No, it's not pro-Israel.' Pro-Israel is getting to safety and security. So changing the direction of being pro-Israel is what motivates me."

According to this same staffer, representatives in this group deem it "essential to work with strongly pro–two state groups like IPF, APN, Brit Tzedek, and others." He drew a direct connection between resolution of the A-I and I-P conflicts and combating Islamist extremism, saying: "My boss also says 'Isn't it in the US's best interest that we are trying to calm the Arab-Israeli and Israeli-Palestinian stuff down. Doesn't this work best for better relations with our allies, against al-Qa'eda, against even shooting at soldiers in Iraq?'" He also took a look at the basic contours of "peace" and what it would take to get there. "We believe the Clinton parameters are sound," he said. "[My boss] won't tell them [the protagonists] what the final Israel-Palestine borders should be, but there's (1) the Taba Accords; the Clinton parameters; (2) We aren't ever going to get there without a strong US role; and (3) It's Congress's job not to screw this up."

As this staffer went on to indicate, Democrat House members in this category were happy to work with the Republican Bush administration's constructive efforts for I-P peace, while deriding those seen as not constructive and engineered by AIPAC-backed Dems. "When Pres. Bush does something right on Israel-Palestine, [my Democrat boss] openly and publicly lauds him for it," he said. "By contrast, you should take a look at the 'Dear Mr. President' letter by [Democrat Reps.] Blunt and Hoyer that got 300 signatures putting all the obligations on the Palestinians, not Israel."

Another interesting, overlapping bloc of supporters in this cluster is comprised of Californians and other West Coast House members. Numbering roughly 14 members over time, with 10 or 11 of them consistently sticking out their necks,[155] they constitute a large percentage of the cluster's activists. During most of this study, its members were white (8 members), African American (2), Hispanic (3), and Asian (1); men (6) and women (8); Democrats (13) and one Republican. Almost all were of Catholic or Protestant backgrounds; almost all had served more than five terms, and were heavily geographically bunched around San Francisco, Los Angeles, and San Diego. They represented a diverse group, entirely free from ethno-religious ties to the conflicts with the sole exception of Rep. Issa.[156] Moreover, if one moved up the Pacific coast, one could easily add Oregon's Earl Blumenauer and Peter DeFazio, as well as Washington's Jim McDermott and former Rep. Brian Baird—all Democrats—to this list.

Most people in this cluster, significantly, are ensconced in "safe districts," but many remain wary of potential blowback from their questioning of Israeli government policies. When I asked one staffer, "Is there a price to pay?" he responded: "There's always a certain amount of fear. I personally haven't experienced AIPAC's power. Whenever you have a well-organized lobbying organization with email effectiveness, of course, you have to consider and expect the consequences. So 'scared' would be too strong, but [the boss] was concerned. He really felt the need to take a stand. He's gotten increasingly tired with AIPAC taking the hard line on things relating to Israel. Things come up every two months; we assume they're written by AIPAC; not that they're necessarily wrong, it's just that they overreach."

This view, I believe, is indicative of the nuance and differences of opinion that exist even within this group of Arab and Palestinian empathizers.

Finally, one other potential source of recruits for this informal cluster can be found among libertarians. They sometimes vote along with members of this group but are primarily motivated by the belief that the US should not "go in search of foreign entanglements." Many libertarians think the US has been too quick to stick its nose into foreigners' business. One staffer noted,"Mr. [Ron] Paul (R-Texas) is passionate about foreign affairs. He's a very independent thinker. He's very much guided by the principle of noninterventionism. He's a libertarian. Mr. Paul has regularly questioned our huge aid package for Israel, and he has suffered blowback from hard-line pro-Israel groups."

These sentiments raised the question as to whether or not the success of the "Tea Party" types in the 2010 elections—the addition of 62 Tea Party types— might have brought reinforcements to this camp. Concerns of this nature in right wing pro-Israel circles were, for the most part, reasonably quickly abated, as discussed later.

Estimates of how many House members in this cluster really know and care greatly about the issues in focus here range from the high single digits to mid-teens. There are a few dozen others who will sign "Dear Colleague" letters or back House resolutions introduced by the activists, but as a staffer said, they will usually "not be willing to stick their necks out on issues like those in the smaller group do." Who's willing to stick their necks out in 2013? "Only people like Lee, Capps, Ellison, McDermott, Conyers, Moran, Blumenauer, Moore, Price, McCollum, and maybe a few others," said a highly informed staffer. On some occasions, with support primarily from other progressives, this number can balloon up to the mid-fifties', like it did during the "Gaza 54" letter of January 21, 2010, which called upon Pres. Obama to lift Israel's siege of the Gaza Strip and was signed by 54 House members. (The "54" included nearly all of the reps listed in the first cluster.)

AMBIVALENT "MIDDLE ROADERS"

A few dozen House members, representatives with moderate to greater levels of knowledge about A-I and I-P affairs, have staked out a position of calculated ambivalence. They know and care a fair amount about Middle East issues, but they are not inclined to cast their lots heavily with one side or the other. While not standing consistently with strong, two-state advocates, they refuse to take the "pro-Israel" default mode adopted by hundreds of their fellow congresspersons. Seemingly caught, in their minds, between a rock and a hard place, they choose to adopt an arm's-length position with respect to the major protagonists, keeping their fingers crossed that any political blowback will not trouble them too greatly. From staffers in this small, nebulous informal grouping, one hears arguments like the following.

"My boss initially had no real expertise on the Middle East. He has helped refugees [from two countries] and traveled. He wants a two-state solution, but how do you get there? He was, is, skeptical. The [Israeli] security fence? Okay, build it, but let's talk about the route. So he takes flack from both sides. He didn't get involved in the Hamas right to vote issue. He was sort of caught in the middle."

"The boss has said, 'If I lived in Israel, I would not be a Likudnik' [a right wing Israeli]. He meets with AIPAC and other groups. There are no confrontational aspects like with [Rep.] McCollum. We don't get a lot of feedback on his votes."

"[My boss] gets support from both a strong Jewish American group and a strong Arab American group. He has a strong belief in a secure Israel and an independent Palestinian state. The ADC and AAI: I think they try. I try to tell them how to lobby, but they're just not that well organized or as active as the pro-Israel groups."

"He is the quintessential moderate and independent thinker. He knows Middle East issues as well as anyone. He's had 30 years in public life, almost two decades as a congressman. He listens well to his constituency, and then formulates his own views. His position is constantly evolving. He's a good rep of the district—his response to people who challenge him is that he sent out questionnaires and found husbands and wives who answered differently. For every issue, he meets with both sides. On the Arab-Israeli conflict, he meets with AIPAC, Churches for Middle East Peace, and AJC. I haven't met with ZOA in quite a while."

"My boss is hesitant to sign off on all these 'Dear Colleague' letters—I imagine they mostly come from the Mideast subcommittee of HIRC. I think he relies a lot on senior staff and staffers for their views on these issues. He's quite learned on foreign affairs. He wanted to be [and is serving] on HIRC. It's the one committee he wanted to be on. He has no further aspirations regarding committees. He's very open-minded about Arab-Israeli stuff. We took a pass on the Hamas letter; people among the staff members decided not to pass it along to him."

"He has a more independent view; not pandering. He sympathizes with the call for the US to be an honest broker in the Middle East."

I checked these House members' ideological dispositions, and most have liberal or slightly to the right of liberal orientations. Some "middle roaders" will back their colleagues from the aforementioned Arab/Palestinian sympathizer clusters in response to what they perceive as overly aggressive Israeli government behavior, such as more egregious military undertakings against Lebanon or the Palestinians, or saber rattling against Iran. In short, they can bump up the number opposing AIPAC-backed initiatives, or backing pro-peace initiatives, to the mid-fifties or the sixties', but this occurs rarely. As matches descriptions of their behavior, there are not many "activists" in this cluster, so some may question the degree of their "care" for matters in this issue area. And most in this group do not shy from criticism of Palestinian, Arab, or Iranian actors whenever they deem it necessary.

SELF-PROCLAIMED STEADY SUPPORTERS OF ISRAEL; BUT WHY?

My next informal category of House members includes individuals who profess steady support for Israel, but for and from whom there is no really clear explanation for that stance and definitely no real passion in their pro-Israel posture. This is the mushy middle. From these congresspersons' staffers, I heard comments like the following.

"General factors affecting the congressman's behavior include first, domestic political considerations—like AIPAC, etc.; second, the State Department's position; third, the president's position—as the one who sets the major parameters of foreign policy."

"[Congressman X] is a [war] veteran. He's very focused on defense and military affairs and serves on the Armed Services committee.

He's very well connected with the Pentagon and has good relationships with [important Pentagon officials]. He's a supporter of Israel, but he understands the costs to the US for that support. I don't discuss details about the conflict with him. Matters, letters, get vetted by me before they go up to him. I won't show him every single pro-Israel letter. It's not important to sign every single letter; it's not intellectually or politically helpful to us or to Israel."

"He's pro-Israel. What's the basis? I'm not exactly sure what his position is based in. It's pretty much black and white what he thinks. The congressman is very conservative. We have a conservative district."

"You know what you're going to do. Yes, we're in favor of Israel; no, not Hamas. We take the lead from the committee on foreign policy. As regards Israel, it's the default position. We wouldn't go to the wall on these issues for him. It's only as important to him as it is to his constituents. We have a reasonable-sized Jewish community. We have a growing Arab community . . . The congressman is a prodigious reader; he's very familiar with all these issues on his own. His Israel stance is not public, but it stems from his constituency, which speaks a lot about it. He still has a measure of independence from all these issues; he has no hard-core position on the Middle East yet because he's too new to the job. He likes to see both sides."

As one can see, it's difficult to narrow down what motivates the IME conflicts-related behavior of individuals in this "group." It is the most nebulous of my categories. Most are concerned, but do not exhibit great care about the IME conflicts; and most, but not all of its members, are not highly informed about these conflicts. Checking their backgrounds, most are Republicans and conservative Democrats from less urbanized districts where constituent concern with Middle East issues exists but is not strong, thereby granting a greater measure of independent movement. In addition, their backgrounds show that no compelling, personal, ethno-religious factor is in play. Still, these House members' views do reflect their sense that the "pro-Israel" dispositions of their party leaderships, who possess the power to shape their personal political futures, is a strong consideration. Political pragmatism is heavily in order, along with sound recognition that the US's "special relationship" with Israel, whatever its complexities, is safeguarded by both executive and legislative leaders. By my estimation, there are a few dozen House members in this category. As their staffers say, they voice care and concern, primarily for Israel, and possess a modicum of knowledge about Mideast matters, but they don't really seem to know or care a great deal about Israel's Middle East conflicts.

ISRAEL'S "STRONG SUPPORTERS"

Next within the context of "those who care" comes a large group of congress-persons whose commitment to Israel is "strong." Their commitment is based on a hodgepodge of factors, but what stands out is one or more of the following factors: (1) their Christian or Jewish religious values; (2) for some, their Jewish ethnic identity; (3) their recognition of Israel as the only true democracy in the region, a democracy surrounded by authoritarian bullies; and/or (4) their strong security and defense-oriented concerns, more commonly deriving from a conservative or neoconservative foreign policy orientation on the Mideast. Members in this cluster can be placed in specific subgroups.

Christian Zionists: Evangelicals, Old School Baptists, and Religious Conservatives

For anyone who has read studies on the nexus of US domestic politics and the IME conflicts, the American evangelical community's role is very well known. For most evangelicals, Israel's contemporary existence represents a fulfillment of biblical prophecy, a clear sign that the "end of times"—including the second coming of Jesus Christ—is upon us. Therefore, a curious yet very powerful alliance has been established between many evangelicals, or so-called Christian Zionists, and right wing Jewish Zionists and Israelis.

Less well known to students of IME conflicts is the degree to which religiously devout Christians, coming from diverse denominational and ethnic backgrounds, hold a special place in their hearts for Israel as home to God's "chosen people." During my interviews, I found these religious sentiments to be very strong. Among many elderly African American congresspersons, religious belief combines with fond memories of support provided by progressive American Jews to the civil rights movement, such that sentimental bonds with Israel run deep. In some cases, they are so profound as to be impervious to challenges, even those made by fellow minorities and based in appeals to uphold the basic human rights of Palestinians and Arabs. Moreover, many in this cluster, both blacks and whites, are largely ignorant of the Palestinians' history and plight. Here are some examples.

"[My boss] has a steadily pro-Israel belief. Also, his own personal belief is anchored in his political beliefs—a people's right to self-determination. He has a hard-line view. He's a very religious man. He reads the scriptures morning and night, but I don't think this alone is what defines his position. It's more of an empathic connection [to Israel]. If I get kicked out of my house, I'd be really pissed. He's not well traveled [and he's in his mid-50s]. He was a businessman. When he saw [the movie] *Munich*, it was the first time he'd ever been touched by a Palestinian's viewpoint. These issues were always out of his scope [before coming to Congress]. Unless you're on HIRC or have concerned constituents regarding foreign affairs, then foreign affairs is near the bottom rung for most people in Congress."

"He's definitely considered a friend of Israel. I know there's a safe characterization regarding the Palestinians, or view of the Palestinians, by the Congressional Black Caucus [CBC] as a reflection of what blacks in the States go through, so on resolutions supporting Israel, CBC members may either vote present or against [AIPAC-supported measures]. But there are no particular individuals within CBC who are leaders on this issue. The Arab-Israeli conflict stuff doesn't rank high for most of these members. Hardly anyone, maybe no one in Congress, is anti-Israel." [N.B. This flies in the face of some of the evidence of African American activism discussed earlier.]

"He's been strongly pro-Israel—basic growing up. These are our friends; they're surrounded by hostile powers. We're their critical ally in a strategic sense. He traveled to a rally here over Soviet Jewry [many years] ago. But since coming to Congress he has not shied away from dealing with Jordan, Egypt, etc. We meet with Syria, too, but with them we agree to disagree. Now he sees dialogue is important with all. He takes a carrot and stick approach with foreigners—you want us to help you, but you've got to . . ."

"We are overwhelmingly pro-Israel. We have good relations with AIPAC—he tours the country for them, but we have good relations with APN's people, even though we're slightly more hard core than them. He's Irish Catholic; his father taught them they were spiritual Jews. He believes in a two-state solution. He believes there has to be a viable Palestinians state with viable borders and then borders could open up. There needs to be an end to terrorism. He supports having Jerusalem as the capital of Israel, but he has no full position on this issue."

"The boss is pro-Israel. Why? He has a religious perspective. I think he's pretty near the evangelicals—his religious foundation drives his position on the matter. He also has a natural repugnance to suicide bombings. From a military perspective, I don't think anyone has the right to pass judgment on another's right to exist [sic]. So, if you look at Iran, we're pro-Israel, but this issue is very complex. I don't think our relationship with Israel is a liability, really; I don't think matters with the Arab world would be that much better because there are such big cultural differences."

It is clear that certain conservative, Christian religious beliefs cause many members to care a great deal about Israel's fate. If one does a little math here, extrapolating from my random sample, some 10 percent, or 44 House members, could be placed in this "Strong Supporters" camp in the mid-2000s. Again, I am not talking here about Israel's diehard evangelical supporters in the House. One half decade later, the arrival of Tea Party types would have brought its own injection to this group, as some 40–50 percent of Tea Party types have evangelical, religious orientations. And as one can also see from the quotes, Christian Zionists in general often adopt the language of neocons and "clash of civilizations" types. As a secular humanist, I have reservations about how many people in this group actually "know a lot" about the conflict because their views are most heavily based in biblical interpretations. Their "care" seems real; and in the eyes of the beholder, it is divinely inspired.

In light of the previous discussion, I decided to make two graphs. I took my House staffer interviewees and divided them into five groups on the basis of their bosses' stated religious identity, with Number 5 representing House members who gave no religious identity. I then charted the relationships between the estimated percentage of the time House staffers told me they spent on all "foreign affairs" (Graph 1) and "on the IME conflicts" (Graph 2). Here is what this effort yielded:

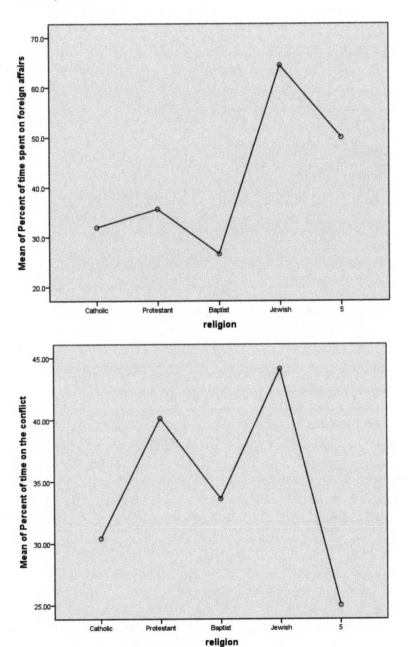

The graphs pretty much speak for themselves in terms of the groups' priorities. To be fair, any individual House member's office, regardless of the representative's religious orientation, might have a staffer who works a lot on these issues. That said, I do find the results of this analytical effort intriguing. I'll make two final comments in conjunction with the figures. First, do notice that even though the Baptist group scores lowest on foreign affairs in general in Graph 1, its score rises considerably for time spent on the conflict. That would help substantiate the earlier point that Israel holds a special place for conservative, religiously devout House members, as is characteristic of many Baptists. Second, I'll simply assert here that greater time spent examining the Middle East conflicts does not necessarily translate into adoption of the soundest policies. As a professor, I would like to think that greater empirical knowledge still places its possessor(s) in a stronger position to argue one's case vis-à-vis one's interlocutors. But I'm also well aware that a harsh reality of today's American society and culture is that rational thought does not always carry the day, as may be "in play" with this cluster's policymaking.

SECULAR-MINDED, STRONGLY COMMITTED TO ISRAEL; "LIGHT BLUE"

"On a lot of this stuff, the difference between Israelis and Palestinians, it's like cowboys and Indians. You're always going to root for the cowboys."
—former, longtime staffer for a leading "light blue" House member

Many House members in this "strong supporter" category are from Jewish backgrounds. There were 26 Jewish House members in 2005–2006 and 27 in 2011–2012. Like most American Jews, Jewish House members are disproportionately liberal in their political orientation; 24/26 were Democrats in 2005–2006 (with one R, and one I), as were 26/27 in 2011–2012. The one R was House Majority Leader Eric Cantor; the Independent was Bernie Sanders of Vermont, who is a socialist. Many of these individuals are not heavily religious in their disposition or practice, but their Jewish identity is strong, heartfelt, and translates into a fundamentally solid commitment to Israel's welfare. Individuals who most quickly come to mind, some of whom have retired since 2005–2006, are/were House members Reps. Gary Ackerman (D-New York), Howard Berman (D-California), Barney Frank (D-Massachusetts), Nita Lowey (D-New York), Adam Schiff (D-California), Allyson Schwarz (D-Pennsylvania), Debbie Wasserman-Shultz (D-Florida), Henry Waxman (D-California), Robert Wexler (D-Florida), and others. Several are/ were recognized as among the "best and the brightest" in the House. Most certainly "care" about the IME issues, but they are not uniformly knowledgeable about them.

There are/were also many non-Jewish House members readily identified by staffers as "very strong supporters" of Israel, people such as Reps. Dennis Cardoza (D-California), Steve Chabot (R-Ohio), Ric Keller (R-Florida), Ed Markey (D-Massachusetts), Doris Matsui (D-California), Dutch Ruppersberger (D-Maryland), Steve King (R-Iowa), and many others. Indeed, this cluster is the biggest of the five groups, or at worst in a tie for first place with the "Steady Supporters, but Why?" group. From staffers associated with and/ or knowledgeable about such individuals, I collected the following comments.

"She has a background as a strong supporter of Israel and its right to exist. [She has close family members] who fled the Holocaust. She sees clearly the need for a secure Israel and strong US-Israel relations."

"As for [the boss's] attachment to Israel: I don't have a sense that it's strategic. It can't not be emotional; but mostly it's from a moral perspective—what Jews went through, yes, but they're a shining example of democracy in the area. They had their leader assassinated [Rabin] and there was still stability. You can be fully critical of your own government in Israel; not in the Arab countries. This is a compelling moral reason for supporting Israel. My view of the Middle East has been shaped by [the boss's] eyes."

"The congressman is obviously far more concerned with [another committee's] issues, but his commitment to Israel is strong and based in a strong moral and ethical obligation to protect Israel as a democracy. He takes his cues from NORPAC on how to size up appropriations for Israel. He also refers heavily to the party conference and HFAC staffers. The Arab-Israeli conflict is a peripheral issue for Armed Services—where he invests most of his efforts."

"He has a strong connection to Israel from birth. For Hamas stuff, we take the president's line. He and the president are on the same wavelength. There's been no follow-up yet from groups that disagree with us. He's out of the loop on this Hamas stuff. If Ros-Lehtinen asks him, he'd probably get on board. Ros-Lehtinen has her reasons for taking a tough line on these matters. His position became my position very quickly. He'll tell me what his view is and what information he needs and even where to get it from."

"The congressman—90 to 95 percent of his belief is based in the view that Israel is a democracy and a good ally . . . .[Former congressman X] came from this district. He left a legacy of helping Soviet Jews, etc. My boss's emotional attachment to Israel comes from this legacy. Also, US interests and the history of ties to Israel are crucial for him. My boss leans more toward AIPAC because it's viewed as representing the views of the broad Jewish community more than others, and it does more for US-Israel relationship within our (US) broad security goals. We also listen to others. We signed the letter to Condi Rice that Brit Tzedek and IPF put out; but we also sign on to the AIPAC stuff. Overall, he thinks it's important to back the Israel-US relationship. He's supporting the Ros-Lehtinen stuff on Hamas because he sees this as pro-peace. Brit Tzedek and IPF are not in favor of pushing this legislation because they think it will punish the wrong people. The boss thinks it will just punish Hamas, which rejects the peace arrangements and is a terrorist organization."

"My boss is a strong supporter of Israel. They don't need to lobby me; they just come to say thank you. His position: he's pro-Israel because he was in local government and as a candidate running for office many candidates get sent questionnaires. These questionnaires ask very partisan questions by AIPAC, such as 'Do you defend Israel's right to self-determination?'"

The quotes above are highly revealing on two counts: first, they offer considerable insight into what motivates members of the "light blue" group; second, they reveal a high frequency of tension between "light blue" representatives and their own foreign policy staffers, with the latter often questioning the soundness of what they see as their bosses' lopsided commitments to Israel.

In essence, the "light blue" cluster represents a mix of individuals, some with strong ethno-religious ties to a democratic Israel, and an even greater number of individuals motivated by a combination of other factors. Most of the latter individuals' attachment derives not only from a shared, strong appreciation for Israel as a democracy, but as a strategic partner and fellow combatant in the US and the West's "war on Islamist extremists." Former representative now Senator Mark Kirk (R-Illinois) represents an interesting case of a non-Jewish member of the "light blue" camp in the mid-2000s who trended "dark blue" from then on. I'll save lengthier discussion of his case for the chapter on Appropriations, but it merits noting here that he is a former military intelligence official, thus highly knowledgeable about defense issues, and also comes from a state with a large, active, right wing pro-Israel community.

Part of what separates "light blue" members from their "dark blue" colleagues is their greater moderation and pragmatism. An UNRWA official I interviewed met with Rep. Berman, and the latter went on for two minutes talking about how in his opinion UNRWA shouldn't even exist. Berman then said, "But that's all academic. Now let's see what I can do because these people [the Palestinians] exist and you need to feed them."

Finally, it's also important to note that many House members in this cluster have chosen to go with the flow of Israeli politics. Accordingly, they have remained wary of and aloof from the more aggressive peace agenda of J Street and other groups. They tend to "roll" with AIPAC. Staffers of key figures here individually and independently voiced a common refrain to the effect that "It is not our [the US] role to negotiate for the Israelis; the details will be worked out as part of a final status agreement. We were in favor of the [1993] Oslo Accords, and then the Taba Agreement and the Clinton parameters [of 2000–2001], [both advocated by Labor party leadership], but now, after the second intifada, we're okay with Sharon's leadership. We're happy to work with whomever the Israelis elect."

Among most in this group, there is a strong sense that at the end of the day Israel leaders will be compelled to accept the creation of a Palestinian state, one that meets secular and moderate Palestinians' aspirations. But it's not only fair, but important, for the reader to ask whether or not their optimism will withstand the test of time. The years pass and have borne witness to a rightward shift in Israel's political culture, bringing the election of right-to-extreme right wing–laden Israeli governments, none of which desires the creation of a Palestinian state that meets minimalist, moderate Palestinian goals. Individuals with racist track records—people whose beliefs make these otherwise staunchly liberal humanist Democrats cringe—have held ministerial posts, the equivalent to US cabinet posts, for years on end in successive right wing Israeli governments. West Bank settlement has continued apace, severely testing the breaking point for any two-state solution. Despite these developments, these "strong supporters" stay their course.

PRO–RIGHT WING ISRAEL: "DARK BLUE"

Last but not least are the House members who make up the most unflinching supporters of Israel, members whose positions place them in lockstep with those on the right, or often, even far right wing of the Israeli political spectrum. Indeed, as discussed later, at times they promote policies that go beyond what right wing government leaders in Israel deem desirable. At the time of my research effort in 2005–2006, this included members such as Ileana Ros-Lehtinen (R-Florida), Tom Lantos (D-California), Brad Sherman (D-California), Eliot Engel (D-New York), Shelley Berkley (D-Nevada), Louie Gohmert (R-Texas), and Anthony Weiner (D-New York). These members play(ed) a disproportionately strong role in the initiation of "Dear Colleague" letters and resolutions designed to take the pulse of their fellow members, all the while advancing views espoused by AIPAC or farther right wing pro-Israel groups like ZOA. Ros-Lehtinen, Engel, and Sherman have carried this torch into the early 2010s.

For some individuals in the "dark blue" camp, their attachment to Israel is deeply rooted in family history, their Jewish ethno-religious identity, and a profound motivation to do whatever they perceive to be in Israel's best interest. Let's begin with the late Rep. Lantos. During this study, Lantos was—and is likely to remain—the only Holocaust survivor to serve in the US Congress. Born in Budapest, Hungary, in 1928, Lantos witnessed Nazi German oppression firsthand. Arrested by German occupiers because he was a Jew, he was forced into a prison labor camp. He escaped; was captured, badly beaten, and returned to the camp; only to escape once again. He made his way to a safe house set up by the now celebrated Swedish diplomat Raoul Wallenberg, where he remained until Hungary's liberation. When he eventually made his way home, he discovered that his mother and other family members had all been killed in the Holocaust, a fate shared by some 450,000 other Hungarian Jews. While a university student in Hungary, Lantos won a Hillel Foundation scholarship to study in the United States. He moved to the US, earned degrees from the University of Washington and the University of California, Berkeley, became an economics professor at San Francisco State University, and ran for the US Congress and was elected in 1980.

During his lifetime, Lantos made dozens of trips to Israel. He consistently used his position on HIRC/HFAC to steer issues in what he viewed as a pro-Israel direction. A veteran staffer stated in the mid-2000s that for Lantos, "His priority issues were: (1) the Arab-Israeli conflict; (2) Iraq; (3) Iran; and (4) Saudi Arabia." But Israel remained, for Lantos, his great passion. As one former staffer told me, Lantos stated on one occasion, "Every day I say to myself, what can I do to help Israel today." He combined his unique status as the sole Holocaust survivor to ever serve in the US Congress with his passionate commitment to Israel and carved out a special status with regard to Middle East matters. The former staffer quoted above added that, on another occasion, Lantos, speaking to colleagues, asserted: "Trust me. On these [Mideast] issues, I speak with absolute moral authority." House members' deference to Lantos in this issue area will be noted in numerous staffers' comments elsewhere in this book.

A second important figure in the "dark blue" camp during most of this study was Congresswoman Shelley Berkley. Berkley's connection to Israel was also rooted in her Jewish identity and was Holocaust-based. As noted in one press report: "In telling of her lifelong support for Israel, Berkley . . . told of her maternal ancestors being Sephardic Jews from Salonika, Greece, and her paternal ancestors being Ashkenazic [*sic*] Jews from the Russian-Polish border regions. Jewish communities in both regions were wiped out by the Holocaust . . . Last year, the congresswoman was part of the US delegation that attended the observance in snowy weather marking the 60th anniversary of the liberation of Auschwitz. She described that event in personal and emotional terms: '. . . That, my friends, the very fact that any of us survived to tell the tale is a testament to the survival of our people.'"[157]

Shedding insight on the attitude of Berkley's "dark blue" view vis-à-vis the

Christian evangelical supporters of Israel, a staffer, himself Jewish, said, "As regards [Berkley's] response to the evangelical crowd—[she] has been at their events and spoken; they're huge supporters of [her]; they're way to the right."

On some issues, one staffer, in synch with his "dark blue" boss, supported positions acceptable to a broad range of groups, like many of the Clinton parameters, but on others—no return of the "old city" of Jerusalem; Arafat as solely responsible for the failure of Camp David in 2000; taking cues, as he told me, from MEMRI reports—the staffer adhered to "dark blue" positions and points of reference. These positions are unacceptable to moderates of all stripes who advocate a mutually acceptable "two-state" solution.

Eliot Engel is another member of the "dark blue" team. Representing the 17th district of New York, Engel has many constituents for whom the welfare of Israel represents a major cause of concern. Engel is also Jewish, and strongly identifies with Israel. As a long-standing member of HIRC/HFAC, Engel has played a key role in advancing bills and resolutions that are designed to promote and safeguard support for right wing Israeli governments and that undermine efforts by successive US presidents to improve relations with the Palestinians and other Middle East nations. From very early on in his House tenure, he introduced measures calling for recognition of Jerusalem as the "undivided capital of Israel," a call running counter to long-standing US foreign policy and international law. In recent years, Engel has offered consistent opposition to the Israel-related policies of his fellow Democrat Pres. Barack Obama. In 2013, with Rep. Ackerman's departure, he became Ranking Member of HFAC's Middle East and South Asia subcommittee. The following excerpt from *a New York Observer* article provides some insight into Engel's thinking on Middle East matters: "Engel said he didn't understand, tangibly, what [PA Pres.] Abbas could offer in return, and said he disliked the new tone and policy of the Obama administration. Engel once championed Hillary Clinton as an irreducible supporter of Israel in New York, but disapproved of the statements she made against settlements. Engel argued that the Obama administration's demands risked making a mockery out of the authority of Israeli Prime Minister Benjamin Netanyahu."[158]

A veteran HIRC/HFAC staffer noted, critically, of Engel's policy that "It's so Israeli right wing. Engel, for example, makes off the wall comments. His role in Congress is to be to the right of Likud. This springs from his own convictions and that of his constituents."

A fourth, fervently "pro-Israel" figure was former Congressman Anthony Weiner. Much the darling of the liberal news media—like MSNBC—prior to his forced retirement from Congress due to his involvement in a sex scandal, Weiner's zealous commitment to right wing Israeli positions on conflict-related issues caused consternation among many observers, who couldn't square his strongly progressive views on domestic issues with his arch-conservative position on the A-I conflict. As commentator Jo-Ann Mort wrote,

> [Weiner] is consistently the most conservative voice in Congress regarding Israel and the Palestinians, siding with the most extreme elements among the Israeli settler population (for whom there is strong support in his district and some West Bank settlers probably even hail from there). His politics on this issue are way out of sync with his cultivated image as a liberal. . . From the day that Anthony Weiner entered Congress, he has sought to end all aid to the Palestinians, no matter who is in charge . . . Weiner has consistently portrayed himself as a staunch supporter of Israel, but the support he has shown is to the most extreme elements inside Israel. . . . His opinions, as he expresses them, are way out of the US American Jewish mainstream, though they probably do reflect opinion among many of his constituents in Brooklyn.[59]

Yet another member of the "dark blue" team is California Democrat Brad Sherman. Rep. Sherman's behavior and views on the conflict are such that numerous on and off-the-Hill sources describe him as "whacko" and "crazy." A veteran staffer described Sherman's worldview and behavior in less colorful but telling terms: "Mr. Sherman is Jewish and was raised to be pro-Israel. He is a Zionist, but not slavishly pro-Israeli. He starts off as someone who has grown up in that milieu. Sherman takes a measured distance from groups like AIPAC. He was raised to be pro-Israel."

Just as the tiny group known for its empathy for the Palestinians has its non-ethno-religiously defined and motivated members, so too does the "dark blue" group. At the top of the list here is Rep. Ileana Ros-Lehtinen (R-Florida). At the time of my interviews in 2005–2006, Ros-Lehtinen was already serving as chair of HIRC's subcommittee on the Middle East. After spending some years in the minority opposition, she became chair of the full House Foreign Affairs Committee in 2011, following the regaining of House majority power by the Republicans in the 2010 legislative elections. In 2013, she had to step down from the full committee chairmanship due to the Republican Party's service limits, but she returned to chairing its Middle East subcommittee.

In 2006, a highly knowledgeable staffer characterized her views as follows.

> "Her big issues/concerns include freedom and human rights issues in the world. She's a female chairing the Middle East subcommittee. She's a political refugee herself. She's an ethnic minority herself. She fled Cuba at nine years old with her family. Her experience as a political refugee has always driven her to push for human rights and democracy. She's very conservative and very security focused, but her concern for human rights offsets these more conservative "extreme" positions. She has embraced Jordan because of the king's commitment to open up and create slots for women in parliament, etc. By doing this, she sends a message to the Egyptians that if you want bilateral free trade agreement, then you're going to need to perform more like Jordan and Bahrain to get the support. With the Saudis, she thinks they should get no access to the subcommittee unless you make progress with regard to (1) terrorists and (2) human rights and religious freedom. Access to the subcommittee is important because access is everything in this town. . . . The 'closed door' has always been her policy. . . . Those in the more conservative camp want more direction against Iran—you can't take military action against everyone, but they favor sanctions that are actually implemented— sanctions on Iran; sanctions on Syria."

These heavier sanctions came to pass in ensuing years, with Ros-Lehtinen playing a leading role. And by the early 2010s, people in the pro-peace camp were speaking of Ros-Lehtinen in the harshest, most unflattering of terms, as discussed later. An elder staffer presented a milder critique in 2012: "Ros-Lehtinen has a very Manichean view, shaped out of the nexus of her personal background and the Cold War. That's the conventional wisdom about her perspective. She's very progressive on many other issues. In that way, she's a lot like Lantos was. Lantos had a very stark view of human nature. But Lantos was generally for human rights; with Ros-Lehtinen the Manichean view translates into her being against things." Another staffer said, "Ros-Lehtinen takes a militantly pro-Israel position."

Ros-Lehtinen is not the sole "dark blue" player with a non-Jewish American background. Evangelicals like former Majority Leader Tom DeLay (R-TX), Mike Pence (R-IN), and Ted Poe (R-TX) featured prominently in the mid-2000s. They were backed by nonevangelicals, like Peter King (Catholic; R-NY) and Joseph Crowley (Catholic; R-NY), who were still in office eight years later. At a ZOA dinner event in November 2003, Rep. DeLay—who at the time was the most powerful man in the House—delighted his right wing pro-Israel audience by recounting how when he had stood atop the Israeli-occupied Golan Heights and looked south in the direction of the Israeli-occupied West Bank, "I didn't see occupied territories, I only saw Israel."

All of the aforementioned House members work(ed) very closely with "dark blue" House members in support of right wing pro-Israel bills and resolutions. Almost all of these members, according to staffers, are also highly motivated by their constituents and by the events of September 11. (One must remember that I initiated this study just 4 to 5 years after 9/11.) They, and many of their colleagues, act as though the US is indeed locked into Samuel Huntington's "clash of civilizations," with the Arab/Iranian/Islamic world at the top of the list of US enemies. The need to combat Islamist extremist-based terrorism, in their worldview, places the US in the same boat with Israel, necessitating close military cooperation and intelligence sharing to combat a common foe. There seems to be little sense that the US's unqualified support for Israel has engendered hatred of the United States.

Who else should be mentioned in this group? Ted Deutch (D-Florida), for one. Deutch, who is Jewish, arrived in Congress in 2011, filling the seat vacated by Rep. Robert Wexler. By 2013, Deutch was serving as ranking member on HFAC's Middle East and South Asia subcommittee. One staffer said, "Deutch is 'dark blue.' He's got a lot of Jewish constituents back home. He and Engel are like a tandem." Several staffers also told me Rep. Joe Pitts (R-Pennsylvania) was a very hard-line in his support for Israel. In May 2012, Rep. Pitts's office sent a letter to a constituent, signed by Mr. Pitts, in which Pitts stated that he was against recognizing the Palestinian Authority and that the best route to peace would be for Israeli Prime Minister Ariel Sharon and Palestinian Pres. Yasser Arafat to negotiate a resolution of the conflict. Arafat had died in 2004, and Sharon had been in a coma since 2006. Pitts's staffers, embarrassed, said that a form letter had been sent, but the mistake seems to shed light on the true level of "care" being given this issue.[160]

Finally, here is one more staffer's comments on another non-Jewish House member closely related to the "dark blue" camp. They combine an interesting mix of security concerns, "clash of civilizations"–like logic, racist stereotyping, and vitriol. The staffer said:

> "Arabs say very clearly they'd like to see Israel pushed into the sea, etc. Look at the PLO charter. George Habbash and Abu Nidal were very clear about all this. They're nut jobs like the president of Iran today. They're making a boulevard for the Hidden Imam to walk down; Ahmadinejad's a whacko. The average Muslim thinks Israelis are dogs and should be killed. The Palestinians don't want coexistence or a Palestinians state. To me, it's a very simple issue. You can't make peace with somebody who doesn't want peace. Israelis have consistently made concessions. Our diplomats keep trying to make Arabs look better than they are, but [the congresswoman] is a very strong supporter of Israel. She has a relationship with AIPAC, but her relationship with JINSA is more important."

During this study's time frame, there have been roughly 30–40 "dark blue" House members according to my interview-based estimates. All work to support right wing Israeli government policies, including Israel's ongoing settlement policies. Its recent core group is comprised of Reps. Ros-Lehtinen, Engel, Sherman, Berkley (until early 2013), Cantor, and Deutch.

THE "DEFAULT POSITION"—TAKEN BY THOSE WHO DON'T CARE

The great majority of congresspersons neither care nor know much about Middle East matters. Congresspersons whose constituents, in general, do not consider foreign policy issues important are left a greater degree of flexibility in how they deal with these issues. (Although as we've seen a very small number of powerful donors can and do make a big difference, and many members are pressured to make it look like they care out of fear of being "primaried" or opposed in the general election by potent "special interests.")

What is both interesting and important is that for most House members with little interest in foreign affairs, the default position is a "pro-Israel vote" as defined by the dominant pro-Israel lobby, AIPAC. "[His] subcommittee keeps him very busy. He has very little time for foreign affairs issues. There's a large Jewish community in [one of our major cities], but he's a very independent thinker; no consulting of others. But most of the time he votes pro-Israeli."

Unless newly elected congresspersons bring strong sentiments about the conflicts to their new job, they are more inclined to take the "pro-Israel" default position as well. Staffers would tell me things like: "He's a freshman; he's not a leader on these issues. It's premature to say how much importance this issue may take on for him. He weighed in with the press on the [2006] Hamas election issue; he took the same position as the administration, which was a pro-Israel one." Another staffer noted, "These issues aren't really all that important to our constituents, but we feel pretty safe going with a pro-Israeli position."

Despite the arrival of J Street, staffer interviewees in the 2011–13 time frame indicated that not that much had changed in the way their peers in most offices were behaving in the IME issue area. One quick, highly noteworthy exception being the way Congress rejected the Obama administration's call for authorization of warfare against Syria in fall 2013. On that occasion, J Street stood largely on the sidelines, and perhaps suffered a setback for doing so. FCNL, APN, and others mobilized a war-weary, debt-ridden public to contact their congresspersons and resist Pres. Obama's call for tougher action against Syria, for which Obama himself had enlisted AIPAC's direct support.

That said, there is little to suggest that the "default mode" has been rendered defunct, so it makes sense to ask how one explains this behavior—the recourse to the "default mode"? I have adopted several ways of approaching this question and offering answers. First, as we saw in chapter one, a great number of House members will "stand with Israel" because of an affinity with other democracies and due to other derivatives of their "standard" American political socialization experience. Second, many are pressured to "support Israel" or suffer the electoral consequences. They adopt the "default position," bowing to pressure from the dominant lobby, and/or accede to requests from, at times, a handful of vociferous, often well-heeled constituents. A staffer said, in spring 2013, "Frankly, we sign off on a lot of the pro-Israel stuff because I look to protect the boss and find the right path to protect his longevity. If we see there are 150 people who have cosigned an AIPAC-backed letter or bill, it's pretty easy to sign on."

Third, all members have a partisan identification, and both parties' leaderships have strong vested interests in adhering to acceptance of Israeli government policies as also discussed in chapter one. Fourth, while party identifications and loyalties help explain voting behavior—and readily suggest certain political ideological orientations to most observers—there are richer ways of classifying congresspersons' ideological positions. One can then compare their ideological classification with their behavior on Middle East matters.[161] Worded differently, many members' behavior on Mideast issues may be explained by a tendency to see these issues through their political ideological lenses. But in addition, where their ideological values do not seem to match or predict their voting behavior on Middle East matters, this may make it easier to discover what other factors are causing some members to part ways with their ideological brothers and sisters on Mideast affairs.

When one engages in this exercise, what does one find? First, House liberals are more active on Middle East issues than House conservatives. Second, when one looks at members' behavior across ideological camps, one sees clearly that ethno-religious "blood" is thicker than political ideological "water." A disproportionate percentage of those standing in opposition to their political ideological brothers and sisters is made up of House members motivated by ethno-religious factors. Among liberals, for example, Reps. Jan Schakowsky, Henry Waxman, Ed Markey, Brad Sherman, Ted Deutch, Adam Schiff—and in previous Congresses Gary Ackerman, Howard Berman, Barney Frank, and Jane Harman—abandon their "Strongly" and "Somewhat Liberal" colleagues to support many or most right wing pro-Israel letters, resolutions, and bills. While most of the aforementioned members are "light blue," some like Sherman and Deutch are "dark blue" supporters of Israel. At the same time, Arab American members like Charles Boustany and Darrell Issa tend to part ways with their staunch and even "Extremely Conservative" colleagues to back letters and measures more supportive of "Arab" causes. In short, from all appearances, family and ethno-religious socialization make a difference, although one must also note that constituent sympathies are playing a role with some, if not all, of these congresspersons.

When I examined the voting records of all House members at both ends of the ideological spectrum, using a scorecard provided by the *Washington Report on Middle East Affairs* and relevant data gleaned from Internet searches, I found that of the 21 members in the "Strongly Liberal" camp for whom there were data, 13 were strong two-state solution proponents, while 8 were not. Of the 54 members in the "Somewhat Liberal" camp for whom there were adequate data, 24 were sympathetic to moderate Arab/Palestinian causes, while 30 were not. At the other end of the spectrum, in the "Extremely Conservative" camp, only 2 individuals in the group of 75 displayed sympathy for moderate Arab and Palestinian causes. In brief, liberals are much more likely to abandon their ideological peers than are conservatives. All of these findings basically confirmed the data produced by my own survey.

THE IMPACT OF HISTORY

Having dragged on for nearly one century, the Arab-Israeli and Israeli-Palestinian conflicts represent issues that are far from new to many members of Congress. Moreover, for those congresspersons who have followed these issues, whether more attentively or from a greater distance, the twists and turns of these conflicts have created their own lasting impressions. This is significant because their perceptions of the protagonists—whether one is talking about countries or specific individuals—have been shaped by these historical developments, especially for those House members willing to move beyond knee-jerk or stereotypical assessments of those countries and their representatives. Let me provide a few examples.

Just as Egypt's Pres. Sadat altered US public opinion of Arab leaders, so were congresspersons' views changed. Consequently, there are those in the House and Senate who remained steadfast in their commitment to high levels of US military and economic support to Egypt as a reward for Sadat's 1979 peace treaty with Israel. Israeli Prime Minister Yitzhak Rabin received kudos from most House members for signing the 1993 Oslo Accords. Similar, positive sentiments among congresspersons were created by Jordan's King Hussein, especially once his pro-American orientation and propensity for moderation were consolidated by signing the 1994 Israel-Jordan peace treaty.

Matters are not so simple as regards the Palestinian nation and major Palestinian actors. It was more difficult for veteran congresspersons to transition from the perception of Yasser Arafat as a "terrorist" to Arafat as serious peacemaker. Indeed, even as Arafat made his way down the peace path, more supportive, open-minded congresspersons were quick to accept negative judgments of Arafat, such as those that followed the "failed Camp David summit" of summer 2000, a failure Pres. Clinton clearly laid at the doorstep of Arafat. It helped matters little that it took almost exactly one full year for US State Department officials who were present at this summit to publish an enlightening account on its proceedings, clearly indicating that Arafat was not deserving of such blame.[162]

The "failed Camp David summit" of 2000 would be followed by the second intifada, and a more protracted, rightward shift in the Israeli electorate. But no event could exceed in importance that of September 11, 2001, which brought the Mideast conflicts literally crashing down on Americans' heads. This was a watershed, historical event, the likes of which caused many congresspersons to embrace a more "clash of civilizations"–like mind-set, with all the attendant consequences for relations with various parties of the Middle East and beyond.

I will remind the reader here that congresspersons' perceptions are heavily colored by numerous factors on the Hill. Beyond whatever biases are predominant in the mainstream media, congresspersons are more subject than the average American citizen to biased information; that is, information provided by the most powerful interest groups, acquired from skewed congressional hearings, or passed to them by biased party leaders and other congressional colleagues.

SUMMARY COMMENTS ON HOUSE MEMBERS' BEHAVIOR

It is easy to name the congresspersons on both ends of the "A to Z" spectrum. On the strongly pro–two state solution, pro-moderate "Arab" side, one finds the very small number of House members with ethnic or religious ties to the region. They are supported, and at times even outdone in terms of activism, by members with strong human rights orientations who recognize the legitimate grievances of the Palestinians, other Arabs, and other peoples of the Middle East. There are perhaps no more than 10–15 individuals who have considerable knowledge and exhibit ongoing concern for Palestinian rights, but on occasion several dozen other House members—mostly "middle roaders"—do come to their support, constituting a group of 54 to 60-some persons. Meanwhile, at the other end of the spectrum, there is a "rival" cluster of individuals of considerably greater size. It includes most of the Jewish American House members; roughly 20 of them are of the "light blue" persuasion, with about 10 of the 20 actively involved in the issues covered in this study. To this group, one may add the 6–8 Jewish and handful of non-Jewish members of a "dark blue" orientation who are heavily involved in Mideast matters.

The roughly 20 "light and dark" blue activists have a strong support group of close to 80 House members, drawn from across the political ideological spectrum. From voting records, it is easy to ascertain that as many as 58 House members of various liberal persuasions lend support to the "light and dark blue" camp. Many Jewish American House members and others—like some religious African American "civil rights" generation members—part ways with the humanitarian concerns of their political ideological brothers and sisters to side heavily and consistently with Israel, even backing the strongly right wing Israeli governments that have been in place for most of the past three and one-half decades. And again, many of these are governments that have included members, the equivalent of US cabinet officials, who are identified as racists by a significant percentage of Jewish Israelis.

Another way of thinking about these numbers is as follows: if just 40 strong "pro–two state solution" activists could enlist backing from the roughly 110 liberals, they would have 150 supporters. This never happens! In fact, they rarely get half that number! By contrast, the strong and unflinching supporters of Israel can capture 207 supporters from various conservative camps, about 45 from the middle ground of the ideological spectrum, and even pick up as many as 105 liberals, for a grand total of 374. What is interesting is that none of the 37 "extremely conservative" camp supporters of Israel comes from a Jewish American background. This means that there is a plethora of conservative Christians, from mainline Baptists and Catholics to evangelicals, who are typically also national security "hawks" and/or team up with secular-minded "security hawks" to back right wing Israeli governments.

On the basis of my personal interviews, I have calculated the following distribution of views in the House.

HOUSE MEMBERS' SENTIMENTS

Sympathy for moderate Arabs, Palestinians:	13 percent (roughly 57 members)
"Middle of the road" stance:	16 percent (roughly 69 members)
Strongly supportive of Israel; but why?:	26 percent (roughly 113 members)
Very strong supporters of Israel:	40 percent (roughly 174 members)
Members w/ no position; too new on the job:	5 percent (roughly 22 members)

Total 435

These calculations are based on the assumption that the "bosses" of all those interviewed "care and know" about the conflict. This assumption is erroneous, as I have demonstrated, and therefore the numbers extrapolated for the entire House don't match staffers' widely shared views that "300 members" don't really care or know that much; or that "two-thirds of the members [c. 287] just go with the flow."

But as it turns out, I believe the guesstimates of 287–300 just going with the flow—which means, for the most part, doing what AIPAC tells them to do, were very close to the mark. How so? When one adds the number of known Arab/Palestinian sympathizers or solidly "pro–two state" solution advocates—roughly 57 members—to the number of solidly pro–right wing Israel supporters—93–94 members, the total is 146–148. Subtracting 148 from 435, the result is 287, or exactly two-thirds of the chamber! This is just under the 300 figure, or 69 percent, and almost spot on the two-thirds, 66 percent estimate. Please understand that I am not claiming here that 146–148 House members actually "care" and "know" the IME conflicts. Hill cognoscenti would think me crazy to make such a claim. So let me state that there is a big discrepancy between the number who "care" and the number who are genuinely "knowledgeable." I think most of them do "care" about these conflicts, but for a great number of them, their knowledge is limited or even impaired by their viewing these conflicts through religiously or ideologically colored lenses. This problem obviously extends to include even the activists at both "ends" of the A–Z spectrum, but in my opinion afflicts a higher percentage of those in the "Z camp" than in the "A camp" because of ethno-religiously based political socialization factors.

Who are the others—the 287 members? Because most activist members are clustered in coastal states and "blue" states, my thoughts turn most quickly to the "red" and "purple" states throughout the country, comprised of many states of the Deep South, the central Midwestern agricultural heartland, and the mountain states. There are 161 Republicans from "red" (76 representatives) and "purple" (85) states, and another 64 Democrats from "red" (42) and "purple" (22) states, who are all "strong supporters" of Israel. This accounts for 225 of the 287 seats, and leaves a mere 62 seats to be "picked up" from "blue" states. This is no difficult task in that many "blue" states have multiple, conservative pockets. For representatives from such backgrounds, where constituent interest is very low, support for Israel emanates from their vision of Israel as the sole regional democracy, matches their conservative or neo-conservative foreign policy and related security concerns, and—never to be underestimated—represents the path of least resistance.

UNDERSTANDING SENATORS' BEHAVIOR ON THE IME CONFLICTS

Before presenting my own "A–Z" categorization of senators, I wish to note first that staffers provided what were to me shockingly low figures for the number of senators who really cared and/or were knowledgeable about Middle East affairs. Again, one low estimate was "five or six at best," and this came from 2013 interviews with two veterans of the House and Senate, both of whom are highly knowledgeable about Middle East affairs. When I suggested as many as twenty, they both were quick to exclaim, "No way!" In an effort to substantiate their claim, they came up with what I conceded constituted one clever measure by noting, "Take, for example, the tea or coffee, events sponsored by the Senate Majority Leader when there are official visits by foreign dignitaries," one of the staffers said. "These are by invitation only from [2013] Sen. Reid's office, sometimes done in conjunction with Foreign Relations. So except for when [PM] Netanyahu or King Abdullah [of Jordan] come, they can't get more than four or five senators to show up. There's just not enough interest." In passing, I will add here that several Senate staffers told me what one of these two said, that Sen. Reid himself, the majority leader, "has zero interest in the Middle East."

When I asked a knowledgeable Senate staffer what his thoughts were on this topic in 2013, he smiled, reflected, and said, "These things are heavily driven by staff, even though the bosses are the key decision makers. Off the top of my head, I don't know any senators who know the Middle East really well."

I'll conclude this section by reemphasizing the point that even on the Senate side of the Hill, one finds a few neophyte staffers who are working hard to get a feel for the issues and their own senator's beliefs and policy positions.

CATEGORIZING THE SENATORS' BEHAVIOR

In categorizing the senators' behavior, one may again start with the assertion that there is no one in the Senate who holds views of an unquestioningly pro-Arab or pro-Palestinian nature. In the same vein, there is no senator who harbors ill will toward Israel to the point of wishing to see its destruction. In brief, this is a null set on the Senate side, just as it is on the House side.

Strong Empathy for the Palestinians: A Club of One or Two in 2005–2006; Almost a Null Set by 2011–2013?

During the 2005–2006 round of interviews, this category was a "Club of One," or at best two. There is no doubt that Senator Lincoln Chafee (R-Rhode Island) was in this category and that his interest, orientation, and level of activism set him apart from all of his Senate colleagues in this issue area. One staffer noted, "Chafee has an extremely principled opinion on the Middle East. He's the only one to voice concerns about our myopic foreign policy . . ." A second Senate staffer opined:

"Sen. Chafee has been very critical of the administration. He blames Bush for being insufficiently engaged in Middle East peace efforts and he's been quite critical of Israel. This represents a big change from when Sen. Brownback was chairing the committee."

And a third staffer said:

"On the 2006 Hamas election, Chafee's position is an evolving position. He's very upset at the US—great rhetoric about a two-state solution. We coulda shoulda worked with Abu Mazen [Mahmoud Abbas] on various items: 1) the route of the barrier; 2) prisoners held without charges; 3) going through the barrier. We needed to strengthen the [Palestinian] moderates. He's very frustrated by the US not helping them and that this led to Hamas's victory. Others argue against this point."

The only other individual who was broadly perceived as close to Chafee in this issue area was Sen. John E. Sununu (R-New Hampshire). Sununu, son of former governor and Bush White House counsel John H. Sununu, is of Palestinian-Lebanese Christian Arab descent. During his one term in the Senate, he alienated fellow Republicans by taking a strong stance against the USA Patriot Act. One staffer said, in 2006, "Greater clarity as regards his position on the Arab-Israeli conflict will come up over the next few months, but Sununu is very thoughtful, and engaged, on these issues." However, Sununu, even if more attentive to Arab and Palestinian concerns than his Senate colleagues in general, was not perceived by Senate staffers as being as committed to offsetting the strong "pro-Israel" bias as was Chafee.

Here is how an unsympathetic Senate staffer spoke of Chafee and Sununu: "Chafee is in a league of his own. No other senators speak in a pro-Arab manner like Chafee; he's definitely out of the mainstream. Sen. Sununu, perhaps because of his background, is more sympathetic, but people can understand where he's coming from." By which he meant unlike Chafee.

By 2012–2013, both Chafee and Sununu were long gone. Chafee had been defeated in his 2006 Senate bid by Sheldon Whitehouse, who took a stronger "pro-Israel" position and received stronger backing by AIPAC and others. Former Sen. Chafee subsequently ran for governor of Rhode Island and was elected as an Independent. He also joined the advisory board of J Street in 2008, thus keeping a hand in conflict-related matters. As for Sununu, he was defeated by Jeanne Shaheen in 2008, with the latter similarly strongly backed by AIPAC. Sununu went into business and academe.

By 2013, in the estimation of some strong pro–two state groups, Sen. Dianne Feinstein had perhaps entered this category. Staff at FCNL, for example, described her as their "champion" in the Senate. They were inclined to grant Sen. Jeff Merkley (D-Oregon) favorable recognition as well, but were at a loss to describe other senators in such terms.

Senate "Middle Roaders": Supportive of Israel, But Occasionally Circumspect

Beyond these two individuals, one moves on to a category of senators who, at a minimum, express support for Israeli, but are not immune to lodging criticism against Israeli government policies and practices. Many of these individuals have been around for a long time and are nearly "bulletproof" from an electoral vantage point and therefore are able to adopt more independent-minded positions on a broad range of issues, including that of the Arab-Israeli and Israel-Palestine conflicts.

A few senators, most of whom were either sure of or allegedly not concerned about their electoral base, enjoyed a large measure of decision-making freedom in this issue area. "[The senator] is different from most senators," one staffer said. "I would not classify him in the vehemently pro-Israel group. Israel is a strong ally, but we need to moderate our support for Israel and look to our interests with other countries." Another staffer noted that his boss was motivated by religion to be more evenhanded. "He wants to put people at the same table to talk out issues. It's not Christian to be backing oppression. There's a need for compassion and dialogue in Christ-like behavior. . . . He wants to be and is tough against terrorism, but he still wants to be compassionate and evenhanded." The same staffer added:

> "My boss is very much an independent, free thinker. He doesn't care whether he gets reelected. He fears a horrible, fiscal calamity. He's a genuine Christian thinker; this guides his thinking. He wants to put people at the same table to talk out issues. It's not Christian to be backing oppression. . . . We need to concentrate the fight against takfiri and Wahhabi types—not 'Muslims' as the people write in. [The home state] is a very pro-military state; there are many bases."

A good number of senators, their electoral comfort zone notwithstanding, were also described as wary to grant anyone a blank check, including the Israelis. Here's a sample of these views. One staffer said, "She believes we've had an ally we can rely on in the Middle East and they appreciate our support, but sometimes our relations with Israel have caused problems for us in the Middle East." Or as another put it, "My boss is capable of criticizing Israel's behavior, but we are still strong supporters of Israel in general."

Finally, for some senators, "distance" and independence from these issues is claimed on the basis of greater interest in other concerns. Staffers said the following to this point: "He is interested in the Middle East and the Arab–Israeli conflict, but his two priorities are on other issues"; "[The senator] is [extremely active on another committee] so his work on Foreign Relations pales by comparison."

The group of middle roaders also included independent-minded Jewish American senators, especially those more supportive of the Israeli left and Labor Party than its right wing elements. "The senator is Jewish," one staffer said "He's very moderate. He's not a regular practitioner of Judaism. He's a twenty-first century thinker. He's an absolute believer in Israel and Israel's right to exist, but Israel has responsibilities. He's more Labor than Likud in his orientation. He's pro–two state solution. The senator is a very religious man—he strives to do what is good. He has great respect for other religions. He is driven by what he thinks is right."

Some staffers described their senators' independence as based in "national interest" and/or humanitarian values. One staffer said his/her boss's position was "What is in the US interest? . . . She is not in lockstep with the AIPAC types. When she says she is a supporter of Israel heart and soul, she means it, but I don't think she feels constrained. She can't abet Hamas in any way, but she's got strong humanitarian values."

In short, the group includes many independent-minded, moderate senators, ranging from liberal Democrats to moderate Republicans. I cannot name their names without basically revealing the staffers' identities, thereby violating my pledge to them. Senators in this group don't always support AIPAC-backed measures, but are far from immune to doing so. By my tally, there are about 30–35 senators in this category.

STRONG SUPPORTERS OF ISRAEL, WITH A PRAGMATIC BENT

Moving into this category, one finds a group whose support for Israel is close to unwavering, but not to be taken completely for granted. Some of this "difference" is attributable to these staffers' unwillingness to sign off on all the policies coming from right wing Israeli governments. Some staffers also alluded to their bosses' pragmatism as a critical component of their strong support for Israel: "He's a very pragmatic guy. He likes to ask how policies will impact people you're disagreeing with"; "[The senator] is a big picture kind of person. He is Jewish. He has a strong sense of engagement. He believes you can't have economic security without political security"; "He [the senator mentioned in the prior quote] tends to be more of a realist, and an internationalist. . . . My boss is Jewish, but he's evenhanded. Israel will have to give up something—it's best to have a two-state solution."

Pragmatism, of course, may be induced by a variety of factors. For senators who have presidential aspirations, a strong commitment to Israel seems de rigueur, so much so that it might make some senators look like they belong in the category to follow. One staffer commented on this phenomenon, saying, "Sen. Rubio hopes to be president someday, so he'll stumble all over himself to look pro-Israel." Sen. Rubio is far from the first, nor will be most likely be the last, to exhibit such "pragmatic" behavior.

The size of this "pragmatic, strong supporters" group increased at the expense of the group of "unflinching supporters of Israel" following the 1993 Oslo peace process. One staffer said the number of senators who are unflinching supporters of Israel declined from 25 in the 1990s to 10 in 2006. The staffer attributed this decline to the fact that "AIPAC basically opposed Oslo. This is when it started. We had a wholesale [home state] Jewish abandonment of AIPAC. AIPAC was left as a much more conservative group, and Peace Now blossomed." This claim is somewhat exaggerated. Even if AIPAC's influence was somewhat diminished in the mid-1990s, it rebounded solidly in conjunction with the 2000 "failed" Camp David summit and subsequent intifada, and the events of September 11, 2001.

But in the early 2010s, pro-peace groups have brought people like Sen. Durbin into this group, and others would place Sen. Feinstein here as well. As noted earlier, they have been attracted by the stronger pro-peace orientation of J Street, thereby partially distancing themselves from the tougher, right wing pro-Israel AIPAC line. By my estimate, there were about 45–50 senators who fit into this category during the 2005–2013 time frame.

UNFLINCHING SUPPORTERS OF RIGHT WING ISRAELI GOVERNMENTS

Senators Lieberman, Susan Collins, Chuck Schumer, Jon Kyl, Rick Santorum, James Inhofe, Barbara Boxer, Eric Coleman, Sam Brownback, Frank

Lautenberg, and Daniel Inouye. These were the names of Israel's most hard-core Senate supporters in 2005–2006. (Back then, Sen. Durbin might have been included in this group, and in even earlier times Sen. Levin. Others could have made arguments for Sen. Feinstein's inclusion in this group as well. But Durbin's and Feinstein's recent association with J Street represents a move into the category discussed above.) By 2013, among the hard-core types, Brownback, Coleman, and Santorum were no longer present; Inouye and Lautenberg passed away. All the others remained in place, and new names such as Robert Casey Jr. (R-PA), Mark Kirk (R-IL), and Lindsey Graham (R-SC) picked up where others left off.

It's interesting to examine the factors that brought various senators to this cluster. Some staffers described their boss's pro-Israel stances as having unclear origins. According to one staffer:

> "[The senator] is extremely pro-Israeli, even though coming from a state with a very small Jewish population. Our constituents tend to be more skeptical with regard to Israel, but [the senator] sees Israel as the only democracy in the Middle East and an essential ally in the war on terror. [The senator] sees the Israelis as all alone in the world . . . We've often wondered where the attachment comes from. Perhaps it's the influence of colleagues; e.g., Sen. Santorum, who does a lot on religious freedom and organizes Republicans and Jewish roundtables; also Sen. Kyl . . . . The only issue area where [the senator] deviates from moderation is [the senator's] strong pro-Israel support."

Others see their boss's policy stances as originating in personal views. One staffer for a Jewish senator said:

> "He's very much into small, successful steps. He hoped Gaza would go peacefully, etc., but nothing positive has happened there. Terrorists have been elected; now what do we do? It's a very different situation. We don't discuss final status issues. I would tell him to avoid these issues because you won't be able to get people to the table. There's too little room for negotiation. The right of return [of diaspora Palestinians] is a nonstarter for Israelis. With regard to Jerusalem, it's a very difficult issue, but I can't see one party getting it all.

I think my boss comes to this issue area with strong personal views, so it's very hard to lobby him on this."

Sen. Daniel Inouye (D-Hawaii) served in the US Senate from 1963–2012; that is, through most of this study, and he was a powerful voice on Appropriations as discussed in a later chapter. His commitment to Israel was long-standing and unbending. He also was backed heavily by pro-Israel campaign donors during his lengthy career. A staffer attributed his long-standing support to his service in World War II. "In World War II he was with an Asian-American battalion," the staffer said. "He was among of the first troops to free Dachau. He didn't see it directly himself, but his friends did. In 1959 he became a congressman, asked for a Pentagon briefing, and discovered we knew nothing about the concentration camps, so he's felt we owe them the protection of Israel."

Sen. Samuel "Sam" Brownback (R-KS), who served in the Senate from 1996–2011, has been described as a Christian Zionist and evangelical. According to one report, he began to be influenced by the thinking of Michael Horowitz, a neocon at the Hudson Institute, in the late 1990s.[163] In addition, as one Senate staffer described him: "He comes from the fundamentalist Christian side of the party. . . . His starting point is his firm belief that the Jewish people have the biblical right to the land, so they have the right to live there. He believes it's all theirs, but on a practical basis, he believes it's the right of the Israeli government to do what's necessary. Democratic processes should determine what Israelis themselves see as necessary. So if they want to give back land, okay. He disagreed with giving up the land. He was against their giving up the land of the West Bank, but he's always supported the Israeli government's decisions to withdraw."

Yet another senator's pro-Israel was described as motivated by his religious beliefs. "The senator is solidly pro-Israel," the staffer said. "He has made three or four trips to Israel and he doesn't travel much. His trips to Jerusalem were particularly significant as a [devoutly religious man]. It's sometimes tough for him—he gets caught between the church's views and politics."

To conclude this section, it's instructive to take a look at how several Senate staffers saw their "unflinching" bosses. Here are three comments made independently in summer 2013 by veteran Senate staffers The first comes from a staffer who saw eye-to-eye with his "unflinching" boss: "I'd rather have a democratically elected Israel as a partner in the Middle East than just about any other regime sitting there—they're partners and we can trust them and fight with them." But two other staffers, behind closed doors, presented a starkly different picture. One stated: "There are many veteran staffers here who have a hard time accepting the strong pro-Israel positions of their bosses"; the second asserted, far more poignantly, "Some senators here put the national security of Israel ahead of that of the United States." When I asked if he would attach any senators' names to that statement, the staffer demurred.

All told, 12–13 senators could be placed in this box in the mid-2000s. In 2013, their number was roughly the same.

SENATORS' HISTORY AND KNOWLEDGE BASE, AND SPECIAL RELATIONS WITH FOREIGN ACTORS

As with House members, through trips to the region or official visits by dignitaries to the US, senators have established favorable personal relationships with regional actors, from kings and presidents to other representatives. Examples abound. One staffer told me that Pennsylvania's Sen. Arlen Specter had built closer ties with Syria's Assad family, one that influenced his behavior. Another staffer said of his senator, and others: "The senator has established a relationship with the King of Jordan; there's a lot of people up here very protective of Jordan." Former Egyptian Pres. Anwar Sadat had many friends in the Senate; and Sen. Leahy (Vermont), for example, spoke frankly with Sadat's successor Pres. Mubarak. Senators can have strong, usually positive relationships with Arab leaders and their countries, without in any way forgoing strong commitments to Israel. Meanwhile, others learned to be skeptical of Arafat. One staffer said of his boss, "She probably gave Arafat the benefit of the doubt, [but] she didn't trust him." In contrast, other senators, of course, have sewn special ties with Israeli officials over the years, like that of former Sen. Kyl with Benyamin Netanyahu.

The senators' bonds, overall, have been strong enough to weather serious challenges or, alternatively, to give rise to great senses of betrayal and breaches of trust. And the senators are in a better position to learn if they have been wronged. They enjoy access to information that is not available to their House counterparts. As a Senate staffer pointed out, "Almost nobody up here has a security clearance, but senators do. They see a lot. We [staffers] get informed in the most cryptic, guarded way." Actually, House members do get secret intelligence briefings at times, too, but a greater percentage of senators are likely to have access to classified information. A caveat here is that classified information may prove misleading, but this does not alter the significance of senators' relatively privileged access to such information and its potential impact on their perceptions and decision making.

THE SENATORS IDEOLOGICAL DISPOSITIONS AND VIEWS OF THE IME CONFLICTS

How do senators' ideological positions—using a spectrum that runs from strongly liberal to strongly conservative—match up with their sympathies vis-à-vis IME issues?[164] And how does the senators' overall "disposition" compare to that of House members? One notes (see endnote 10) that the number of senators who display some combination of sympathy for non-Israeli actors or a greater willingness to criticize the Israeli government is very small; that is, one person, at best, in each ideological camp. This means that there is less sympathy for moderate Arab/Palestinian causes or criticism of Israeli policy among liberal senators than there is among liberal House members. However, the overall percentage of senators with at least a modicum of concern for this issue area is much higher than in the House. This is not surprising in light of two factors: (1), what senators must go through to get into office in the first place due to the higher stakes and higher level of vetting; and (2), the lengthier terms they serve, and thus lengthier exposure to the issues after they've been elected. As in the House, there is more activism at either end of the spectrum. There are a greater number of conservatives who are activists in the Senate compared to the House.

The finding that ethno-religious "blood" is thicker than political ideological "water" rings true again in the Senate, especially on the liberal end of the picture. A very large number of those who demonstrate unswerving support for Israel are Jewish Americans: Senators Ron Wyden (D-OR), Boxer, Blumenthal (D-CN), and Al Franken (D-MN) among strong liberals. Senators Ben Cardin (D-MD), Schumer, and to some extent Levin are in the somewhat liberal camp. In earlier times, Sen. John Sununu would have been noteworthy here at the other end of the spectrum; that is, a conservative senator bucking the unquestioningly pro-Israel position of fellow conservatives.

To sum up, the beliefs and behavior of US senators cover the same range of views found in the House, but there is definitely a different mix. Again, unsurprisingly, there is no one who espouses an anti-Israel position in the Senate. Perhaps more noteworthy, at the beginning of my research effort, only one individual, Sen. Lincoln Chafee, was widely perceived as strongly, consistently, and actively sympathetic to Palestinian and broader Arab concerns and grievances. His motivation appears to have been based entirely on humanitarian values and principles. As my study neared conclusion in 2013, no senator "fit" in this category as did Chafee; only Sen. Feinstein received a noteworthy nod.

The "middle roader to consistent supporter of Israel" ground is robust among senators. With their six-year terms of office, and the power of incumbency placing many of them in an even more enviable position, they seem to benefit from a greater degree of independence of judgment in this issue area compared to their House colleagues. At the end of the day, when the votes are taken, they do vote heavily for AIPAC-endorsed resolutions and bills, so few are bucking the tide in any serious manner. Many senators, however, are cognizant and appreciative of the roles played by other governments in the region—primarily, over a broader historical sweep, the Egyptian and Jordanians ones—and they work to safeguard American relationships with those regimes in the face of efforts to cut back US aid disbursements in their direction.

The Senate—the more august body—contains its fair share of fervent backers of Israel. Many—but far from all of these individuals—are motivated by religious and/or ethnic considerations, whether as conservative Christians, Christian evangelicals, or Jews. Some, haunted by the Holocaust, clearly perceive Israel as an essential safe haven for the Jewish people. And the group of Israel's unflinching supporters is rounded out by security hawks like Senators John McCain and Lindsey Graham.

Last but not least, senators from across this spectrum are mindful of Israel's democratic values and institutions and feel a certain moral obligation to defend Israel as a crucial democratic ally in a very turbulent and high-valued geostrategic region of the world. Some see Israel as a steadfast ally in the "clash of civilizations." But the bottom line here is that, as in the House, a significant percentage of senators neither care nor know all that much about the IME conflicts. Ethno-religiously inspired senators notwithstanding, most of them hail from the middle of the country and the deep South. And the overwhelming majority of them adopt the "default mode" to vote for AIPAC-backed policies.

Chapter Six

HOW HOUSE MEMBERS MAKE MIDEAST POLICY

I'll now examine how the pieces of the congressional action puzzle come together to affect congresspersons' behavior in making Mideast policy. I have chosen to focus more heavily on four committees. In this chapter, I will look at the House Committee on Foreign Affairs (HFAC; formerly the House International Relations Committee, HIRC). In chapter seven, I'll cover the Senate Committees on Foreign Relations. And in chapter eight, I will examine both the House and Senate Appropriations committees. Out of the myriad issues and activities engaged in over the time span of this research effort, I have chosen to look more closely at congressional activity in response to the 2006 election of Hamas and the 2011–12 attempts by the Palestinian Authority to acquire formal recognition at the United Nations. A caveat before proceeding: any redundancy in the use of earlier quotes here and in ensuing chapters is perfectly intentional; the reader will now see certain quotes in the context of congressional action.

REMEMBERING THE MOBILIZATION OF BIAS

Data on campaign financing can be quite telling. As the reader saw in chapter two, the nexus of campaign finance donations, elections, and the acquisition and retention of positions of power appears striking. Again, the focus there was primarily on recipients of funding by "pro-Israel" donors because that's where nearly all the action is.

For our purposes here, it should be made clear that many individuals on these lists required no "financial incentive" to adopt a "pro-Israel" position; they've done so because it's engrained in their personal political socialization experiences, or because they see standing with Israel as in the strategic interest of the US. But in an important regard, that's not what matters. What matters is whether or not this assistance provided them a special advantage at least once, if not on numerous occasions, to defeat their election opponents, and whether or not this support incentivized continued "pro-Israel" behavior. Beyond this observation, there is, on the surface, somewhat of a "chicken and egg" problem here as regards the list of career recipients. Did the money flow to those already sitting in positions of influence, or was their rise in congressional prestige and acquisition of greater positions of influence acquired as a result of the assistance? With many congresspersons, it's actually quite easy to discern what came first, as the reader will see. But whatever the causal connection between campaign finance assistance and congressional behavior, there has been an excellent return for the donors on almost all of these investments, as shall now be demonstrated.

THE HOUSE: MESSAGES AND MOTIONS

In Congress, the task of congresspersons is to engage in interest articulation and to legislate. In both chambers, there are many ways members go about mobilizing support for a broad range of issues, from silly and symbolic ones to the most serious and sublime. In the balance of this chapter, I discuss how House members enlist support for their causes, beginning with the circulation of "Dear Colleague" letters and other forms of communication and move on to the introduction and passage of resolutions and bills relating to key Middle East affairs.

"Dear Colleague" Letters

One way House members try to get out front on a particular issue is to write a "Dear Colleague" letter and circulate it to elicit support. In any given week, a flurry of letters appears covering a broad spectrum of issues.

Staffers respond in a variety of ways to these letters. One approach—one that struck me as particularly surprising—is for staffers to take matters into their own hands and "bury" the letter. One staffer said, "Matters, letters, get vetted by me before they go up to [the congressman]. I won't show him every single pro-Israel letter—like the Hamas election letter—I didn't even pass it along to him. It's not important to sign every single letter; it's not intellectually or politically helpful to us or to Israel."

More commonly, it is the boss who has taken a wary or disdainful posture vis-à-vis "Dear Colleague" letters and has instructed his staffers to act as gatekeepers. "My boss is hesitant to sign off on all these 'Dear Colleague' letters—[in this issue area] I imagine they mostly come from the Mideast subcommittee members of HIRC," one staffer said. "I think he prefers to rely a lot on senior staff and staffers for their views on these issues." Many members and staffers also feel strongly that to sign too many letters dilutes the value of the congressperson's signature. As one staffer noted, "With the 'Dear Colleague' letters and cosponsorships, we try to keep it limited so that it means something."

The justification for "deep-sixing" many of these letters is ready-made by their sheer quantity. According to one staffer, "There are stacks of 'Dear Colleague' letters every day; most just get lost in the shuffle." Accordingly, office SOP for how many of these letters are dealt with can be gathered from the following comment. "As a general rule, we don't sign on to a lot," a House staffer said. "Every week the LD and the three LAs sit down to go over the 'Dear Colleague' letters. One, we look at the 'Dear Colleague' letters on a bill, and two, we look at calls from our constituents on a bill. Number two [the constituents' views] takes priority over number one."

By 2012–13, the use of the Internet had facilitated circulation of "Dear Colleague" letters to an abusive point; that is, it had opened up the floodgates. This caused some House members and staffers to retreat to older methods to get letters taken seriously.

"Dear Colleague" letters relating to IME conflicts are, by all accounts, commonplace. Many staffers chalk this up to congresspersons seeking to score points with constituents and lobbyists by demonstrating that they are "doing something" to address various issues and that they are trying to raise their colleagues' level of consciousness. The bulk of these letters reflect right wing pro-Israel viewpoints; and many are seen as serving as a way of gauging other members' level of commitment to Israel. In many offices, the standard response is to go with the flow; in essence, this is the "Dear Colleague" letter default mode. Consider the following quote from a staffer: "'Dear Colleague' letters and resolutions, we're pretty willing to sign on to pro-Israel items. We have so little interaction with the region; the LD or someone else may go ahead and sign us on. Any time a pro-Israel thing is up, he knows how to vote most of the time. Most D's are supportive of Israel. There's nothing to gain or lose by voting for pro-Israel things, so in part it's a party solidarity matter.

Israel is the only democracy, yes; but in our eyes this doesn't need to be and isn't articulated because it's such a nonissue for our constituents."

Staffers and their bosses send "Dear Colleague" letters to a range of recipients. For example, some letters are addressed to top executive officials, such as the president, secretary of state, or foreign leaders. Members of Congress often cross party lines to laud or criticize executive branch policy responses to new developments. One middle-of-the-road member's staffer noted how his office "covered" itself along these lines. "We signed the letter to Condi Rice that Brit Tzedek va Shalom [the predominantly Jewish American, pro-peace organization] and IPF put out; but we also signed the AIPAC-backed letter," he said. "Overall, he thinks it's important to back the Israel-US relationship." On balance, however, staffer interviewees made it clear that letters with an AIPAC imprimatur are far more likely to evoke stronger positive reactions.

At times, aggressive letters have a polarizing effect, and give rise to dueling "Dear Colleague" letters. Alternatively, people may pile on, circulating their own, complementary letters. As a "dovish" congressperson's staffer noted in a 2006 interview: "A lot of the time it's like playing pickup basketball. Members and their staffs find issues and see who wants to play. Last week there was the Swiss/Red Cross issue—whether there's a need for a new symbol [other than the cross]. [One office] picked up on this and sent a letter to the Swiss. We decided to play on this issue. We got 45 members to sign on—most were Jews, many New Yorkers—to a 'Dear Colleague' letter. I contacted AIPAC, the AJC; they didn't go to the mat on this one, but they contacted a few members. We got 45 signatures in one week and sent the letter off to the Swiss. [When things like this work out well] we can put out a press release later if there's a victory."

As Al Kamen wrote in his *Washington Post* "In the Loop" column, contributions made by lobbyists to these letters can be quite direct, but these connections usually remain unknown to the broader public. Here is what Kamen wrote in mid-May 2009.

> . . . House Majority Leader Steny H. Hoyer (D-Md.) and Minority Whip Eric Cantor (R-Va.) sent out a "Dear Colleague" e-mail Tuesday asking for signatures "to the attached letter to President Obama regarding the Middle East peace process." The letter says the

usual stuff, emphasizing that Washington "must be both a trusted mediator and a devoted friend to Israel" and noting: "Israel will be taking the greatest risks in any peace agreement." Curiously, when we opened the attachment, we noticed it was named "AIPAC Letter Hoyer Cantor May 2009.pdf." Seems as though someone forgot to change the name or something. AIPAC? The American Israel Public Affairs Committee? Is that how this stuff works?[165]

The answer to his question is, in many cases, a resounding "Yes!"

Before moving beyond this section, it's worth mentioning again a letter that 54 House members sent to Pres. Obama in January 2010, a time frame during which Israel and Egypt's blockade of the Gaza Strip was producing a humanitarian disaster for Gaza's Palestinians. The "Gaza 54" were calling upon the Obama administration to pressure Israel and Egypt to lift their blockade, decried by objective observers as "collective punishment" contravening the Geneva Conventions. The letter called for allowing Gazans improved access to clean water, fuel, construction materials, medicine and health care products, and sanitation supplies. To put this letter in perspective, that it garnered 54 signatures—almost all progressive Democrats; just under one-eighth of the House members—was viewed as a significant achievement in pro-peace circles. There was no policy upshot to the protest letter, but as noted elsewhere, more vulnerable signatories like Joe Sestak (PA), Donna Edwards (MD), and others were targeted by AIPAC elements in the 2012 election campaign.

HOUSE RESOLUTIONS

"There really aren't many votes taken on Middle East issues.
Mostly there are just resolutions."

Successful "Dear Colleague" letters might lead to sponsorship of a resolution, usually a nonbinding resolution, designed to yield a "sense of the House" on a specific issue. Other resolutions emerge sui generis. Here again, there is a proliferation of resolutions, nearly all of which run in a "pro-Israel" direction, and most are decided by a voice vote. "Almost every other week there's some kind of nonbinding resolution to show support for Israel," a staffer said. "[My boss] signs on even if sometimes some measures are seen as silly."

The staffer who informed me of Rep. Moran's story also offered a serious, substantive "punch line" as regards House practices on these resolutions:

> "One can characterize Moran's flare-ups by specific historical incidents. You can find one or two per year 'Sense of Congress' pro-Israel resolutions; these are stand alone, leadership driven, 'Sense of Congress' resolutions. These resolutions are put on the suspension calendar so you don't need to go to the Rules committee to get them put on the agenda. It [this procedure] is supposed to be used for early in the week, noncontroversial bills, not things considered controversial like this, and these resolutions, which need a two-thirds vote, do pass overwhelmingly. The Jewish diaspora has enormous clout up here. And there's a primal fear here of rocking the boat. Overseas, in foreign countries, all of this leaves really negative impressions regarding the US as an 'honest broker' or not. The fear and misunderstanding is embedded in this institution. I've heard so many people, fellow House members, like after the peace vigil, come up to me and say they understand what he [Moran] really meant, etc., but felt they couldn't stand with him. It was too risky."

While in office (1999–2011), Rep. Anthony Weiner (D-NY) steadily proposed resolutions designed to put a damper on US relations with other countries he perceived as unfriendly to Israel. For example, HR 3289 of October 14, 2003—Fiscal 2004 Supplemental Appropriations for Iraq and Afghanistan/Vote to Bar Saudi Arabia from Receiving US Financial Assistance—was one of many similar efforts (it ultimately failed to pass 193–233). As Progressive Punch reported, "During debate on the $87 billion supplemental spending bill for Iraq and Afghanistan, Congressman Weiner (D-NY) proposed an amendment which would have prohibited any funding included in the supplemental bill from being used for loans to Saudi Arabia. The Saudi government, Weiner argued, played an important role in financing the 9/11 hijackers, has funded suicide bombers in Israel, and, consequently, should be excluded from any US financial assistance."[166] The idea that the "Saudi government played an important role in financing the 9/11 hijackers" is so ludicrous as to provoke the issue as to what motivated Weiner to lodge such a claim. Had Osama bin Laden set foot in his home country, the Saudi government would have had him beheaded. Yet 192 other House members signed Weiner's resolution.

On occasion, resolutions are introduced that reflect concern for people or issues affecting the interests of Palestinians, Arabs, or their supporters, but these resolutions are a harder sell. For example, Rep. Brian Baird (D-WA) introduced a measure praising Rachel Corrie, one of his constituents, for her courage. Recall, while participating in a protest movement in the Gaza Strip in March 2003, Corrie, a young American pro-Palestinian activist, was run over and crushed to death in broad daylight by an Israeli bulldozer. Baird's resolution, however, "didn't go anywhere," said a Washington (State) staffer.

Resolutions run the gamut from lighthearted to serious. In any given House session, there will be many resolutions calling upon House members to congratulate Israel on the occasion of its 60-something birthday or, more seriously, condemning Hamas and Islamic Jihad for firing Qassam rocket attacks at Israeli civilians. Typically, domestic politics looms large behind many resolutions. As one veteran staffer with broader historical perspective stated in 2005, "The Republicans have been very smart by bringing up resolutions supporting Israel. A few years back the D's had the lead on these issues, but no more. It's much more of a bipartisan thing today." At the forefront of many resolutions have been HIRC/HFAC leadership elements such as Ileana Ros-Lehtinen and Eliot Engel.

There is also a fair level of personal gamesmanship that congresspersons play in voting for resolutions. In 2013, a season staffer said, "With many of the resolutions forwarded by [Rep.] Ros-Lehtinen or extremely pro-Israel members, people vote for it because they know it's not going anywhere in the House, or they know that the Senate will beat it down. In the back of your mind as a House member, you know that it's never going to become law, so you can please the leadership and your constituents without damaging US foreign policy. What becomes tricky is when people press and want to make this stuff the law."

Despite this gamesmanship, House members would do well to remember that even resolutions they take lightly are not similarly viewed abroad. "The resolutions do matter abroad; they're paying attention," one staffer commented. "They carry more weight abroad than here." And many staffers and their bosses do see harm in the "pro-Israel" bias of many House resolutions.

"The passage of so many pro-Israel resolutions causes well-informed, dovish congresspersons to throw their hands up in the air in frustration because they see congressional leaders abusing their prerogatives to limit debate over controversial, conflict-related issues and steamroll acceptance of pro-Israel measures," one staffer noted, referencing the fact that the resolutions do not need to go through the Rules committee to get on the agenda. As he also observed: "House resolutions are usually one-sided. You could find one or two per year sense of Congress resolutions; these are stand alone, leadership driven, sense of Congress resolutions. They are put on the suspension calendar, so you don't need to go to the Rules committee to get it put on the agenda; it's on the floor with tight parameters for debate. It's supposed to be used for noncontroversial bills, not controversial matters.

One of the more powerful statements on the potentially pernicious impact of right wing pro-Israel resolutions was made on the House floor on February 17, 2005, by Rep. Barney Frank (D-MA). Frank believed that Yasser Arafat's death, combined with Ariel Sharon's courageous order to withdraw from the Israeli-occupied Gaza Strip, had created a new, hopeful moment for proponents of a two-state solution to the I-P conflict. But Frank, who took great pains to place the burden on all parties—Israelis, Arabs, Palestinians, and Europeans—to shoulder responsibility, went on to state:

> "But there are also things that friends of Israel should refrain from doing, and that brings me to this Chamber right here, Mr. Speaker. Explicitly, I think we should resolve that those on the right wing in Israel who object to Prime Minister Sharon's decision to withdraw from Gaza and to begin a withdrawal from the West Bank and to begin a process that we hope will lead to a Palestinian state, we have got to be careful that they do not win in the United States House of Representatives what they have lost in the Knesset [Israel's parliament], because they are going to try and they will, unfortunately, have allies here. We have a history here of people in this body and in American politics taking the overwhelming support that exists for the Nation of Israel's existence and for Israel's cause and manipulating this in ways that I think are not intended to have a negative effect on the chances for peace, but certainly can have that."[167]

Frank proceeded to give the example of how, in 1995, when Prime Minister Rabin of Israel was still alive and there were strong prospects for peace, the House of Representatives had overwhelmingly passed a resolution demanding that the US embassy in Israel be moved to Jerusalem. Frank said that he knew that this effort was consciously designed and timed to undermine the peace process. In addition, Frank noted that on June 23, 2004, House Concurrent Resolution 460, which he admitted voting for while holding his nose, suggested that Israel should not have to withdraw from most of the West Bank. Frank describes himself as "troubled" both by his specific vote because of its message and by the method by which the vote, in general, was brought up.

> "[My vote] would be fatal to the peace process and therefore damaging to Israel's own legitimate best interests. [And] it did not give sufficient recognition to what ultimately should be the Palestinians' result in this process. It stated the legitimate concerns of Israel, and it left silent some of the concerns of the Palestinians. Of course, it came before us unamendable and you had to vote yes or no. This is the kind of dilemma we had. I hope we will now determine, Mr. Speaker, that the members of this House will not be put in a position of voting on an unamendable resolution with only 40 minutes' debate which will be the truth, nothing but the truth, but not the whole truth, and which will perhaps be designed to undercut the peace process."

By nearly everyone's account, Rep. Frank's plea has, in general, gone unheeded.

Resolutions reflecting the power of right wing pro-Israel elements are on full display when Israel has used its superior military might in conflicts with Palestinian or Lebanese opponents. For example, following Israel's three-week, 2008–2009 war with Gaza's Palestinians, in which both Israel's government and Hamas were accused of war crimes in the UN requested Goldstone Report, the House passed a nonbinding resolution, H. Res. 867, condemning the report by a 344–36 vote.

PASSING A BILL IN THE HOUSE

"Bills don't come to the floor unless they're going to pass."
—a veteran staffer

The overall procedure for enacting a bill is often lengthy, and many more times than not results in failure. All players understand the difficulty of the game. Put simply, any bill placed in the legislative hopper will usually be assigned to the committee(s) deemed most appropriate for discussion and deliberation. Once in committee, it will be passed along to the most fitting subcommittee. A bill can, accordingly, languish and die at the subcommittee or full committee levels, never making it to the floor of the House for consideration and debate. Should it arrive on the floor, the vagaries of partisan politics may leave even a sound bill savaged. But should it succeed, then the bill still has to survive the same process in the Senate and, ultimately, either be signed by the president or be so strongly backed as to override a presidential veto.

For our purposes here, I have chosen to examine more carefully what happens to proposed legislation in its earlier stages. I will begin by looking at the processing of issues in the relevant House committees.

Dynamics of the House Committee on International Relations (HIRC); now the House Committee on Foreign Affairs (HFAC)

"Who carries the water for Israel? HIRC people are the authorizing agency; they shape the debate to protect Israel and denounce countries that are critical of Israel. Also, there are Jewish members who are very partisan for Israel; they're not necessarily religious, but for them it's a calling for protection of the homeland. Policies, issues, funding, etc., emanate from HIRC committee debate and discussion. And some members are motivated by fear in how they vote—AIPAC's litmus test is 'Do you support Israel or not?' And it's a zero sum game; either you vote for Israel or against Israel on all issues."
—veteran staffer

The House committee that deals with foreign affairs has undergone yoyo-like name changes. The committee was formally named the House Committee on International Affairs from 1975 to early 1979. Its name then changed to the

House Committee on Foreign Affairs, was renamed the House Committee on International Relations from 1995–2007, then returned to being the House Committee on Foreign Affairs in January 2007. When I conducted my interviews in 2005–2006, everyone referred to the committee by the HIRC acronym, and in 2011–2013 they were calling it HFAC.

A brief aide-mémoire is in order before examining this committee's activities. The "mobilization of bias" concept is very useful in this context: if a deliberative body has come under the control of a group of individuals espousing a particular ideological orientation or set of interests, then that body is likely to embrace the associated positions and policies. The reader should also remember that competition among House members for a seat on this committee has remained low. Only a small number of House members are strongly interested in serving on this committee, first and foremost because there is no "pork" to bring home to their constituents. House members who are highly motivated to serve on the committee face little competition; they find it easy to obtain and retain not only their full committee seats, but their favorite subcommittee assignments as well. In turn, this permits them to acquire a greater level of familiarity with the issues at play and, others things being equal, enhances the likelihood they will be shown greater deference by new committee colleagues and fellow House members in general.

Which Members Had Clout on House Foreign Affairs?

For political scientists, there are a couple of ways to ascertain who has clout or influence in decision-making circles. One is to look at who the formal holders of power are: this is referred to as "positional analysis." But "positional analysis" does not always reveal who the power holders or most important actors are, and so political scientists also have recourse to what is called "reputational analysis"; that is, asking well-informed individuals whom they perceive to be the most influential actors. In this study, I employed both approaches and found that at times there was/is considerable overlap, and that at other times, more powerful figures aren't occupying the most important posts, such as committee chairmanships.

The following chart shows which individuals held the two key posts, i.e., were formal holders of power, on the House's foreign affairs committee from the 103rd Congress (1993–95) until the 112th Congress (2011–2013).

HOUSE COMMITTEE ON INTERNATIONAL RELATIONS (HIRC)
HOUSE FOREIGN AFFAIRS COMMITTEE (HFAC)

Congress	Year	Chair	Ranking Member
103rd Full	1993–95	Hamilton, D-IN	Gilman, R-NY
103rd EurME		Hamilton, D-NY	Gilman
104th Full	'95–'97	Gilman	Hamilton
104th EurME		Burton, R-IN	Torricelli, D-NJ
105th Full	'97–'99	Gilman	Hamilton
105th WHemi		Gallegly, R-CA	Ackerman, D-NY
106th Full	'99–'01	Gilman	Gejdenson, D-CT
106th WHemi		Gallegly	Ackerman
107th Full	'01–'03	Hyde, R-IL	Lantos, D-CA
107th MESA		Gilman	Ackerman
108th Full	'03–'05	Hyde	Lantos, D-CA
108th MECA		Ros-Lehtinen, R-FL	Ackerman
109th Full	'05–'07	Hyde	Lantos
109th MECA		Ros-Lehtinen	Ackerman
110th Full	'07–'09	Lantos	Ros-Lehtinen
		Berman, D-CA	Ros-Lehtinen
110th MECA		Berman	Pence, R-IN
		Ackerman	Pence
111th Full	'09–'11	Berman	Ros-Lehtinen
111th MECA		Ackerman	Burton, R-IN
112th Full	'11–'13	Ros-Lehtinen	Berman
112th MESA		Chabot, R-OH	Ackerman

EurME = Europe and Middle East; WHemi = Western Hemisphere; MESA = Middle East and South Asia; and MECA = Middle East and Central Asia

When I asked who the most influential actors on Middle East matters were on HIRC in the mid-2000s, knowledgeable House staffers from both parties gave the following names. For the Republicans, HIRC Chairman Henry Hyde, and Middle East and Central Asia subcommittee chairwoman Ileana Ros-Lehtinen were cited most often. Other, noteworthy Republicans included Chris Smith (NJ), Dan Burton (IN), Steve Chabot (OH), Darrell Issa (CA), Dana

Rohrbacher (CA), Ron Paul (TX), Tom Tancredo (CO), Joseph Pitts (PA), Mike Pence (IN), and Peter King (NY). Again, Hyde and Ros-Lehtinen were deemed the most influential of this group. Hyde was almost but not completely lacking in criticism of Israeli government policies; Ros-Lehtinen is among the "dark blue" supporters of Israel. More details on both of them are presented below.

Among the Democrats serving on HIRC, Ranking Member Tom Lantos (CA), Gary Ackerman (NY), and Howard Berman (CA) were seen as having the most clout. Others cited by staffers included Eliot Engel (NY), Robert Menendez (NJ), Sherrod Brown (OH), Brad Sherman (CA), Robert Wexler (FL), Joseph Crowley (NY), Earl Blumenauer (OR), Shelley Berkley (NV), Adam Schiff (CA), Barbara Lee (CA), and Betty McCollum (MN).

There is no rocket science behind the several, nonetheless necessary, observations that need be made here: (1) The preponderance of influential HIRC actors are from East and West coast states, many of which have a large number of Jewish American constituents; (2) Many of the Republicans are evangelical or other religiously motivated people: Burton, Tancredo, Pitts, and Pence; (3) Many of the Democrats are Jewish American House members with "light blue" (Ackerman, Berman, Schiff, Wexler) and "dark blue" (Lantos, Engel, Berkley, Sherman) orientations; (4) Thee is only one person of Arab heritage—Issa; (5) A few of the Democrats are progressives, namely Blumenauer, Lee, and McCollum.

In essence, for many years, the House's foreign affairs committee has been "stacked" with and dominated by staunchly pro-Israel House members—people with a commitment to Israel much more intense than the pro-Israeli orientations of Americans in general, of many Jewish Americans, and of most American House members as well. At the full committee level, one has to return to the years of Chairman Lee Hamilton (chairmanship 1993–1995) to find a chairperson who was considered evenhanded. His successors Benjamin Gilman (1995–2001), Henry Hyde (2001–2007), Tom Lantos (2007–2008), Howard Berman (2008–2011), and Ileana Ros-Lehtinen (2011–2012) all exhibited, or continue to show, staunchly pro-Israeli orientations. They were all at least "light blue"—Gilman, Hyde, and Berman—if not "dark blue"—Lantos and Ros-Lehtinen—in their orientation and management of the full committee's affairs. Hyde, a conservative Catholic, had his moments of tension with right wing Israeli governments over the construction of the West Bank security wall because it cut through areas that negatively affected Christian Palestinians' as well as others' lives and livelihoods, but he otherwise remained a strong supporter of Israeli government policies, including those of right wing Israeli governments. In 2011–12, with "dark blue" Ros-Lehtinen in charge, the committee was even more firmly predisposed to abet the very right wing Israeli government of PM Benjamin Netanyahu.

Ed Royce (R-CA) became the HFAC committee chairman in 2013 after Ros-Lehtinen had to step down due to service limits. Jennifer Rubin interviewed Royce shortly after he assumed his post and was able to shed light on Royce's orientation.[168] Royce began the interview by noting that his keen interest in world affairs derived in part from his father's World War II participation, including the liberation of Dachau; and Rubin later noted that "The revelations of the Holocaust's horrors had a 'significant impact' on the way Royce views the world and the critical role of American power."[169] In the same interview, Royce spoke boldly of beefing up efforts to pressure Iran to abandon its nuclear weapons program to aid our Israeli ally, and complimented his predecessor Rep. Ros-Lehtinen for her great work. With regard to the role Congress could play in shaping Mideast policy, Rubin noted:

> While the executive has great authority on foreign policy, Congress controls the purse strings. He [Royce] intends to pursue what he calls "conditionality." He explains, "One piece of legislation was the anti-incitement [bill] that I and [Rep.] Howard Berman tried to pass to tie aid to the Palestinian Authority to a set of criteria to require the end of [terrorist] incitement." He points to TV and textbooks that still perpetuate virulent anti-Semitism and call for Israel's destruction. "The attempt is to create leverage to move behavior," he explains. That should carry over to other countries, he explains, noting he is meeting later in the day with a group of Egyptians who are gravely concerned about the turn in the Morsi regime.[170]

Interestingly, a veteran staffer with a critical eye saw Royce as "not having much interest in this neck of the woods [the Middle East] because his favorite issues are East Asia, trade, sub-Saharan Africa, and terrorism." The staffer added, "He's considered a 'safe' chair from right wing pro-Israel forces because he's inclined to take his cues from [Republican] party leaders like

Reps. Cantor and Boehner." In brief, Royce appeared most likely to toe the line drawn by Rep. Ros-Lehtinen.

The same "light blue" to "dark blue" mix has been in place among full committee Ranking Members (RM) over time, as well, at least from 1999 until now. Hamilton, obviously no enemy of Israeli interests, was RM from 1995–1999; he was followed in that post by Gejdenson, Lantos, Ros-Lehtinen, Berman, and Engel. Gejdenson was born in a WWII Displaced Persons camp in Germany in 1948, and his family moved to the US. Interestingly, this man, who remained totally committed to Israel's welfare throughout his entire life, was deemed too friendly to pro-peace, pro-Labor forces in Israel and therefore as harboring animus toward Israel's more hard-line, right wing, pro-Likud elements. His disposition reportedly ruffled AIPAC officials' feathers, and they contributed to his 2000 electoral defeat. Anyway, since early 2001, the full committee's RM has been "dark blue" in orientation with the exception of Rep. Berman, and needless to say Berman's calling was simply one shade lighter. For all his experience and relative moderation, Rep. Berman always had Israel's "back," as evidenced by the successful resolution he sponsored in January 2009 that offered Israel nearly unanimous congressional support for its aforementioned Gaza War clubbing of Palestinians in the Gaza Strip. (The Palestinian to Israeli death ratio was well over 100, and roughly one-third of the Palestinians killed were children.)

Similarly, the key House foreign affairs subcommittee—first named "Europe and the Middle East" and later "the Middle East and South Asia"— has long been dominated by individuals whose commitment to Israel ranges from strongly supportive to unquestioning. And the level of commitment has remained unwavering regardless of the policies implemented by successive Israeli governments, including the mostly hard right wing governments of the past thirteen years. Again, one would have to return to the years when Lee Hamilton chaired the subcommittee, 1977–1994, to find a greater measure of balance coming from the chairperson. Gilman ("light blue") effectively chaired both the full and subcommittee slots as well from 1995–2001, when the Republicans' own three-term limit forced him to bequeath the full committee chairmanship to Henry Hyde.

Since the 105th Congress (1997–99), Gary Ackerman ("light blue") has served as RM of the Middle East subcommittee for all but four years, during the 110th and 111th Congresses, when he stepped into the subcommittee's chairmanship. He was succeeded in the subcommittee chairmanship by Ros-Lehtinen ("dark blue") for the 108th and 109th Congresses, and following the two terms served by his successor Ackerman the subcommittee chairmanship reverted to Republican control under Steve Chabot of Ohio. One may also note that while Ackerman was chairing the subcommittee, the RMs for the 110th and 111th Congresses were respectively Mike Pence and Dan Burton. Both are self-described "born again" Christians, for whom the veneration and protection of Israel takes on a special spiritual calling. Both can be placed in the "dark blue" camp.

In sum, the chairs and RMs of HIRC and HFAC, as well as of the relevant Middle East subcommittee, have been held for many years by either Jewish Americans or Christians whose ethno-religious backgrounds shape their worldviews in a pronounced manner. The only slight outlier here may be Ros-Lehtinen, the Irving Moskowitz–funded Republican with an ironclad commitment to right wing pro-Israel positions. Using my slightly different formula, the House full committee's chairmanship has been firmly controlled by "light" and "dark" blue figures from 1995 to the present, and the same is true of the full committee's RM slot from 1999 until the present. As for the relevant subcommittee, the same story holds for its chairmanship from at least 2001 until the present and its RM from at least 1997 until the present. In 2013, the subcommittee's RM went to a leading "dark blue" figure: Eliot Engel.

In consequence, as a staffer working for a "dark blue" HIRC member assessed the committee's disposition in 2006, "It's unanimously pro-Israel." The staffer added, "There are no Jewish Republicans on the committee, but all Jewish Democrats on the committee are a strong pro-Israel group."

Another committee staffer in 2006 noted a stark change in the modus operandi of the committee protagonists. "Mr. Hyde is not Mr. Gilman. Things are very different now. Mr. Gilman was principled. He was a nice old man; he cared. He was very supportive of things normal people would support. But it's so extreme now. It's as if all the pain and suffering of the Palestinians is their own fault. Members like Engel, Sherman, and Ros-Lehtinen all take such extreme positions."

Because most congresspersons have not seen membership on House foreign affairs as a plum position, competition for that committee is significantly lower than that for resource-rich and/or power-wielding committees. Therefore, the committee's lower status opens the door to individuals with strong personal and/or constituent-driven interest in particular aspects of foreign affairs; and no one need recuse oneself. These factors appear to play themselves out in stark fashion when it comes to subcommittee assignments.

House members are expected to serve on more than one committee, so foreign affairs may represent a secondary or tertiary choice for many, with their level of interest and time commitment to the committee's proceedings affected commensurately. Thus, a veteran staffer interviewed in summer 2013, acutely interested in Mideast affairs, failed to recognize the names of the "bottom half" of HFAC's members. "I think they're almost all new," the staffer said. "The turnover among HFAC members shows there's less interest; it shows how low priority this committee has become. If your committee can't get out an authorizing bill, you're making no impact."

Many staffers were even more disparaging in their evaluations of some HFAC members' foreign affairs acumen. Here are three quick examples: "On HFAC, you'll find a lot of people who sound like Sarah Palin did in Katie Couric's interview"; "Many members on HFAC don't even know there are Palestinian Christians"; "We had a House rep, I won't name him, on a trip to Gaza; he had no idea about security issues, Israel's blockade, etc. He didn't know anything at all."

Because many members serving on this committee are not well versed in Middle East history and politics, they depend heavily on staffers or colleagues to equip them with information. In my opinion, this renders all the more pertinent an observation shared with me by a former HIRC committee staffer who focused on Middle East issues. "In personal offices, look at the full HIRC members' staffs and probably 80 percent of them have worked at AIPAC or have a very tight relationship with AIPAC," the staffer said. "Also, people [staffers] go from Congress to AIPAC or ZOA. For example, Matt Mandel, who worked for [Rep.] Engel, is now at AIPAC."

Composition of the HIRC Subcommittee on the Middle East and Central (later South) Asia; and the State of Play

A younger staffer, helping walk me through the legislative process, noted, "Any piece of legislation goes through the subcommittee, the committee, then to the floor. On the floor, it's very unlikely for there to be 'open rules' because then anyone could introduce an amendment. Pretty much everything that comes up [to the floor] has either gone through the subcommittee and the committee, so they and they alone [members of those committees] have had the chance to work it up, and most items are long-standing policy, like the Iran Freedom markup; so there's little that appears that is open to floor debate. During markups, some sessions are open, you can submit amendments, etc., but much depends on what the Rules committee [Rules and Administration] will allow you to do. The House operates on its own rules. Everything is pretty planned. Any amendment that finally 'gets in' and is debated on the floor has to go through the 'rules process' and people on the Rules committee have a majority partisan status and bias."

This comment highlights the significance of committee and subcommittee memberships and whatever predispositions exist therein, as well as the ability of leadership on the Rules committee to play an interventionist role. It opens the door to a "tyranny of the majority," or, perhaps more accurately, "a tyranny by the majority's leaders."[171]

For many years, Middle East matters were covered under a subcommittee entitled Europe and the Middle East, or the Western Hemisphere. In 2001, when Henry Hyde (R-IL) replaced Ben Gilman (R-NY) as chairman of HIRC in the 107th Congress, Hyde created a Middle East subcommittee—Middle East and South Asia—with Gilman in mind. How so? Because Gilman was described by veteran staffers as "not wanting any competition in this issue area, and Mr. Hyde's creation of the new committee was more a function of trying to satisfy the 'needs' of five or so of the most powerful members on the full committee." When Gilman lost in 2002, Hyde shifted the structure of the committee—its title changed to Middle East and Central Asia—and Ileana Ros-Lehtinen (R-FL) stepped in as the subcommittee's chairperson. These chairpersons, in turn, are powerfully positioned to steer the legislative process. As a veteran, high-ranking Democratic staffer described it: "With the drafting of legislation, there's a fair amount of competition among members; many want to be the first out of the gate on issues. There is a partisan slant to this stuff; Republicans are a bit slow to take up Democrats' initiatives unless it's a nonbinding resolution. This [2006] is an election year, so people are looking for angles to appeal to the Jewish community. Also, if we can take a jab at the president [Bush] or embarrass the Republican majority, we'll do it. All of this is in play all the time, and it only becomes accentuated during an election year." In short, new resolutions and bills are not taken simply on their merits; partisan perceptions and calculations are shaping views of legislation from the get-go.

With these factors in mind, let's look at the composition of the HIRC Mideast subcommittee's membership. During my initial wave of interviews in 2005–2006, on the Majority side there were ten individuals, led by Ileana Ros-Lehtinen (FL-9th term). She was backed by Steve Chabot (OH- 6th term; Thaddeus McCotter (MI-2nd term); John Boozman (AR-3rd term); Connie Mack (FL-1st term); Jeff Fortenberry (NE-1st term); Jo Ann Davis (VA-3rd term); Mike Pence (IN-3rd term); Katherine Harris (FL-2nd term); and Darrell Issa (CA-3rd term). Note that with the exception of the chairperson and vice chairman, all the other subcommittee members were only serving, at most, in a third term. That means all had fewer than five years of experience on the job.

The foreign policy orientations of the Majority's subcommittee members deserve special consideration. As noted earlier, at the head of the table in 2005–2006 sat Rep. Ros-Lehtinen. In terms of potentially relevant family history, her maternal grandparents were Sephardic Jews of Turkish background who had taken up residence in Cuba and been active in Cuban politics. As a young girl, Ros-Lehtinen, along with other members of her family, fled Castro's Cuba; thus she acquired firsthand experience with some of the ordeals of political oppression and exile. But what precisely motivated her to adopt a stridently right wing pro-Israel position was unclear to many. On the surface, her childhood experience might just as easily have caused her to be more empathetic with Palestinians in light of their own tragic history of dispossession. That said, it makes sense from a global historical vantage point that she acquired a conservative, pro-democracy, antisocialist and anticommunist perspective early on in life. And due to many PLO-affiliated groups' assistance from the Soviet Union and the socialist/communist world, her distaste for the longtime, dominant PLO would flow naturally from this worldview.

Ros-Lehtinen's political orientation has been discussed prior, but I'll add one observation. Some believe Ros-Lehtinen's political orientation to be of a pragmatic nature. A House staffer said, "Yes, Ros-Lehtinen is a leader on many of these issues. She's motivated by her desire to be chair of the full committee when Hyde steps down, so she plays to this issue." Voicing a similar sentiment, a highly knowledgeable staffer, who had worked for the Republicans said, "There are many incredibly rich Jews in her district. Many are

Democrats, but others are conservative on Israel, like her big donor, Irving Moskowitz. I think she calculates that if she's on their side, they won't put up a candidate against her."

It's worth repeating, as noted here and detailed earlier, Rep. Ros-Lehtinen has been very well taken care of by right wing pro-Israel campaign contributors. But whatever the explanation, Ms. Ros-Lehtinen chose to identify herself with the Israelis as political underdogs and valuable allies and has become one of the most ardent pro-Israel hawks in the House. She takes, as one staffer said, "a militantly pro-Israel position." As will be amply demonstrated below, she has used her considerable power to sponsor House resolutions and bills that right wingers would consider unfailingly beneficial to the interests of Israel.

Next, Rep. Chabot, despite his greater seniority, in the mid-2000s, was not a focus of people on the Hill in the context of Middle East matters. He certainly was not considered a "go-to" guy on this issue in that time frame, although there were indications that he was acquiring greater knowledge of Middle East issues and becoming better acquainted with its major players through trips to the region. As one staffer noted in 2006, "He's traveled widely; met all the players. He had only traveled to Europe before Congress. He and [Rep.] Wexler just came back from Egypt—January 2005."

One half decade later, as will be discussed, Chabot was chairing this same subcommittee, and Ros-Lehtinen had become the chairwoman of the full committee. Chabot has never posed any problems for Israel's right wing governments.

Mr. Pence, a relative newcomer to the House and the Middle East subcommittee, was and remains well known for views heavily shaped by his deeply Christian values. One of a small group of Christian evangelicals holding morning prayer sessions in each other's offices, Pence could be counted upon to adopt strong right wing pro-Israeli positions anchored in his own religious beliefs. Jo Ann Davis, another Republican subcommittee member, held similar views. A veteran Democrat staffer, commenting on the power of evangelical voices among the republicans, stated in the mid-2000s that "the vast majority of members are not following these issues, [but] the Republicans would turn to Tom DeLay [R-TX; House Majority Leader], who was very active in foreign affairs. You could very much put him in the Armageddon camp; it frightens me and Gary [Ackerman]—they [evangelicals] love Israel for different reasons." The staffer continued:

"Mike Pence, too, is very active. He goes to Israel and he comes back and offers resolutions supporting the security fence, etc. You get some people whose religious views are determinative; for example, at a subcommittee meeting in 2004 with the room full of Arab ambassadors, when the discussion came around to the Arab-Israeli conflict, Jo Ann Davis (VA) declared, 'I support Israel because my Bible tells me so.' There was an audible gasp from the Arab guests. Her position resonates nicely with her evangelical constituents, the position comes easily to them, but again, they're not active like Pence."

Subcommittee members Katherine Harris (R-FL) and John Boozman (R-AR) were also attached to the evangelical camp. Boozman would be elected senator in 2010, much to AIPAC's approval.

Darrell Issa, the self-made millionaire of Lebanese Christian ancestry, was one of the House's self-identified "Gang of Four." That said, Issa was inclined to work with Chairman Hyde, but also with Democrats on the subcommittee, in his efforts to advance positions more sympathetic to Arab interests. And as a "hawkish" conservative Republican, he did not always see eye to eye with "dovish" congresspersons on Middle East issues.

Congressman Fortenberry, just in his first term, spent some time in Egypt during his years as a student but had not manifested any noticeably stronger sensitivity to Arab voices in his early years in Congress. Rep. McCotter was seen as ultra-conservative, a strong anticommunist crusader type, and very hard-line vis-à-vis Islamist parties like Hamas and Hizballah. On these bases, he developed a close, cooperative relationship with Ms. Ros-Lehtinen over time and was very supportive of her stridently pro-Israel positions.

On the Minority side of the HIRC Middle East subcommittee, there were eight individuals: Ranking Member, Gary Ackerman (NY-12th term), Howard Berman (CA-12th term), Eliot Engel (NY-9th term), Joseph Crowley (NY-4th term), Shelley Berkley (NV-4th term), Adam Schiff (CA-3rd term), Ben Chandler (KY-2nd term), and Dennis Cardoza (CA-2nd term). The Minority subcommittee membership reflects a number of interesting attributes. First, it has little in the way of geographic dispersion. Of its eight members, six are from either New York or California. Second, nearly all of these subcommittee members hail from districts with large Jewish American populations, a great number of whom are very vocal in their unbridled support for Israel. Third, most of these subcommittee members are known for their strong personal devotion to Israel, whether as a product of their own ethno-religious identity, strong political convictions, or both. And fourth, in contrast to the Majority subcommittee members, these Minority members, in general, were far more experienced in Congress and in this issue area.

While all of the Minority HIRC Mideast subcommittee members may be said to be strong supporters of Israel, at least seven of them held a particularly strong, self-professed attachment to that state. For example, a staffer described Ackerman as follows: "Ackerman is heavily influenced by his Jewish roots and upbringing. He comes to his views through a self-informed process; he goes to the region often. He came to his views not due to AIPAC but because he is culturally and institutionally a leader on these issues. He explains to other people what the picture is. Many Democrat members will approach him and ask him why he's opposed to Weiner or Berkley on a certain issue, for example. I place him a little left of center."

With regard to other figures, the same senior staffer noted:

> "If you want to get a feel for specific resolutions and bills, you should just look at things like SAA, or the bills on Saudi Arabia, and see who cosponsors them. Mr. Engel coauthorized the SAA. Engel follows his own instincts on Mideast and Israeli affairs. He was strongly supportive of the militantly pro-Israeli Ros-Lehtinen. Engel favors a two-state solution, but the devil is in the details. Engel sees Jerusalem as remaining the indivisible capital of Israel, for example, and he has supported the security fence. He felt Oslo [1993 Peace Accords] was the right idea, but that the particulars were not worked out properly. Weiner's position is driven by the Lubavitchers [Hassidic Jews] in Brooklyn Heights [New York], who believe the rebbe is coming. His position is very heavily constituent driven. Cantor is the only Republican Jew in the House. I don't know him well, but I think he's got more on his agenda than Israel. He's very ambitious. He comes from rural Virginia, so he has his evangelists there undoubtedly. We like to get his name on bills because he's a Republican big shot."

Because the Democrats' Steering Committee is ultimately responsible for making committee membership selections, it means that the Steering Committee has played its own role in creating this strong, pro-Israel lineup.[172] Interestingly, for example, I was told by well-informed staffer interlocutors that Dennis Cardoza was picked by the Democratic party's Steering Committee to block Cynthia McKinney's effort to be a leader on HIRC in the 109th Congress (2005–2006). As noted elsewhere, McKinney had raised the ire of Israel's supporters by strong pro-Palestinian statements, and she was successfully targeted by AIPAC for defeat in her electoral district in 2002. When her opponent decided to seek a Senate seat in 2004, McKinney ran again for office and won, and she requested HIRC membership upon her return to the House. This placed the Steering Committee, chaired by Nancy Pelosi, in a ticklish position.

Lest one wonder whether or not there are House members acting as best they can as "gatekeepers" to HIRC membership, the answer is "Yes." And a prime example is provided by McKinney's case. According to standard operating procedures among House Democrats, any person who leaves Congress due to electoral defeat and then comes back can reclaim his or her seniority. One staffer said this presented problems, noting that the party "leadership really struggled with this. One reason Rep. Cardoza is there [on HIRC] is because he was picked to block [McKinney's] candidacy. The House leader— Dennis Hastert—has been a poster boy for pro-Israel stuff, and Cardoza has signed all the ["Dear Colleague"] letters as hoped for. So Cardoza represented a sound, alternative choice. Insiders saw Cardoza's candidacy as designed to block McKinney."

The longevity of some individuals on HIRC/HFAC's Mideast subcommittee is noteworthy. In 2006, both Ackerman and Berman were each already in their twelfth terms, along with Engel, who was in his ninth term; all enjoyed a wealth of subcommittee experience. Of these three, Engel was widely viewed as among those most likely to initiate "Dear Colleague" letters, resolutions, or bills that were supportive of right wing US-Israeli interests, although Berkley had performed strongly in this capacity as well after her arrival in the House.

The presence of so many "pro-Israeli" elements on the subcommittee as a whole guaranteed them a minimum winning coalition. Typically, this factor has been of lesser relevance because so many other subcommittee members hold concordant pro-Israeli views; the subcommittee was one, according to many staffers, where there was a very strong sense of bipartisanship on issues relating to the A-I and I-P conflicts because of the overwhelmingly pro-Israeli sentiments of its members. Again, of all the subcommittee members, only Darrell Issa of California was commonly identified as someone who possessed and expressed greater sympathy for Arab and Palestinian perspectives, and of course even he did/does not espouse an anti-Israel position. Indeed, staffers said Issa sometimes voted for resolutions and bills that cut against certain Palestinian positions to undercut attempts to label him as too pro-Palestinian.

By the 112th Congress (2011–2012), Chabot was chairing the subcommittee, with Pence, Fortenberry, and Mack (FL-4th term) still in place. Mack, himself, as a senator then House member, has a long track record as a strong, even hawkish supporter of Israel. Fortenberry was showing signs of greater attentiveness to arguments by "two-state solution" advocates. New members with the Majority Republicans included: Joe Wilson (SC-6th term), Ann Marie Buerkle (NY-1st term), Renee Ellmers (NC-1st term), Dana Rohrbacher (CA-12th term), Donald Manzullo (IL-10th term), Michael McCaul (TX-4th term), Gus Bilirakis (FL- 3rd term), Tom Marino (PA-1st term), and Bob Turner (NY-1st term). Note how many were first-term representatives. All of them followed AIPAC's line.

The 112th's Democrat subcommittee members included stalwarts Ackerman at RM, as well as Dennis Cardoza and Ben Chandler, but old-guard figures like Engel, Crowley, Berkley, and Schiff were gone. Importantly, Engel remained on the full committee, as well as on Energy and Commerce. The others had moved on to "A" committees: Schiff had moved to Appropriations, Crowley and Berkley to Ways and Means. New members on the HFAC Middle East subcommittee included Gerald Connolly (VA-2nd term), Ted Deutch (FL-2nd term), Brian Higgins (NY-4th term), Allyson Schwartz (PA-4th term), Christopher Murphy (CT-3rd term), and William Keating (MA-1st term,). Deutch and Schwartz were strongly committed to conservative positions on Israel. Again, one should note the junior status of these members.

If one needs a clear example of the "mobilization of bias" theory in operation, one need look no further than HIRC/HFAC. For the umpteenth time, this committee is seen as a "no pork, no play" B-level committee; competition for committee membership is not strong. Yes, there is the occasional House member who finds this a dream committee, even though his or her constituents could not care less, but such people are few and far between. This greatly facilitates HIRC/HFAC committee membership for those with particularly strong self-motivational or constituency-driven agendas. Thus, when one examines its composition, and more specifically that of its Middle East subcommittee, one finds a very interesting state of affairs. To some, one can rest assured that the subcommittee is in safe hands; for others, the foxes are guarding the henhouse. An ardent, keen, external observer of what happened to HIRC over time has been Khalil Jahshan. As Mr. Jahshan noted, "They [pro-Israel forces] became intoxicated with their own power. There was a gradual move to stack the committees and take over chairmanships. They wouldn't have dared do this 25 years ago, but by the mid-2000s things were very different."

So what? Does the composition of the House Subcommittee on the Middle East and Central Asia and full Committee on International Relations memberships make any difference? In a word, yes; in three words, very much so. All bills are initially referred to relevant subcommittees. Thus, any bill that touches on foreign policy issues relating to IME conflicts is likely to be submitted to the Subcommittee on the Middle East and South Asia. Any other issues relating to that region are fair game for closer subcommittee scrutiny and initiatives as well. In either case, the subcommittee's work takes on its own importance in the legislative process because many of its members serve as major sources of information, cue providers, and reference points for House members in general, as well as primary initiators of "Dear Colleague" letters, resolutions, and bills. In fact, as one House staffer from a less interested office went so far as to state: "In our office, we would see it as disrespectful to the members on HFAC for us to initiate stuff."

Key HIRC/HFAC Staffers

A brief note on key staffers on HIRC/HFAC is in order. In general, HIRC/HFAC committee staffers are bright, intelligent, and hardworking. The Majority chief of staff and Minority staff director are typically older, more knowledgeable, and more experienced than House staffers in general, and they can be very influential.

In 2006, Hillel Weinberg was HIRC's Majority staff director. By the mid-2000s, he had been on HIRC for four years. Growing up, he had spent one year at Hebrew University in Jerusalem, but decided not to stay there. He attended Yale, where he studied mostly American government, earning an M.A. and a Ph.D. from that prestigious university. He then attended law school at the University of Virginia. His previous experience had come with the Committee on Europe and the Middle East (1985) under Rep. Gilman (R-NY). He learned of a permanent position with Sen. Rudy Boschwitz (I-R; MN) as foreign policy and budget staff director, worked there until Boschwitz lost in 1990, then did some work consulting for the State Department Human Rights Bureau during the years of Pres. George Bush, the elder. When Bush I lost, Weinberg worked as a tax counsel to Sen. Dave Durenberger (R-I; MN) until the latter retired due to a small scandal. Gilman brought Weinberg back to the committee before the November 1994 election. Gilman wanted to head the subcommittee, and Weinberg worked as an advisor on budget and staff oversight, picking up some Middle East-related assignments. When Gilman shifted to the Middle East subcommittee, Weinberg ran it for him.

Beginning with the 107th Congress, a Europe subcommittee and a separate Middle East subcommittee were created, and Weinberg worked for Gilman's Middle East subcommittee with two others from Gilman's staff. He also worked for Rep. Hyde on several regional issue areas and did Gilman's international affairs staff work. When Gilman retired, he went back to the full committee, with Ileana Ros-Lehtinen becoming chairwoman of the subcommittee. Weinberg was thus working for HIRC Chairman Hyde, with a supervisory role over the subcommittee on the Middle East. On the House side, this work involved the territory from Egypt to Iran.

The Minority staff director was Alan Makovsky. Makovsky had studied history at the University of Michigan and Princeton University, specializing in Turkish and Middle Eastern affairs. His scholarly pursuits included residences in Turkey, Israel, and Egypt. From 1983–94, he was a State Department official, serving in the Bureau of Intelligence and Research and working on Turkey and the Middle East. He worked for some years at the Washington Institute on Near East Policy (WINEP), and eventually was recruited to fill the Minority staff director slot. He remained in that position, or served as Majority chief of staff, until 2013.

In the mid-2000s, according to one staffer, HIRC work "was divided up by country and/or issue areas, such that there was a foreign aid guy, a public diplomacy guy, a 'drugs and thugs' staffer, and economic issues staffer, plus people who know China, Africa, and so forth." On the "country side" for the Middle East, Weinberg was the lead figure, backed up by several other staffers. Yleem Poblete, Rep. Ros-Lehtinen's staffer, was the Middle East subcommittee staff director.

One key staffer described the flow of information among majority staffers as "not terribly disciplined." The staffer added, "There are newspaper clips—as in internal messages from newspapers; some people have a hobby of doing this. Someone inside the administration sends me articles, and I get hundreds of emails." Top staffers guided information-gathering efforts, including soliciting expert testimony for briefings and hearings. For example, one such staffer said, "We're taking a big look at foreign aid right now. [Weinberg] has called for a GAO study on Egypt through the chairman, and is inviting in expert testimony." The same staffer noted, providing some insight to inner workings, "It's not so easy to work out expert testimony on some countries, like Egypt, for example. There's an article in the *Christian Science Monitor* regarding Egyptian aid; Ned Walker [well-known US diplomat] quoted it, so I called him. I need to go to former officials to get more critical commentary. As regards think tanks, we shop locally for the most part because of the simplicity. You do get the same old people testifying on issues because of this; for example, Matt Levitt of WINEP gets called a lot as an expert on terrorism."

The key staffers Weinberg and Makovsky were exemplary and emblematic in many regards. Both had impressive academic credentials and years of valuable experience and/or field research. Both also came from strongly pro-Israel backgrounds, anchored in their own Jewish ethno-religious identities and close cooperation with unflinchingly pro-Israeli individuals and institutions. A person working for the Majority staff, who approached matters from a different perspective, felt isolated and described the work environment as "hostile."

The Calling of Expert Witnesses and Hearings

Committee briefings and hearings are potentially of great value and significance. A briefing differs from a hearing in that a briefing is less formal and there is no official stenographer present as there is at a hearing. Both provide forums in which expert witnessed are called to offer testimony, thereby hopefully enlightening House members and staffers alike and providing the opportunity for additional debate and discussion. Thus, a potential, important task of the subcommittee chairperson—Ros-Lehtinen in 2005–2006; Steve Chabot in 2011–2012; and the RM Ackerman for both periods—is to engage staff members in soliciting individuals to provide expert witness testimony on panels designed to enlighten House members on the great regional issues of the day.

Hearings are set up by committee staff, with the chairperson and RM's staffers working somewhat collaboratively. If there are three expert witnesses being called to testify, then the chairperson's staffers will usually pick two, and the minority or ranking member's staffer(s) will be allowed to pick the third. Other committee members can go to the chairperson and call for a hearing on an issue if they wish, but they must secure the compliance of the chair. Wrangling occurs, therefore, both within and between Majority and Minority staff members of the subcommittee and full committees over the expert witnesses that are selected. It thus becomes instructive to see which individuals are called upon to educate House members in briefings and hearings, with an eye to remembering that the subcommittee's chairperson and RM play the dominant role in determining who is called upon to provide expert testimony and advice.

Under Chairwoman Ros-Lehtinen's watch at the subcommittee level (in the mid-2000s), the subcommittee either heard from an expert witness and/ or conducted a hearing roughly once every two weeks. (Names of the participants are printed in the *Congressional Record* and are readily available from the thomas.gov site.) In brief, individuals called upon to testify or provide expert witness testimony before the House during this time frame typically held strongly right wing pro-Israel backgrounds or were of a "light blue" pro-Israel orientation. Very few experts provided critical commentary on Israel's policies, and this during a period when Israel's government was dominated by hawkish, right wing elements, as it was again in the 2011–2012 time frame. Because House subcommittee briefings and hearings represent occasions for the political instruction and socialization of congressional members, the skewed nature of the witnesses meant that little to no opportunity was being provided for subcommittee members in general to hear from experts possessing alternative points of view.

This state of affairs sometimes yields its own ironic moments. This author was present on one occasion in the mid-2000s when an expert witness, Ilan Berman of the National Defense University, was trying to impress upon subcommittee members the need to adopt a more confrontational posture vis-à-vis Iran. During the Q&A, Rep. Howard Berman asked the expert Ilan Berman why it was necessary to move with such speed against the government of President Ahmadinejad. The scholar answered that, given Ahmadinejad's responsiveness to the needs of the poor, if he were allowed to stay in power for any length of time he might gain wider popular support, making it more difficult to dislodge him from power. Rep. Berman smilingly submitted the rhetorical rejoinder, "So in other words we should get rid of him before good governance sets in?"

When I visited the Hill in February 2011, HFAC had a briefing on the revolutionary upheaval in Egypt and Tunisia. The three witnesses included the neoconservative Elliott Abrams, WINEP's Rob Satloff, and Dr. Martin Kramer, a highly academically credentialed right wing Zionist. Again, the lineup of expert witnesses left almost no opportunity for committee members to hear important, alternative views. Several staffers indicated that Ros-Lehtinen's principal aide, Yleem Poblete, had to be assigned a large measure of responsibility for these selections, as well as for other briefings and hearings. Ros-Lehtinen's staff was described by many staffers as "dysfunctional because they can't talk to State or schedule meetings with various people without Yleem's permission."

The parade of largely likeminded witnesses, in and of itself, induces tunnel vision rather than a broadening of the ideational horizons of subcommittee members. Perhaps even more important, failure to use the subcommittee as a forum for congressional oversight and debate on executive branch policies during the mid-2000s left the subcommittee derelict in the eyes of many. This was perhaps most striking in the dearth of hearings held on the Iraq War. Many staffers were quick to note that bias commonly entered the picture regarding briefings and hearings during this time frame. "There are clear party biases in the selection of people for hearings, just as there are often clear, personal biases in the selection process for committee memberships as well," one staffer said. "Tom DeLay [Majority Leader] is a Christian Zionist; Tom Lantos is very pro-Israel. There's always a bias."

With Ros-Lehtinen chairing the subcommittee once again in 2013, it was expected that the same bias in expert witness selection would return in full effect. In one of the last interviews I conducted, an off-the-Hill observer said that "a spring 2013 hearing on Syria represented a pleasant aberration because it had witnesses with diverse viewpoints and was actually worth attending." In other words, for most briefings and hearings, most staffers felt that if the picture had changed at all it was for the worse.

THE STATE OF PLAY ON HIRC/HFAC: WHO PUSHES AND PASSES THE BILLS AND RESOLUTIONS?

Given the strong conservative, right wing pro-Israel bias extant at the sub-committee level, the possibility of more balanced policies emerging from it has been nil. Hypothetically, even if more serious debate had occurred regarding the Palestinians' legitimate rights or Arab states' grievances, once taken up by the full committee, these matters would run into a buzz saw of other strongly pro-Israel voices. In the mid-2000s, those voices included those of "dark blue" RM Lantos and a generally compliant Chairman Hyde. Again, Hyde was capable of some criticism of Israel over treatment of the Christian Palestinian community, but that seems to be where his sympathies ended, and he rarely took any forceful action to protect even that minority community's interests against Israeli government policy. Other conservative voices among the Republican majority on the full committee—people like Peter King, and evangelicals Dan Burton, Thomas Tancredo, and Katherine Harris—would join the chorus of Democrats to drown out minority dissent by the likes of Republicans Ron Paul and Darrell Issa and Democrats Earl Blumenauer and Betty McCollum. Less activist members simply espoused the full committee's majority consensus, as indicated by a staffer who stated, "My boss has no significant Jewish or Arab population. This means he's able to approach the conflict objectively, in a nonparochial manner. He believes strongly that Israel is a strong US ally, and that we have strong moral and ethical obligations to protect Israel as a democracy."

How did staffers perceive HIRC members in the mid-2000s? Here are some of the views that I harvested from my interviewees. To begin, one has a group of staffers, constituting a strong majority, who see things as satisfactory. Speaking in 2006, two veteran subcommittee staffers working for right wing pro-Israel members, told me:

> "There's a few bomb throwers on the committee. But people have so much respect for the Majority and Minority leaders—Hyde and Lantos. There are few contentious markups. Issues are such that people can work together. There's lots of mutual respect on the committee; it's probably one of the least contentious committees. It's a real bipartisan committee—HIRC. Hyde and Lantos set the tone from the top."

"Lantos and Hyde have worked remarkably well together to many people's surprise. [My boss] and Lantos's thinking is quite alike on International Relations issues, including the Middle East. You should just look at letters, resolutions, and bills and see who is cosponsoring each other's initiatives, who teams up. For example, if Hyde and Lantos team up, they'll get most congresspersons to go along with them."

Nonetheless, staffers with critical—even harshly critical and cynical views—were not hard to find. I heard the following from staffers.

"We've made more statements condemning the Palestinians Authority than anything else we've done. There's a sort of competition among HIRC members to sponsor legislations. No one wants to be saying they're against Israel. It's a suicidal thing to do. Why hang yourself supporting something you know is going to fail?"

"It's so Israeli right wing. Engel—with his aide Jason Steinbaum— they make off-the-wall comments. Brad Sherman's office, too. I think Engel's role in Congress is to be to the right of Likud. It springs from Engel's own convictions and that of his constituents. As regards Lantos, you should go to the HIRC website and look. Whether it's the full committee or the subcommittee—maybe it's not like 'kill the Arabs,' but . . . AIPAC is very powerful."

"MEMRI and WINEP—there's so much information. Every week they have briefings on the Hill. How are they set up? People get a call from AIPAC on whatever, saying they've got a guy who just did this study on Hizballah . . . MEMRI does one meeting every two months—they talk and show vile footage from the Arab media. Their presentations are always about how disgusting, etc., the Palestinians and the Arabs are. Staffers and HIRC people will all show up for these briefings."

As one veteran staffer, working for a "dark blue" House member in 2006, noted, the timing of the introduction of bills touching on Arab-Israeli and

Israeli-Iranian matters is noteworthy; the AIPAC annual conference is timed to correspond with the critical moments in the formulation of HIRC/HFAC, Appropriations, and other committees' deliberations. "If you want to get a sense of how things work, and who stands where, look at all Foreign Ops and foreign authorizing bills," the staffer said. "Look at aid to Egypt—is it military or foreign aid, and look at how people line up on this. Look at the Lantos amendment; look at the Berkley-Crowley amendment; look at how both tried to hamstring aid to Egypt. On the SAA—go back to the previous, 107th Congress; look at who signed and when. Look at the dates of the past AIPAC conferences. For every year, you'll note huge jumps signing on after the AIPAC meetings. It's all done on a scale that is unprecedented by anyone."

A POIGNANT EXAMPLE: PASSING HR 4681 IN 2006

In order to provide a blow-by-blow description of how a specific piece of I-P conflict-related legislation was passed in the House, I have chosen to focus on House Resolution (HR) 4681, passed in 2006. I've selected it because staffers pointed to it as one of the most important and more controversial pieces of legislation processed by the House at the time of my initial research effort. I also chose it because the language it contained, as will be seen, was strongly opposed by Pres. George W. Bush's administration.

In January 2006, Hamas's candidates scored a stunning, surprise victory in Palestinian Authority parliamentary elections. Officially designated a "terrorist" entity by the US and other governments, Hamas would be coming to power in the PA via democratic elections. How were members of Congress to respond?

HR 4681—the Palestinian Anti-Terrorism Act of 2006—was initiated by Rep. Ileana Ros-Lehtinen in response to Hamas's victory. Introduced in the House on February 1, 2006, backed by AIPAC, and enjoying heavy bipartisan support, it acquired 294 cosponsors. Once placed in the House hopper, the House leadership (the Speaker's people) sent it to several House committees, including HIRC. HIRC's full committee's leadership referred it to the Subcommittee for Middle East and South Asian Affairs. Again, Rep. Hyde was then chairman of the full committee; Rep. Lantos was RM. On the subcommittee, Rep. Ros-Lehtinen was chair; Rep. Ackerman was RM. I was fortunate to have been on the Hill conducting interviews before and after the vote on HR 4681 was taken. Therefore, I can offer a sample of staffers' views of how they and their bosses looked at this bill and how they responded to external interests, from "Dear Colleague" letters, through HIRC, to the floor debate.

To begin, as a staffer said, "[T]here were dueling 'Dear Colleague' letters over HR 4681: anti-4681 letters by Blumenauer, LaHood, and Capps, plus one or two others; versus pro-4681 letters by Waxman, Lantos, Ackerman, and others. Also, APN and other lobby shops, entered the fray, disputing AIPAC's facts over 4681." The Ros-Lehtinen bill, backed by AIPAC, gained rapid traction and attracted numerous cosponsors, as seen. Here's how two AIPAC-leaning offices reacted. Note, as the passages are read, with whom the staffers conferred, or did not consult.

> "We just recently signed on to the Ros-Lehtinen bill. AIPAC itself brought this bill to our attention via a phone call. 'Take a look at it, please,' they asked. I read it, and researched it; I called my IDF friend and had a long conversation about Hamas and Israeli public opinion. Me, personally, I see a lot of negative repercussions from the bill, but it fits the congressman's past and present position and he signed on. Unfortunately, in this job in Congress, people want to see you do something—just take action. We also listen to others. Overall, [the boss] thinks it's important to back the Israel-US relationship. He's supporting the Ros-Lehtinen stuff on Hamas because he sees this as pro-peace. Brit Tzedek and IPF are not in favor of pushing this legislation because they think it will punish the wrong people. The boss thinks it will just punish Hamas, which rejects the peace arrangements and is a terrorist organization."

> "I think we got on HR 4681 due to a conversation with the Baltimore AIPAC guy. You get so many emails, 'Dear Colleague' letters, you have to have a way to sift through that. So we'll ask, 'What does Howard [the AIPAC guy back home] think about it?' Whether it's the Saudi bill, the Hamas bill, whatever. Lobbyists only get so many asks—they know if they get you to go out on a limb for them . . ."

It's important to note that the introduction of this legislation coincided with AIPAC's huge, annual meeting, so more than just organizing phone calls AIPAC had hundreds, perhaps even thousands, of members fanned out across Capitol Hill to push for HR 4681. Thus, as a conservative Republican's staffer noted:

> "During the big AIPAC convention, a guy named Rob came in to see us. Iran and funding for the PA were the two big issues. We had a very friendly exchange—'good to see you again this year,' etc. He said: 'Thanks, I've noticed that you're on board about Iran, but why aren't you cosponsoring the Hamas Ros-Lehtinen bill [HR 4681]?' I said: 'We see no real reason or need to do so; you know where our sympathies are; there's nothing to worry about.' Meanwhile, regarding Arab groups, etc., we got press releases from CAIR, but they didn't have any function I know of. [Did you hear from other pro-Arab or pro-Palestinian groups?] None that I can think of, or to the extent that I'd remember their names. I find this strange, actually, but maybe it's because we're from a small state."

One staffer felt morally conflicted by his Republican boss's intention to back 4681. "US aid was provided before the Hamas election," he said. "Now what? I believed Hamas might win because they provide the social services. We get AIPAC visits; phone calls regarding Hamas. I have to talk to the boss about our position. I pointed out that this position is antithetical to Bush's position. Yes, we're not too happy with Bush's position overall, but there's a need for humanitarian aid. They [AIPAC] said you can't legitimize a government that calls for 'our death and destruction.' I told them, you need to talk. A 'Talk with the IRA'–type approach to this is necessary."

A staffer working for a Democrat, who would vote yes, held similar sentiments. The staffer said, "We're trying to make AIPAC happier, but only after their dragging us to agreement or our signing on. The congressman is very supportive of their concerns, but the question is, does the legislation make sense? What's the issue? Israel's survival? Peace? I think it's only a matter of time before we have to succumb to the Hamas-related legislation. We're holding off; it doesn't seem like it is good legislation. AIPAC people came in to the office two weeks ago during their big conference, but there is no groundswell of support for their views back home."

In contrast, staunch opponents of the bill, albeit few in number, expressed serious reservations. A staffer said of Rep. Price, "When we saw the bill [4681] coming up on the calendar and we told him it would cut most aid, he found it too extreme and he asked for more information and his opinion crystallized. He collaborated with Capps, and circulated two 'Dear Colleague' letters." Another staffer for a Hispanic House member shared his doubts about 4681, stating, "Members who had anti-4681 views thought the bill was superfluous, designed more to make an accentuated point of view on these issues. The president could already freeze aid to Palestinians, block UN money, etc. The president already had the power he needed, so the administration said it didn't need it [4681]."

In one office commonly sympathetic to Palestinians grievances, the boss and his staffers met with AIPAC representatives, but the encounter left them with a bad taste in their mouths. According to a staffer, "AIPAC people also came in to meet with the congressman to lobby 4681. There were six of them, two from the district. The youngest was a high school student. The congressman was clear he wouldn't change his mind—he opposed their recommendations—he just told them, 'Thank you for your time.' It seems as if more junior people had been sent. The high school student spoke to the congressman in a condescending tone."

Meanwhile, many staffers looked for cues from leadership and HIRC committee staffers, in whom great trust is placed. A staffer said, "Work gets done by the committees and their professional staffs. They're very experienced; they do all the heavy lifting. If a HIRC member calls, for example, Ros-Lehtinen, then we'll take a look at it. We'll also discuss what [Rep.] Rohrbacher thinks. If [Rep.] Ron Paul sends a letter, we'll throw it in the trash. He's a zealot."

Noteworthy was that many who deferred to leadership on the committee willfully accepted hawkish views. As one staffer said of Ros-Lehtinen, "We're often likely to agree with her hawkish view, and we backed her on 4681."

Members and staffers in these opposition circles mulled the consequences of opposing 4681, calculating the potential electoral backlash, as is discussed below.

THE HIRC SUBCOMMITTEE MARKUP ON HR 4681

"Dark blue" House members sprang into action to shape this legislation and leave their prints on the markup. A staffer for a "dark blue" member noted,

> "Regarding Ros-Lehtinen's [4681] bill, the problem is that Hamas is
> a terrorist organization. Most people agree that US taxpayer money

should not go to a Hamas-led government, but aid flows through many channels—UNRWA, CARE, ICRC—to the Palestinians. Everybody is on the same page—that bill [HR 4681] will get at least 400 votes, but the devil is in the details. And here is where constituent concern, etc., kind of ended. The question arises: How to deal with the issue of humanitarian aid to the Palestinians? Can we all agree we don't want a crisis there? So Shelley Berkley put forward an amendment to strike the section on blocking aid to NGOs. The new wording stated that the Bush administration, after consultation with Congress, can provide aid to the Palestinians. Then Sherman tried to modify this. In the end, both proposals were rejected. Interest groups are very influential in crafting legislation, but at markups some significant changes can occur. On this bill, Ros-Lehtinen probably worked very closely with AIPAC, I would assume."

Notably, the HIRC subcommittee "markup" debate over HR 4681 was almost entirely between "dark" and "light" blue supporters of Israel. The only meaningful exception came in comments from Mr. Issa, and his intervention was made in a very delicate way. So, in spring 2006, HR 4681 sailed through the committee vote, opposed by only two members, one of whom was Betty McCollum (D-MN). But even this subcommittee vote created an opportunity for another "demonstration effect." For having the temerity to buck AIPAC and vote no on 4681, McCollum's office received a menacing phone call from an AIPAC official, in which she was accused of abetting "terrorists." By coincidence, I was in the House congressional office buildings within 24 hours of these events unfolding, so I dropped by McCollum's office to seek an interview with her staffer. McCollum was standing in the office lobby. She was visibly shaken; she looked like a deer caught in the headlights. But McCollum did not take the AIPAC call lying down; instead, she went on the offensive, taking her story to the broader public and firing back at AIPACs high command. She also later voted with 36 others against the measure when it came up for the full floor vote.

This incident inspired the following, critical expose by Richard Silverstein. "Now the *Forward* provides us with a perfect example of Aipac's worst 'take no prisoners' style," Silverstein wrote. "The fact that it [HR 4681] wasn't a unanimous vote didn't sit well with the bullies at Aipac. So they decided to make an example of Rep. Betty McCollum (D, MN) . . . Amy Rotenberg, an active member of the organization from Minneapolis, called McCollum's chief of staff, Bill Harper. Aipac sources said that the purpose of the April 7 call was to express disappointment over the congresswoman's vote against the bill. According to Harper, Rotenberg said that 'on behalf of herself, the Jewish community, Aipac, and the voters of the Fourth District, Congresswoman McCollum's support for terrorists will not be tolerated.'"[173]

As noted above, McCollum struck back. She sent a letter to Howard Kohr, AIPAC's executive director, demanding a formal, written apology, and barring AIPAC reps from setting foot in her office until she received one. To mend fences, Rep. Ackerman was brought in to arrange a meeting between Kohr and McCollum. As Silverstein wrote, "It should be noted that Ackerman is usually a sure-vote for Aipac and indeed he supported HR 4681. But most pointedly, he objected strongly to the tactics used against his colleague calling them: 'reminiscent of the Taliban.' It sounds like . . . McCollum caved to Aipac (though one can hardly know what went on in the meeting) . . . But I still applaud her for getting pissed as hell at this brutish behavior that is so common for the pro-Israel group."[174]

When I returned to Washington, D.C., for another round of interviews in spring 2012, I inquired about Rep. McCollum's level of engagement on Mideast issues. The answer I received from numerous on and off the Hill sources was that it had declined somewhat. She may have been adopting a lower profile running in to the 2012 electoral cycle, but the perception in some circles was that she had "learned her lesson" and had been behaving in a less obstreperous manner from the perspective of hard-core, right wing, pro-Israeli elements. That said, McCollum continued to show herself capable of opposing AIPAC-backed policies.

THE FLOOR "DEBATE" AND VOTE

One staffer who, along with his boss, opposed the bill went to great lengths to explain his pique over how the bill had been treated in terms of limiting floor debate. As he informed me, the Majority can limit debate in the House through the Rules Committee. A second way to limit debate is to consider the bill under suspension—this means no amendments are possible and debate is heavily curtailed. Such a bill requires a two-thirds majority to pass. The Majority leadership brings the bill to the floor in suspension, but then there are no amendments and there is very limited debate time.

As this staffer told me: "Look at the National Defense Authorization Act— over $400 billion was at stake—it was deeply scrutinized in the Senate; it got 200 to 300 amendments, and had 2 to 3 months' debate. Over here in the House, by contrast, there were only 20 amendments and one to two days of debate. Far fewer amendments are offered in the House today because it will be to no avail. People are not committed in the House to considering a bill like 4681 on its merits, versus bowing to outside pressure. 4681 is complete posturing and playing to narrow constituent interests."

The staffer added, "This legislation—4681—was shoved down our throats. It was originally on the calendar for 45 minutes of debate. This is a joke [such a short amount of time]. This will affect the lives of millions of people."

In the end, 4681 was brought to the House floor under a suspension of the rules on May 23. No amendments were possible. It received just three hours of floor debate. Despite appeals by nine House members to vote no—with many quoting APN talking points—the full floor vote on 4681 proceeded, creating its own stories. Both parties' leaders entered the fray, calling upon leadership elements to "whip" the members to vote for 4681; the Democrat leaders "whipped" their members to vote in favor of Republican Ros-Lehtinen's bill. One staffer commented on the political pragmatism that guided the Democratic leadership to get Democrats to vote in favor. "Pelosi and the leadership . . . didn't want to have Democrats voting against or not voting—they considered this low hanging fruit that needed to be plucked. They didn't want to show poorly compared to the R's on this. It could cost them support at election time; they saw great symbolic value in 4681, if not much on the merits." In other words, symbolic values and electoral considerations trumped the merits of legislation that would affect the livelihood of millions of Palestinians. And for some staffers, like this one, the "big issues" were left untouched.

> "The vote on 4681 was a no-brainer, but it begged questions on related matters. For example, we recently got a 'Dear Colleague' letter on Iran. It seems like Tel Aviv wants to have veto power over the US's Middle East policy. Matters can be a little bit frustrating. There seems to be an inevitable downward spiral that Israel is going through—they and their allies seem to be looking to us to pull them out of this. By building the wall and calling for a two-state solution,

the Israelis have put off the demographic problem maybe for a generation. But they could still be a minority in their own country by the end of this century. When they become a minority in their own country, well, look at what happened in South Africa. Sooner or later they'd have to prevent the Arab Israelis from voting, so how does the US react? How does Israel react?"

Meanwhile, progressives, and more forceful pushers of peace, had a different perspective. As noted earlier in this book, one staffer expressed the view that

"My boss's vote on 4681—he takes that underdog perspective and applies it to most things. He wouldn't want to be in a group of nine people voting against a terrorism bill, of course. On this one, it was helpful to have the IPF, APN, and the US Campaign material, as well as Mrs. Capps's statement—I thought, okay, we're good to oppose this. There's no fundamental anti-Israel position here, but people can and do make this difficult on purpose by playing the anti-Semite card; like Dershowitz's position versus Chomsky. People have been hit with that mud, and it's mud that sticks."

A staffer with a Hispanic House member, who had voted against the bill, was asked if there was any price to pay for the Nay vote on 4681. "The urban legend on that is Cynthia McKinney," he responded. "One of the peace groups told me there were other things going on in her case as well. Also, she was further out on a limb. But there is a fear of AIPAC as a powerful constituency. There's no real concern by us about a challenger being financed, but you certainly don't want to agitate them and be their enemy. It would look very bad to disparage Mr. Lantos given his personal story. This hangs over the debate, as well."

Regarding potential blowback, another veteran staffer said:

"His instincts are pro-Palestinian, pro-Arab. He recognizes it's the kind of thing that can get him in trouble. He recognizes the potential for trouble. He gave me a letter to the editor [of a home district newspaper] about his HR 4681 vote. The letter was from his opponent. Informal comments on this [his vote] have been made by friends, etc., back home. This is the first time it's coming up in a campaign. There are Jewish attorneys in [the home state] voicing expressions of concern; there's muttering about this. . . . Three to four years ago the Israeli consul general from L.A. was in [our home state] and gave a public speech to the principal Jewish congregation, and he really ripped my boss and this did get media coverage. Isn't this unethical behavior by an ambassador? It made my boss angry for a number of reasons and this faded, but . . . So there's always an awareness of a possible political blowback. Also, the [pro-Israel lobby's] lower level of organization in [our state] could change, and this might pose problems. But it's not what's in [the home state] that matters; it is fear of out of state funding that is the big concern. I'm not aware of specific cases elsewhere, but there's a generalized sense that this is dynamite—a 'toe the line on this' or else kind of thing."

Reflecting on how these factors affected his boss's perceptions, the same staffer added, "The boss describes it as a constant low-level muttering in the cloak room over this. Many [representatives] react by saying 'this is bullshit; it's not worth the fight.' He's still very supportive of Israel's right to exist and Israel's security. He always votes for the foreign aid bill to Israel; and he's very supportive of R&D with Israel like with the Arrow project; and he's had informal contacts with many Israelis, including Likudniks. But he can vote against AIPAC-sponsored bills. He thinks the US needs a more balanced policy that recognizes that Palestinians need their own state. We believe Israel is being unreasonably intransigent in a lot of instances."

Similarly, another staffer responded to my query about opposition to 4681 as follows:

"There is always a certain amount of fear. I personally haven't experienced AIPAC's power. Whenever you have a well-organized lobbying organization with email effectiveness, of course you have to consider and expect the consequences. So 'scared' would be too strong, but [the boss] was concerned. But he really felt the need to take a stand. He's gotten increasingly tired with AIPAC taking the hard line on things relating to Israel. Things come up every two months; we assume they're written by AIPAC; not that they're wrong, it's just that they overreach. Why is there a need to go so far beyond what reasonable people would support that it's just chest beating? So this 4681 was seen as an opportunity to strike back, take a stand."

Expanding on his comments to cover other issues, this same staffer also opined:

"We [the boss and I] think Mearsheimer and Walt make a simplistic argument about the power of the pro-Israel lobby . . . The strongest factor for most Americans is most Americans' socialization. They look at the Israelis and the Palestinians and say, 'Who looks the most like me?' Add to this the Christian fundamentalists and eschatologists who see Israel as a pawn on God's chessboard. These two factors represent a stronger source of support for Israel. Groups like AIPAC then focus this support like using a magnifying glass to turn it into a bright burning point. If AIPAC was so powerful like Mearsheimer and Walt say, the US would have a formal mutual defense pact with Israel like with Japan and others."

At least some progressive bosses and staffers were annoyed by fellow progressives who did not side with them. One staffer said, "Jewish members like Sander Levin [sic] and Barney Frank—they caught us off guard with their support for 4681."

This staffer's response also demonstrated just how arcane these issues can become with regard to congressional procedure, and milking those procedures to political advantage.

"The bill was placed on the suspension calendar—the Tuesday calendar—so it was voted on without amendments. There was a visa provision in the original version; also an item about Financial Services—stuff had been included that needed clearance from the IFI [International Financial Institution]. Sensenbrenner of the Judiciary Committee took the bill off suspension to mark it up and deal with the visa issue; they did this very quickly. I told [some people] that we should have jurisdiction on the IMF/World Bank money in the provisos because we have IFI jurisdiction. Rep. Frank said, 'Okay, let's talk.' Then we went to mark up the bill on the IFI and World Bank stuff. [We] negotiated with HIRC to waive our referral if they would remove the democracy governance provision, but they didn't want to do this. [We] said, 'Okay, then we'll call for a markup sometime; I don't know when.' So they relented in order to make sure the bill got to the floor [where they knew they'd win any vote]. Lantos agreed that the democracy governance bit shouldn't be there. So the issue will get sorted out in conference; and the Senate version [McConnell-Biden] is more palatable to us. It was in the IFI and the Bilateral Aid sections where the problems were. So it [democracy governance] was stricken from the IFI section of the bill, but remained on the bilateral side. This was where and how they relented. It will not, then, be likely to remain on the bilateral side either when it comes to conference [the conference committee]. So the language was put there by people who don't really want a Palestinian state because they're trying to establish conditions that can't be met. [Rep.] Frank actually played a very active, interesting role here behind the scenes. Again, this was done by telling or reminding Lantos that Egypt, Jordan, etc. weren't democracies either."

Perhaps the most ironic, amusing, and still somewhat revealing story relating to the vote went as follows: "[Congressman X] actually missed the vote [on 4681] this morning—he missed the vote because he was talking to the AIPAC guy. If we're not on the right place on this vote, people—our opponent—will take this single issue with him and play on it. AIPAC has a scorecard—you can look at the AIPAC website at election time—and they send it to their members. This is not a big deal for us, but it would be for targeted members. It is, nonetheless, important to us because we have a large Jewish constituency and we hear from them on a regular basis."

The vote on HR 4681 was lopsided, as one might have surmised by extrapolation from the huge number of its cosponsors and its strong backing by HIRC full and Middle East subcommittee leadership and members. The "Yeas" counted 361 (210 R's; 150 D's; 1 Independent); the "Nays" were 37 (31 D's; 6 R's). Nine members answered "Present," and 25 registered as "Not Voting." Keep in mind that the administration of Pres. George W. Bush and the State Department saw HR 4681 as superfluous, undesirable, and even counterproductive to overall US objectives. Yet 210 of Bush's fellow Republicans voted for it, and were joined by the overwhelming majority of House Democrats.

Additional analysis of the May 23, 2006, vote is instructive. Focusing on the 37 "Nay" votes, one discovers that at least 20 of those votes came from the Progressive Caucus of the Democrats. Reps like Neil Abercrombie, Earl Blumenauer, Lois Capps, Michael Capuano, Peter DeFazio, Lloyd Doggett, Sam Farr, Maurice Hinchey, Marcy Kaptur, Dennis Kucinich, Betty McCollum, Jim McGovern, Jim Moran, David Obey, David Price, and Jim McDermott stand out. Overlapping with these progressives were numerous minority House members, collectively representing 9 of the 37 Nay votes. There were six Congressional Black Caucus (CBC) members—John Conyers, Carolyn Kilpatrick, Barbara Lee, Cynthia McKinney, Gwen Moore, and Mel Watt—alongside three Congressional Hispanic Caucus (CHC) members— Xavier Becerra, Raul Grijalva, and Nydia Velazquez; all are Democrats. Four Republicans voted against the bill: Walter Jones, Jim Kolbe, Mac Thornberry, and Wayne Gilchrist. Three of the four members of the "Gang of Four" voted against it: Reps. Dingell, LaHood, and Rahall. And the libertarian Republican Ron Paul rounded out the 37 "nays." Of the nine who answered "Present," eight were CBC members and one was Hispanic; so all nine were minority members. Finally, of the 25 "Not Voting," standouts included "Gang of Four" member Darrel Issa and Patrick Kennedy; for Issa, this was a perfect example of his reluctance to stick his neck out on all of these votes to avoid the appearance of having truck with an Islamist extremist organization.

A BRIEF NOTE ON OTHER HIRC CONCERNS

The "main event" of the 2000s was the US invasion of Iraq in 2003. The "brainchild" of Bush's right wing pro-Israel, neocon advisers, the war would drag on beyond the end of the decade, incurring a huge cost in US "blood and treasure." But while US forces searched for Saddam Hussein's trove of WMD, the House, and HIRC leaders in particular, busied themselves with initiatives against other "terrorist states" in the region. Rep. Eliot Engel presented the Syrian Accountability Act (SAA) in April 2003, an act seeking to end Syria's large military presence in Lebanon, prevent Syria's alleged development of WMD, and block Syrian support for "terrorism." Engel's effort culminated in enactment of the Syrian Accountability and Lebanese Sovereignty Restoration Act, which became US law on December 12, 2003.

In the same time frame, plans for Iran were already being cooked up. These plans were brought forth on January 6, 2005, when HR 282, the Iran Freedom Support Act, was introduced by Rep. Ros-Lehtinen. The bill acquired 360 House cosponsors, but other House members were wary. As one high-ranking House staffer urged me to examine HR 282, and noted: "A lot of people on the right in Israel and in the American Jewish community are pushing, but the bill's a lot like the 1998 Iraq Liberation Act—funneling money to the INC [Iraqi National Congress]—so [my boss] is reluctant to sign on." The bill passed the House on April 26, 2006, by a vote of 397–21, but died in the Senate where, as staffers informed me, its opponents thought the bill stifled diplomacy and represented an effort to set the stage for war against Iran like the 1998 Iraq Liberation Act had for the 2003 war against Saddam Hussein's regime. Comparable bills had also been introduced against Iran in the 108th and 109th Congresses: HR 5193 and HR 6198, respectively. As regarded SAA and the bills on Iran, one seasoned staffer noted that

> "All knowledgeable persons saw these initiatives as inspired and backed by AIPAC and the Israeli government. As a former staffer for a key HIRC member said in 2006, 'Now there's no trust between the Democrats and the Pentagon because of what's happened in Iraq. Also, AIPAC was in bed with these guys, so one needs to be wary. A good portion of the Democrats feels this way. There's some angst among Democrats about AIPAC. And there's angst in AIPAC as well [because they think] we went to bed with the neocons, but now we're wondering how to get out of it. A war against Iran might only get ten Democrats to support it today.'"

HFAC: THE STATE OF PLAY IN 2011–2013

In the years between my 2005–2006 and 2011–13 research trips to Washington, D.C., several major events unfolded. One huge development was the December 2008–January 2009 Gaza War, launched by the IDF to end years of sporadic rocket fire upon southern Israel by Palestinians in the Gaza Strip and to destroy tunnels used for smuggling weapons into Gaza from Egypt's

Sinai Peninsula. During this Gaza War, some 1,163–1,417 Palestinians were killed, well over half of whom were civilians; thirteen Israelis were killed, four by friendly fire. The massive destruction of homes, schools, businesses, and infrastructure in the Gaza Strip, combined with enormous disparity in loss of lives, brought a torrent of international protest against Israel's actions. Members of the US House (and Senate) saw matters differently, and a resolution sponsored by Reps. Ros-Lehtinen and Berman, HR 34, "Recognizing Israel's right to defend itself against attacks from Gaza . . ." passed by a vote of 390 to 5, with 16 abstentions and 21 voting present. Those not voting "aye" found the resolution almost completely lopsided, providing no references to Israel's years of illegal settlement activity nor Palestinians' other legitimate grievances. When the United Nations' "Goldstone Report" was issued in September 2009, Rep. Berman led another effort—H.R. 867, backed by AIPAC—that won broad support in the House (344 "ayes" vs. 36 "nays"), condemning that report as biased against Israel and lacking in stronger criticism of Hamas. The "Goldstone Report" was approved in the UN General Assembly by a vote of 114 countries in favor, 18 opposed, and 44 abstentions. Beyond the US and Israel, those registering their opposition included Israel's traditional stalwart supporters in the United Nations: the Marshall Islands, Micronesia, Nauru, and Palau.

In May 2010, the Mavi Marmara, a humanitarian aid ship bringing aid to Gaza from Turkey but suspected by Israel of arms smuggling, was boarded by the IDF in international waters. Nine activists on board were killed. Both incidents sparked widespread international outrage against Israel's actions, and the latter brought a severe rupture in Turkey's relations with Israel. But the US Congress stood by Israel through these events and others, like the August 2010 Israel-Hizballah border clash. And in fact, during the 2011–2013 research time frame, the state of play in Congress, if anything, only hardened in its commitment to Israel. As one highly concerned House staffer said to me in February 2011, "The special interests have taken up residence here. There's not much going on; it's hardwired. You find the facts to suit the argument."

HFAC and its Middle East subcommittee were still heavily dominated by right wing pro-Israel elements. One staffer emphasized that some change in office capabilities and staff had been induced by the Tea Party's budget cuts. "Members' staffs have been cut by roughly 15 percent over the past three years," the staffer said "In January 2013, so many good people have left or been furloughed." Of even greater significance, pro-peace forces on and off the Hill bemoaned the 2011–2013 composition of HFAC's leadership, specifically targeting their handling of Mideast issues. "We're trying to get a room on the Hill right now—like a Foreign Affairs room—to offer an information session," one off-the-Hill activist noted in February 2011. "I've always been able to book a room without any problem, but now . . . Ros-Lehtinen's office is vetting everything and if they don't like the [lobby] group you can't even get a room."

With Rep. Ros-Lehtinen chairing HFAC in 2011–12, then with Engel as RM of the full committee and Ros-Lehtinen as chairwoman of the subcommittee from 2013 on, "dark blue" members held key posts in this time frame. But much attention was given to change produced by the 2013 departure of two "light blue" giants, Ackerman and Berman. A moderately progressive staffer commented on their departure, saying:

> "The loss of Reps. Ackerman and Berman represents a big blow to Middle East peace efforts. They were more sensible folks among the Jewish caucus; this creates a void within the Democrat caucus, too, that hasn't been filled. They had unimpeachable pro-Israel credentials, but were fair-minded. Sherman and Engel do not represent an upgrade. Back in 2003, when Tom DeLay was so powerful, I thought things couldn't get worse. Today, I look at those times and recognize that a certain level of bipartisanship existed then compared to today. Then, we could get bipartisan cosponsors on most anything, but now, even in Appropriations, things are very divided along partisan lines."

Important, pro-peace advocates off the Hill echoed this lament.

> "Losing Ackerman and Berman has decimated HFAC. Sure, they were both solidly pro-Israel types, but they were serious and could be constructive. Now HFAC is more than ever a home to grandstanding. Both in the House and Senate, filling the shoes of Ackerman, Berman, Kerry, and Lugar is not an easy thing to do. Look at almost all of the hearings that are held in the House. It's almost always just the pro-Israel regulars from WINEP, the Hudson

Institute, and AEI [American Enterprise Institute], of course, but it's gotten even worse over the past year [2012–13]. There were silly seasons and sessions before; now it's just pure silly. Only the sessions on Syria have been interesting."

It's useful to recall here that committee and subcommittee leaderships make a difference because so many other rank-and-file members are likely to take their cues from these individuals. Moreover, the leadership has large control over the legislation that emerges from an issue area.

Developments in the Middle East during 2011–13 had a definite impact on the House, and Congress in general. The 2011 revolutions of the Arab Spring, the protracted crisis in Syria, the "revocoupion" ousting Pres. Morsy in Egypt in 2013 all brought a mix of optimism, concern, and consternation. For example, the Arab Spring, late 2010–early 2011, caught the attention of US legislators, and a hearing was called by HFAC Chairwoman Ros-Lehtinen to ascertain its portents for the region and IME conflicts. This was the hearing I observed that featured the neocons Elliott Abrams and Dr. Martin Kramer, as well as WINEP's Rob Satloff. As a person who has spent over six years of his adult life living and conducting political research in Egypt, I found the session far from enlightening, and it was pathetic to observe the obsequious behavior exhibited by some House members in their exchanges with Mr. Abrams.

On balance, the monumental changes occurring in the Middle East and North Africa brought mostly confusion. As one observer stated, "The changes in the Middle East and North Africa have tempered Congress. They don't know what to do because they don't know what's going on. And also I think people are just tired of the Israel-Palestine conflict; they feel there's nothing they can do."

Perhaps the most noticeable change in terms of US policy focus had been a shift away from the A-I and I-P conflicts to the perceived threat to Israel from Iran and its primary Arab ally, Syria. In early summer 2013, prior to the "revocoupion" in Egypt, a staffer said, "Iran has been completely overshadowing anything else happening in the Middle East." Although immediate events were most determinative of this shift in focus, it represented a pitch delivered to the wheelhouse of new Majority leader, Eric Cantor of Virginia, a darling of neoconservatives. As a veteran staffer commented in summer 2013,

"Cantor has an outsized role on this [Iran] issue. Cantor has made a political calculation to use this as a 'wedge' issue, a partisan issue to make Obama look bad. And Ros-Lehtinen plays along, just throwing fire left and right and coming up with a whole series of the most inflammatory initiatives: move the US embassy to Jerusalem; cut aid to the Palestinian authority; cut aid to Egypt or condition aid to Morsy's government."

Spring 2012 saw interesting language relating to Iran and Israel inserted into the 2013 National Defense Authorization Act (NDAA). In May, the House voted overwhelmingly (401–11) to reject "any US policy that would rely on efforts to contain a nuclear weapons-capable Iran" and voted that it was a "vital national interest" of the US "to prevent the Government of Iran from acquiring a nuclear weapons capability." This position was much more hawkish than the Obama administration's, which sought to distinguish between Iran's acquisition of a nuclear weapons capability versus Iran's possession of a nuclear weapon.[175] Also passed (411–2) in the House in May 2012 was HR 4133, "The US-Israel Enhanced Security Cooperation Act," sponsored by AIPAC, which stated that Congress supports the "unique and special" relationship between America and the Jewish state.[176]

Bedrock support for Israel continued on into spring 2013. During this research trip, a heavily interested House staffer told me in a very matter of fact tone, "Here's how it works on HFAC. The lobby tells certain committee members, 'This is what we want; we want these items.' The members then turn to committee staff and request the items, and this is how it gets written at the committee level. The committee staffers work with the ['pro-Israel'] lobby to get a draft of the bill, and even the final draft of the bill. It's rare to have an opportunity to amend the bill because most of the time it's rammed through by a voice vote. Big items, bills, sometimes get a debate, but it's hardly a real debate. [Who participates in these debates?] It's the same cast of characters—whoever wants to go down there and get their brownie points."

For many years, AIPAC's legions have brought three "asks" with them to their meetings with congressional leaders at the time of their annual conference. In spring 2013, one "ask" was support for HR 850, a Ros-Lehtinen –sponsored resolution against Iran that not only sought to tighten sanctions beyond what the Obama administration wanted, but also included "antiwaiver language"; that is, expressly not including standard language that allows presidents critical wiggle room in their interpretation of congressional legislation. One staffer saw HR 850 as "a trial balloon to see how far the House could tie the president's hands." HR 850 acquired 350 cosponsors, and quickly sailed through HFAC, but in its May 2013 markup it acquired a few problematic additions to its original version: (1) language that would facilitate a backdoor opening to a complete oil embargo of Iran, an extremely hawkish position bruited about in mid-2012, but dumped then because even Sen. Menendez said it was too extreme; (2) the anti-presidential waiver language; and (3) language raising the formal US-Israel relationship to an unprecedented status. (Somewhat surprisingly, and to the dismay of about ten House members, J Street was initially lending its support to HR 850. Their posture reinforced fears among some that J Street represented an "AIPAC lite.") On a motion to suspend the rules and pass the bill, HR 850 passed on a July 31, 2013, vote of 400 to 20, with one person voting present, and was sent to the Senate. I make note of it because the resolution demonstrated once again just how far leading House members were pressing for policies they deemed beneficial to the Israeli government. A Jewish American staffer depicted item number 3 above as "silly business." The staffer added, "Let's stumble over ourselves to show much we love Israel, our BFF, bestest friend forever."

Some measures introduced in the House, initially deemed far-fetched, were revived in the early 2010s and took on great significance even though still considered "wild" and "crazy" proposals by many. For example, legislation introduced by Sen. Robert Menendez in 2013 picked up where an earlier "wild" House initiative had failed. As one commentator said, "The new bill cosponsored by Menendez goes beyond previous attempts to show support for Israeli policy towards Iran. The last such attempt was a 2011 proposal from Reps. Michele Bachmann (R-MN) and Louis Gohmert (R-TX); it would have 'approved' any strike Israel performed. Menendez and Graham's proposal is all the more threatening in that it is backed by credible legislators, albeit known hawks against Iran, and is ostensibly bipartisan."[177]

Although HFAC's focus had shifted significantly in Iran's direction by the turn of the decade, the Palestinian issue would not go away. Particularly upsetting to many HFAC members in the early 2010s was that the Palestinians, having despaired of the US as an honest peace broker, decided to take their grievances to the United Nations. Related diplomatic initiatives triggered a rapid mobilization by AIPAC and other lobbies to block this initiative, and members of Congress responded with alacrity. (Pro-peace advocates APN,

FCNL, and others viewed the Palestinians' bid as understandable and constructive.) In July 2011, several months before the Palestinians presented their application to the UN, Rep. Ros-Lehtinen sponsored HR 268, which had acquired 356 cosponsors, and passed by a vote of 407–6. Major measures introduced in HR 268 included provisions calling for the suspension and/or cancellation of US funding for the United Nations should that body respond favorably to the Palestinians' request. Great pressure was placed on the Obama administration to stop the Palestinians' initiative dead in its tracks. This effort "paid off" for Congress and Obama's White House, which also fought the Palestinians' unilateral effort, when the Palestinian bid for statehood met insurmountable resistance in the UN Security Council in fall 2011.

Where the effort fell short, however, was in forestalling recognition of the Palestinians' call for membership in other UN bodies, like the UN Educational, Scientific, and Cultural Organization (UNESCO). Both before and after the Palestine Authority was granted UNESCO membership in late 2011, there was a flurry of activity in the House (and Senate, as discussed later) to block and then condemn this development. This took the form of threats to cancel US funding of "guilty" UN bodies, followed by activation of previous legislation designed to punish the UN for any formal elevation of the Palestinians' UN presence in the absence of a negotiated settlement with Israel. One staffer noted, "The AIPAC people were out 100 percent to push punitive measures on the Palestinians for taking their case to the UN." These measures are covered in the section on the Senate's response to these developments.

THE IMPACT OF HOUSE BILLS—OR—SO WHAT?

Does all of this work to pass legislation in this area end up making a difference? House staffers are divided in their opinions. As revealed by the following quotes, many take rather disparaging views of what Congress's impact is on US foreign policy. Some see Congress as being, or as having made itself, insignificant. Others still find that Congress's behavior does have an impact, more commonly a negative one, on foreigners' views of the US government in general. And finally, there are those who believe that Congress, on important occasions, sets the parameters of foreign policymaking by the executive branch. The following set of quotes comes from 2006.

"I think the House Committee on International Relations today is very lacking in power. I think the committees have no influence on what happens. The Republican leadership has been indiscrete and indiscriminate in just jumping over them. Power is flowing from Karl Rove, just walking over Congress."

"All the votes are political, not really all that helpful. It's political posturing. For the most part, I don't find Congress's role helpful. If you're pro-Israel, you'd take heart that Congress is pro-Israel, but on a policy level it's not helpful. There's no substance, no teeth to much of what Congress does. We're obviously going to give Israel the military and political support they need. We won't be seen as an honest broker. My overall view is that it's political posturing—peacock feathers. The Arabs look for scapegoats; they blame the US or use the conflict to defeat domestic critics. If Congress did change its position, it might not change matters in the Middle East. However, I do think Congress's position makes a difference. House activity is more for House members' constituencies. Lots of the bills wouldn't make it on the floor if the White House really opposed it today. I think the real political actors out there know that the House and Congress in general is a sideshow."

"The president is the commander in chief, but Congress plays an important supporting role. We provide the money. We play an important supporting role and foreigners lobby Congress very extensively. I don't want to oversell it, but yes, we play a role. You should go work at State or the NSC [National Security Council] if you really want to have an important role [in foreign affairs]. But Congress can set the parameters; and the White House hates this. Maybe Congress wants to restrict trade or use sanctions against rogue nations; the White House hates this. . . . The White House can also use Congress as foreign interlocutors. The same exact thing is being played out now regarding Iran—as the 1986 and 2001 Libyan and Iran sanctions bills. The administration hates this; it ties their hands. I'm not sure the administration will embrace this, but eventually they might come around."

"Look at the Ros-Lehtinen bill on Iran and the one she did on Syria last year. If you want to get a sense of its importance, look at the SAA to see how it ties hands. The president said, 'Please don't do this,' [but they ignored him]. Rep. Anthony Weiner was very involved; he's got to be working with Ros-Lehtinen's committee staff. Ultimately, the executive branch is influenced. Congress cuts the checks, but with SAA, they went beyond this and determined the president's options."

"Look at Lantos—he wants to either cut back aid to Egypt or shift it from military to economic aid. Every year Lantos's amendments set the bar higher for the Egyptians—it's more and more of a struggle [to pass aid for them]."

In the 2011–13 time frame, this mix of views held strong.

"Overseas, in foreign countries, all of this leaves a really negative impression regarding the US as an 'honest broker' or not. The fear and misunderstanding is embedded in this institution."

"The work of the DoD [Department of Defense] and State does filter down and affect who has clout in the House; for example, the first Appropriations bill was usually defense, now homeland affairs is. There is difficulty in passing a State Department authorizing bill— there's an abdication of responsibility to the executive branch. If the House passes something, that does send a message to the rest of the world; and if some of these crazy proposals get through the Senate and are signed by the president, then it's the law of the land, and that's a whole different ball game."

"Ros-Lehtinen has made a lot of noise, but now she's become too extreme. It's gotten to the point where others don't want their com-mittee to become like HFAC. HFAC has no clout. The House in general has allowed the authorizing bill for foreign affairs to become a big joke. Everyone adds on their amendments to the joke. The Senate process has almost broken down this way too."

"I think Congress, when we have resolutions, letters, etc., it does set the parameters. The Iran sanctions are a very good example. They determine or set the parameters of the debate in a way the administration may not want."

Last but not least, here's a former veteran staffer's 2013 take on Congress's efforts to block PA President Mahmoud Abbas's bid for statehood in the United Nations. "On the Palestinian statehood issue, Congress took steps not necessarily in the interest of the US," the staffer said. "In essence, Congress took formal positions telling and rewarding the Palestinians to use violence by creating the perception that they'll just get punished by cuts in US assistance if they go the peaceful route via the United Nations."

Chapter Seven

HOW SENATORS MAKE MIDEAST POLICY

A BRIEF, HISTORICAL BACKGROUND NARRATIVE

One of the more memorable chairmen of the Senate Committee on Foreign Relations was Sen. Jesse Helms, a Republican from North Carolina. A powerful conservative in the Senate for decades, Helms assumed and held the committee's chairmanship from 1995–2001. During his years in the Senate, as a veteran staffer put it, "Helms went from being staunchly anti-Israel to becoming less dogmatic, versus his retained dogmatism on other countries, like Cuba." Way back in 1973, for example, Helms had actually proposed a resolution demanding that Israel return the West Bank, seized by Israel during the 1967 Arab-Israeli war, to Jordan, and that Palestinian Arabs receive a just settlement for their grievances. He also called for a break in US relations with Israel in 1982 because of Israel's military invasion of Lebanon. Then, abruptly, Sen. Helms's position flipped. One major cause of the fundamental change in Helms's views on Israel derived from his 1984 election travails. According to numerous Hill observers, Helms's campaign opponent Gov. Jim Hunt accused Helms of having "the most anti-Israel record of any member of the US Senate." Pro-Israel PACs, responding allegedly to prompts by AIPAC, dumped so much money into the race against Helms that it became the most expensive Senate race ever. Although Helms won, his victory was much narrower than in previous elections. Fewer than 87,000 votes made the difference out of more than 2.2 million cast. In response, Helms decided to never again risk being placed in AIPAC's crosshairs.[178]

Another cause of Helms's change of heart grew out of the rise in political power of Christian fundamentalists. Helms, who had very conservative religious views, had helped found the Moral Majority in 1979. He was very close to the major, national evangelical figures Billy Graham, Pat Robertson, and Jerry Falwell. As the views of these men moved in a hawkish, pro-Israel direction in the late 1970s and early 1980s, so did those of Helms. Christian fundamentalists trumpeted Israel's reappearance as a fulfillment of biblical prophecy, setting the stage for the second coming of Jesus Christ. Falwell began preaching that "To stand against Israel is to stand against God," and some Israeli leaders felt buoyed. As highlighted in an Institute for Policy Studies report:[179] "Prime Minister Begin of Israel called Rev. Falwell in 1981 after the Israeli bombing of an Iraqi nuclear facility to rally a favorable response from the American public. Falwell gave a sermon on behalf of Israel and asked the most influential of the 80,000 preachers associated with the Moral Majority to do the same. In 1982 Ron Godwin announced that the Moral Majority was going to lead tours to Israel 'to transform as many concerned American citizens into well-informed, educated friends of Israel as possible.'"[180] When Moral Majority leaders encouraged US voters to register for the 1984 elections, they also asked them to vote for candidates who strongly backed Israel; and in February 1985, Falwell led a group of nearly 1,000 to Israel to meet key Israeli politicians.[181]

One veteran Senate staffer chose to take me on a trip down memory lane, recalling observations of Helms's 1990s metamorphosis. I think it interesting to share this staffer's somewhat lengthy account because it reflects the degree to which some senators, even those holding chairmanships, may fall under the influence of staffers and special interests, or a combination thereof. According to the veteran staffer, "At least two of Helms's aides were either incredibly influential in his metamorphosis and/or major beneficiaries of it. One influential figure was James Lucier. Another was Danielle Pletka. Lucier was far right wing, and earlier on, while serving as the Minority staff director for Republicans on the Middle East, had put his ultra–right wing perspective into play. Lucier had the attitude that 'The senator [Helms] will vote the way we tell him to.' Helms eventually had to let Lucier go—he was too far to the right, even of Helms. For example, Lucier was tied up with the investigation of the Reagan–Oliver North Iran-Contra 'October surprise' issue."[182] (A second, veteran staffer informed me that Helms had serious health issues in this time frame, enabling staffers like Lucier to "run amok." Helms did undergo quadruple-bypass surgery in June 1992, but he dumped Lucier in January—that is, much earlier—in that year.) Pletka, who was born in Australia, had worked as a correspondent with the *Los*

Angeles Times and *Reuters*; she had been posted in Jerusalem from 1984–1985. Republicans brought her on board as a senior professional staff member for the Near East and South Asian subcommittee, and she served there from 1992–2002. "Pletka, herself, was far to the right, too, but she wanted zero to do with this cloak and dagger stuff," recounted the first staffer. "But she [Pletka] could have been helping defend a fellow neoconservative, [Elliott] Abrams [convicted of wrongdoing in the Iran-Contra scandal]. Whatever the case, this [scandal] consumed our efforts for almost a year."

Sen. James Jeffords (R-Vermont) acquired the Middle East subcommittee's RM role in this time frame, and traffic to his office increased markedly, from visits by ambassadors to interest group representatives. When preparations were made for briefings, Minority staffers working for Jeffords talked to Pletka and her colleagues. The veteran staffer said, "Things were almost always bizarre because Dany [Pletka] was so rough on people. She was very antagonistic and tried to vet the hearings. She would handpick the people for the hearings, although Jeffords's staffers could get some people in. She softened somewhat over time; she was young and incredibly smart; she spoke Arabic, Hebrew, and another language. Lucier, by contrast, wouldn't allow anyone else to come in. He was very pro-Israel; 'Palestinians were all terrorists,' etc., but fortunately he was even more preoccupied with Cuba, the Contras, and so forth."

Did Pletka, in turn, also effectively come to run Helms's show from behind the curtain, as had Lucier beforehand? And if so, was she abetting any "special interests"? Another senior staffer, who did not, I will note, have the ringside seat held by my principal storyteller, knows Pletka well. He averred that "She had lots of influence with the senator [Helms], and she spoke often with him. No one pulled punches. But to my knowledge, she didn't manipulate him in any way." But he added, with a coy smile, "Dany is, of course, her own person. But she may have views very similar to certain groups." When I asked him for clarification as to which groups, he begged off, but it seemed obvious from the interview's context that he was referring to the neocons and right wing pro-Israel groups. (In recent years, Pletka has taken up residence at the neoconservative American Enterprise Institute think tank, which routinely promotes right wing pro-Israel policies.)

When Lucier was let go, "the Admiral"—Navy Rear Admiral James Nance—took his place. The Admiral was an old, childhood friend of Helms and was brought in to clean house. "He bent over backwards to be fair and balanced," noted the veteran staffer. "He didn't get excited about politics. And the Senate debate as a whole improved significantly." The Admiral became Helms's guy. Dick Lugar, a fellow Republican, was a strong, moderating force with Helms; Jeffords, a Republican (who would turn Independent in 2001), was to the left of Lugar. "During Helms's tenure, [Claiborne] Pell [D-RI], who retired in 1994, was the [full committee] RM; he was infirm in his later years, and Helms ran right over him," according to the staffer. "Once Joe Biden took over from Pell, there was much more activist opposition." Helms finally retired in 2002, and Lugar became Foreign Relations Committee chairman. Lugar was "more moderate, loved foreign policy, and had been waiting for a long time for the chairmanship."

The same veteran staffer/narrator quoted above also provided a candid look at how some senators acquire their positions on Senate Foreign Relations, as well as their level of knowledge about foreign affairs. First, serendipity—many would call it bad luck—can determine who lands in an important post. "[The senator] got his Middle East subcommittee assignment in [the 1990s] because he was the last guy in the door," the staffer said. "Everyone else got to pick ahead of him; they all had seniority over him. All of this came at midterm and people were settled in, and people didn't want to switch."

Second, neither knowledge nor experience is a prerequisite. As the staffer said, "Prior to the 1990–94 experience I knew nothing—zero—about the Middle East and suddenly I'm on the subcommittee. [The boss] also knew zero about the Middle East." The staffer was able to get up to speed quickly. "Everyone calls you; the phone rings off the hook. So we met with all the principals—all the ambassadors. AIPAC were the first ones on our doorstep. We already had a relationship with them, but of course now it intensified. Before [the senator's] appointment, they came two times per year; this changed to once every three weeks."

Third, as indicated above, everybody—and their brother and sister, it seems—will seek access to those in positions of power, so astute staffers look for intelligent spokespersons for a range of interest groups to make contact with and try to get a handle on what's going on in the Mideast. To this point, the staffer said he made contacts with Mubarak Awad of the Palestine Research Center; Graeme Bannerman a Mideast expert who had worked for the State Department and the Senate Foreign Relations Committee; the president of the Lebanese American University; and representatives at Peace Now, Churches for Mideast Peace, APN, and AIPAC.

Still, even for those trying to broaden their horizons, in almost all staffers' minds AIPAC had a leg up on all the competition and maintained the most contact.

"DEAR COLLEAGUE" LETTERS AND SENATE RESOLUTIONS

As is true in the House, "Dear Colleague" letters and resolutions are "penned" in relative abundance and range from matters trivial and symbolic to those of great gravity. When I asked my Senate interviewees which senators were most likely to write "Dear Colleague" letters or introduce resolutions relating to the Arab-Israeli conflict in 2005–2006, thereby acquiring a reputation for activism, one staffer pointed out Senators Coleman, McConell, and Biden, adding that their letters are "all in the same [pro-Israel] direction." Another staffer waxed more expansive, observing that "There are so many people vying for the lead in the Senate on pro-Israeli positions. Sen. Kyl is very big. He and Coleman cochair the US-Israel Inter-parliamentary committee, so they plan CODELS—exchanges with [the Israeli parliament] Knesset members—one time per year, as well as other events. Feinstein is their Democratic counterpart. Lieberman is a key figure in general as well. Among the Democrats, Lautenberg is very active; and Schumer is a big player. Santorum is a leader on the Iran issue. Clinton is out front on this, especially on Iran. As regards Republicans, Brownback does Arab-Israeli stuff; Voinovich a little. Chafee is the only one who will ever get out there—the only one who criticizes Israelis for the IDF bombings, etc. Sununu can be a big figure, too, but he's more of a moderate; he looks at both sides of the issue. He's not much of a leader on stuff. I don't see his name out there."

Two other staffers emphasized how Christian religious motivations affected this area of activity. Said one: "There's a weird mix of people initiating resolutions because of Christian fundamentalist interests—like Brownback and people from the South and the Plains states—who are often in the vanguard on these issues. Initiators of 'Dear Colleague' letters and folks who are active on religious liberties include Santorum, Gordon Smith, Sam Brownback, Evan Bayh, and Mr. Coburn."

Many of the activist senators were perceived as hawkish on Middle East matters, as noted by a variety of staffers. "Nelson is very hawkish," one staffer said. "He and Lieberman, many others, including Clinton, are very hawkish on Iran and wanting to keep the military option on the table. Prior to the

Hamas election [January 2006], Nelson and Talent circulated the 'Dear Colleague' letter trying to block Hamas's participation in the election."

As one can readily ascertain, these senators fall into one or more of the following categories: (1) individuals in top party leadership positions: Senators Biden, Clinton, Lieberman, McConnell; (2) Jewish Americans and/or senators who represent states with large Jewish constituencies: Senators Boxer, Clinton, Coleman, Feinstein, Lieberman, Schumer, Nelson; (3) Christian evangelicals and/or senators from states with large evangelical constituencies: Senators Bayh, Brownback, Coburn, Kyl, Santorum, Smith, Talent; (4) national security hawks: as named above, but including Senators McCain and Graham. The "outliers" are Chafee and Sununu, with the latter possessing his own ancestral connection to the conflict. In contrast to those in the House, Senate Foreign Relations committee members are not particularly prolific in writing "letters." A Foreign Relations committee staffer interviewed in 2012 said, "'Dear Colleague' letters in this issue area don't come out of our committee. Sen. Kyl and Sen. Kirk are more active in this regard." Both Kyl and Kirk are ardently pro-Israel right wingers.

In the Senate, "Dear Colleague" letters and Senate resolutions are seen to have value as "attention-getters." Speaking candidly, one staffer told me that "there's pressure to deliver 'copy' to the senator because what's written may be read on the Senate floor." In other words, as was true in the House, letters and resolutions become an easy, relatively cost-free way to score points with one's constituents and other interested parties. It's "cost-free" because, as most staffers will rather cavalierly admit, "they're letters and resolutions, so they don't really matter to the players on the Hill."

There's a variety of motives for signing "Dear Colleague" letters or voting for resolutions. As a Senate staffer noted in 2006, "Votes on Israel don't come up a huge amount. It's normally votes on resolutions, or requests to sign letters. . . . This can be tactical as a signature to signal the president, etc., and as a pressure valve for congressional actors, too, to write a letter and persuade others to sign on. So it's instructive to look at letters and resolutions on Iran, Syria, etc.; see who the original cosponsors were and which senators signed on. Some folks may sign on due to pressure."

In speaking of "pressure" to sign the letters, there was widespread agreement among Senate staffers in both the mid-2000s and early 2010s as to its most common source, with most uninhibitedly acknowledging AIPAC's dominance. One aide to a Senate Foreign Relations committee member in

2006 said, "Look at the bill on Iran right now. AIPAC is making it very clear they want us to sign on. We developed another bill as an alternative. This is our proposal, our bill, we've sponsored it. Some senators have signed on. There is no coordinating mechanism up here to talk about who else is doing something comparable; that is, presenting an alternative view"

Another staffer said in 2006 that AIPAC's ability to apply pressure is affected by each senator's level of vulnerability, or how—in my words—"bulletproof" they are. So when he explained "how the game's played," he covered the spectrum from the 10–20 senators who need AIPAC's support—those who are vulnerable like Talent,[183] Santorum, Bayh,[184] Schumer, Boxer, and to some extent Feinstein—to the senators who do not—those solid like McConnell, Mikulski, Durbin, and Nelson of Florida. The staffer said that "some senators have a mixed relationship with AIPAC: Feinstein waxes hot and cold with them; Levin also goes back and forth," whereas others "don't need or get AIPAC support, people like Byrd, Hollings, Leahy, Chafee, and Jeffords." But, as most senators need campaign finance help, the staffer's proviso that "AIPAC has so much ability to raise money that at the end of the day you'd need to get people raising enough money on the other side [to compete with their influence]" speaks volumes. Only the few senators with no concerns about money may escape this pitfall.

In 2013, little had changed. For the pro–two state crowd, Senators Feinstein and Durbin's acceptance of J Street support had made some difference, but overall, few observers on and off the Hill disagreed with a veteran Senate staffer's view that "Not that much has changed from five or six years ago. There's no question that AIPAC is the dominant lobbying group." On a more controversial note, the same staffer said of AIPAC: "The pressure they apply is often just over the top. There's no reason for them to be constantly pushing as hard as they do on all of these issues. It's just not helpful."

AIPAC-backed letters do not receive unanimous support. In 2009, an AIPAC-backed letter presented by Senators Bayh and James Risch was left unsigned by 29 senators, including a few more moderate Jewish American senators like Feingold, Kohl, and Feinstein. They had been urged by APN and IPF to see the Bayh-Risch letter as too lacking in balance; to wit, while calling upon all Arab states to normalize relations with Israel, and the Palestinians to tighten their security measures, the letter completely ignored Israel's failure to stop West Bank settlement activity. But I mention this letter primarily to provide some perspective; that is, that AIPAC's opponents hailed the 29 "missing signatures" as a significant victory. Neutral observers would quickly recognize the other 71 signatures as no small measure of support.

As regards resolutions, the Senate typically sees a plethora, nearly all of which are designed to show support for Israel. In the latter 1990s and 2000s, one of the most active senators as regards the introduction of right wing pro-Israel resolutions was Sen. Brownback of Kansas. The reader will recall that Brownback, whose Senate career spanned 1996–2010, is a staunch social conservative, inspired by evangelicalism and Christian Zionist thought. Just prior to his arrival in the Senate, that chamber had passed the Jerusalem Embassy Act of 1995 by a vote of 93–5. (Senators Robert Byrd, Chafee, Mark Hatfield [R-Oregon], Spencer Abraham [R-Michigan; an Arab American] and Jeffords voted "nay"; Sen. Bill Bradley [D-New Jersey] did not vote.) The 1995 act called for the United States to move its embassy from Tel Aviv to Jerusalem, a move that would violate international legal standings on Jerusalem's status as Israeli occupied territory, dating from the 1967 Arab-Israeli war. The 1995 act included a presidential waiver of the sort discussed earlier, permitting the US president to refrain from fulfilling the act's primary objective on the grounds of national security. Every president, from Clinton through Bush and Obama, has exercised such a waiver when presented with comparable bills. After Brownback's arrival in the Senate, he could be counted upon at the beginning of nearly every new Congress (1999, 2003, 2005, 2007, 2009) to introduce a resolution calling upon the president to relocate the US embassy from Tel Aviv to Jerusalem, and recognize Jerusalem as the "undivided capital of Israel." To this end, he usually had the backing of Senators Tom Coburn, Susan Collins, Mike Crapo, John Cornyn, Kyl, Lieberman, Santorum, Specter, and Gordon Smith. Brownback also repeatedly sought to remove the presidential waiver embedded in the 1995 act. On March 16, 2010, during the acrimonious standoff between Pres. Obama and Prime Minister Netanyahu over Israeli settlement activity, Brownback sided with the Israeli prime minister against the US president, sardonically asserting, "It's hard to see how spending a weekend condemning Israel for a zoning decision in its capital city amounts to a positive step towards peace."[185]

While many "older guard" aggressive supporters of Israel were no longer in place by 2012–2013, other senators, like Lindsey Graham, Mark Kirk (or his staffers), James Risch, and on many issues Barbara Boxer, had stepped forward to introduce hard right wing, pro-Israel initiatives, as will be discussed more fully below as well as in the chapter on appropriations.

PASSING A BILL IN THE SENATE

Given the difficult hoops through which a bill must jump in order to become a law of the land, the introduction of bills in the Senate is far less common than that of resolutions. As we saw in the House, it is important to review who has occupied the key seats on Senate Foreign Relations over time. The chart below offers a quick overview.

SENATE COMMITTEE ON FOREIGN RELATIONS; CHAIRS AND RANKING MEMBERS, FULL COMMITTEE AND NEAR EAST SUBCOMMITTEE

Congress	Year	Chair	Ranking Member
105th Full	'97–'99	Helms, R-NC	Biden, D-DE
105th NESA		Brownback, R-KS	Robb, D-VA
106th Full	'99–'01	Helms	Biden
106th NESA		Brownback	Wellstone, D-MN
107th Full	'01–'03	Biden	Helms
107th NESA		Wellstone, D-MN	Brownback
108th Full	'03–'05	Lugar, R-IN	Biden
108th NESA		Chafee, R-RI	Boxer, D-CA
109th Full	'05–'07	Lugar	Biden
109th NESA		Chafee	Boxer
110th Full	'07–'09	Biden	Lugar
110th NESA		Kerry, D-MA	Coleman, R-MN
111th Full	'09–'11	Kerry	Lugar
111th NESA		Casey, Jr., D-PA	Barrasso, R-WY
112th Full	'11–'13	Kerry	Lugar
112th NESCA		Casey, Jr.	Risch, R-ID

NESA = Near Eastern and South Asian Affairs;

NESCA = Near Eastern and South Central Asian Affairs

In discussing the leadership positions presented in the table, I'll begin by noting that all the senators on this list, unsurprisingly, steadily expressed a commitment to Israel's long-run welfare and security. As shall be seen, the level or intensity of commitment has varied among these individuals, but the only one on the list who was more circumspect and posed probing questions about specific Israeli policies was Sen. Lincoln Chafee. And no objective observer would describe Chafee as hostile to Israel.

Second, one should notice that for every Congress, the most relevant chairmanships on Senate Foreign Relations have been held by at least one if not two individuals with a deep, unflinching pro-Israel commitment deriving from a religious or ethno-religious background. This "distinction" is most visible among the chairpersons and/or RMs of the subcommittee on Near Eastern and South Asian Affairs. Senators Brownback, Wellstone, Boxer, Coleman, Casey Jr., Barrasso, and Risch have filled these "slots," and all share(d) relevant religious or ethno-religious inspired orientations. Wellstone was Jewish, and a strong liberal Democrat and progressive voice on nearly all issues, but he earned high marks from right wing pro-Israel groups when it came to matters relating to Israel. Boxer, a liberal Democrat, is Jewish and has always been a pit bull for Israel, as was equally true of the conservative Republican Coleman, who is also Jewish. Senators Brownback, Casey Jr., Barrasso, and Risch all approach(ed) IME issues from varying Christian Zionist positions, and all espouse(d) right wing, pro-Israel policies. All of these senators are or were very heavily AIPAC-approved.

Again, in the mid- to late-2000s, the full Senate Foreign Relations Committee was chaired by Sen. Lugar (R) of Indiana and its RM was Sen. Biden (D) of Delaware. They remained locked in these top two positions, changing hats as chairman and ranking member with the R vs. D Senate power shifts, until Biden received a higher calling and became Obama's vice president in 2009. Their key staffers enjoyed a reputation for a more dispassionate, objective approach to the conflict than their predecessors in Helms's crew. A seasoned Democratic staffer noted of the Republican Lugar, "When Lugar took over he fired everybody on Jesse Helms's staff. They were all a reflection of their basic priorities. Helms's staff was extremely partisan. With Lugar's staff, it's hard to tell which party the people are from. The Minority committee staffers work for Biden, of course; and Biden and Lugar work extremely well together."

On the full committee in 2005–2006, Lugar's fellow Republicans included

Chuck Hagel (NE), Lincoln Chafee (RI), George Allen (VA), Norm Coleman (MN), George Voinovich (OH), Lamar Alexander (TN), John Sununu (NH), Lisa Murkowski (AK), and Mel Martinez (FL). For the Democrats, Biden's fellow Democrats included Paul Sarbanes (MD), Chris Dodd (CT), John Kerry (MA), Russ Feingold (WI), Barbara Boxer (CA), Bill Nelson (FL), and Barack Obama (IL). (The reader can see that, despite its smaller membership size, Senate Foreign Relations has broader geographic dispersion, pound for pound, than House Foreign Affairs. There's somewhat higher representation of people from the Midwest versus the East and West coasts, and a lower percentage from New York and California.)

How did Sen. Lugar perform as chairman? Lugar's loyalty to Israel was questioned by his victorious 2012 primary opponent, and as aforementioned knowledgeable staffers told me this had indeed contributed to his loss. Nonetheless, across his many years as a senator, he was generally perceived as a solid friend of Israel, and even some ZOA members lent him support in 2012, as also noted earlier.

Influential right wing supporters of Israel saw Hagel as problematic. According to a 2010 *Commentary* article, "The *Washington Jewish Week* report[ed] just how serious is the opposition and aversion to Hagel [by right wing backers of Israel]: 'I would regard him as the bottom of the class as far as Israel goes,' said Morris Amitay, a former executive director of [AIPAC] and treasurer of the Washington PAC, a pro-Israel political action committee."[186] And of course these sentiments are revealing if one's searching for reasons why Pres. Obama's nomination of Hagel as secretary of defense was so hotly contested by right wing pro-Israel forces in 2013. But through my behind-closed-doors interviews, I learned much about Hagel's sentiments; as a well-informed staffer told me in the mid-2000s, "Sen. Hagel is capable of criticizing Israel's behavior, but he is still a strong supporter of Israel in general." Chafee and Sununu were seen as being the most empathetic to Palestinian and Arab views among their Republican colleagues, but their stances were more than offset by fellow Republicans Coleman, Allen, Murkowski, and Martinez. As discussed earlier, all four latter senators were recipients of significant campaign finance support from pro-Israel PACs, whether they needed this form of "encouragement" to back Israel or not.

Among the committee's Democrats, Biden was long seen as a very strong supporter of Israel. According to M.J. Rosenberg, a former AIPAC staffer,

Biden "is about as close to the pro-Israel community as any member of either house," is "rated 100 percent by AIPAC," and "When he goes to the synagogues in Florida, he goes not as a visitor but as 'mishpocha' [family]. The Jews simply love the guy."[187]

Kerry, Dodd, and Sarbanes were also seen as strong to very strong supporters of Israel. Although Kerry has accepted exceptionally little in the way of contributions from pro-Israel PACs,[188] he was still seen as holding views largely concordant with AIPAC's. Feingold was a strong, if not obsequious, supporter of Israel as well. Meanwhile, during their thirty-year careers as congresspersons, Dodd, Sarbanes, and Boxer each racked up over $247,000, $220,000, and $239,000 respectively in campaign contributions from pro-Israel PACs. Boxer and Nelson (the latter with over $43,000 in pro-Israel PAC support per year since just 2007) are considered among the senators least likely to question Israel's policies, including those of recent, hard right wing Israeli governments.

As for the Near Eastern and South Asian Affairs subcommittee, in 2005–2006 it was comprised of R's Chafee (chairman), Hagel, Coleman, Voinovich, and Sununu; with the D's represented by (RM) Boxer, Sarbanes, Nelson and Obama. This lineup represented one of the few periods in the subcommittee's recent history in which there were senators more empathetic to moderate Palestinians and Arabs and inclined to push for "space" between Israeli and American interests; namely, Chafee, Sununu, to some extent Hagel, and to a lesser degree, the "freshman" Obama. But again, Coleman, Boxer, Nelson, and Sarbanes were happy to team up to keep that "space" minimal.

SENATE FOREIGN RELATIONS STAFFERS' VIEWS OF THE SENATORS

As regards the Senate committee's staffing arrangements, these have always granted an upper hand to the Majority party, like in the House. One subcommittee member's staffer pointed out in 2006 that "Only the top four Democrats on the full committee are allowed committee staffers: Biden, Sarbanes, Dodd, and Kerry." So often senators serving on the Middle East subcommittee have just one staffer who is working in their office on foreign relations issues writ large. For example, the staffer quoted in this paragraph was the only one in his senator's office working on foreign affairs, which he clearly felt was inadequate. Another senate staffer with excellent academic credentials, working for a Near East subcommittee member, voiced frustration about his workload. "By academic training, you write long pieces," he said. "Here you have to write short pieces; do background, analyses, and recommendations in one page, double-spaced—the more concise, the better. Analytical memos are different, but the emphasis is always on clarity, precision, and comprehensiveness, but short. There's a huge emphasis on time. Time is everything. You have minutes to brief your boss, so you have to present orally quickly as well. The academic training doesn't teach you to go quickly and how to multitask. There are over ten big issues to deal with per day. As a Hill staffer, your time is not yours. If there's a meeting called right now, I'm gone [from this interview]. My phone rings off the hook all day long. I work 60 to 65 hours per week."

Asked whether "special interest" groups provided language for bills being proposed, this staffer responded, "It's hard to say what percentage of staff letters and so forth come from outside. With regard to the origin of the Syria Accountability Act [2003], I believe Rep. Engel's staffer was the chief writer of that act." But many staffers made observations similar to those a veteran Senate PSM shared with me in a 2012 interview, "The language in many letters, resolutions and bills is penned by AIPAC. Sen. Kirk's staff make no bones about how they treat Israel policy; and Bob Menendez's staff is not even changing the language from AIPAC drafted materials. I tell them, 'Come on, can't you at least use a little imagination.'"

How did Senate staffers view the Foreign Relations committee's senators? Which ones were reputed to be the "sharper knives" in the Senate Foreign Relations Committee box? Staffers mentioned Lugar, Feingold, Sununu, and Biden. Other senators had a reputation for specific countries or issue areas. One staffer said, "On Iraq and Afghanistan, Hagel is quite sharp"; another said that Chafee is known for asking "pretty tough questions" of Condoleezza Rice on issues concerning the Israeli security barrier.

A quick note about Chafee and Israel: when I asked a staffer if Chafee might take election heat for questioning Israeli policies, he responded, "A far right Israel Jewish group has already given money to his opponent. APN, Brit Tzedek, IPF all appreciate what he is doing, they all say. It will be a tough election, but things feel good." But the staffer was wrong, Chafee lost; and his opponent was backed strongly by right wing pro-Israel donors, as was discussed. When I interviewed Chafee, I asked him if he felt his Senate campaign had been done in by right wing pro-Israel actors. He said, "No," but I'll note that he was just gearing up for his gubernatorial campaign in Rhode Island, which he went on to win.

Specifically concerning the A-I conflict, another Senate staffer with a high academic pedigree saw the following senators as most influential: Lugar, Biden, Brownback, Boxer, Dodd, and Hagel. The staffer also mentioned Kerry's staffer Nancy Stetson, saying, "She is one of the real serious professionals up here on the Hill." Another, highly informed reaffirmed Biden as the most influential member. "People do look for his views," the staffer said. "Biden's a leader here." A few highly knowledgeable staffers even saw Biden as playing a dominant, perhaps even domineering role among Democrats. As one noted, "Sen. Biden really seems to be steering the ship himself. Relations between the Senate and staff need to be worked on and improved. There is some dependence on us [PSMs], but more for details, not strategy. Biden does seem to know more about the countries than our inside the beltway folks do. You should look into one hearing in particular that we had about Syria for the SAA, when Biden stated for the record how frustrated he felt regarding discussion of the reform issue in Syria. Biden said, exasperated, 'Not one of you has mentioned the 1,000-pound gorilla: the Arab-Israeli conflict.'"

KEY STAFFERS ON THE SENATE FOREIGN
RELATIONS COMMITTEE

By broad consensus, the role of Senate PSMs was deemed very valuable. "Many decisions are made at subcommittee levels on Biden and Lugar's staffs; they'll have a lot to say on policy," a staffer said. Another concurred: "Staffers here are crucial. Biden and Lugar's Foreign Relations staffs are very important." But as the second of these staffers suggested, Lugar's PSMs seem to have been permitted greater freedom and influence than Biden's. And another PSM said, "Lugar's staff has broad power on issues." He didn't say the same of Biden's PSMs, and he was in a position to know.

In 2005–2006, the Senate PSM names that tripped off the tongues of staffers holding Senate foreign relations portfolios were: Puneet Talwar, the Democrats' Minority professional staff director, Dan Shapiro (in Democrat

Sen. Bill Nelson's office), Paul Grove (Republican Sen. McConnell's foreign policy aide), and Kim Savit (senior PSM for the Middle East, Central and South Asia on the R's Majority staff). As a reflection of how talented these people are, Talwar was recruited by Pres. Obama for his National Security Council (NSC) to cover Iraq, Iran, and the countries of the Persian Gulf. Dan Shapiro, who had come out of Rep. Lee Hamilton's HFAC staff stable, had also staffed with Sen. Feinstein, sat on Pres. Clinton's NSC as congressional liaison, and worked for Sen. Nelson before eventually returning to the NSC as Pres. Obama's senior director for the Middle East and North Africa. In 2011, Obama appointed him the US ambassador to Israel. Grove has become Minority clerk for the Foreign Ops subcommittee of Senate Appropriations, and Savit opted for academic pastures in Colorado.

In 2005–2006, the Majority staff director for the full Foreign Relations committee was Ken Myers; the Minority staff director was Anthony Blinken. For Near Eastern and South Asian Affairs, the Majority PSM was again Ken Myers, and the Minority PSM was the aforementioned Puneet Talwar. Tony Blinken moved into the White House as national security adviser for his Senate boss turned vice president, Mr. Biden. Ken Myers worked for Senate Foreign Relations through 2012, moving back to the position of the full committee's Minority staff director after the D's regained control of the Senate in 2007.

In 2005–2006, there were just two full-time Minority Foreign Relations Committee staffers dealing exclusively with the Middle East—Puneet Talwar and Perry Cammack. Of the two, Talwar was older, seasoned, and seen as possessing greater Middle East expertise. He is of Indian descent and knew how to speak a little Arabic. Cammack had recently arrived on the job and was learning Arabic. (Years later, in May 2012, Cammack was brought on board at the Department of State's policy planning staff.)

One PSM described himself as a "filter for information," reading about two hours per day, most of which involved just staying on top of daily news and meeting often with various people and representatives from NGOs. Importantly, he complained that it was "hard to look at long-term stuff; the bigger picture gets lost." He indicated that the State Department was the best source of information. PSMs, he noted, could request classified information, and many PSMs go through security clearances, despite there being no classified information in their office. The Department of Defense was also a point of reference, but the Pentagon folks were "very secretive by nature, so it's hard for me to get information from them."

When asked how he saw the committee members, the PSM didn't hold back. "There's a strong centrist bloc of Republicans—Hagel, Lugar, etc., but further down the roster there's some Republicans on the committee who have a tough, unfair view of Arabs and perhaps some Democrats who do as well," the PSM said. "There are two to four hard right Republicans on the committee. There are no neocons in the Senate, but hard right, yes. Trent Lott, for example."

SENATE BRIEFINGS AND HEARINGS

What do the "nuts and bolts" of setting up Senate hearings look like? Mid-level PSMs don't recruit people for the hearings, in general. They make recommendations to their subcommittee superiors, like a Puneet Talwar, who would then confer with his counterpart, Karen Savit. Talwar and Savit, in turn, would take their recommendations to the full committee's staff directors—for the Majority R's Ken Myers and the Minority D's Anthony Blinken. Myers and Blinken would confer to decide who would be brought in. They would also talk with Lugar and Biden, because it could be high-ranking officials like Sec. of State Colin Powell or Sec. of Defense Rumsfeld being brought in to testify. To offer the partisan dimension to this discussion, for the Democrats, Senators Reid, Levin, Biden, and Rockefeller were the top folks who would get together and brainstorm on Iraq, and Talwar would be there with them.

Individual senators may request a hearing. The PSMs will ask the senator whom he or she would like to invited, and the senator will get suggestions from visitors, committee staff, NGOs in the area, or from area think tanks like Brookings, CSIS, etc. PSM types will put a list together, and the committee's chair or RM will say "these people—so and so—look good." And the PSMs will also contact the White House and State Department for suggestions.

A veteran staffer shed light on which senior PSMs were playing strong roles, and why. "Committee staffers have institutional memory and bring structure to the process," the veteran said. "They have more experience and a longer history of experience. The [Minority] committee has 2 or 3 guys, mainly 1 or 2 doing Arab-Israeli stuff, and if you're going to the Middle East guy to ask, 'What are you doing today?' Right now [2006], he's going to answer 'Iraq.' PSMs carry a ton of power and influence. For example, you should try to see Pat Garvey. Patrick worked on stability and reconstruction for Iraq and Afghanistan, incentivizing people to send staffs overseas. So if you're going to do something on Iraq, he's the go-to guy on this and other work. On the Arab-Israeli stuff, Kim Savit is often the lead."

When I asked if there was partisan balance regarding briefings, the same staffer noted:

"We feel oftentimes they forget there is a Minority party and they [the Majority Republicans] try to steamroll us. I will note that Lugar and Biden worked out an agreement to cooperate well and control the agenda. They get an equal say as to who the witnesses are, but the Republicans have veto power, ultimately. Partisan pressures are maintained on Lugar and Biden, of course, with regard to hearings. Our thinking is changing regarding the recruitment of experts for testimony; we think Washington think tanks bear a bit of the responsibility for getting involved in Iraq in the first place, especially AEI [the American Enterprise Institute] and the Heritage Foundation. CSIS might have provided better input; and we see the need for more outside voices like Biden did earlier, during the eight months we were the Majority party, back in 2002–2003. I find WINEP very useful as long as you understand they have a bias, whereas AEI and Heritage may bring little real expertise in on some subjects. In my own opinion, I think Arab voices are not heard quite enough."

How do the staffers view these hearings, as well as the roles played by key Foreign Relations committee members and other influential senators? Some complained that many senators display considerable diffidence about these briefings and hearings. A staunchly pro-Israel senator's staffer observed, "State Department people are often hosted by the Senate, but many senators don't attend. Hearings provide opportunities to be on the record for both senators and the witnesses. [My senator] really listens at the hearings; he has a good attendance record, and he's very attentive." A staffer for a more independent-minded senator noted, "Regarding hearings, there's some bias built in, but you have to take things issue by issue. You can always follow up with questioning if you think there's bias. I think you get a fair sense of what's going on from many people. The Pentagon or administration people on Iraq aren't necessarily going to tell you the gritty truth."

This staffer added that "[Senators] George Allen and Lamar Alexander are more party liners; some may not care to understand the issue to the core. Lugar and Hagel choose their battles; they're very thoughtful. With most people, it's issue by issue. There's waning bipartisanship in the Senate. The Dems are crying wolf a bit too much. [Sen.] Obama is very good. In hearings, people usually don't ask questions unless they know what the answer will be."

With greater regard to the substance of hearings, Senate staffers complained of the dearth of hearings on major issues during the mid-2000s. "There have been no hearings on Israel this year," one staffer said. "If you don't have something nice to say about Israel, you don't hold a hearing. Everybody but Chafee is in lockstep with Israel. Chafee was willing to criticize the White House's endorsement of the Gaza plan." Staffers and other interested parties were especially dismayed over the great shortage of hearings on the Iraq War. Again, most chalked this up to the Republicans not wanting to hold hearings during which Bush's Republican administration figures might well be embarrassed.

At times, experts appear on the Hill to share their wisdom about particular issues, sometimes in less formal settings. Many staffers make it clear that they yearn to hear and learn more from unbiased figures. One such opportunity was provided in the mid-2000s, when former CIA analyst Michael Scheuer appeared. A veteran staffer said of the meeting:

> "There was a huge turnout by staffers—about 50 or 60 staffers were there. Usually just a bunch of young, hungry kids turn out, it's pretty pathetic, really, but Scheuer's testimony was at 3 pm without food and still there was a huge turnout. Scheuer kept arguing that US support for Israel is the genesis of support for bin Laden. He kept asking, 'Why does the US support Israel? We must ask ourselves. Is our support to Israel really worth it?' There is no support for intervention anywhere—Iran, Syria; the coalition they were trying to build has fallen apart. Pro-Israel groups, AIPAC, etc., Lieberman, all feel we can impose our will vs. Kerry, Biden, and others who disagree. But many people here are afraid of the other shoe dropping, especially on the House side, and all this has to do with politics. The merits of

the policy are of second and third tier to politics, unfortunately. The public can smell the opportunism."

An aide to a Jewish American senator observed, in 2012, however, that promoting open dialogue is not frequently desired in talks with outside experts. "Post–9/11 there's been little debate space regarding Israel's position and what's the proper way to handle the Arab-Israeli conflict," the staffer said. "When Biden had hearings before, on Iraq, they were less scripted, so they were more helpful. There's a lot of pressure on Capitol Hill to not have this kind of hearing. People often stack the hearings—lining up speakers recommended by AIPAC and ZOA. They want the hearings to help reinforce the point they're already making. There's pressure to have something deliverable at the end. You have to be careful about being undecided in having an open mind in public because then all kinds of people will be lobbying you if you say the wrong thing."

SENATE BILLS AND RELATED HEARINGS; FOCUS ON THE RESPONSE TO HAMAS'S ELECTION

As is true in the House, in any given year there are not likely to be that many actual bills relating to the A-I or I-P conflicts per se. Important bills passed during the early to mid-2000s included those aimed at increasing the pressure against Israel's primary regional adversaries, including Syria, Iran, and of course Iraq. Although some bills are constructive in nature, many are reactive and punitive. Major international developments beget calls for action, however, as with the unexpected, momentous, game-changing January 2006 electoral victory of Hamas. Thus, it seems useful to slow down and study how senators responded to that event.

A staffer who knew Sen. Chafee commented on his reaction. One such person said, "His first reaction to Hamas's winning was one of great depression. How do we get from 'Oh boy, look what we've got now' to policy is the big question. [Diplomats] Robert Malley and Dennis Ross fear that if Hamas fails due to US influence, this could complicate matters. We still care about the Palestinians. We still want peace between the Palestinians and Israel. It's in the US interest to find a solution."

Chafee did step up to the plate to play a more activist role in this time frame, supporting the Bush administration's decision to keep the door open for diplomacy and constructive relations with the Palestinians, especially the moderates. Even in offices of senators known as "strong supporters" of Israel, I heard appraisals like the following one. "She recognizes the need to appreciate the Palestinians' position and that we can't be too reactionary when it comes to Hamas's election," one staffer said. "She has a sound appreciation of the importance of how we handle these issues—how it could impact on our relations with other countries; so we can't just engage in quick, knee-jerk reactions to developments like Hamas's election."

Echoing the belief in not making a knee-jerk reaction, a moderate Jewish American senator's staffer said, "We haven't duked it out yet over Hamas [here in the office]. At first we were saying Hamas should be left out, but political realities there have made us shift. There's obviously a problem with democracies bringing radical Muslims to power." On balance, most senators and their staffers appeared to be caught off guard, and their initial reactions were of a 'what the hell do we do now?' character.

Again, House members' rapid response to the election produced HR 4681. As noted earlier, this bill included very tough provisions, many deemed unacceptable by a broad range of legislative and executive officials. In the Senate, there were mixed views, but many senators responded with concern and alarm to HR 4681, seeing its provisions as excessive. And it's noteworthy that a significant part of this confusion derived from mixed signals being sent by right wing pro-Israel actors themselves, as discussed shortly.

Jockeying in the Senate over how to legislate a response to Hamas's election was intense and generated a flurry of activity. Folks on the Senate side saw the Ros-Lehtinen bill, replete with its tough conditions, sailing through the House and sought ways to either jump on board or counter it. Although numerous proposals were batted about in the Senate, the Senate bill that quickly acquired greatest support was the McConnell-Biden bill, S 2370. Thus, the chairman of the powerful Foreign Ops subcommittee of Senate Appropriations, McConnell, teamed up with the RM of Senate Foreign Relations, Biden. Both "strong supporters" of Israel, their bill was designed to defuse some of the major friction points embodied in HR 4681, about which a senior Senate staffer told a media source, "Senate leaders view the House bill as 'insanely irresponsible.'"[189] Some staffers even believed the Senate bill would not be brought to a floor vote because senators disliked 4681 so much that they didn't want to create the need for a conference committee in which senators and House members would have to work out some consensus.

To determine how best to deal with the new Hamas government, the Senate Committee on Foreign Relations assembled a group of genuine heavyweights—James Wolfensohn, Robert Malley, and Dennis Ross—to provide expert testimony. Wolfensohn, former president of the World Bank, and Malley, former NSC member and Middle East adviser to President Clinton, were known to hold positions more in line with that of the Bush administration and the State Department; that is, they believed that wiggle room should be left in any legislation to allow for State's continued, constructive contact with non-Hamas Palestinian leaders. Ross, a key figure on the conflict spanning the presidencies of Bush, Clinton, Bush, and Obama, was known to adopt policies closely in line with AIPAC. According to a key staffer, Ross's inclusion on the panel "had been secured by a very strong supporter of Israel on the Foreign Relations committee. We picked Dennis Ross to testify. [My boss] likes and respects him. He's close to [the senator's] thinking."

For those urging a more prudent approach than that being championed in the House, it was hoped that Wolfensohn, Malley, and even Ross would bring a sober look at the consequences of terminating US aid for Palestinian schools, medical clinics, and other organizations under the supervision of a Hamas-elected government; and/or of barring diplomatic contact with all officials of the Palestinian Authority. In fact, even Israeli government officials began expressing concern that too harsh a response—like the bill being pushed by AIPAC's best friends in the House—might put Palestinians on a path to starvation, making it incumbent upon Israel to cover these costs. These Israelis argued that "at this point the bill [HR 4681] could end up limiting the diplomatic flexibility of the new Israeli government in dealings with the new PA regime. In addition, Israeli officials said, the bill may place the onus of providing for the well-being of the Palestinian population on Israel, the occupying power in the territories. The bill could also result in the cancellation of several internationally funded aid programs in which Israel has a vital interest, in fields such as public health, water and sewage."[190]

Of course, all three of the expert witnesses were coming from a totally pro-Israel perspective. So when Wolfensohn expressed concern that harsh measures might result in a million starving Palestinians, his views were consonant with views held by many Israeli officials. Still, in effect, these expert witnesses' testimony did serve as a useful brake on the House bill, as demonstrated in these descriptions of how Senate staffers, assigned the task of responding to Hamas's victory, performed their duties in real time.

One key staffer for a Middle East subcommittee member described the maelstrom he was entering at the onset of this episode. "There's little time to sit down; I'm almost always running down the hall," he said. "I'm now working on a line-in line-out text to modify this [Hamas bill] text. I'll tell [my senator, who's seen as more sympathetic to the Palestinians] to look at this, then we'll have a slightly longer conversation to see what issues really need to be addressed, perhaps using Wolfensohn, Malley, and Ross's comments to point to. Then we'll need to get the State Department to present a viewpoint. I know that State doesn't support this [HR 4681] despite AIPAC saying it does. I've heard this—these are private assertions by AIPAC that I've heard from other offices' staffers. I still haven't heard it from AIPAC directly."

Just one week later, the same staffer told me:

> "AIPAC is coming to see me [this week]. They'll probably say this [their language regarding Hamas in the McConnell-Biden bill] is more flexible, but it's a fake flexibility. You have to see the strings attached on humanitarian aid. Take education funding, for example. Biden says 'we should build schools,' but under the terms of his own bill's language [McConnell-Biden], you can't build schools. OFAC [Office of Foreign Assets Control with the Treasury Department] would have to sign off on these allocations. You'd have to deal with Hamas for school construction, and dealing with Hamas is formally prohibited. Even Dennis [Ross] said we need to get money in to pay salaries, but all of this would run into the same dead end if you look at the language in the [McConnell-Biden] bill. Teachers, doctors, etc., non-Hamas types will suffer also because we'll need to differentiate between Hamas and the other Palestinians somehow."

Another staffer provided the following tour d'horizon, depicting the issue's complexity. This staffer believed that the Bush administration had presented a sound policy—a logical policy on Hamas—one which followed up well on the Ross, Malley, and Wolfensohn recommendations. Some $400 million would be redirected toward UNRWA (UN Relief and Works Agency) or held in abeyance. Senate staffers had spoken at length with State Department officials about humanitarian aid and all had agreed there's still a fine line between humanitarian aid and taking pressure off of Hamas. For example, prior to the 2006 election, Fatah had put 30,000 new people on the payroll. Few were inclined to feel obligated to help the PA meet this new payroll burden. One staffer said, "Maybe Hamas will make things easy and fire them all, but this is unlikely if Hamas is smart. I wouldn't want to be Hamas right now. The EU has fallen into line with pressures, too. Perhaps Iran will pony up [to help Hamas; which Iran eventually did]; we'll see."

How would this Senate action play out? One staffer had been told by Sen. McConnell that he wouldn't use a supplemental as a vehicle for his bill, but in the end, McConnell went ahead to use a supplemental to cover the three points: to make Hamas "recognize Israel; renounce terrorism; and recognize past Palestinian commitments." All told, there were now five bills under consideration: (1) the Ros-Lehtinen–Lantos bill that had been marked up in HIRC; (2) McConnell-Biden, which had not yet been marked up; (3) Rep. Kolbe's Appropriations bill, a related bill which had already been passed in the House; (4) McConnell's language in a Senate supplemental Appropriations bill; and, (5) Sen. Judd Gregg's bill, which he ended up voting against himself because it had been so burdened by other members—some $10–$15 billion in add-ons. A potential sticking point with the leading contender—McConnell-Biden—was its references to Israel as a "Jewish state," highly provocative and controversial because at least 20 percent of Israel's population is Palestinian Arab. As a staffer said, "This wording is likely to raise the ante. Will the State Department endorse this? There are one million Arabs in Israel. AIPAC put the 'Jewish state' language in, people tell me."

A third Senate staffer presented his own edifying outlook on S 2370, especially with an eye to explaining factors affecting many "less concerned" or otherwise heavily preoccupied senators' behavior, and which lobbyists were weighing in on the issue.

"The senator [my boss] has not yet decided whether to support the McConnell-Biden bill; her schedule weighs heavily on how much time she even has. She was too focused on the budget last week to deal with this issue. I may have to draft her a memo on it. She has spoken with constituents on this issue. We have discussed the House versus the Senate's versions of the bills on Hamas. She'll probably listen to me and just take a decision. The AIPAC folks met with [the senator] the day the bill by McConnell and Biden was introduced. I can only surmise they spoke against it [McConnell-Biden], since it's meant as a foil to Ros-Lehtinen's bill in the House. I met with the ZOA yesterday and they reiterated it's in our best interest for Hamas to fail. Everybody says we can't provide aid and deal or negotiate with terrorists, but it's a democratically elected government, so what do we do? In fact, we're having an office debate over this issue and whether Hamas can achieve a monopoly of force. I had Presbyterians in here talking about a West Bank hospital that gets $200,000 per month from the PA. If you pass legislation that affects the PA, this will get cut off. The AIPAC rep is here every six to eight weeks, but even more often if there is pressing legislation like this. Look at the security wall—that was last year's big issue—this issue went to the ICJ [International Court of Justice], sent there by the UN General Assembly. The supporters of Israel went apoplectic about this. There were letters to Kofi Annan and the boss signed on. Personally, I thought the letter's demand to stop this was pretty absurd: the secretary-general couldn't stop this [sending the matter to the ICJ]. Meanwhile, we get church people and others telling us of the negative impact of the wall on farmers, and so forth. But back to the Hamas thing, here we're talking about aid, money; with the wall, it's a different thing."

A third Senate staffer compared HR 4681 and S 2370. In doing so, he not only helped shed light on the arcane language of the Hill, but clarified how much is at stake in how bills are worded.

"Look at the differences between the Ros-Lehtinen bill and the McConnell-Biden bill. The three big issues on the McConnell-Biden bill are: (1) The need for a broader national security 'carve out' or waiver, which involves what Hamas needs to do or change to get money and recognition. We need to make them recognize Israel's right to exist, renounce violence, and reaffirm commitment to all preceding Palestinian documents. By a 'carve out,' I mean whether or not to make the waiver broader; (2) Should there be a sunset on the bill? Should we make it a five-year bill and reissue it in five years if Hamas gets reelected, or revisit this issue if Hamas changes or there are other changes? And (3) What to do about travel/contacts with the Palestinians by US officials? Do we really want to paint all Palestinians with the same brush? Everyone was pretty much like-minded on Hamas. [Sen.] Boxer was browbeating Wolfensohn by reading the Hamas charter [which calls for Israel's destruction]. Wolfensohn knows it; it's not necessary."

And finally, here, a fourth Senate staffer sized up the bills, concentrating on McConnell's as a counter to HR 4681.

"This is where we are now. A Hamas government is being formed. There's still ten days to two weeks until the Israeli elections, so we must wait and see until this plays out. There are three Senate resolutions/bills out there regarding Hamas. Then you've got the [House] Ros-Lehtinen bill that cuts off all aid. The McConnell bill is seen as an alternative to this. It's meant to slow down the whole process. My sense is the McConnell bill gives the Bush administration as much leeway as possible—it will enable some Palestinians to travel, and offer some representation to the Palestinians. Part of the rationale of the Senate bill is to offset the Ros-Lehtinen House bill, so it buys time. It plays that tactical role. Cosponsors for the McConnell bill reflect much bipartisanship."

Somewhat later in the game, in the offices of a fifth senator, a consistently avid "supporter of Israel" and of AIPAC initiatives, the "take" on McConnell-Biden was now one of resignation. It reflected the fact that AIPAC, CUFI, and other right wing pro-Israel forces, now perhaps encouraged by Israel's government, had reconciled themselves with S 2370's passage. "We signed the McConnell-Biden bill," the staffer said. "The Jewish lobby was very much behind this. We got contacted by AIPAC people back home and here in D.C. and were urged to sign. The RJC [Republican Jewish Coalition] also urged us to sign it."

In the end, the McConnell-Biden bill, which itself, after all, contained many provisions ensuring that Hamas and the PA would be kept in a tight box, was passed in the Senate by unanimous consent in June 2006. It was sent to the House, where it was approved. By year's end, President Bush signed it into law.

How did staffers evaluate the overall effort and outcome? Many senators and staffers were pleased that the "insanely irresponsible" H.R. 4681 had been stopped in its tracks. But most were not oblivious to the domestic political considerations motivating Sen. McConnell and others, as indicated by this staffer's observations.

> "McConnell-Biden significantly revised the Ros-Lehtinen bill that the House passed. It's like making sausage. They had input from Leahy and Sununu to temper it, and this revised version—S 2370—was passed by unanimous consent. If you make a side-by-side comparison of the original bill and the present bill, you'll see interesting changes. Some senators, like Sen. Leahy, wanted it to match the [Middle East] Quartet's position [the United States, Russia, the European Union, and the United Nations]. As for McConnell's role, he's in leadership, so he needs to be cognizant of political needs; he needs to cater to members who need to demonstrate their support for Israel. Don't forget that McConnell is potentially the Senate Majority leader. [Our senator] is different; he doesn't feel the need to demonstrate strong support for Israel."

Others were left wondering just how much the Palestinian people would suffer as the result of its passage, as reflected in this staffer's musings.

> "Now this bill [McConnell-Biden] prevents money from going directly to the PA and also prevents money from going to schools for meals, etc. It prohibits contact with all NGOs and any organizations affiliated with Hamas. Our USAID folks are not allowed to work with the Ministry of Health folks, for example. We had a briefing on this that was organized by Sen. [Ted] Kennedy. He had brought in the UN Human Rights Commission, CARE, and other NGOs. Much of the focus has been on how basic human needs are not being addressed."

TAKING STOCK IN 2005–2006: SO WHAT? IS THE ROLE OF CONGRESS IMPORTANT?

When I put this question to my staffer interviewees, almost always near the end of my interview, I received what ultimately constituted a broad range of responses. In some cases, staffers waxed reflective on not just the relationship between Congress and the president, but also congresspersons', especially House members, need to mollify constituent concerns. One staffer clearly disapproved of his own boss's behavior.

> "From an I.R. [International Relations] student's perspective, you see Congress as an uncontrollable child on many issues, but sometimes you realize Congress is accountable to the American people more than the president is, and should weigh in. I always ask, 'Is Congress being helpful in backing the administration?' But I also refuse to sign on to stuff because some person is trying to get their name on something for domestic political considerations, things that might hurt the administration and its objectives. Examples to me are people trying to cut off funds to the PA and providing no flexibility on this issue, or acting like [Sen.] Santorum does on Iran. There are people out there advocating their own positions very successfully, but they may represent very narrow interests, like rabbis and Jews in [our home, Midwestern state] who weigh in about how Jerusalem is being treated. There are many heavy hitters at events by AIPAC and the RJC [Republican Jewish Coalition]. With my boss, of course, [for these groups] on all of this it's like preaching to the choir."

A second staffer presented another disparaging view, in 2006. "With respect to the significance of Congress, I think there's not a lot of impact," the staffer said. "There's little to moderate impact, especially as things have become more partisan. There's no modern day Republican like a Sen. Fulbright questioning the administration's policy. If you had a president from one party and the other party controls Congress, we might have more criticism and a greater role by Congress on foreign policy." A third Senate staffer issued his own bleak assessment of Congress's role, saying, "Congress only does two things well: (1) nothing; (2) overreact. There's not a lot of long-range planning, especially on the Hill."

At a minimum, the staffers' comments show disillusionment with the ability of the Senate/Congress to behave constructively and productively, and that this is especially true of output by the Foreign Relations committee. In this regard, it is particularly useful to read what a Senate staffer had to say about why McConnell played such a big role with this important bill, and what this had to say about the dysfunctional nature of Foreign Relations. The reader will recall my earlier discussion of authorizing committees' failure to pass bills out of committee due to partisan discord and other factors, and how this empowers the Appropriations Committee. The Senate staffer helped shed light on this recurring problem in stating:

> "It's interesting that McConnell took the lead on the Senate Hamas bill; it's probably because a staffer had a strong interest in the issue. McConnell is chairman of the Foreign Ops subcommittee, so there was concern that he'd drag his feet there as well as on the Supplemental. McConnell had said that he wasn't going to attach the Hamas bill to the Supplemental, and the bill was sent to Foreign Relations and not to Appropriations as it should have been, but it was going to loop back to Appropriations anyway because they [on Foreign Relations] can't get out an authorizing bill. Why no authorizing bill? Because people on that committee with axes to grind will gum it up or add on something controversial. Last summer the House passed [an authorizing] bill, but in the Senate it became so controversial due to additions that Lugar just pulled it from the floor."

All matters considered, many Senate staffers seemed to suggest that where the Senate is shaping policy, its impact is either small and/or negative. And in the end, in this case, there was very little discussion of the practical implications of this legislation; that is, its negative impact on NGOs and others trying to deliver basic services to the Palestinians.

THE SENATE FOREIGN RELATIONS COMMITTEE
OF 2011–2013

In 2011, the full Foreign Relations committee membership changed significantly. With the Democrats now holding the Majority, Sen. Kerry chaired the committee, backed up by fellow D's Barbara Boxer (CA), Robert Menendez (NJ), Ben Cardin (MD), Bob Casey Jr. (PA), Jim Webb (VA), Jeanne Shaheen (NH), Chris Coons (DE), Richard Durbin (IL), and Tom Udall (NM). Of these members, Boxer, Menendez, Cardin, Casey Jr., and Durbin represented a bloc of "very strong supporters" of Israel. Lugar (IN), still on the committee, now served as RM. Fellow R's included Bob Corker (TN), Jim Risch (ID), Marco Rubio (FL), James Inhofe (OK), Jim DeMint (SC), Johnny Isakson (GA), John Barrasso (WY), and Mike Lee (UT). Risch, Rubio, Inhofe, Barrasso, and DeMint were also all "very strong supporters" of Israel, unlikely to question right wing Israeli government policy. The bipartisan group of "very strong supporters" represented a combination of senators with Jewish American roots and/or strong home state Jewish communities, senators with evangelical Christian beliefs and/or strong evangelical communities, security hawks, and a few presidential hopefuls.

Sen. Casey chaired the Near Eastern and South Asian Affairs subcommittee, with Boxer, Menendez, Cardin, Coons, and Udall in support roles. Jim Risch was RM, backed by Corker,[191] Lee, Rubio, and Isakson. Barrasso bowed out to Risch in the Near Eastern and South Central Asian Affairs subcommittee's ranking member slot. Barrasso had become RM for the Public Lands and Forests subcommittee on Energy and Natural Resources, obviously a more critical role for his Wyoming constituents. He was still on Foreign Relations but moved over to other subcommittees.

In the 2011–2013 time frame, as noted earlier, Congress's attention had shifted considerably; its focus was now more heavily on the perceived threat to Israel posed by Iran. This shift was much to AIPAC's liking, as well as that of Israel's right wing government, as it took the focus off A-I and I-P affairs. The Iranian threat had taken on its own significance due to continued fears of the country developing a nuclear weapons capability and because of Iran's ability to project power via Syria, as well as directly, into Lebanon. In Lebanon, the Iranian government has backed heavily several of Israel's nemeses, with the coreligionist Shi'ite Hizballah at the top of the list. Consequently, senators circulated a torrent of "Dear Colleague" letters and introduced many resolutions and bills aimed at countering the Iranian challenge.

As we saw in the House, Senate activity in this area was far from new. Many senators, prompted by AIPAC and right wing Israelis alike, had been placing Iran in their crosshairs for many years, as discussed earlier. I will add here what one staffer advised me to do back in 2005 when I asked him what bills were especially interesting to know about. "You should look at S 333, the Iran Freedom and Support Act of [February] 2005, which supports the Iranian people and condemns the government," he said. "It authorizes $10 million to promote 'change' in Iran. It is sponsored by [Sen.] Santorum and has 43 cosponsors. Clinton and Lautenberg are cosponsors; there's domestic politics at play here. S 333 indicates that we have all the ingredients to create democracy in Iran by nonviolent means. Dems like Stabenow, Levin, and Bayh have signed on. Specter has not; neither has Schumer. Some people are comparing this to what happened before going to war against Iraq."

Also, as additional background, in the summer of 2006 attention was focused on the Syrian-Iranian surrogate in Lebanon, Hizballah. Following Hizballah's abduction of Israeli soldiers along the border, Israel responded powerfully, launching a full-scale assault on Hizballah's forces in southern Lebanon. The Senate promptly passed Senate Resolution 534 in support of Israel and its right to self-defense. Sponsored by Majority Leader Bill Frist, with 43/44 D's and 19/55 R's cosponsoring the resolution, the resolution passed on a voice vote. The lone Democrat who did not cosponsor was Max Baucus, who was absent because he was attending the funeral of a marine nephew killed in Iraq. Interestingly, many R's, including Senators Lamar Alexander, Chafee, Coburn, Larry Craig, Pete Domenici, Mike Enzi, Judd Gregg, Hagel, Lugar, and John Warner did not sign on to this bill. It is doubtful that they actually opposed the measure and that they would have voted against it if the ayes and nays had been taken. Regardless, various right wing pro-Israel interests took them to task for this "slight" or oversight. In yet another response to events in Lebanon, a bipartisan letter, signed by 88 senators, called upon the European Union to declare Hizballah a terrorist organization. (The Senate effort was matched by a House letter that contained 209 members' signatures.) This time, twelve Republican senators refrained from signing, including Lugar, Hagel, and Warner, all of whom were then chastised as follows:

> "Most troubling, the top two Republicans on the Senate Foreign Relations Committee, Chairman Richard Lugar (R-IN) and Senator Chuck Hagel (R-NE), and the top Republican on the Senate Armed Services Committee, Chairman John Warner (R-VA), were not among the 88 Senators who signed the letter. When it comes to

Israel and the Jewish community, the hypocrisy of Republicans in Congress is just overwhelming. 'How is it that Republicans in the Senate can claim to be supporters of Israel when almost 20 percent of their caucus—including their top two Members on the Foreign Relations Committee and top Republican on the Armed Services Committee—apparently does not think that Hezbollah should be on the E.U. list of terrorist organizations,' asked NJDC [National Jewish Democratic Council] Executive Director Ira Forman. 'While Democrats are out there trying to punish Israel's enemies and ensure that she has a right to defend herself, these ten Republican senators have no problem with the international community treating Hezbollah as a legitimate organization. Shame on them.'"[192]

Why didn't these Republican senators sign on? Some staffers and off-the-Hill observers in D.C. suggested that the senators were troubled, as was the international community writ large, with Israel's excessive use of force in Lebanon. The Israeli Air Force, to give one example, had bombed critical Lebanese infrastructure, including oil storage facilities, producing the Mediterranean Sea's largest ever oil spill and causing an ecological disaster along the Lebanese coast. A Palestinian refugee camp was bombed, and Lebanon's power grid and communications systems were also extensively damaged by Israeli bombs. Overall, the punishment inflicted on Lebanon and Lebanese citizens in general, not just Hizballah-related Lebanese, was so great as to cause almost all citizens of Lebanon, including Sunni Prime Minister Fuad Siniora and other long-standing Lebanese enemies of Hizballah, to show solidarity with Hizballah. Lebanese of many stripes actually rejoiced over the black eye inflicted by Hizballah's elusive fighters upon the IDF during the brief war. One veteran Hill staffer said, "When the Israelis chose to broaden the war, hitting non-Hizballah targets, including the Christian heartland, they put the pro-American Siniora government in a tight spot, angered the Lebanese American community, and created a lot of controversy. The Israelis crossed some red lines with their behavior, and some senators took notice."

Three specific developments redirected congresspersons' attention away from the Iran-Syria-Lebanon axis toward I-P issues: (1) The Palestinians' 2011 bid for United Nations recognition and membership as a state.(2) UNESCO's October 2011 decision to grant the Palestinians full membership in that organization. (An effort that, if achieved, would confer automatic membership for the Palestinian entity in other international organizations, such as the World International Property Organization [WIPO], as well as open the door to similar recognition of the Palestinians in the World Health Organization and sundry other international bodies.) And (3) Israel's late 2012 announcement to push ahead with settlement construction in E1, the land zone adjacent to Jerusalem, whose development by Jewish Israelis would effectively block the creation of a contiguous Palestinian territorial entity on the West Bank. Significantly, Israel's E1 announcement followed the UN General Assembly's November 29, 2012, vote granting Palestine Non-Member Observer State status in that body.

What made the first two developments immediately problematic for the US government was that legislation passed by Congress in the early 1990s closed the door to US government funding of any UN organization that recognized the Palestine Liberation Organization (PLO) and/or a Palestinian state in the absence of formal Palestinian recognition of Israel's right to exit. Specifically, Public Law 101-246, Title IV, &414, February 16, 1990, 104 Statute 70, 1990, prohibited the appropriation of funds "for the United Nations or any specialized agency thereof which accords the [PLO] the same standing as a member state." And Public Law 103-236, Title IV, &410, April 30, 1994, 108 Statute 454 barred funding to any UN body "which grants full membership as a state to any organization or groups that does not have the internationally recognized attributes of statehood." Both of these public laws, passed by Congress, followed on the heels of 1989 Senate and House efforts like Senate bill S 763,[193] which were designed to ensure the PLO's "compliance with commitments to stop terrorist activities and to recognize Israel's right to exist," in addition to Senate Resolution 875 and House Resolution 2145, both of which contained language similar to that found in the public laws of 1990 and 1994. Sen. Robert Kasten, Jr. (R-WI) was the primary sponsor of S 875, and Rep. Tom Lantos sponsored HR 2145. In a nutshell, recognition by any UN body of the Palestinians' right to statehood or their achievement of statehood status would trigger a suspension of US funding to the "offending" UN body under these laws. (I'll just note in passing that it was Sen. Kasten who was to be a major recipient of campaign funds that AIPAC's President David Steiner was soliciting from one Haim Katz. Katz surreptitiously taped and released to the public the conversation, much to AIPAC's embarrassment. The conversation can be found on-line and makes for an interesting read.

By 2011, the Palestinians had seen 18 years pass since the signing of the 1993 Oslo Peace Accords without any clear indication of the peace process bearing fruit, as well as the past two years during which negotiations with Israel had been frozen while Israeli settlement activity on the West Bank continued. Israeli authorities, for their part, argued that they had no clear partner for peace, given the often bloody Fatah-Hamas rift in the Palestinian camp, Hamas's refusal to recognize Israel, and the fact that Palestinian authorities were either abetting or proving themselves incapable of stopping Hamas's and/or Islamic Jihad's shelling of Israeli sites and citizens with Qassam rockets. In these circumstances, altered and energized by the late April 2011 reconciliation between Fatah and Hamas, the leaders of the PA appeared determined to take their case for statehood to the United Nations and other international bodies.

In general, the Senate (and House's) response to the Palestinians' bid for recognition at the UN was immediately condemnatory and depicted the bid as an attempt to circumvent the Palestinians' earlier agreement to resolve the conflict through a negotiated settlement with Israel. As early as May 2011, Senators Cardin, Collins, Bob Casey, John Thune,[194] Menendez, and Risch introduced Senate Resolution 185, which opposed Palestinian efforts to seek unilateral UN recognition and reiterated language akin to Sec. of State Hillary Clinton's April 2009 formula according to which the United States "will not deal with or in any way fund a Palestinian government that includes Hamas unless and until Hamas has renounced violence, recognized Israel, and agreed to follow the previous treaty obligations of the Palestinian Authority." Some 87 senators cosigned the resolution, and it unanimously passed in the Senate on June 28. On the occasion, Democrat Majority Leader Sen. Harry Reid said, "A negotiated settlement of the Israeli-Palestinian conflict should come through direct Israeli-Palestinian negotiations . . . A fair beginning to good-faith talks also means the Palestinians cannot simply stop by the negotiating table on their way to the United Nations to seek recognition as a state."[195]

But PA leaders pressed forward with their objective of attaining UN recognition during summer 2011, and in response, the modes employed by US senators to thwart this effort diversified. For example, in late August 2011, Senators Menendez and Rubio used their Latin America connections, urging the presidents of Colombia, Panama, and Costa Rica to oppose any UN resolution put before the UN General Assembly regarding recognition of a Palestinian state. Similarly, in mid-September 2011, Senators Coons and Isakson, respectively chairman and RM of the Foreign Relations subcommittee on Africa, sent letters to 23 African presidents to reject any unilateral bid for statehood by the Palestinians.

Ultimately, the intense domestic and international lobbying effort against UN recognition of Palestine paid off. By fall 2011, it was clear that, beyond the US threat of using its UN Security Council veto, the PA would not be able to secure enough Security Council votes to override such a veto. Moreover, pressure placed on UN General Assembly members also stymied efforts to bring the issue to a vote there. Still, PA leaders registered a major victory on October 31, 2011 when UNESCO's members voted 107–14, with 52 abstentions, to approve the PA's request for full membership. Because of the aforementioned public laws, the Obama administration was legally bound to freeze its funding of UNESCO—$66 million (22 percent of the total funding, the US the largest provider of its funds). Among the senators who were more outspoken on this development were "pro-Israel" stalwarts Susan Collins and Lindsey Graham. Collins sardonically said that at a time when the US had a total debt of some $14 trillion, it was particularly hard to justify continued funding of UN organizations run amok. For his part, Graham, RM on Senate Appropriations' State and Foreign Ops, said: "This could be catastrophic for the US-UN relationship. This could be the tipping point."

UN recognition of the PA came at a price. It set in motion all previous laws passed by the US Congress requiring cancellation of US funding to UN bodies guilty of granting such recognition. No new US legislation was required. Speaking even more menacingly in response to the UNESCO development, Sen. Lindsey Graham said Congress was considering termination of all US funding for the PA—$550 million in fiscal 2011—despite his acknowledgement that support for the PA was still sound policy. *Foreign Policy* reported that Graham said, "I don't think that's in our near-term or long-term interest, but that's what's going to happen, that's where this thing is headed . . . The world has to make a decision . . . . If the UN is going to be a body that buys into Palestinian statehood . . . then they suffer. It's a decision they make."[196] Sen. McCain also chimed in, saying, "They've made a decision and they will pay the consequences for their decision. . . . US tax dollars are not going to be spent, if I have anything to do with it, on organizations that take the measures they've taken."[197]

On the other side of the aisle, senior Senate Democrats mostly fell in line, with a party spokesperson informing *Foreign Policy* "they either support cutting funds to UN organizations that grant membership to the Palestinians, or at least don't plan to do anything about it."[198]

How did more peace-oriented US groups see SR 185 and what went on in conjunction with its passage? For the most part, one needed to go outside official government circles to find more biting criticism of this development, including that dished out by individuals like the people at APN, whose love for Israel is unquestionable. At Americans for Peace Now, staff made clear that "This resolution was one of the main focal points of AIPAC lobbying on the Hill last month [April 2011] and in the days since, with strong pressure on members to cosponsor. Members of Congress understand that whether or not they cosponsor this kind of measure will be 'scored' by AIPAC . . . A little over a month of lobbying yielded a total of 89 cosponsors; so 90 senators if you include Cardin [the bill's sponsor]. APN strongly opposes S. Res. 185, along with its House version, H. Res. 288."[199]

After the Senate passed SR 185, Mairav Zonszein, an Israeli-American and native of New York City, wrote, "The resolution . . . reasons that US policy is committed to a two-state solution through negotiations and thus any unilateral action by the Palestinians is counterproductive . . . This is a ridiculously insulting double standard. Israel has been taking unilateral actions for decades with impunity, actions which have drastically changed facts on the ground and continue to undermine the very notion of negotiations. Can you imagine the US making aid to Israel contingent on anything it does?"[200]

From the moment the US laws sprang into effect, enormous problems were posed for the White House and US diplomacy. Freezing UNESCO funding portended deleterious consequences for US programs in sundry developing countries, placing at risk programs designed to meet the needs of the poorest of the poor around the planet. This prospect was brilliantly parodied by John Oliver in a March 15, 2012, segment on Jon Stewart's *The Daily Show*, in which Oliver drew attention to how the decision might affect the welfare of small children in a UNESCO-funded school program in Gabon.[201]

Defunding the UN posed problems for Pres. Obama's administration on numerous fronts. It brought friction with the international community in general, starting with UNESCO and the UN. It brought cries of protest by all NGOs that would be negatively affected. It produced strong denunciations from all countries that feared disruptions of program funding and the attendant consequences. And it heightened tension between the White House and Congress. In mid-January, 2012, *UN Watch* reported that, "One [UNESCO official] confirmed that the administration of US President Barack Obama has been seeking ways to effect a waiver of the law that mandates immediate cessation of Washington's contributions to any UN agency that allows Palestinian membership. But this official added that the one key person holding out is Congresswoman Ileana Ros-Lehtinen, who chairs the Foreign Affairs Committee."[202]

By February 2012, the Obama administration was making clear its hope to work with Congress to restore funding to UNESCO despite that organization's recognition of Palestinian statehood.[203] With Rep. Ros-Lehtinen vociferously sustaining her opposition, the administration became more aggressive in March, when Sec. of State Clinton, to use Hill vernacular, "blew the hold" placed on most US aid for the Palestinians. As staffers explained, even though Congress holds the "power of the purse," "these 'holds' can be seen as more of a courtesy extended by the White House to Congress, or not." In response to Clinton's move, key congressional actors relented. As reported by CNN, "Two powerful Republicans in the House of Representatives released restrictions Friday on the disbursement of US assistance to Palestinians that the congresswomen had been blocking in Congress. . . . Rep. Kay Granger, chairwoman of . . . House [Foreign Ops] . . . , said she was releasing a hold that had been in place since August on all of the $147 million in congressionally appropriated money for the Palestinians. [Elsewhere] House Foreign Affairs Chairwoman Ileana Ros-Lehtinen partially lifted her block for more than half of the funds to be sent."[204]

But for Obama's administration, the grander conundrum continued well on into late spring of 2012. One approach taken by its State Department, itself reflective of the Israel lobby's power, was to appeal to Jewish American interests to gain backing for a presidential waiver. In late April 2012, Assistant Secretary of State for International Organization Affairs Esther Brimmer went "hat in hand" to speak to the American Jewish Committee of Greater Miami and Broward County. The choice of venues was highly revealing. After a lengthy disquisition designed to demonstrate how and why the Obama administration had been defending Israel's interests in the UN and affiliated organizations and how it had maintained its opposition to the Palestinians' unilateral bid for statehood, Brimmer finally got around to making her pitch for AJC's support to secure greater breathing room for the US president's foreign policy making. "Ultimately the withholding of funding at UNESCO and elsewhere could lead to the loss of voice and vote in these international organizations, undermining the US's ability to advance its interests," she said. "It would also have a devastating impact directly on organizations like the World Health Organization, which relies heavily on US contributions to prevent deadly pandemics from spreading globally and to the United States. The WHO is also essential to the global progress made against malaria, HIV/ AIDS, and polio."[205] As Brimmer went on to say, the Israeli government had steadily expressed its profound appreciation for the US administration's efforts to defend Israel's interests in the UN, as well as stated how damaging it would be if the US were no longer fully capable of playing that role. Taking a powerful tact, she asserted, "We cannot afford to cede the floor to emerging powers and adversaries, such as Iran and Syria, which do not share our values and would be more than happy to undermine US and Israeli interests. These countries want nothing more than to see the United States retreat from the UN, withdraw from UN bodies, and lose its influence and leadership positions and potentially its vote in key UN bodies."[206]

Just one month later, in May 2012, this multidimensional struggle shifted battlegrounds as the issue of continued funding for the UN Relief and Works Agency came into focus. UNRWA was set up in 1949 to assist Palestinian refugees after their expulsion from Palestine due to the warfare surrounding Israel's 1948 creation. Once again, AIPAC was in the middle of this struggle. "As usual, the American Israel Public Affairs Committee (AIPAC) is taking the lead in lobbying various Senate offices to support an amendment to the 2013 State and Foreign Operations Appropriations Bill introduced by Senator Mark Kirk of Illinois that would require the US government to confirm the number of Palestinians who receive assistance from UNRWA," the Palestinian Policy Network reported. "But the real goal of the amendment is clear: It is an attempt to redefine the number of Palestinian refugees receiving aid from UNRWA with a view to limiting its budget, which is heavily dependent on US aid."[207]

An UNRWA official who preferred anonymity, however, saw these matters slightly differently. It's true, he told me, that as this article reported, a switch in the definition in the direction of what Sen. Kirk was proposing would leave as few as 30,000 Palestinians on the list, whereas the current definition covered some five million people: the original refugees and their descen-dants.[208] But he said this was not the "real goal" of the Kirk amendment. Why? Because one of the thorniest so-called final status issues associated with the I-P conflict's successful resolution—alongside sovereignty over Jerusalem; water rights; final borders; and security concerns—is that of Palestinian ref-ugees' "Right of Return," a right emblazoned in international law. So as the official said, "If Kirk's amendment could miraculously make five million Pal-estinians disappear, then this would lay the groundwork for additional steps to eliminating the 'Right of Return' issue. At UNRWA, we didn't think this amendment originated with AIPAC; rather we had the sentiment it was a question of the foxes guarding the chicken coop."

Ultimately, Sen. Kirk's amendment was thwarted by the Foreign Ops chairman, Sen. Leahy. As I will detail in the chapter on Appropriations, Sen. Kirk, and/or his staff, may have spent far too many of his chits in introducing this amendment. But the entire effort reflected, once again, the influence wielded by "pro-Israel" actors, as well as those efforts' impact on US foreign policy and the United States' image abroad.

Last but not least, the United Nations General Assembly vote on November 29, 2012, represented a significant breakthrough for Palestinians. The lopsided vote reflected Israel and the United States' isolation in the world community: 138 members voted in favor of the resolution; 9 opposed it; and 41 countries abstained. In the "no" column, in addition to Canada, the Czech Republic, and Panama, stood supporters of Israel in the UN, such as the Marshall Islands, Micronesia, Naura, and Palau—countries that most Americans would either not know or not recognize as independent nation-states.

Israel's pique over the General Assembly vote was quickly demonstrated by the announcement of plans to move ahead with settlement construction at E1 on the West Bank. How did the US Senate respond? In essence, Sen. Dianne Feinstein was the sole voice audibly opposing the Israeli government's plans for E1. As M.J. Rosenberg wrote:

> It is then not surprising that Feinstein is so upset about the Netanyahu government's decision to proceed with planning for the development of the area between Jerusalem and Ma'aleh Adumim, the area known as E1. She understands that building Jewish apartment houses and

shopping malls in E1 would kill the two-state solution to the Israeli-Palestinian conflict by cutting Ramallah and Bethlehem off from East Jerusalem and from each other. . . . There can be no Palestinian state if Palestinian territory is divided into three little cantons—the northern West Bank, the southern West Bank and Gaza—all walled off from the historic Palestinian (and Jewish) capital of Jerusalem. And, of course, that is what Netanyahu and the Israeli right is determined to achieve. Yes, she is one of those legislators (there aren't many) who puts the national interest before the need to raise money for the next campaign. In that respect, she is decidedly old school.[209]

Most senators, however, lined up to initiate or endorse legislation designed to punish the Palestinians should the latter utilize their new status to press claims against Israel in the International Court of Justice (ICJ) or International Criminal Court (ICC).

"Having earned the observer non-member status, Palestinians will enjoy access to UN agencies and the International Criminal Court (ICC) where they could file complaints against Israel. The biggest fear I have is that the Palestinians achieve this status it won't be very long before the Palestinians use the United Nations as a club against Israel," Sen. Lindsey Graham said.[210]

The senator's statements raised the question of why Israel's authorities would fear Palestinian recourse to the ICJ and ICC if Israelis had not violated international law(s).

That Israel's right wing government had helpful elements in the US Senate was placed in evidence in early July 2013. Two former Hill staffers, now working in Washington, D.C., as UNRWA officials, met formally with a PSM for Sen. Corker. Behind closed doors, the PSM, Trey Hicks, presented his own rendition of the A-I conflict's history, using right wing/religious references to the West Bank as "Judea and Samaria," and talking about how Israel should "finish the job" in terms of its conquest of that land. Said one of the UNRWA officials, "Here he was, in essence advocating that Israel engage in ethnic cleansing of the West Bank to two UNRWA diplomats. We couldn't believe what we were hearing."

Shifting to another Senate Mideast-related matter, the power of AIPAC and other right wing supporters of Israel was also on display in the effort to block Pres. Obama's appointment of former Sen. Chuck Hagel as secretary of defense in 2013. All Hill cognoscenti could see that AIPAC hardly needed to lift a finger as its key Senate allies, led by Senators Graham and McCain, skewered their erstwhile colleague and fellow Republican, Hagel, for his past willingness to pose tough questions relating to right wing Israeli government policies. Sen. Kirk's deputy chief of staff, Rich Goldberg, was "outed" by *Roll Call*'s Meredith Shiner as leading a secret campaign against Hagel, and a former Senate staffer told me he did so without Sen. Kirk's knowledge or consent. All of this opposition despite Hagel's almost always having voted in favor of continued aid to that state. Staffers and observers on and off the Hill gave much credit to J Street for expending resources in Hagel's defense, and they described AIPAC as telling members of Congress behind closed doors that they did not support Hagel's nomination, but preferred to "keep their powder dry" and not expend too much of their own political capital to defeat Obama's nominee.

More intriguing were AIPAC's efforts to push pieces of legislation that would have given a full green light for the use of military force against Iran. Senate Foreign Relations leaders Graham and Menendez took the lead in introducing S. Res. 65 in March 2013, which off-the-Hill opponents labeled "the backdoor to war resolution" because its language would require the US to back Israel in any military effort undertaken to prevent Iran from acquiring a nuclear weapons capability. Sen. Corker's office, abetted by Sen. Rand Paul's, got the language amended in the Senate Foreign Relations committee markup, inserting the role of Congress in the authorization of military action against Iran, along with a requirement that Israeli military action would have to be seen by the US government as "legitimate," as can be seen by viewing the official copy of the revision of the resolution section 8.

> (8) [Congress] urges that, if the Government of Israel is compelled to take military action in legitimate self-defense against Iran's nuclear weapons program, the United States Government should stand with Israel and provide, in accordance with United States law and the constitutional responsibility of Congress to authorize the use of military force, diplomatic, military, and economic support to the Government of Israel in its defense of its territory, people, and existence.

Barring the introduction of these amendments, the resolution, which passed the Senate in May 2013 by 99–0, would have given strong support—although it was a nonbinding resolution—to the possibility of Israel unilaterally initiating armed hostilities against Iran, with the US president being called upon by Congress to "provide diplomatic, military, and economic support" to Israel. The revised language brought specificity to Israel responding to an Iranian nuclear weapons program and left little wiggle room for the president to determine how to respond to Israel's actions, with Congress entering the picture to vote up or down to authorize any US military action. But as one staffer asserted, pointedly, "Even though the bill was watered down before it passed by a vote of 99–0, it still showed the US was giving Israel the keys to drive US foreign policy on Iran. Insert any other country's name in the equation with the original resolution, and people would accuse you of sedition!"

Sen. Graham's critics also pointed out that in presenting this same resolution, Graham described it as an affirmation of a policy already endorsed by Pres. Obama. In fact, Graham was twisting the president's language from his speech before AIPAC in 2012, with Graham stating, "the real issue is making it clear all options are on the table and that we have Israel's back. That's what the president said at AIPAC last year; 'We have Israel's back.'"[211] As reported by the *Washington Post's* Jennifer Rubin, based on a phone interview with a candidly speaking Sen. Graham, the senator saw this Senate initiative as a critical component in a grander strategy on Iran, involving a resolution pledging support to Israel if it acted.[212]

How was the language in the original resolution changed? How were specific passages stricken? Quiet pressure was successfully brought to bear by off-the-Hill forces in spring 2013. This resulted, as an APN spokesperson told me, "in the green light being changed to a tepid yellow one. Sen. Corker was convinced by APN and other off-the-Hill forces favoring diplomacy over force to alter the language; and Sen. Menendez, who could have fought to block the amendment, chose not to do so." All keen observers on and off the Hill saw this as a small yet significant victory against AIPAC-inspired legislation. But even in victory—and in ironic testimony to AIPAC's overall, ongoing reach and influence—when one of the victorious rival lobbyists asked a certain journalist how and why he had missed their successful effort and had thus failed to report on it, the journalist responded that "the development hadn't been covered in the AIPAC press release, upon which, he somewhat sheepishly confessed, he'd been relying too heavily."

Chapter Eight

APPROPRIATIONS

"Look at Appropriations, it's where the rubber meets the road."
—numerous staffers

HOUSE APPROPRIATIONS

"Among House members, one can distinguish between people [congresspersons] who make a lot of noise and people who make an impact. The people who make a difference are the appropriators—the members who sit on the Appropriations Committee. Its chair and subcommittee chairs are the people who write the bills that determine who gets the money. The 'noise makers' are the House authorizers: the people who sit on the other committees [such as House Foreign Affairs]; the people who are pandering. As the saying goes, 'Authorizers give you work; appropriators give you money.'"
—a veteran staffer

As I progressed through my interviews, I was advised time and again to interview staffers who worked for congresspersons serving on the Appropriations Committees, or "Approps." This held true across both legislative chambers, Senate and House. As an extra nod to the power and special status of Senate and House Appropriations committee members, many staffers, in both time frames, concurred with a peer who noted, "Committee assignments are everything in Congress. People here say there are three political parties in Congress: Democrats, Republicans, and Appropriators."

Appropriations, in contrast to HFAC, is an "A" committee, a plum committee assignment. It is one of the quintessential "bring home the bacon" committees. Competition for membership on Appropriations is thus far more intense and acquisition of chairmanship or RM status at the full or even subcommittee level is highly coveted.

The following chart offers a look at which individuals held the most powerful positions on the House Appropriations from 1997–98 (105th) to the present.

HOUSE: APPROP'S FULL COMMITTEE AND FOREIGN OPERATIONS SUBCOMMITTEE FOR 105TH THROUGH 113TH CONGRESSES

Congress	Year	Chair	Ranking Member
105th Full	1997–99	Livingston, R-LA	Obey, D-WI
105th For. Ops.		Callahan, R-AL	Pelosi, D-CA
106th Full	'99–'01	Lewis, R-CA	Obey, D-WI
		Young, R-FL	Obey
106th For. Ops.		Callahan	Pelosi
107th Full	'01–'03	Young	Obey
107th For. Ops.		Kolbe, R-ARI	Lowey, D-NY
108th Full	'03–'05	Young	Obey
108th For. Ops.		Kolbe	Lowey
109th Full	'05–'07	Lewis	Obey
109th For. Ops.		Kolbe	Lowey
110th Full	'07–'09	Obey	Lewis
110th For. Ops.		Lowey, D-NY	Wolf, R-VA
111th Full	'09–'11	Obey	Lewis
111th For. Ops.		Lowey	Granger, R-TX
112th Full	'11–'13	Rogers, R-KY	Dicks, D-WA
112th For. Ops.		Granger	Lowey
113th Full	'13–'15	Rogers	Dicks
113th For. Ops.		Granger	Lowey

Because party leaderships are concerned with gaining and maintaining control of Congress and its key committees, a certain synergy emerges that affects heavily the selection of Appropriations' chairpersons and RMs. Considerable care is therefore given to filling these leading roles because powerful "special interests" are not just watching but actively seeking to influence the selection process; that is, to stack the deck—to mobilize bias—in their favor. Needless to say, "special interests" are also active in either fostering or maintaining strong relations with these individuals and other committee members after they have taken up these positions. Thus, the appropriators are very heavily lobbied by "special interest" groups.

When I began this study (2005; 109th Congress), Rep. Lewis, representing the Republican Majority, was chairman of the full committee, while Rep. Obey, a Democrat, was its ranking member. Rep. Young replaced Lewis as full committee chairman for the second session of the 106th Congress. Rep. Kolbe (R) was chairman of the State, Foreign Operations, and Related Programs subcommittee, or as it's called—"Foreign Ops"—and Rep. Lowey (D) was its RM. Foreign Ops is the key Appropriations subcommittee for the interests of this study due to its role in determining funding for the State Department, US Agency for International Development (USAID), the Peace Corps, and numerous other programs involving foreign countries and organizations. So in terms of "positional analysis," the key figures on Appropriations were Lewis, Obey, Young, Kolbe, and Lowey.

By 2011–13, several notables had retired or moved on: Obey and Kolbe had retired, but many familiar faces remained on the full committee. On the Republican side, Rogers (fifteenth term; chairman of Appropriations), Lewis, Young, and Wolf were still major figures on Appropriations, with both Lewis and Wolf on the Foreign Ops subcommittee. For the Democrats, Rep. Norm Dicks (WA; eighteenth term) had become RM of the full committee, but Lowey remained RM of Foreign Ops. Meanwhile, Rep. Kay Granger (R-TX; eighth term) had become chairwoman of Foreign Ops.

Important House appropriators are showered with more than just prestige, office traffic, and attention. Mark Kirk, David Obey, Nita Lowey, and Steny Hoyer rank among the House's highest lifetime recipients of pro-Israel campaign donations. Kay Granger, who served as RM on Foreign Ops in the 111th Congress (2009–10), became its chairwoman with the 112th Congress in 2011 and holds that position as I write. According to CRP, although Granger received no appreciable amount of pro-Israel campaign finance contributions for the 2007–2008 election cycle, she garnered a total of $33,500 from pro-Israel PACs and individuals in 2009–10, and $25,000 in 2011–12.[213] All of these individuals, in their hearts and minds, may have just been engaging in rational policymaking in the national interest; their positions might not have been affected one iota by campaign finance support. But there the money is, and it is not a small amount. It has flowed to people on Appropriations more than to House members sitting on most other committees.

Just as one must go back to the mid-1990s and Rep. Lee Hamilton's chairmanship of HFAC to find more evenhanded treatment of Middle East matters on that committee, one must retreat to the late 1990s, the 105th and 106th Congresses, to find an individual serving in a key Appropriations post who took a tougher stance vis-à-vis funding for Israel. To wit, Rep. Sonny Callahan (R-Alabama), chairman of Foreign Ops, tried to hold then Israeli Prime Minister Netanyahu to the latter's own direct July 1996 pledge to the US Congress that US economic aid to Israel—$1.2 billion per annum—would be phased out beginning in 2000. All that came of Callahan's efforts was a temporary, first time ever capping of foreign aid to the Middle East as a whole at $5.4 billion by the committee.[214] Callahan moved away from his chairmanship, but did not exit the House, and he caused another kerfuffle in 2002 when he sought to cut $200 million in emergency assistance to Israel and $50 million in humanitarian aid for Palestinians from a supplemental appropriations bill. Speaking on the House floor, Rep. Callahan announced, "I am going to offer amendments as we go through the bill to strike all of the aid to Israel that was included here without any request from Israel, without any request from the administration, without any requests from anybody. But someone within this beltway decided since we were going to have a supplemental bill, they were going to get some pork in it for Israel."[215]

For threatening these cuts, Callahan came quickly under fire by "pro-Israeli" actors like Ira N. Forman, executive director of NJDC, who took special umbrage at Callahan's use of the term "pork" in the context of support for the "Jewish state," and called on party leadership to dress down their fellow Republican.[216] Callahan retired less than one year later at the age of 70. The point here is that "hiccups" like Callahan's have been the exception rather than the norm.

When I asked in 2005–2006 which House Appropriations members were deemed most important on Middle East matters—thereby engaging in reputational analysis—there was near unanimity over the power and influence of Jerry Lewis (R; 14th term), Jim Kolbe (R; 11th term), David Obey (D; 19th term), Joe Knollenberg (R; 7th term), Nita Lowey (D; 9th term), Frank Wolf (R; 13th term), Steny Hoyer (D; 13th term), and Mark Kirk (R; 3rd term). Note the length of terms of these individuals, with the exception of Rep. Kirk. As a veteran staffer pointed out, "You don't usually get to become an Appropriations member without many years of experience. This is true in both the House and Senate." The high "reputations" of most congresspersons derives in part from their lofty, formal committee positions and length of tenure, as would be expected from positional analysis. As the figure above shows, there is relative stability in key positions on House Appropriations. Once you capture the prize, you hold on to it as long as you desire and are able, thereby reinforcing your power and influence. Thus, several of the most powerful House members by "reputation" are also on the "positional" chart: Lewis, Kolbe, Obey, and Lowey. Other "reputedly" powerful figures included Reps. Wolf and Hoyer; both ranked fifth among the 37 R's and 29 D's respectively on Appropriations' full committee. But there were reps that did not occupy formal positions of power on the committee, like Rep. Kirk, who were powerful by reputation. I have already provided some commentary on Kirk's sentiments and "attachments" to right wing pro-Israel interests, but Kirk's case will be examined even more carefully later in this chapter.

By 2011–2013, among the strong "reputational" figures, Obey and Kolbe had retired, as noted above; Knollenberg had been defeated in an election; and Kirk had been elected to the Senate. But most of the other individuals remained in place, and Kay Granger (R-Texas) had joined this "group."

THE APPROPRIATORS: WORKLOAD AND PROCEDURE

In both of this study's time frames, appropriators were seen as being assisted by highly astute staffers, among the best in the House. As Rep. Obey remarked, "You can't run the place without staff. Members have hundreds of responsibilities, so if you're going to be running a committee, without their support you would get nowhere."

Interestingly, and again also indicative of these staffers' special status, Appropriations staffers in general are described by many veteran staffers as "owing their allegiance to the Appropriations member who picked them, not to the member's political party."

The work done by appropriators and their aides passes annually through various stages, some marked by a lull, others by great intensity. January through March are the slow months for appropriators; in early April Appropriations work and project requests start up in earnest. May is busier; by May and June most bills have come to the floor for debate. This makes June and July the busiest months of the year. Congress is in recess during the month of

August, but staffers continue to work. If bills are not passed in both chambers, they're sent to the joint House-Senate conference committees in September, October, and November. As regards conference committees, one staffer said, "Most issues are worked out before the conference committee meets. We [staffers] have formal staff meetings. We go through all the differences until we've resolved almost everything. The conference is usually just a formal exercise. Leaderships will cue us when to start negotiating—then it could take about one and a half weeks."

Appropriations committee meetings are not always behind closed doors. Private citizens can get into the room for markups, which means that the lobbyists, too, are actually in the room. Staffers told me that lobbyists will actually pay people to stand in line or sit on chairs all night outside House congressional office buildings on D Street to ensure the lobbyists get a seat at some markups. Once in the room, lobbyists can communicate with others in the room, and the stakes are high in many of these sessions. One staffer instructed me to observe the gallery during any hearing. "You'll see constituents who leave after thirty seconds because they don't understand or they're bored," the staffer said. "The only people remaining seated are lobbyists. Staffers have to stand up against the walls for quicker access to their members. Lobbyists now communicate with House members with their phones. They'll signal, 'You don't have to talk any more.'"

Another staffer pointed out the enormous potential for improprieties. "The lobbyists can't speak publicly at markups, but they can be consulted by the reps at the markups—they can whisper in people's ears, etc., or use Black-Berries or iPhones to communicate their thoughts to the staffers, and the congresspersons," the staffer said. "Special interest actors would pay you [a staffer] $5,000 for the subcommittee report, which is not to be seen by people before it goes to the full committee."

One can readily understand the implications of many of these reports for the stock values of traded companies. A veteran staffer informed me that staffers can buy and sell stock whenever they want, and he knew of a staffer who profited from his intimate knowledge of land usage issues. After all, what's at stake in these committee markups can be of great financial importance. I was walking down a hallway in the Cannon House Office Building, passing by a room where one such markup was being held. A 30-something lobbyist with a look of sheer panic and frustration on his face said loudly to his colleague, "If [Rep. X] keeps talking like that in there, we're fucked."

A major reason that Appropriations has come to acquire greater significance in the realm of Arab-Israeli and other affairs is that due to partisan friction many years went by without the successful passage of a foreign aid authorizing bill by either HFAC or Senate Foreign Relations. As one staffer commented, "HFAC has become a frickin' debate society. So in practice, appropriators play a tremendous role because HFAC can't get a bill out." These characterizations held true into the early 2010s, when another staffer, speaking of HIRC, said, "Approps has taken over their work, the authorizers' work, because they can't get a bill out."

Illustrating the major difference between HFAC and appropriations, another staffer said, "There's a huge difference between authorizing and appropriations. Their [appropriators'] bills have to pass every year. They have more power, albeit less time. It's very easy to get something in a bill if an appropriator wants it."

This disparity across committees in the ability to marshal funds causes friction. As one staffer put it, "There's a battle between [the other, House] committee chairs, the authorizers, and the appropriators. The Appropriations people often end up being able to write their own checks or determine where the money goes because authorizing bills haven't been passed by both bodies [that is, the House and the Senate]." So in essence, as many staffers noted, there's a tension in Congress between authorizers and appropriators with the latter always having the upper hand. The Appropriations Committee wields a lot of influence, so authorizers feel like they're left holding the short end of the stick.

In the minds of many staffers, many of Congress's problems reside in Appropriations. In 2005–2006, the full Appropriations Committee had ten subcommittees. The ten subcommittees' chairs were so powerful that they were nicknamed "the cardinals." (In 2007, two new subcommittees were added, and the power of the now twelve cardinals remained largely intact.) Each "cardinal" drafts his or her subcommittee's bills and holds markups, and language can be inserted at both the subcommittee and full committee levels. So-called placeholder language can be inserted, too, at both levels.

The "cardinal" who oversees matters relating to foreign aid expenditures is thus chairperson of the Foreign Ops subcommittee. In the House, Mr. Lewis and Mr. Obey, again respectively the chair and ranking member of the full committee in 2005–2006, attended all subcommittee markup meetings—all ten of them—so these meetings were scheduled at different times to enable their presence. However, It was very clear from an interview I had with Mr. Obey that the full committee chair and RM typically cannot stay on top of the details the way the subcommittee chairs can.

It's important to understand how the Appropriations process works. The appropriators have the text of the bill (from the authorizing committee, like HFAC) on one hand and the committee report on the other. One must note the difference between the "bill" and the "report." A bill is passed by the authorizers; the report specifies where the money is to go; it's written by the Majority; it's not amendable; it gives specifics. In other words, the text of the bill says, for example, there's a lump sum for housing. The committee report then spells out how this lump sum will be spent, and people cannot amend this on the floor. No names are affixed to the earmarks in the committee reports. These meetings are "open rule", which means a member can offer any amendment. However, a member can amend only the text of the bill and not the committee report, and all the earmarks are put in place in the committee report. (The reader will undoubtedly recognize "earmarks" as those add-ons most commonly identified with congresspersons' efforts to provide "pork" or benefits to special interests.)

Providing additional insight to committee procedures and the politics of markups, a staffer in 2005 highlighted the crucial role played by House leadership and the influence of the strongest special interest group, "With HIRC, AIPAC has an open door. But they don't have an open door to Foreign Ops. So AIPAC works a lot through the Speaker's office to get at the Foreign Ops people. Foreign Ops people have to listen to the Speaker's office. On some issues, people are real puppets . . . . But the committee listens very closely to House leadership on any Appropriations issues. Just look at who sponsored the anti-Palestinian stuff; they're all from the leadership level—people like [Majority Leader Tom] DeLay, [John] Boehner, and [Eric] Cantor."

Another staffer, helping round out the picture as regards committee markups, stated: "There are voices that will support Palestinians. During Foreign Ops hearings, the State Department and USAID will come in and talk about how policy is being shaped. Then, the context and focus of remarks by these people and [Secretary of State] Condi Rice will serve as the context for the markups. The bill will go to the full committee, then amendments will be offered at this level by those carrying water for the IR [HIRC] types. You cannot legislate via an Appropriations bill. Yet there are insidious ways that Appropriations committee members act on behalf of IR types, and sometimes this produces scintillating debate."

Efforts at legislating via Appropriations bills also can and do occur during the earlier, markup phase; that is, provisos may be inserted in markups that can have interesting, and at times far reaching, consequences. For example, one staffer noted, "What goes on in a markup is very interesting. Look at what happened in February 2005. Rather than give money to the Palestinians, they gave money to [the philanthropic, Women's Zionist Organization of America] Hadassah to build hospitals. I can't explain this and don't want to because it would be too disturbing." Hadassah, by comparison, was already super well endowed. The staffer who told me this happened to be liberal and Jewish and was disgusted by this outcome.

Markups on the Middle East, according to staffers, are often contentious. Because many members are trying to score points with AIPAC or other interest groups, there's usually some language in a bill that is new that a few members see as too biased toward Israel. As one staffer remarked, "A very small minority will get upset, like Jesse Jackson Jr., and Obey in the past . . . There was a big fight a few years ago when we put in new language over funds for Palestinians. When it comes to funding for Palestinians, people get emotional about it."

The Appropriations Committee grew in importance during the course of this study because with Congress in general failing to pass new budgets annually, the discretionary power of the appropriators was all the more greatly enhanced compared to that of members of other committees To this point, a staffer in 2013 said, "Because there is no new budget, the appropriators work up a 'continuing resolution' [CR] based on the existing budget. Often you get just the chairman, the ranking member, and their staffs sitting down to work out the details of the CR. Usually the chairman and ranking member attempt to accommodate the requests of other rank-and-file members on Approps, unless it's a crazy proposal, so others do retain some influence due to this practice. But the authorizers and others usually get cut out of the game."

A DISCUSSION OF KEY HOUSE APPROPRIATIONS PLAYERS: "WATER CARRIERS" AND OTHERS

On Appropriations, specific individuals acquire the reputation among staffers of "carrying the water" on certain issues or for certain countries. There are bosses and staffers alike who take umbrage with the phrase, but it is one I found to be in common usage. Thus, broadening our scope for a moment to give examples, Jesse Jackson Jr. and Frank Wolf were seen in the mid-2000s as the House Appropriations' "water carriers" on matters relating to sub-Saharan Africa and the Sudan. Rep. Knollenberg did so for the Armenians. Chairman Hyde "carried the water" for Colombia to fund drug interdiction. I'll note here that a 2013 interviewee, unfamiliar with this study's scope, said, "You're missing the point by focusing your questions on individuals, like who the 'water carriers' are, on specific committees. The problem is much bigger than that; it's the lack of knowledge people in general have about the conflict and/ or their unwillingness to do what is right. It doesn't matter who's on these committees because these bills and resolutions supporting Israel are going to pass by overwhelming votes anyway."

The staffer's point is well taken, but I disagree with his negative assessment of the value of examining who sits on Appropriations and its Foreign Ops subcommittee. I need only remind anyone of the "attention" focused and showered on these committees and their members by all concerned parties, both on and off the Hill. In brief, I don't believe the money flows heavily to these specific individuals as pure acts of generosity.

Moving beyond this rejoinder, with regard to the Middle East, not all "water carriers" need be Appropriations members. That said, there was widespread agreement among staffers in the identification of Nita Lowey, Mark Kirk, Steven Rothman, and to some extent Adam Schiff—all on Appropriation—as the primary "water carriers" for Israel in the mid-2000s and beyond (for those members still on the Hill in the early 2010s). As shown above, all have been significant recipients of campaign contributions from pro-Israel PACs. After settling into the House, Congressman Kirk was seen as a principal conduit for AIPAC-drafted measures. One staffer said in 2006, "It's Kirk who puts forward AIPAC's ideas and amendments." The staffer also identified other committee members closely connected with AIPAC: Kolbe, Knollenberg, and Lowey.

The full committee's chairman, Bill Young (R), and ranking member Dave Obey (D) were known to weigh in on the subcommittee to support continued aid for Egypt and Jordan, and they typically refrained from running interference against funding for Israel. Obey and others could and would override repeated efforts by "dark blue" House members like Tom Lantos to cut funding to Egypt out of their recognition of Egypt as a steady, helpful ally. Obey's behavior here, it is important to state, was supported by many Labor and right wing government officials in Israel itself, not to mention the US Departments of Defense and State. Obey himself told me that he never had any major disagreement over A-I matters with Lowey, who again was widely seen as a pro-Israel "water carrier." In this regard, Obey and Lowey's behavior generally held true over time, perhaps a fortiori, for aid to Jordan's kings; but again this aid has been seen as beneficial by even most right wing Israeli governments. A corollary here is that a "pro-Arab" member of the "Gang of Four" on House Appropriations like Rep. Ray LaHood could easily promote assistance to Jordan, but he would still be hopelessly outnumbered by other committee members if he and others pushed for less assistance for Israel. In a word, the committee "deck" was stacked.

In 2011–2012, Rep. Lowey remained firmly in place on the Foreign Ops subcommittee as ranking member, backed by Reps Schiff and Rothman. Kirk, with especially heavy campaign finance backing from right wing pro-Israel sources in 2010, had been elected as one of Illinois' two senators. To repeat, Knollenberg, Kolbe, and Obey had retired. Meanwhile, Foreign Ops Chairwoman Granger, a Republican, had become a steadfast ally of Democrat and RM Rep. Lowey on most matters relating to the Middle East. Indeed, Granger and Lowey had already earned recognition as a new dynamic duo, engaging in behavior, detailed below, all very supportive of Israel and, in practice, presenting a bipartisan challenge to the Obama administration.

On the House Appropriations full committee in 2011–12, the collective presence of Reps. Moran (VA), Price (NC), Farr (CA), Lee (CA) and McCollum (MN) did present the possibility of a bloc opposing AIPAC-guided policy. Moran and Price were also both on Foreign Ops, and both had/have usually taken positions sympathetic to the Palestinians. But the full committee chair and RM—Rogers and Dicks, respectively—and subcommittee chair and RM—Granger and Lowey—all commanded greater formal power and considerable respect, so what they wanted they readily got. At the subcommittee level, Granger and Lowey could count on strong backing from Lewis, Wolf, Rothman, and Schiff, and at the full committee level most everyone else typically just fell into line. This situation did not change in any significant manner with the arrival of the new House members in 2013.

A number of factors cause House members to seek service on the Appropriations committee. After all, this is an "A" committee; it distributes enormous funds. But as regards the narrower focus of this study, the presence of Appropriations members with strong allegiances to specific foreign countries clearly holds its own significance. With this factor in mind, I will double down on earlier remarks and share some characterizations and commentaries from staffers about former and current House Appropriations members.

Nita Lowey has been a stalwart supporter of Israel on Appropriations, identified by many as a "water carrier" for Israel. Lowey is commonly described as willing to listen to all sides and arguments on the issues; in other words, she is not extreme in her views. Yet her commitment to Israel can only be characterized as unshakable and has remained so over all of her years of service and all the changes in Israeli governments. She is Jewish, and many of her White Plains, New York, area constituents share her deep concern for Israel's welfare. She has long supported funding for peace-oriented Palestinians and other Arab actors. But as a dovish staffer observed about Lowey (and Steve Rothman), "Ms. Lowey is an avowed supporter of Israel—she's Jewish, unabashed, but not a raving zealot; so is Mr. Rothman—he's cut from the same cloth. But both Lowey and Rothman are very concerned about Palestinian terrorist activities. To them, no behavior by Palestinians in response to Israeli behavior is justified. If children die from rubber bullets, well they shouldn't be demonstrating . . . Lowey will say [PA Pres.] Mahmoud Abbas needs to be supported or else we'll get another Arafat, but still she'll say to Abbas, 'You need to get your people in line or else.' Egypt and Jordan's efforts to crush terrorists are not enough, they [Lowey and Rothman] think, 'you need to eliminate the madrasas there.'"

Here's an example of how Lowey has come to right wing Israeli officials' assistance. In March 2010, just as her fellow Democrat Vice President Joe Biden arrived in Israel on an official visit, Israel's Interior Ministry announced approval of the construction of 1,600 housing units in East Jerusalem. Such activity is considered illegal by virtually the entire international community.

Prime Minister Netanyahu apologized for his ministry's announcement, claiming ignorance, but his apology was not taken at face value in D.C. The announcement was condemned by the US administration, seen both as damaging to US efforts to advance the peace process and as a major affront to Pres. Obama. But for her part, Lowey was quick to salve the wound in US-Israel relations. Citing Lowey's characterization of the new tensions as a "hiccup," the *Jerusalem Post* reported, "'There is no question in my mind that the 10-year memorandum of understanding is solid,' Nita Lowey . . . said of the decade-long US aid plan under which $3 billion will be going to Israel this year. 'There is strong bipartisan support for Israel in the Congress that will not falter.' She said that continuing support is also in place when it comes to the US commitment to Israel maintaining a qualitative military edge over its Arab neighbors and other forms of military coordination. 'The military cooperation, the intelligence cooperation, the focus on Iran, is solid and strengthens every year,' said Lowey, who also sits on the House Intelligence and Homeland Security committees. And, using Netanyahu's nickname, she stressed, 'Bibi has the support of Congress. It is solid. It is secure.'"[217]

The same *Jerusalem Post* peace went on to state that well over half of the House's members had signed a letter to Sec. of State Clinton "affirming their support for the US-Israel relationship and urging the two countries to quietly resolve any differences."[218]

What of Rep. Kirk? Because Mr. Kirk had earned the reputation as a primary "water carrier" for Israel, it makes sense to examine what has motivated his behavior. The description that follows is based on his track record and statements made to me by knowledgeable staffers. After earning a master's degree from the London School of Economics, Kirk went to work on Capitol Hill in the latter 1980s, eventually becoming chief of staff to Rep. John Porter (R-IL). While there, he worked with the Human Rights caucus, founded by Porter and run by Rep. Lantos. A key issue then was the "refusenik" issue, which had a home base in the Jewish American community in Illinois. Kirk became concerned with these issues and traveled to Israel. He joined the US Navy Reserve in 1989 and was pressed into stints of active duty over ensuing years. At the same time, he worked with the State Department in the very early 1990s. From 1995–2000, Kirk worked for Rep. Ben Gilman, an ardent Zionist—albeit not ardent enough for right wing pro-Israel types as discussed earlier—and traveled to Israel many more times. He also went to Kosovo, where a priest had been killed, and he got to see the first concentration camp in Kosovo. All of these experiences left a very powerful impression on him. Kirk came to appreciate how, in his view, the US-Israel defense relationship strengthens both countries. During his navy reserve duty, Kirk served in Naval Intelligence; he thereby acquired a military strategic mind-set, came to describe himself as a "national security hawk," and became an important figure in Congress on national security issues.

As regards Kirk's views of Israel, as a staffer put it, "I've never heard him articulate a position that would place him [ideologically] in Israeli politics. He's very much an American ready to work with whichever government is in power in Israel." So as Israeli governments have become more right wing and have included individuals from parties labeled as extremist and racist by many Israelis, Mr. Kirk has remained a stalwart supporter. As a congressional staffer told me, "Israel is a core part of my life and Kirk's personality, too. It's dear to Kirk as well. He is a key member on Foreign Ops. That's where all the money for Israel comes from, and it's very important to know how to work the committee."

Although not heavily identified as a "water carrier" for Israel, another consistent supporter of funding for Israel has been Rep. Denny Rehberg (R-MT). I include Rehberg in this discussion simply because he has served many "tours of duty" on Appropriations, and because his behavior seems typical of many of his peers; i.e., he doesn't bring any strong, personal, ethno-religious connection or concerned constituent base to the issue area, so it's interesting to see how staffers have viewed his behavior on Appropriations.

Rehberg arrived in Congress "very interested in foreign affairs, and he wanted to get on Foreign Ops because of this." In 2006, a staffer noted, "For Rehberg, this represents a niche compared to the governor and the senators from Montana, who are not interested in foreign affairs. There's no real interest in this in his home state [Montana]. His interest dovetails nicely with Bush's focus on foreign affairs."

This staffer provided an interesting snapshot of how a young member on Appropriations like Rehberg would play the game; how the Foreign Ops subcommittee is commonly perceived compared to other Appropriations subcommittees; and the "gatekeeping" role party leadership plays in selecting the subcommittees' members. "On the Foreign Ops subcommittee, he's a new member, better to be seen and not heard, so better to go along with the chairman and work behind the scenes if need be," the staffer said. "He'll voice his opinion on some issues, and hopefully the chairman hears him. On markups and committee votes, you're gonna vote with the chairman, so he's gonna support Kolbe on the Foreign Ops subcommittee. Out of the ten subcommittees, Foreign Ops is a tertiary level subcommittee . . . Foreign Ops sends nothing home. There's no bring home the bacon ability. The Steering Committee of the Republican Party determines who goes where on the committees; they're the gatekeeper, so you need to keep the higher-ups happy. Appropriators will sit on other committees whose issues resonate for their constituents, like those dealing with energy and water, or the military subcommittee if they have a military base. But Rehberg is on Foreign Ops because he's interested in it. The line is drawn in the sand. He's gonna be with Israel. He's always gonna fund their requests."

REFLECTIONS FROM A FORMER COMMITTEE CHAIR AND RM, REP. OBEY

Rep. Dave Obey served for many years as either chairman or RM on House Appropriations. Obey was definitely not identified as a "water carrier," but I find his role on Appropriations and his track record on Middle East affairs intriguing, instructive, and emblematic and therefore worthy of lengthy commentary. Obey hails from a district in north-central Wisconsin where hardly any constituents prioritize Middle East affairs. After receiving a B.A. in political science, Obey studied politics at the graduate level, with a focus on the Soviet Union and international relations, so he arrived in Congress in 1969 with a much better understanding of Middle East affairs than most. As Obey told me, "I formed my views long before I became a member of Congress or was on Appropriations. I've been a lifelong supporter of the peace process, so at times I've had considerable skepticism about players on both sides."

It's interesting to see how Obey made his way onto Appropriations. Still in his early thirties, he was tapped "just by luck" by Rep. Wilbur Mills to fill an opening on Appropriations. He was 24 years younger than the next youngest person on the committee. At the time, Clarence "Doc" Long (D-MD), who was seen by many as being in AIPAC's back pocket, was chairing the Foreign Ops subcommittee. According to Obey's longtime aide in Wisconsin

Jerry Madison, "When Long lost election and retired in 1985, AIPAC went apeshit. They didn't want Obey to be the next Foreign Ops chair because Obey would tell the AIPAC folks exactly what they didn't want to hear. Sen. [James] Abourezk, a leader on Arab American issues, was one of Obey's best friends in Washington, D.C."[219] But back then, when AIPAC's power wasn't as great as it has been for many decades now, Obey was able to surmount this opposition to become the lead Democrat on Foreign Ops.

While Obey proved he would and could block aid to Syria for not jumping on the Camp David peace wagon, and while he proved he would and could deal toughly with intransigent Palestinians, right wing pro-Israelis' fears of Obey were confirmed in the early 1990s when he backed Pres. Bush's tough line against Israeli West Bank settlement activity and consolidated his warmer relations with moderate Israeli leaders. As Obey told me, "[PM] Rabin and I became reasonably good friends; and [President] Shimon Peres and I certainly became good friends. The last time I saw Rabin, he shooed everyone else out of the room and said, 'I just ask you two things. Please do not let Israel's well-meaning friends in the United States prevent you [Obey] from continuing good relations with the Palestinians; otherwise all will be lost. And would you please keep AIPAC off my back. I don't need their help. I'm a big boy and I can do this [what needs to be done] by myself.'"

The story speaks volumes about Rabin's perception of AIPAC and the degree to which its leaders sought to derail the Oslo peace process. Obey's Rabin-inspired behavior, in turn, engendered considerable friction with AIPAC and other congressional actors. Reelected in 1994, his most difficult election ever, he became RM of Appropriations in January 1995 due to the 1994 electoral Republican "revolution" and the R's regaining Majority control. In a subsequent House floor fight, Obey accused the new Speaker, Newt Gingrich, of abetting right wing Israeli policies. According to Obey, Gingrich replied, "You don't understand, Dave. I am Likud."

Obey recounts with considerable pride his toeing the line against knee-jerk support for Israel, but from the mid-1990s forward it seems that he rarely contested spending measures for Israel in any significant manner. In light of his early to mid-1990s run-ins with AIPAC when he was sitting on Foreign Ops, it's interesting to see that the biggest amount of pro-Israel funding he ever received came in 1990, $60,199 (he ranked number 5 in all of Congress). Assistance from "pro-Israel" sources then dipped to $18,650 in 1992 and $17,200 in 1994,[220] when he was fighting the good fight on behalf of Mr. Rabin. The numbers, it seems, suggest that some pro-Israel elements were trying to punish him.

Rabin was assassinated by a Jewish fundamentalist in November 1995, and in May 1996 the hard right wing Likud leader Benjamin Netanyahu was elected Israel's prime minister. For the record, during my interview, Mr. Obey displayed no reluctance to express his lack of fondness for right wingers like Prime Ministers Shamir and Netanyahu, but while not always marching in lockstep with AIPAC positions—for example, he was one of the 37 House members voting against HR 4681 in 2006—he did adopt a largely mainstream, nonobstructionist position with regard to US aid for Israel from the mid-1990s through the end of his career. As he told me, he could not remember ever having any major disagreement with Nita Lowey on funding for Israel—although Lowey, of course, voted for HR 4681—and Lowey, to her critics, has been Israel's "water carrier" as RM or chair of Foreign Ops from the mid-1990s until the present.

For the 1996 and 1998 electoral cycles, Obey's campaign finance receipts from pro-Israel sources bounced back up to slightly over $34,000 for each cycle. What percentage of the total campaign funds raised did this sum represent? The answer for 1998, to give one example, was just a little under 5 percent of the $800,827 raised for Obey's campaign.[221] This is not an indispensable amount, but as we saw in the "Getting Elected" chapter, it's far from insignificant. During the election cycles of the 2000s, support from pro-Israel PACs to Obey did dip into the realm of insignificance; it decreased to the $3,000 to $8,500 range, and was more often on the low end of this range. In no cycle did any countervailing, "pro-Arab" funds of significance flow to his campaign. All told, however, during his impressive, 42-year House career, Obey amassed over $200,000 in campaign finance support from pro-Israel sources before his retirement. And thus one can ponder: did any of this assistance cause Obey to forget Prime Minister Rabin's plea along the way?[222]

When I asked obliquely about the influence of campaign finance on congresspersons' behavior in general, Mr. Obey said, "No, I don't think that's the case at all," and he went on to offer his own explanation of what shapes his colleagues' behavior, which I will present below. But when Obey himself returned to how much time congresspersons now spend raising funds, I asked again if this didn't mean that money does in fact make a big difference. He first responded by saying, "Welcome to the world of politics," then he added:

> "Jews, Turks, Greeks, Armenians; there are so many groups [in this country]; but I don't think this is what drives policymaking behavior. I voted with labor, for example, because I believed in it. I have very little patience with people who argue that money makes the difference or explains the behavior. In a district like mine, management can push harder than workers, but I still voted with workers. It's not a shock that many New York members are going to support Israel because they grew up in that kind of community; just like in Michigan people back Arabs. That's the way the country works."

So put succinctly, for Obey, money is not decisive. Rather, a congressperson's personal, principled beliefs are likely to determine his or her policymaking. And of course, congresspersons must be mindful of the major concerns of their districts' constituents. But what else can one take away from Obey's experiences and observations? How best can we explain his behavior? I'll answer those questions by trying to put myself in Obey's shoes, based on his comments, and then I'll leave the reader to grapple with how best to interpret what influenced his behavior.

To begin, given his lofty position in Congress, and the myriad battles he had to fight, Obey may have been largely ignorant of how much money he was receiving from pro-Israel PACs. Or worded slightly differently, one would need to know exactly how consciously, if at all, Mr. Obey went about dialing for pro-Israel PACs' dollars, instructed others to do so, or was informed of such contributions, and I didn't go there in the interview. Others who have spoken with him told me that he was not very aware of such donations. So it's possible that the laser focus on the Middle East and pro-Israel PACs' money might lead an analyst like me to err in attaching too much importance to campaign finance numbers in his or comparable congresspersons' cases.

Reflecting on the "big picture" of Congress's role on Middle East matters, Mr. Obey said: "The problem with Congress is that Congress comes at [these Mideast matters] from the opposite direction compared to me. Congress has always been much more inflexible on these issues than I think it should be. Look at what's happening on Iran now [late 2013; early 2014]. I see members wringing their hands on Iran; Congress should sit back and give the administration some time and space to carry out its initiatives." Clearly Mr. Obey feels Congress can hamstring executive branch efforts. But moving beyond that observation, when I asked for him to elucidate what he thought caused the "hand wringing," he responded, "It's the squeaky wheel that gets the grease; ginning up support for negative positions is much easier in Congress. Within the American Jewish community—I'm convinced that there are many more pro-peace types than one might think. This is one problem. It just isn't true of the American Jewish community that they oppose more peaceful efforts."

Implicit, in his comment, is that pro-Israel interests that are not in the pro-peace camp represent the "squeaky wheel." Does campaign finance fit into the "squeaky wheel"? To this point, I asked, "Don't campaign contributions make a difference in this regard?" He responded, "No, not at all."

Now let's look at how Obey spoke of the handling of annual Middle East appropriations. He began by noting that Appropriations is usually following up on policy orientations sent to them by the HFAC authorizers, while recognizing that the appropriators have the power to balk and block certain recommendations coming to them from HFAC. "Appropriations tries to work on consensus," he said. "It's a fiscal committee; not a policy committee. So as regards the level of aid for Egypt, the Palestinian Authority, Israel, etc., there's certainly a consensus about not changing the Camp David [1979 peace treaty] funding, except at times like when [Israeli PM] Shamir was pushing West Bank settlements and the Bush administration tried to hold up the loan guarantees [to get the Israelis to stop]."

As regards the nuts and bolts of processing items placed before Appropriations, he said, "You get 30 like-minded people, sit them down, and they produce like-minded views. [There are 50 people on House Approp's.] This is what happens. Most microdecisions are made at the subcommittee level. We set the dollar amounts and if there's something the subcommittee people do that causes concern, then the full committee will sit down and work out a solution . . . There were no major policy differences between me and the [Foreign Ops] subcommittee folks. Our views were consonant most all of the time."

This comment makes one wonder who the 30 people are; how most, if not all, ended up on specific committees and subcommittees; and what they do once they've arrived there. Again, when I asked him if he saw any "pro-Israel" bias or regarded Nita Lowey, for example, as "water carriers" for Israel, he said, "I don't agree with the 'water carrier' label. I've seen Nita stand up to oppose items by the noisiest elements. Yes, Nita is a very strong supporter of Israel, but she's always mindful of her responsibilities to the broader whole. Our positions weren't identical, but I can't think of an occasion when we had a major disagreement." But this means that he himself was, in the final analysis, approving policies favorable to right wing Israeli governments.

The level of aid for Israel and Egypt, as a reward for their signing the 1979 Camp David peace accords, was $3.2 billion and $2.2 billion respectively, making them for many years the two largest recipients of US foreign aid. And this was out of a total foreign aid bill that typically amounted to $20–$25 billion for the entire world! Only a few congresspersons challenged this "payout" over the decades. But looking beyond this "peace dividend" to Egypt and Israel, Obey's mention of Pres. George H. W. Bush's pressure on Israel by withholding $10 billion in loan guarantees, which Obey supported, deserves additional commentary. Why? Because the West Bank settlement policies actively pursued by Shamir's fellow Likudniks from the mid-1990s until today were every bit as egregious and in violation of international law as what Shamir envisioned. Yet Obey, along with nearly everyone else, did little to nothing to oppose those policies by blocking various forms of assistance to Israel's increasingly right wing governments from the mid-1990s onward.

At first blush, I was surprised to hear Mr. Obey say that he didn't know much or remember much of the details of appropriations matters touching on Israel from the mid-1990s onward. Speaking with him in summer 2013, his mind still seemed very sharp, so I can't chalk up his forgetfulness to mental fatigue. But again, let's try to put ourselves in Obey's shoes. What he does remember most vividly about Middle East matters dates to the 1984–94 period when he was chair of Foreign Ops: "I had a greater role then; this was back when [Rep.] Charlie Wilson [of "Charlie's War" renown] was very active. After I left Foreign Ops, things changed for me because the Appropriations Committee is different than other committees. It's like 13 separate departments, and operational decisions occurred at the subcommittee level. So after 1994, I dealt with issues, then put them out of my head." One can only imagine how incredibly long the list of issues tackled by Obey was, as either chairman or RM of House Appropriations, and how impossible it might be to remember specific details in any single area of less direct interest and concern.

In this vein, a final observation by Obey struck me as being of greater weight than first meets the eye and speaks to the difficulties a key committee person faces. "In the House, I just focused on my committee," Obey said. "You don't have the luxury of trying to advocate your own narrow views. You focus on getting 218 votes to pass the bill."

Let's chew on Obey's statement for a while. As the chair or RM of Appropriations, Obey dealt with issues covering the entire spectrum of government expenditures. After leaving Foreign Ops, and while serving as chair or RM, he chose to serve as chair or RM of the Labor, Health and Human Services, Education, and Related Agencies subcommittee; in other words, he focused his attention primarily on the subcommittee that spoke most to his heart and head in terms of his own interests and expertise. He gave Middle East issues a much lower priority. Because congresspersons know from the get-go that the dominant pro-Israel groups are likely to get their way; believe that the subcommittee folks need to be trusted, by and large, to set policy in their own issue area; and think that one, as Obey said, doesn't have the luxury of advocating one's narrower view, the rationale for (and an explanation of) Obey's behavior comes more clearly into focus. His statement also suggests that given the complexity of the issues, there's a certain premium placed on doing what's necessary to reach consensus. One doesn't go tilting with windmills.

STAFFERS' APPRAISALS OF HOUSE APPROPRIATIONS

As regards my House staffers' views regarding Appropriations, on balance, and over both of my time frames, most staffers saw members of both the full committee and subcommittee on Foreign Operations as inclined to cooperate on issues in a bipartisan spirit. However, there were a few staffers who took a contrary view, as indicated by the following comment from the mid-2000s. "On Appropriations and Foreign Ops, there is a strong partisan divide," one staffer said. "R's versus D's; it's about philosophical and ideological stuff. If you go to Foreign Ops markups, you'd be shocked to hear what some people say there, like the language they use about the Palestinians and the Arabs; it's not just the drumbeat."

The consensus among staffers was also that partisanship, in general, worsened from 2005 to the 2010s; nevertheless, the "lock" on Appropriations funding by "pro-Israel" elements remained solid. That said, Israel's advantage among Appropriations members was not appreciated by everyone in the

House. As succinctly worded by one staffer, "Israel funding is all pretty automatic. No one is standing up and saying we could probably cut this in half."

Spelled out in lengthier but still questioning language, another veteran staffer pointed out the qualitative differences between assistance to Israel versus aid to other countries. "Within Foreign Ops, issues pertaining to Israel are sacrosanct," the staffer said. "Other money goes to Israel through trade agreements and military purchases, etc. US money goes to them [the Israelis] within 30 days of POTUS [president of the United States] signing the bill; [whereas] money to Egypt is parceled out over time. The rubber meets the road through funding."

The same staffer spoke of the significant differences in debate over this assistance. He and a whole host of his peers agreed that there are different means by which Jordanian, Egyptian, and Palestinian interests are undermined by debate over flashpoints relating to the conflict and by Hamas and others' actions. The staffer said, "Debate doesn't revolve around the legitimacy of interests; for example, a Palestinian state's right to exist, etc., instead the litmus test becomes 'what are you guys doing to protect the interests of Israel? How do we assume that US money is being used to protect Israel, or for democratization [in Arab countries], etc.?' So money for Israel has no preconditions, but money for Egypt comes with preconditions, like telling the Egyptians they have to stop the smuggling [from Egypt] to Rafah [in the Gaza Strip]."

Congressional supporters of aid to Egypt, Jordan, and others can find ways to counter the arguments of the staunchest defenders of right wing Israeli governments. They'll cite the value of joint US-Egyptian military exercises, and the size and weight of Egypt in the Arab world. They'll talk of how animosity to Israel by Egypt has been quelled, and that it's essential to keep Egypt as a friend. They'll also note that Egypt purchases older US military goods; and that Egypt needs money to keep its infrastructure healthy. Meanwhile, Department of Defense people will weigh in via the Defense subcommittee of Approps. And the Pentagon folks will argue, according to a staffer, that "We need to let them purchase x number of planes, ships, etc., and discuss the degree to which there are excess arms they'll sell to Egypt, but not the most sophisticated stuff like with Israel, for fear of a regime change in Egypt."

While many staffers agree with this staffer's assertions, not many are likely to say it out loud. And the "bosses" who agree with these statements are in the minority, and always fighting an uphill battle to retain support for "the other" Middle East states.

TAKING THE BILLS TO THE FLOOR

Bills coming out of House and Senate Appropriations committees that are brought to their full chambers can be subject to debate. As a staffer said, "On Appropriations, people tend to speak with a united voice on many issues. On the committee, most issues get voted with considerable unanimity. Then when the issue gets to the floor, all bets are off. To repeat, Appropriations bills are 'open rule,' so you can make an amendment on the House floor. This offers opportunities for debate on the amendments, and the debate can be quite animated."

It is in these floor debates that "water carriers" who are not members of Appropriations can and do again weigh in if need be. Party leaders will encourage members of their caucus or conference to toe a "pro-Israel" line, and "pro-Israel" resolutions and bills will pass by a comfortable margin. But such debates have become increasingly rare. Efforts can be made to block the aforementioned Continuing Resolutions on a floor vote, but more often than not those efforts fail.

DOES CONGRESS MATTER ON FOREIGN POLICYMAKING? VIEWS FROM APPROPRIATIONS STAFFERS

Most staffers answer this question in the affirmative; and several noted that sometimes people on Appropriations can influence matters with little fanfare. For example, on an action that related to HR 4681, one staffer urged me to examine the language in the March 18, 2006, Appropriations markup. "Mr. Kolbe wanted to prohibit funds from ever being given to the PA unless the PA put an end to terrorist incidents, etc. This passed the House and no one really noticed it; in essence, it accomplished the Ros-Lehtinen bill's [HR 4681] designs before the act. The House approved Mr. Kolbe's language by a 280–180 vote. In other words, Mr. Kolbe and Ms. Lowey did something very quietly that was very dramatic and powerful with very little noise made. By contrast, look at the amount of bills coming out of HIRC; there's a surprising lack of importance with all of them."

Another way to gauge Congress's significance in foreign policymaking is to measure foreign countries' lobbying efforts in the House and Senate. With roughly $2.2 billion in assistance to Egypt at stake many years on end, one can easily understand why the Egyptians invested so heavily in Hill activity. There are many other Middle East and North African nations who benefit from US assistance, among which Israel, Jordan, Tunisia, and Morocco figured prominently. A staffer for one key Appropriations figure remarked that "[The congressman] gets lots of traffic from foreigners. [PA Pres.] Mahmoud Abbas is a frequent visitor. The Egyptians, Jordanians, and Israelis come through a lot also." My interviews with numerous prominent foreign dignitaries, including past and present ambassadors, also brought explicit acknowledgment of appropriators, committee members and their staffers alike, as major targets of foreign embassies' congressional lobbying efforts.

Other nations lobby to lesser success. I crossed paths with the Syrian ambassador to the US in a House congressional office building one day in 2006. At a later date, during a lengthy interview I conducted with him at the Syrian embassy, he spoke at great length not only of the importance of his work on the Hill, but of how certain members of Congress had treated him abusively. He recalled in intricate detail how good faith efforts by his government to comply with US congressional requests on international financial matters had gone unacknowledged and were thereby successfully blocked from producing a positive outcome by Syria's congressional foes. He also expressed his frustration in dealing with many congressmen because of their priorities and, at times, ignorance, recounting that: "I met with a lot of congressmen who told me they voted for SAA because of 'domestic issues' not because of foreign policy concerns. I met with a congressman from Michigan once who told me, 'You know what Syria's problem is? Every time Israel gives back the Golan Heights to you, you use it to shoot at the Israelis again.' I told this to Secretary (Colin) Powell and he laughed." [Israel has never relinquished control of the Golan Heights since seizing it in the 1967 war.]

Finally, I'll add here that staffers often lauded foreign officials for their agility in responding to congressional challenges. One such example offered by a staffer concerned the Egyptian ambassador's response to an amendment to a 2005 bill, HR 4558, that would block aid to countries that voted against the US more than 50 percent of the time at the UN. "The Egyptian ambassador, who is a very smart man, a very political man, said, 'We don't vote against you in the UN; we vote differently.' He said, 'we allow your troops to stay in Egypt; we allow you to use our airspace,' and so on. And the bill was revised."

The following statements offer quick examples of ways in which House members can and do shape the parameters of foreign aid and foreign policy-making by US administrations, and why official foreign representatives view them as influential people to be lobbied.

As regards the nexus of foreign and domestic interest group lobbying, jostling among "water carriers" both within and across committees occurs. One staffer observed, "The most active embassies are those of Jordan, Egypt, Israel, Bahrain, and the UAE. The Egyptians were in two weeks ago; in July there was an effort to try to cut foreign aid, or to move military aid for Egypt to its Economic Support Fund. People like Lantos [and "dark blue" members; authorizers on HIRC] were trying to change the $600/600 million [military aid versus economic aid] mix to a $300/900 million mix. But the Appropriators didn't like it so they blocked it. People on Approps like Kolbe may have weighed in against it, as did so Jesse Jackson, Jr. and Kilpatrick. Lowey [a "light blue" member on Approps] may not have supported it, either. The Egyptians spend 3 to 4 percent of their GDP on their military, so a $300 million cut [as proposed by Lantos] would really hurt them. This is another example of a 'committee vs. committee' power struggle—HIRC vs. Appropriations."

This form of competition, or disagreement, appears with some regularity. The same staffer, working in a "dark blue" office, provided another quick example.

> "You can also see this in the Berkley-Crowley [two more "dark blue" members of HIRC] amendment regarding funding for the Palestinians; they tried to split the aid up into segments with reviews versus one lump sum. But Appropriations favored one lump sum. ZOA [the far right wing lobby] had asked us to do this; [that is, have aid provided in segments, with reviews], pushing for greater accountability among Palestinians. Our amendment did pass pretty overwhelmingly within the entire House."

Direct contact on these matters by US lobbyists, especially AIPAC, also occurs. A veteran aide to a key appropriator, shining a light on domestic special interests' role in the process, put an accent on AIPAC's dominance. The staffer urged me to examine previous Foreign Ops bills, paying specific attention to restrictions on aid to the PLO. "It's startling to see how many different provisions there are," the staffer said. "The vast majority come from AIPAC. It is the 800-pound gorilla. There is a set of items they [AIPAC] have every year. They negotiate with the committee and subcommittee members first . . . . AIPAC must look at who is on the committee and say, 'If we get just one-third of the Appropriations committee to weigh in on this, then we don't have to worry about this much.'"

As another staffer noted, "Israel is the only country that gets its assistance [foreign aid money] up front—in cash. They earn interest on it; the day the bill passes, the money goes into an account and it earns interest before it's spent. About 70 to 75 percent needs to be spent in the US, but it's unlike any other country in the world. Israel just gets the money. The chairman of Approps and his staff write the bill—it all comes down to language, so why does he put different things in there? Members will send request letters every year. Letters are a key part of how people weigh in. The chairman, as best as he can, will try to accommodate them. Not just members of the subcommittee, any member can send a request in. Sometimes there are group letters; for example, Seeds of Peace [which promotes peace by bringing Palestinian and Israeli children together] gets a lot of supporters; a letter that gets 60 signatures will be looked at very seriously. Many members will write letters for Israel; some for Lebanon, some for the Baltic countries."

Jumping ahead to the 2011–2013 time frame, one still found many telltale signs of House Appropriations' power on the international scene. One simple indication is in the flow of communications between the Foreign Ops leadership and the leaders of foreign nations. For example, I learned from key staffers that Rep. Granger engaged in periodic and significant contact with Egypt's Field Marshal Mohamed Tantawi, who for all intents and purposes was ruling Egypt after Pres. Mubarak's ouster in the early 2011 Arab Spring.

When I asked the ambassador of Egypt about Congress's significance in US-Egyptian foreign relations in summer 2013, he told me:

"As regards US aid to Egypt, Congress plays a very important role. This role increases when you have budgetary pressures in the United States like now and the role of Congress becomes even more important. Of course, we have to be in touch with all agencies, like with the Department of Defense and others, but 50 percent of our diplomats focus primarily on Congress, and over 50 percent of the meetings I have personally are with people in Congress. I visit with members and staffers alike on Appropriations, Defense [*sic*; Armed Services], and Foreign Relations. When Congress is in session, I try to spend two full days on the Hill every week from morning until 5:00 p.m., nonstop meetings. I'll take some key staffers to lunch—I don't like to bind myself with protocol—but mostly I'll have lunch with senators and House members."

Elsewhere, remember my earlier discussion of the clash between the House and the Obama administration over continued funding for the Palestinians after their UN statehood bid? The 2011–12 battle over canceling funds for UNESCO provided a fascinating look at Congress's ability to shape not only US Mideast policy, but to do so in a manner that had grave implications for overall US policy vis-à-vis the United Nations. As one very well placed staffer saw these events:

"I came [to this office] as a blank slate. I came here because Appropriations has more of a say, and the boss is on Approps. If the Hill doesn't like something, they can put a 'hold' on it. The power of the 'hold' is significant, and a great example was the recent dustup with the PA. Last year the administration requested $200 million for programs for the PA—more budget support for the PA. Ros-Lehtinen and Granger had concerns over the Palestinian request for statehood issue. The Palestinians walked things back, but then came recognition of the Palestinians by UNESCO and Congress's cutoff in funding occurred. The administration began pressing, 'We need this money. Release the hold.' Now a hold is more of a courtesy than a legally binding thing. The State Department got more desperate; they feared the consequences if the hold was not lifted. [PA] Prime Minister Fayyad called—is he the prime minister or the president? [*sic*]—and said, 'Look, we really need these funds. People aren't allowing me to raise taxes.' So the administration and Fayyad teamed up. Then finally the Israeli embassy and AIPAC weighed in [to lift the hold]. I think this was enough for Granger to release this hold. It became an issue of the security of Israel being threatened, or this is how I saw it. This tipped the balance. It's not as though these were four equal influences, but . . . [Despite these developments] Ros-Lehtinen toed the line, but [Sec. of State] Clinton blew the 'hold' [as the expression goes]."

Another staffer noted, "I've read and heard about AIPAC's influence, but just seeing it in action was really something. Before House hearings, I've seen AIPAC's questions and read them all to prepare the chairwoman. We change them all [that is, the wording], but I hear the same wording from Democrats and Republicans alike at the hearings. So I know the influence of AIPAC is fairly substantial. The Israeli embassy does weigh in also, and they are influential.'"

Another veteran staffer offered this fascinating, insider's rendition of this same episode. "Last year [2011], Speaker Boehner urged committee chairs to present their authorizing bills, and [Rep.] Ros-Lehtinen had her authorizing bill prepared. It contained one section that blocked money for UNRWA, and a section that blocked money for PA security assistance. No matter how much we [concerned officials] talked to people on HFAC, no one was changing their minds. So AIPAC came in—and they said even they didn't want these provisions because Israel doesn't want them either . . . [Rep.] Berman's office picked up on AIPAC's line, so you had Ros-Lehtinen squaring off against Berman! Sometimes I think Ros-Lehtinen and [Rep.] Berkley are being pushed by [the more extreme] ZOA. Ros-Lehtinen's staff member Yleem [Poblete], she won't let people meet with anybody she doesn't want them to meet. I think Yleem is out to lunch. Sometimes I think she's just lost it. She has no respect. You should look at a *Huffington Post* piece being prepared about her. So AIPAC wants her [Ros-Lehtinen] to remove these provisions, and Yleem starts battling with the AIPAC guy in the hallway just a couple days before the markup. Yleem [taking an even more right wing position] is yelling at the AIPAC guy, 'There's no way in hell I'm removing these provisions!' Then the bill came to the markup and the provisions were gone! How did this happen? AIPAC got its way. Who called? The Israeli ambassador? Netanyahu himself? We don't know, but it had to be somebody really high up."

Generally speaking, the same caustic relationship between appropriators and authorizers in 2005–2006 was alive and well in 2011–2012, if not laden with even greater conflict. People saw the extreme positions being advocated by HFAC Chairwoman Ros-Lehtinen, noted above, as so strongly opposed to the foreign policy positions espoused by Pres. Obama as to make almost any authorizing bill that came out of HFAC dead on arrival, if not in the Senate, then in the White House. As one staffer put it:

> "Ros-Lehtinen versus Obama, this is important because Ros-Lehtinen's bills won't go anywhere. But appropriators need to make things happen and work with the White House. Now with Appropriations bills in the House, bills go to the Rules Committee. By law, Rule 21 prohibits authorizing language; that is, introducing policy language, in Appropriations bills. There should be no policy stuff on an Appropriations bill. But nowadays when the bill goes to the Rules Committee, they waive the legal stricture, so in essence, the appropriators have been doing both the appropriations and authorization work. Ros-Lehtinen would be ruled out of order if she tried to offer an amendment to the Appropriations bill. She could only attempt to cut or strike funding; she can't really legislate or authorize something different. So appropriators will carry the day."

Let's now turn to look at what happens in the Senate.

SENATE APPROPRIATIONS

Given the triumvirate of (1) basic, American political socialization—the "natural pro-Israel bias," (2) electoral pressures, and (3) the vetting process encountered by all members of Congress seeking positions on key committees, it is not surprising that Senate Appropriations seats are filled by people with pro-Israel orientations. As seen in the House, considerable care is taken by party leaders, always sensitive to powerful groups like AIPAC, to ensure that senators assuming posts on a committee as important as Senate Appropriations will consistently deliver the goods for Israel. These predilections and proclivities are placed in evidence by a positional analysis of Senate Appropriations' leadership over the past nine Congresses.

SENATE APPROPRIATIONS FULL COMMITTEE AND FOREIGN OPS CHAIRPERSONS AND RANKING MEMBERS

Congress	Year	Chair	Ranking Member
103rd Full	1993–95	Hamilton, D-IN	Gilman, R-NY
105th Full	1997–99	Stevens, R-AL	Byrd, D-WV
105th For. Ops.		McConnell, R-KY	Leahy, D-VT
106th Full	'99–'01	Stevens	Byrd
106th For. Ops.		McConnell	Leahy
107th Full	'01–'03	Byrd	Stevens
107th For. Ops.		Leahy	McConnell
108th Full	'03–'05	Stevens	Byrd
108th For. Ops.		McConnell	Leahy
109th Full	'05–'07	Cochran, R-MS	Byrd
109th For. Ops.		McConnell	Leahy
110th Full	'07–'09	Byrd	Cochran
110th For. Ops.		Leahy	Gregg, R-NH
111th Full	'09–'11	Inouye, D-HI	Cochran
111th For. Ops.		Leahy	Gregg
112th Full	'11–'13	Inouye	Cochran
112th For. Ops.		Leahy	Graham, R-SC
113th Full	'13–'15	Mikulski, D-MD	Shelby, R-AL
113th For. Ops.		Leahy	Graham

The chart reflects several core realities. As in the House, leadership on Senate Appropriations reflects considerable stability. Positions on Appropriations are highly treasured, so once these "plum" positions are obtained, members usually hold on to them as long as they can. Party-imposed term limits force Republicans to abandon their chairmanships after three terms (six years), otherwise the track records of people like Ted Stevens and McConnell would parallel their Democrat counterparts even more closely. The Democrats have no such limits, ergo the longevity of Byrd and Leahy. (Byrd, though respected by many, earned the sobriquet "The Prince of Pork;" Stevens, of course, was the principal in procuring funds for "the bridge to nowhere" in Alaska.)

On Appropriations, positional analysis and reputational analysis go nearly hand in glove. Everyone on the positional list is or was a formally powerful actor and widely recognized as such. Nearly all of the names listed are house-hold names to anyone who follows American politics; they may not know these senators were or are on Appropriations, but they certainly know their names. A few like Byrd and McConnell, whether loved or disliked, were/are legendary figures; only a few, like Gregg, didn't care to stick around long enough to acquire comparable stature.

In terms of narrower, Middle East matters, as we saw in House Appropri-ations, there has been nearly complete uniformity of opinion and support for unfettered funding for Israel, as well as historically strong support to assist Egypt and Jordan—again, the two countries with formal peace trea-ties with Israel. In the Senate, the handling of some Mideast issues has been slightly different than in the House. True, there has been little rocking of the aforementioned boats, but the behavior of several senators merits additional commentary.

First, Sen. Byrd stood opposed to the neocon-inspired war in Iraq and the related loss of blood and treasure. As the reader knows, neocons are avid, right wing supporters of Israel, so Byrd's impassioned stand on the war ran counter to their preferences. But Byrd never blocked aid to Israel.

Second, Senators Stevens and Leahy were both identified by staffers as rec-ognizing the importance of continued funding for Egypt, but again, this was usually consonant with the wishes of even right wing Israeli governments, who saw value in a stable and unthreatening Egypt. Leahy was often trou-bled by the human rights violations of Pres. Mubarak's regime, continues to display comparable concerns with Egypt's postrevolution military leadership, and has steadily pressured Egyptian officials to address such issues. However, in the end he has usually put his stamp of approval on the flow of aid to Egypt, seeing that country as a force for regional stability and a mediator in both intra-Palestinian (Hamas vs. Fatah) and Israeli-Palestinian relations.

Other significant, committee leaders have included Senators Inouye and Graham. As noted elsewhere, Sen. Inouye was a longtime, stalwart supporter of Israel, and Sen. Lindsey Graham has approached Middle East issues from a conservative, even "neocon" hawkish, pro-Israel position.

Because individual senators can play more powerful roles in the Senate, in part due to the power of the filibuster, it's important to study the overall membership compositions of either the full committee or Subcommittee for State, Foreign Operations, and Related Programs (Foreign Ops). What one sees here is that, over time, the respective chairs and RMs have been backed by numerous party members exhibiting a steadfast commitment to the procurement of funds for Israel. Thus, while Byrd was serving as chairman or ranking member, he always had unstintingly "pro-Israel" individuals like Senators Inouye, Durbin, Barbara Mikulski, Tom Harkin, Kohl, and (to a great degree) Feinstein as fellow full committee members. On the Republican side, Senators Stevens and Thad Cochran were backed by Senators Specter, Brownback, and Mike DeWine in this earlier period, all of whom were very strong supporters of Israel as well.

Who were the key positional figures during the 2011–13 period? When Byrd died in June 2010, he was succeeded by Inouye, who was steadfastly pro-Israeli as described above. While Inouye chaired the full committee, his fellow Democrat appropriators included Leahy, Harkin, Mikulski, Kohl, Patty Murray, Feinstein, Durbin, Tim Johnson (SD), Mary Landrieu (LA), Reed (RI), Lautenberg, Nelson (NE), Pryor (AR), Tester (MT), and Brown (OH). And when Inouye died in December 2012, he was replaced by Sen. Mikulski. Over the Inouye/Mikulski period, the ranking member for the Republicans was Thad Cochran, backed by McConnell, Shelby, Kay Bailey Hutchison, Alexander, Collins, Murkowski, Graham, Kirk, Dan Coats, Blunt, Moran, John Hoeven (ND), and Ron Johnson (WI). I name the names because the overall roll call constitutes, almost to a person, a veritable Who's Who? of recipients of major, "pro-Israel" PAC assistance, as shown earlier, and/or individuals with the strongest commitments to Israel in the Senate, as detailed below.

As for reputational analysis of Senate Appropriations' members, staffers concurred that Sen. Inouye's strong commitment to Israel was matched by Senators Kohl, Mikulski, Durbin, Lautenberg, Harkin, and Feinstein. More recently, as ranking member, Sen. Shelby has been working with fellow Republican Senators McConnell, Kirk, Blunt, Coats, and Hoeven. The latter four, all newly elected in 2010, were given solid, positive marks by AIPAC in its Near East Report.[223] This is not terribly surprising, given that the Republicans' committee leaders, McConnell, Cochran, and Shelby, have themselves consistently received high scores from AIPAC, and McConnell and Cochran basically handpicked these new Republican members following the 2010 Senate departures of Gregg, Bennett, Bond, Brownback, and Voinovich. Only a small number of senators has, like Leahy, consistently shown any significant level of concern and understanding for Arab parties like Egypt, whose leaders have worked hard and unfailingly along with moderate Palestinians, to advance a "two state" solution to the I-P conflict.

As evidenced in the House, "pro-Israel" PACs and individual donors have consistently taken good care of most Senate appropriators. Of those listed as "Top Ten Career Recipients" of "pro-Israel" PACs in 2006, one half of them were on Senate Appropriations: Harkin, Specter, McConnell, Durbin, and Reid. Only Specter was absent by 2011–2012. McConnell was not only still on Appropriations, he had become Senate Minority leader. Reid had left Appropriations, but as Senate Majority leader was in a position to influence matters on all committees, not just Appropriations. Meanwhile, Sen. Lautenberg, another "Top Ten" figure from 2006, had joined the ranks of Democrat appropriators and continued to play an influential role until his death in spring 2013. Indeed, pro-Israel PACs have not just showered their attention on Senate appropriators; their campaign finance support has been more like a torrential downpour. Here are figures for pro-Israel PACs contributions to US senators through the end of July 2008, as collected by staff at the *Washington Report on Middle East Affairs* from the Federal Election Commission: Lautenberg (D-NJ): $503,578; Kirk (R-IL): $263,686; Inouye (D-HI): $254,425; Burns (R-MT): $210,210; Landrieu (D-LA): $205,389; Shelby (R-AL): $198,825; Mikulski (D-MD): $198,599; Dorgan (D-ND): $186,350; Murray (D-WA): $182,293; Leahy (D-VT): $134,911; Bennett (R-UT): $133,250; and Collins (R-ME): $109,000. By 2013, according to CRP, career contributions from the "pro-Israel industry" for key Appropriations figures had risen to the following sums: Kirk: $1,340,484; McConnell: $1,072,548; Feinstein: $806,716; Harkin: $779,585; Durbin: $641,566; Inouye: $629,065; Mikulski: $589,559; Lautenberg: $492,507; Brown: $475,395; Murray: $424884; Landrieu: $414,700; Shelby: $350,280; Bennett: $344,200; B. Nelson: $250,373; Murkowski: $185,050; Hoeven: $68,660.[224] Other current committee members include Susan Collins (R-ME) and again Lindsey Graham (R-SC), for whom no contributions from comparable pro-Israel sources appear, but who have both been exceptionally helpful to AIPAC and other right wing pro-Israel interests for many years.

Interviews with Senate staffers show just how solidly the Israel–US Senate Appropriations connection is in place. From a Senate staffer's 2006 statement, we learn what was echoed in so many moderate to right wing pro-Israel senators' offices. The staffer said, "Israel has benefited greatly from US appropriations. The Palestinians are lucky to get $200 million or so and there's always a lot of restrictions." When this particular staffer was asked about special "water carriers" for Israel on Senate Appropriations, the response was:

> "It's so bipartisan on this issue that it's not really necessary. Are there those who feel Israel is not doing enough to make peace? I can't name one in the Senate. Many here feel that: (1) Israel has made a big effort over the past 5 to 10 years to make peace, with the Gaza withdrawal perceived as a strong measure by Israel to address the problem—and yet Palestinian terrorist attacks still occurred and then the Hamas election came. (2) The Palestinian situation has deteriorated greatly due to the [2006] election. (3) The Palestinian relationship with terrorists—overall suspicion of people using terrorism as a method makes them suspect and potential adversaries. For many, the view of terrorists as 'freedom fighters' died with September 11. The conflict is more complicated than that, as you and I know, but not so with the general public that lumps its terrorists together."

The degree to which September 11, the Clinton's "failed Camp David summit" of summer 2000, and the election of Hamas constituted watersheds is evident from the same staffer's additional comments. "Let me make two other points: (1) Congress as a whole is so focused on terror that any other issue gets less attention. (2) The Arab-Israeli issue hasn't changed much at all over the past ten years, so it gets less attention," the staffer said. "The election of Hamas was a continuation of a negative downward spiral dating back to Arafat's poor handling of things. Ten years ago, there were many people more sympathetic or willing to listen to the Palestinians. Everything fell apart after [Israeli Prime Minister Ehud] Barak's offer was rejected. People were persuasive in selling the idea that Barak had made a very serious offer. The perception was that the Palestinians didn't negotiate."

The staffer's depiction demonstrates the propensity of senators and their staffers to accept the dominant view, spread by Pres. Clinton and his team, that Arafat was to blame for the 2000 Camp David summit's failure. To reiterate, this narrative that Arafat was solely to blame, however, was placed in serious doubt, albeit one year after the event, by State Department hand Robert Malley, who was a participant in the meetings.[225] But once again, I got the strong impression from my staffer interviewees that few would have been affected by Malley's account. Moreover, I came away with the belief that very few people on the Hill have the time or energy to look at the big picture. Thus, when I asked the same staffer quoted here, "Does the senator have a clear view on the Arab-Israeli conflict's so-called 'final status' issues?" The answer was: "No, I don't think anyone really does. Some bills come up regarding moving the embassy to Jerusalem. And the growing demographic problem for Israel is a very important dynamic. What will happen when the majority in Israel is no longer Jewish? We don't know."

Finally, on a separate note, it's also interesting to learn how seemingly quickly serious "transgressions" by right wing pro-Israel actors were swept under the rug. One staffer mentioned the Rosen-Weissman-Franklin case, which was described earlier. The staffer said, "I don't think it has affected AIPAC's ability to have access to people or its role in congressional matters. It may have hurt AIPAC's credibility a bit, but so far no real damage has been done. If this were to happen again, however, it could cause real problems."

Like in the House, Senate Appropriations committee members are happily removed from direct appeals by lobbyists. As one staffer said, "On appropriations, we are a bit insulated from the lobbyists. We don't get constituents' calls and lobbyists, but AIPAC, the American Jewish Committee, and ADL requests do go to [our senator's] office, and we hear about these calls. AIPAC doesn't come to our subcommittee level. They have power in senators' offices, but not at our level."

Echoing this point, another Senate staffer with strongly right wing, pro-Israel views noted, "Appropriations, thankfully, is an area where there has been minimal politicking. We try hard to make this [foreign aid] bill what it is—designed to help people in impoverished countries."

Another staffer for a right wing, pro-Israel senator on Appropriations described the way he, his peers, and the senators looked at many Mideast-related appropriations matters as follows: "With regard to the annual foreign aid bill, we don't think about it. We are in many ways a rubber stamp as regards [the 1979 peace treaty] Camp David–inspired money. There's no debate on this. The executive branch, the president, gets what is requested here. It's off the table; no one would think of cutting any of this. Israel is off the table—there's not a lot of control here for us." The same staffer was quick to point out that the treatment of other countries differed. "As regards Egypt, some are attempting to cut back ESF [Economic Support Fund] because this has been seen as tied to progress toward democracy, as though it's a real slap in the face to us that Egypt is not living up to its democracy commitments," the staffer said. "Look at the new bill's language. Egypt cares first and foremost about the military aid, so we're not hitting them where it hurts most. We have rescinded money—about $200 to $300 million—to Egypt because they haven't lived up to democratization progress."

Regarding Jordan, the staffer noted, "It's seen as a very good friend up here. The February 2006 request by the president contained no money for Jordan; none by the executive; none by the House. A hundred million dollars was requested by Senators Frist and McConnell put this in at the request of the Jordanian embassy because of the economic duress in Jordan. This amount was cut down to $50 million in conference at the end of May. But on Appropriations, I think we're very lucky that we're not as tainted by the politics of this issue. We're quite lucky. It says a lot about this committee and Tim Rieser's ability—he's been here 20 years—to maintain an apolitical view on how this committee deals with issues."

ANALYZING THE 2011–2013 FOREIGN OPS SUBCOMMITTEE MEMBERSHIP

Although chaired by the more nuanced Democrat Patrick Leahy, fellow Democrats on Foreign Ops included Harkin, Mikulski, Durbin, Inouye, and Lautenberg (until the latter two senators' passings). The remaining Democrat colleagues, Landrieu and Brown, have also received substantial pro-Israel PACs' support. Their Republican counterparts on Foreign Ops were led by the hawkishly pro-Israel Lindsey Graham, and backed by McConnell, Kirk, Blunt, Coats, Johnson, and Hoeven. Overall, one sees a disproportionately high percentage of senators from conservative Christian, evangelical Christian, and Jewish backgrounds represented on the Foreign Ops subcommittee; and they're positioned alongside other diehard "pro-Israel" senators and hawks. This made for a subcommittee almost unflinchingly responsive to all Israeli government requests. As a veteran Appropriations staffer put it, "No one is going to take money out of appropriations for Israel. No one is that suicidal. Some senators have put the national security of Israel ahead of that of the United States."

THE ROLE OF THE SENATE APPROPRIATORS

Senate Appropriations' role is every bit as crucial as the House counterpart, if not more so, so there is no need to be redundant about some of the mechanics of its operations. But a few caveats and observations are in order. First, as a veteran staffer told me, "The Senate is much more individual based, so even non–Foreign Relations and non–Appropriations people can and do weigh in on issues. They can acquire considerable stature—like a Ted Kennedy. Second, because of their length of terms and their typically greater role in foreign affairs, some senior senators on Approps become every bit if not even more knowledgeable about foreign affairs issues than people in the State Department . . . This is true of the senior staffers as well. Someone like Tim Rieser, who has been there for over twenty years, done the Foreign Ops hearings, etc.; he has traveled the world, met the Dalai Lama; he may know more about some things than even the Secretary of State."

Differences between House and Senate parliamentary procedure affect the power of lobbyists over Appropriations. To this point one staffer said, "If you compare the House and Senate, AIPAC owns the House. This reality [obeisance to AIPAC] is driven by House leadership. Republicans have the majority [in the House]; they control things. In the Senate, one member can hold up matters. Here, in the Senate, AIPAC has power in senators' offices, but they can't affect matters in Appropriations as directly." Nonetheless, there was no gainsaying the lengths lobbyists go to gain influence in the committee. As a northern senator's aide said, "In the Senate, the lobbying effort by Egypt, Israel, and Jordan is even more intense with the people on Appropriations than their effort with the senators on the Foreign Relations Committee."

These statements signify that for appropriators, domestic lobbyists' influence is heavily exercised through their contacts with the senators themselves, and that senators sitting on Foreign Ops can bring a lot to the table. Why? Because on Appropriations bills, and this is equally if not all the more true with relevant Continuing Resolutions, "[House Foreign Ops Chairwoman] Granger and [RM] Lowey basically write the bill with their senior staffers, and the same is true on the Senate side with [Chairman] Leahy and [RM] Graham." Notably, three of these figures, Granger, Lowey, and Graham, are all in lockstep with AIPAC; only Sen. Leahy is not.

STAFFERS' VIEWS: AN EXPANDED DISCUSSION OF "WATER CARRIERS" IN THE SENATE

Although support for all Israeli governments has been nearly unbridled over the years, there are still individuals on Senate Appropriations, despite the one staffer's observation registered above, who have acquired reputations as watchdogs or "water carriers" for certain countries and causes. When I asked which individuals were particularly important role players on Senate Appropriations, these are the responses I garnered.

A Midwestern senator's aide in the mid-2000s spoke of the key players on the committee.

> "At the member level, you should look at what Leahy [Vermont] and Stevens [Alaska] do for Jordan. With Egypt, Stevens is a defender, whereas Leahy has a weird relationship with Mubarak. Leahy defends Egypt, but he has concerns with regard to human rights; so sometimes Leahy aligns himself with Brownback, who doesn't like Egypt. On Israel, Mikulski, McConnell, and Durbin are the core players who care about Israel's money. Leahy's been to Egypt several times; he's been invested in Egypt since the early 1990s, at least. Leahy has actually tried to put conditions on Israel's money. He's always been viewed as an honest broker. Over time, Leahy developed a relationship with Mubarak; he passed notes to Egypt from Bush I. But he really read the riot act to the Egyptians on human rights over the Saad Eddin Ibrahim case.[226] He feels that a viable Egypt will require a vital civil society."

Certain senators, through their trips to the region, may develop special relations that would strike many as out of the ordinary. As discussed earlier, while he was still a player, Sen. Specter, for example had developed strong ties to Syria. One staffer mentioned, "As for the [2003] Syrian Accountability Act—Specter didn't support this because he has/had past ties with the Assad family. He sees the key to peace as passing through Damascus. Specter [who was serving on Appropriations] asked for one hour to talk about SAA in the fall of 2003 before it was passed in order to register his views."

A veteran aide, also speaking in the mid-2000s, spoke of Senator Inouye's and Senator Stevens's leadership on Israel issues in the committee. "Inouye makes sure Israel's needs are met on Appropriations. He does the same for Israel's partners, like Egypt; he protects them as well," the staffer said. "Sen. Stevens and Sen. Inouye are chairman and ranking member of Defense appropriations. They've traveled together, including to the Mideast, and they think alike on Appropriations issues. He may not check with Stevens, but they often come out the same way," the aide said. "Some younger members will follow them if they're not the right wing Christian human rights types like Brownback; so maybe [Robert] Bennett [R-Utah] at times." Numerous staffers said that friction could get created when Brownback backs Israel, but then criticized Egypt. But all agreed that there wasn't anyone on Appropriations who thought aid to Israel should be eliminated. Noted one: "Some liberal staffers or media people are more critical about aid to Israel, but not members."

Not many members on the committee scrutinize Israel's actions. One staffer said that "Specter and Chafee have been keener to examine Israel's role in Congress," but an aide to a Southern senator noted, "I don't know anybody who would say much against Israel on Foreign Ops." This second statement is particularly true when it comes to the issue of aid to Israel. As another staffer mentioned, "I don't think there's anyone on Appropriations who thinks aid to Israel should be eliminated. Some liberal staffers or media are more critical about Israel, but not members."

Some staffers spoke about the members on the committee with reputations as "water carriers." One said, "With Santorum, yes, he's a water carrier for Israel, but I think it's political. He's running the race of his life right now. See the *Washington Post*; he's trying really hard to shore up his base with the evangelicals. Schumer is always a strong supporter of Israel; so are Harry Reid and Lieberman." Another staffer mentioned that "Sen. Kyl is very Israel focused."

Not all "water carriers" are on the subcommittee, however, and other government actors have an opportunity to weigh in. A strongly pro-Israel senator's aide reminded me that "Leahy and McConnell are most active, with their staffs, putting together the proposals in coordination with the House and the White House."

One finds here then, among the alleged "water carriers," a mixed bag of senators. A few—Leahy, Stevens, Specter—appear to be motivated by their attachment to specific objectives, including rewarding parties for their past or potential contributions to Middle East peace. Others fall clearly into the camp of those motivated by their or their constituents' ethno-religious affiliations and sentiments: Brownback, Kyl, Santorum, Schumer, and Lieberman.

By 2011–2013, the Senate Appropriations scene had metamorphosed into an even more solidly right wing pro-Israel body compared to its mid-2000s composition. Gone was former lead Democrat, Robert Byrd, who had questioned US involvement in Iraq and, though never voting to block aid to Israel, did actively oppose resolutions such as those demanding movement of the US embassy to Jerusalem. The committee was chaired by Sen. Inouye, whose strong commitment to Israel has been discussed above; and once again, when he passed away, he was replaced by the staunchly pro-Israel Sen. Mikulski. One can virtually run the gamut of the other Democrats on Appropriations, finding similarly strong backers of Israel along the way. Patrick Leahy, again with a more nuanced approach, chaired the Foreign Operations subcommittee, but his fellow D's included Senators Daniel Inouye, Tom Harkin, Barbara Mikulski, Richard Durbin, Mary Landrieu, Frank Lautenberg, Ben Nelson, Sherrod Brown, and Diane Feinstein. Almost all have been huge recipients of pro-Israel campaign largesse. The only mild sign of "dissident" behavior here from AIPAC's perspective was that Durbin and Feinstein recently proved willing to accept campaign donations from J Street.

Among the Republicans, Ranking Member Thad Cochran (R-MS) was strongly supportive of Israel, alongside fellow Republicans Mitch McConnell, Richard Shelby, Susan Collins, Lindsey Graham, Roy Blunt, Dan Coats, and John Hoeven. And the hawkishly pro-Israel Graham had become RM of Foreign Ops. Perhaps most noteworthy was the addition to the Republicans on Appropriations of Mark Kirk, in whose campaigns and office affairs pro-AIPAC elements have invested very heavily over the years. Kirk, who had acquired experience on Foreign Ops as a House member, garnered a seat on the Senate Foreign Ops subcommittee, alongside fellow Republicans McConnell, Blunt, Coats, Johnson, and Hoeven. His office quickly became very active in "carrying water" for the Israeli government. One veteran staffer said of Kirk's office that "We're quite certain that many resolutions and bills are penned by AIPAC. He and those in his office make no bones about where they put Israel policy."

In 2012 a very interesting situation emerged involving Kirk and his staff. Kirk had a stroke that necessitated surgery, leaving him first incapacitated and then in rehab. His staff, however, continued to introduce aggressive, right wing pro-Israeli measures in Foreign Ops markups and other Senate settings while he was away from the Hill. Thus, at a time when defunding of Palestinian organizations remained a major preoccupation to many right wing pro-Israel interests, numerous, well-informed observers both on and off the Hill echoed the picture painted by one off-the-Hill former Senate staffer, who said:

> "[I] saw outside influences and Kirk's staff as taking advantage of his being in rehab. The LD is known to be very tied to special interests; and people are quite sure the LD is getting stuff from a member of the Knesset and a US lobby. They're shopping this [pro-Israel] amendment around, and the staffer is taking the opportunity to press matters. All subcommittee members are inclined to be deferential and accommodative in a 'Poor Mark Kirk, he really wanted this in the bill' way. Roy Blunt is trying to be deferential. You can't take on someone who's in a rehab center, so it's awkward for Blunt and to some extent Graham. It's awkward for Leahy, too; he knows that he can't put this to a vote because he'll lose. This has put people in a bind. However, the negotiating process may be used to water down the bill. Tim Rieser [the Foreign Ops staffer] and others will find language to water down Kirk's bill. [Kirk's staff] may have cost Mark more than he thinks. Was this the number one thing for him to ask for, to get this but piss off Leahy? Kirk's staff didn't care what State thought, or the Jordanian ambassador thought, that was clear. So Kirk may have cashed in too many of his chits. Leahy knew he could modify it. He'll just put the language in the committee report, and not in the bill. It'll be in the committee report accompanying the bill. If it's in the bill, it becomes law."

To this point, another veteran senate staffer on Foreign Relations noted of Kirk's staffers, "Sometimes when they're hammering Iran I've tried to warn them [Kirk's staffers] about the absence of nuance. But they don't give a shit. There's no nuance at all."

Control of Senate Appropriations was potentially even more important in that partisan bickering in the Senate and Republican control of the House left Senate Majority Democrats either incapable of passing or unwilling to pass a budget, depending on one's view point. Even though the law formally requires passage of a budget on an annual basis, by late 2013 the last budget passed by Congress dated back to April 29, 2009. This standoff "didn't matter" in that specific allocations are in the hands of Appropriations, but as we saw earlier it did mean that the power of Appropriations' members was thus enhanced because Appropriations was called upon to conjure up the necessary continuing resolutions to keep federal funds flowing to all recipients at home and abroad. (When a budget for 2014 finally did pass, it called for $3.4 billion in assistance to Israel, part of the 2009, 10-year Memorandum of Understanding with Israel, making it once again the number one recipient of US foreign assistance.)

HOUSE-SENATE CONFERENCE COMMITTEES

If a bill needs to be ironed out due to differences between the House and Senate versions, then it goes to a conference committee. At such meetings, one finds ten members, five from each chamber, with their staffs. According to one staffer, "Most issues are worked out before the conference committee meets. We have formal staff meetings. We go through all the differences until we've resolved almost everything. The conference is usually just a formal exercise. Leaderships will cue us when to start negotiating—then it could take about 1.5 weeks. By May and June, bills are on the floor. Conferences occur in September, October, or November."

Staffers commenting on the proceedings of the meetings agreed that by the time a conference is held, everything is pretty scripted. House and Senate appropriators do talk to each other across the Hill; and the committee staffers will have already sat down and made deals. As a Senate PSM noted:

> "If there are still problems, these will be taken up and dealt with by the chairs and subcommittee chairs; they'll hash out the tough issues. This is how it's done; and it's done behind closed doors. And this is where the lobbyists, many of whom are former staffers themselves, weigh in with their staffer contacts, trying to find out what's going to be in the conference committee report, and how to influence what's in its language."

I asked one Appropriations staffer interviewee if there is deference shown to the senators by House members in conference committees, and received the following response by one staffer: "It depends on whether it's your issue or not, and how the House has acted," according to one staffer. "For example, it's very difficult for the Senate to try to change something that was big and important to people in the House." It should also be noted that there is room at this stage for executive branch parties to exercise influence. For example, as a staffer said, "Look at the House bill, the Senate bill, and the conference report. You'll see the White House's role, or comments, in the conference report. The White House has the opportunity, with the members' approval, to meet with staff who are writing the conference reports. It allows them to share ideas. Also, one house may want the White House to come in because they may share their view. State or Defense may have their own perspectives, also."

SENATE STAFFERS' PERCEPTIONS OF WHETHER CONGRESS MATTERS ON FOREIGN POLICY FORMULATION

Senate staffers know that they and their bosses play a role in shaping US foreign policy. This was clearly reflected in every interview I had, as evidenced by these statements. As a veteran staffer commented, "Look at Appropriations earmarks. Look at these—like Lantos's in the House; Brownback does the same on the Senate side—look at what they do regarding money for Egypt, the Palestinians, Saudis, etc. Look at how they try to block or curtail it. Does Congress's role make a difference with regard to foreign policy on the conflict? I think so, because we have the money. We write the checks."

Of course, in the end, Senate staffers involved with Appropriations work have experienced the same frustration as executive officials in seeking Middle East peace. In 2012, key Senate staffers saw the situation in the Middle East as so glum and lacking in opportunities for peace as to instill a great lethargy among most senators. "Today [spring 2012] things have gotten so bad and the peace process is so off track—there is no peace process—that no one here sees any need to do anything but pander," one staffer said. "There's no reason to be high-minded; it's just a waste of time. If the Palestinians and the Israelis, or even the [Obama] administration—the negotiator in chief—doesn't say or do anything, if the White House doesn't come up and make their case, then I'm not going to do it. If you [in the executive branch] want a presidential waiver authority to fund the Palestinians, then why aren't you up here pushing for it?"

If the situation looked glum in 2012, then it looked even "glummer" in summer 2013 due to even more violent upheavals throughout the region. As one of the most knowledgeable staffers in Congress observed:

> "The situation in the Middle East has become one in which moderate senators, who care about peace and human rights, have a difficult time having an impact. . . .
>
> "After 9/11 and more recently, I think the situation in the region has become a lot more confusing. We didn't necessarily see the uncertainty that resulted as such a bad thing because it could bring positive developments—turbulence before democratic stability—not that the stability didn't have its merits, of course . . . Ironically, only after the [2011] revolution have we been able to put conditions on aid to Egypt. There is much we don't like about the Morsy government and Morsy himself, but we don't want to act rashly in a manner that would write us out of the process. The Israeli government doesn't support cutting aid to Egypt, and the US military clearly sees Egypt as of strategic significance to the US.
>
> "What else has changed? We've seen more intensive efforts, ad nauseam, to show our support for Israel in recent times, as though this must be chiseled in granite. This takes up more of our time and efforts and distracts us from other problems. It also requires more from us out of our budget, more for an area or region that already was top heavy. This has implications for the rest of the world, about which people will get US assistance. On Appropriations, it's pretty much all in one direction . . . . [Sen.] Kirk is a real zealot—of course now, it's really his staff acting on his behalf. Lindsey Graham has, at times, been in that camp as well. All others pretty much fall in line. If AIPAC urges something regarding the Palestinians or Iran or whatever, then over 80 senators will cosponsor it and it will pass by a voice vote. Plenty of staffers feel they're in a straitjacket put on them by AIPAC, that there's nothing they can do. All the resolutions on Iran are basically inspired by AIPAC or the Israelis and motivated

to force the president to redefine the terms of a military operation against Iran and to do so sooner. And there is increasing use of selective information, and even misquoting of the president, by AIPAC's supporters to gain advantage on these issues."

THE COST OF US SUPPORT FOR ISRAEL

As one of my favorite graduate school professors taught us to always ask, "So what?" Just how much money has the US Congress appropriated to support Israel? Let me begin by answering that question as follows. There's a very small country whose western coastline is demarcated by a well-known body of water. It is indeed tiny. Its land mass is ranked as the 153rd largest among the world's countries, and the size of its citizenry is just over six million. The country is called El Salvador. But there's another country with the very same attributes, especially if one "singles out" the 80 percent of its citizenry enjoying full-fledged rights and benefits, and this second country is called Israel.

Israel, it turns out, receives significantly greater assistance from the US government than does El Salvador. In fact, Israel, a relatively prosperous country, has received far more US aid, both military and economic, than all 42 Latin American and Caribbean countries combined. From the end of World War II until 2012, all Latin American and Caribbean countries received just over $148 billion in 2010 constant dollars.[227] Over the same time period, 1946–2012, US aid to Israel added up to $115 billion,[228] a figure not adjusted for inflation. According to *Ha'aretz*, adjusted for inflation, Israel received $248 billion in US aid between 1948 and 2013,[229] and Israel has received 99 percent of its US aid after 1967. Most of the US's southern hemispheric neighbors, of course, remain among the world's poorest countries. Meanwhile, US assistance has a gone a long way to help Israel become the tenth or eleventh most militarily powerful country in the world.

Finally, some see strong derivative benefits to Israel, and costs to the United States, due to the 1974 Arab oil embargo of the US, the blacklisting of US companies in the Arab world, US engagement in wars in Iraq and Afghanistan, and its ongoing leadership of the "war on terror." These events are all, to a considerable degree, products of hatred of the US government based in its unquestioning support for Israel. When one heads down this path, the cost to US taxpayers skyrockets.[230]

Conclusion

YES. IT'S BROKEN.

In this book, I've presented an analysis of how congressional actors behave with regard to policymaking on the Israel-centered Middle East conflicts. To obtain clear and frank insight in this issues area, I conducted over 200 interviews, most of which were with House and Senate staffers. Put differently, I interviewed extensively the people upon whom the members of Congress depend, with whom they work most closely, and who thus know the congresspersons very well. I believe the staffers "delivered," as did dozens of "off-the-Hill" actors, and a handful of congresspersons. The picture they paint is deeply disturbing to anyone who cares about how policy is made in the US Congress.

As in all political jungles, survival is the leading motivational factor. One does what one must to get elected and, once in office, reelected. There are surely US members of Congress whose behavior is not motivated by such thinking, but not many. To become a player in Congress, to get elected and reelected, nearly all the candidates need money, and lots of it; they also need to make sure money is not used against them. For almost all members of Congress, it's impossible to wrench free of this "carrot and stick" incentivization of their behavior by campaign donors.. As I neared completion of the first draft of this manuscript in January 2014, it was announced that for the first time in US history, the majority of US congresspersons were millionaires. But mega-millionaires and billionaires in Congress—who could, if they chose, fund their own campaigns—were still few and far between. Mere millionaires cannot dream of forgoing campaign finance assistance.

This need for campaign cash places candidates at the mercy of special interests, both on and off the Hill. On the Hill itself, the leadership of both parties desires retaining or regaining majority control; they're motivated to instruct fellow party members to behave in a manner that maximizes support from major donors. Sure, they know members must remain attentive to the desires of their customer base, their constituents, but they also know that large sums of money can facilitate dissemination of "information" by many media outlets that will go far in sustaining voter loyalty. Ultimately, most of Capitol Hill's leaders are dependent upon off-the-Hill resources, and those resources emanate from a range of "special interest" groups and individuals. On some issues, these "special interests" are diverse and dissonant, but in others this is not the case, especially when it comes to their ability to offer large doses of campaign funds.

At times, members of Congress do challenge reigning paradigms. In spring 2012, Senators Barbara Boxer and Bernie Sanders stood before the media to announce to the American public the need for serious reform of the Federal Reserve Board. On the basis of a study they had requested, it was established that directors and board members of many of the nation's largest banks were also sitting on regional Federal Reserve Board directorships. The system, according to Boxer and Sanders, was in dire need of reform lest major financial "foxes" be allowed to maintain their influence over the country's primary financial "chicken coops." Sadly, Boxer and Sanders's effort failed, becoming just one more in a series of failures demonstrating the degree to which Congress is broken. An even more glaring example presented itself with the Newtown, Connecticut, killings, which mobilized the president of the United States and 90 percent of the American public to call for nationwide gun control legislation, only to see the NRA successfully block efforts in Congress to do so. Why doesn't Congress respond? Because of the power and influence of special interests.

In the IME issue area, there is no gainsaying the importance of Americans' political socialization and generally favorable views of Israel. Moreover, many academics and diplomats have long argued that supporting Israel makes geostrategic sense. Indeed, individuals in both major schools of international relations—the idealist and realist schools—have forwarded such arguments. Neoconservative-style idealists, mugged by Samuel Huntington's "clash of civilization" thesis,[231] have seen Israel as a "kin country"—a liberal democratic entity seeking to flourish in a harsh, ever-challenging, authoritarian environment. "They"—the Israelis—are supposedly just like "us"—the Americans. We share the same fundamental values—love of the basic freedoms of expression, religious practice, and assembly—and we must help one another safeguard these individual liberties. If in a previous era we were in the same fight against communism, we are now brothers and sisters in the struggle against Islamist extremism. We are allies in Huntington's "clash of civilizations."[232] Many congresspersons, as we have seen, subscribe to this view.

A realist view was advanced many years ago by a former professor of mine at the University of Michigan, a professor for whom I had considerable fondness. In his book *Israel: The $35 Billion Bargain*,[233] which still serves as a reference point to some, A.F.K. (Ken) Organski argued that assistance to Israel—already the longtime number one annual recipient of US foreign aid when his book appeared—more than paid for itself in terms of benefits gained by the US in its confrontation with the Soviet Union. The Soviet Union is long gone, so Organski's rationale disappeared long ago with that rival superpower's demise. But since 9/11, "realist" policymakers can argue that the "war on Islamist extremism and terrorism" makes it essential to retain Israel as a strategic ally. From this vantage point, Israel represents something akin to an enormous, dependable military advance base situated in close proximity to the jugular vein of the world economy, the major oil and natural gas fields of the Near East. These arguments, too, have broad appeal in Congress.

The logic of both "pro-Israel" idealists and realists fails, however, if one realizes that unquestioning US support for successive increasingly right wing Israeli governments translates into support of Israel's continued illegal occupation of Syria's Golan Heights, of ongoing settlement of lands long designated for a Palestinian state by the international community, of the willful destruction of prospects for a two-state solution, of the repeated inflicting of collective punishment on the Palestinian people, and of the use of hugely disproportionate military force in response to any form of resistance. The logic of those arguments also fails if one realizes that what constitutes one if not the primary cause of widespread animosity toward US policies throughout the Arab-Iranian-Islamic world is precisely this continued, unwavering, unquestioning support for successive Israeli governments. And finally, the logic of these arguments is shaken to its core if one acknowledges that long-standing US support for authoritarian regimes in the region, itself often motivated heavily by those regimes' less threatening relations or formal peace with Israel, constitutes a second major cause of disapproval or hatred of US Mideast policy by people in that region and beyond. On these counts, to keep things simple, one need only look at the "9/11 Commission Report" to see that what motivated the 9/11 perpetrators to attack the United States;—the US's unquestioning support for Israel and for compliant Near East and North African regimes—was at the very top of those perpetrators' list of grievances.

The notion that Congress knows best—that its protracted, largely bipartisan defiance of pro–"two state" moves by both Republican and Democrat White House administrations reflects a better-informed policymaking—is indefensible. As congresspersons' own staffers openly admit, this is a complex issue area about which their own bosses, in general, know very little, and about which most of their bosses care not all that much. Moreover, most staffers themselves lack the time, energy, and inclination to talk their bosses into taking an alternative path. So why do Republican members of Congress repeatedly vote in large numbers against Republican presidents (both Bush presidencies), and why do their Democrat counterparts vote in large numbers against Democratic presidents (Clinton and Obama) on issues about which they collectively, according to their own principal aides, know and care so little? How does one explain this? What motivates them to defy sitting presidents from their own party, thereby not only acutely embarrassing those presidents, but also greatly complicating their foreign policymaking efforts? And what then are the consequences of these clashes between the legislative and executive branches with regard to efforts to make peace in the Middle East? What are the ramifications of the failure to resolve that conflict for US relations with Arab, Iranian, and/or predominantly Muslim peoples and states, and, in turn, for the security of American citizens?

In this book, I have tried to offer insights and arguments for how and why Congress is broken, why the decision-making process is so deeply flawed, and perhaps why congresspersons have behaved the way they do on Middle East matters. In sum, based on the appraisals of congressional staffers and Hill cognoscenti, I have concluded the following.

Many problems are caused by the electoral system and candidates' dependence on fund-raising. Special interests, often representing an extremely small fraction of the overall electorate, affect the electoral process. They weigh in early, vetting candidates through the use of questionnaires and calls for position papers, and winnowing out candidates deemed threatening by providing strong material support for their opponents. The most effective special interests also provide opportunities to sensitize prospective and actual candidates to their concerns. They offer free trips, provide informational materials, and mobilize constituents and professional lobbyists to introduce candidates to their point of view.

Once elected, members of Congress, almost to a person, behave as though the next electoral cycle has begun. They spend great chunks of time "dialing for dollars" or meeting possible donors. They have less time to enhance their knowledge of the issues before Congress, and they tend to "fall back on the politics of the issues." They are on guard to behave in a manner that will sustain the support or minimize the opposition of powerful special interests in the next election. They also know this means paying heed to the special interest–motivated concerns of party leadership and SuperPAC-endowed party superstars.

Newly elected members soon receive visits from lobbyists, replete with new offers of educational trips, professional support, and advice. The most successful lobbyists are seemingly omnipresent. Identifiably powerful lobbyists are ignored at one's peril, as new congresspersons learn very quickly.

Staffers working for members of Congress either already know through prior experience or quickly learn on the job that their workload is incredibly daunting. The huge piles of regular mail and the digitization of communications create an informational whiteout. While many staffers will turn to Congressional Research Services for its less biased reports, their heavy workload causes most of them to turn to party leadership elements or peers working on the relevant committees. But this means, in many cases, that they are requesting insight on how to behave from individuals who occupy specific congressional positions as a product of their special interest obeisance. They're asking the "foxes" what to do.

Equally important, if not more so, the same heavy time constraints—all the more true in an era of budget cutbacks and reduced staff sizes—heighten staffers' reliance upon off-the-Hill special interest groups and lobbyists. There is, in essence, too little time for staffers to read, to learn, and to exercise due diligence. Special interest groups serve the staffers what appear to be excellent talking points on a silver platter. Many staffers are more than happy to ingest the free offerings—what Richard Hall and Alan Deardorff have described as lobbyists' "legislative subsidies"[234]—and move on to another task.

Party leaders are observing their members' behavior and coach them to take positions that maximize the continued goodwill of those special interests of greatest importance to the party. For the great majority with no dog in a specific congressional fight—those who "don't know and/or don't really care" about a particular issue—it's easy and advantageous to sign on to the party's wishes.

Lobbyists and special interest group personnel are also watching intently, scoring congresspersons' behavior, and keeping their concerned memberships informed. If they see congresspersons "misbehaving," they'll let both the congresspersons and group members know. The threat is clear. And if the interest groups of one side in a debate remain largely without serious competition, and possess superior resources, skills, and efficiency, this makes an enormous difference to staffers, their bosses, and congressional outcomes.

Constituent voices are very important, especially on the House side. At times, this creates the possibility for even just a handful of individuals in a particular constituency to influence decisions, potentially to the detriment of other citizens in the constituency, the nation as a whole, and people living far away.

Committees attract memberships that reflect perceptions of their power and value. Membership on the most powerful, "A" committees is sought by nearly all members of Congress. Committees of lesser "value" to many members attract a smaller subset of members, many of whom have personal interest in the issue area or who have constituents with heightened interest in the issue area. In consequence, the structure of most committees, the nature of committee member selection, and the system of committee tenure leave open the possibility for committees' and subcommittees' domination by members motivated by strong personal interests, or members in the thrall of constituent interests and/or "special interest" groups. Individual congresspersons do not have to recuse themselves in the name of the national interest.

Control of committees by members with special interest biases is significant because those individuals use the committees' power and influence—through the issues they place on the agenda, the "expert" witnesses that they call, and the information they disseminate—to affect fellow congresspersons' behavior. The ability to conduct affairs in a manner designed to create genuine learning may be completely lost. Briefings and hearings may indoctrinate more than elucidate.

This combination of factors can result in the ability of an extremely small percentage of American citizens to hold sway over important decision making in Congress. Because Congress has the "power of the purse," this small percentage of citizens can and does exercise considerable influence over executive branch decision making as well.

In the world of French politics, the word "lobby" is a dirty word. It automatically connotes an insidious assault by narrow, parochial interests on the grander, national interests of the republic. In the United States, that's not how most of our politicians feel. On nearly all of these counts listed above, and on nearly all of the big issues of the day, the power and influence of special interests in Congress is on full display. Take an issue; insert a special interest group like Big Pharma, the NRA, major banks, insurance companies, etc. into the equation; and one gets results that defy the wishes and/or interests of the overwhelming majority of the American public. Why and how does this happen? Do the same factors that facilitate many congresspersons' electoral victory assist them in their ascent to important policymaking positions? And do the same "skills" that enable politicians to rise to high policymaking positions—that is, their ability to curry favor with special interests—increase the likelihood of their making special interest–biased decisions across a broad range of issue areas?

As regards Congress's policy performance on Middle East affairs and the IME conflicts, there are many special interest players, but there is only one richly funded, heavily staffed, highly efficient, and supremely effective lobby; its name is AIPAC. AIPAC is the NRA of any issue affecting Israel. For decades, it has been in a league of its own. It is the sole organization focused on IME conflicts that makes its presence felt on every one of the counts listed above for which special interest influence is possible. There are other groups that abet AIPAC on most occasions, such as the American Jewish Committee, B'nai B'rith, NORPAC, ADL, and some evangelical groups like CUFI, and some which prove useful as an even more hard-core right wing fringe foil, like the ZOA, but but no other group successively pressures congresspersons and influences congressional outcomes in this issue area with the same success as does AIPAC. As a current House member noted, poignantly, "When we have some floor votes, some members of Congress will even bring to one another's attention, 'It's an AIPAC vote.'"

It is simply not the case that AIPAC is merely echoing the sentiments of the American public. Let's look once again at how Congress responded to the December 2008–January 2009 Gaza War. While virtually the entire international community stood in condemnation of the death and destruction

Israel was raining down on the Gazan population, on January 8, 2009, the US Senate voted its unanimous consent for Israel's actions. Two days later, the House passed a comparable, nonbinding resolution, with just 5 members voting against it and 20 voting "present." But here's the punch line, as the journalist Glenn Greenwald observed:

> "What makes this accord among America's political class more notable still is how disconnected it is from American public opinion. Last July, a poll from the University of Maryland's Program on International Policy Attitudes found that 71 percent of Americans want the US government not to take sides in the Israeli-Palestinian conflict. Similarly, a Rasmussen study in early January—the first to survey American public opinion specifically regarding the Israeli attack on Gaza—found that Americans generally were 'closely divided over whether the Jewish state should be taking military action against militants in the Gaza Strip' (41 to 44 percent, with 15 percent undecided), but Democratic voters overwhelmingly opposed the Israeli offensive—by a 24-point margin (31 to 55 percent). Yet those significant divisions were nowhere to be found in the actions of their ostensible representatives."[235]

As Greenwald also astutely observed:

> "Given that we hear endlessly from our political establishment that the first obligation of our leaders is to keep us safe—that's the justification for everything from torture to presidential lawbreaking—what legitimate rationale is there for the US Congress to act in unison to redirect worldwide anger against Israel toward American citizens? How are US interests advanced by insinuating ourselves into such an entrenched conflict? Answers to those questions from supporters of the resolution were never required because those questions were never asked. As dubious a proposition as it is, the notion that American interests are inherently advanced by lending unquestioning support to Israel is one of the country's most hardened and unexamined premises."[236]

One must look to the flawed nature of the electoral process, congressional resource shortcomings, and the acquiescence of the major parties' leaderships to discover the factors enabling a "special interest" like AIPAC and its allies to hold Congress in their grip. With respect to its electoral influence, one need only pose a hypothetical question: What would happen to congresspersons' behavior on the IME conflicts if the bulk of campaign finance assistance shifted, diminishing AIPAC's influence and augmenting that of J Street or APN, the Arab American Institute, CMEP, FCNL or Telos? And as regards congressional policymaking, if talk of an "Israel lobby" is perhaps somewhat too nebulous and inclusive, any notion that AIPAC's influence is overblown or, in the final analysis, lacking in special significance is untenable. AIPAC does not win all of its battles, but what team wouldn't love to have a 90 percent success rate—a rate that House and Senate staffers, from across the political spectrum, would have no problem attributing to AIPAC with respect to congressional Mideast policymaking. Small wonder, therefore, that one encounters so many foreigners bewildered by America's Middle East policies—the foreigners don't "get it" because they have such a hard time wrapping their heads around the extent to which those policies are heavily determined by US domestic politics and less so by rational considerations of realities and American interests abroad.

Admittedly, there is great complexity to this issue area and to the big picture. A huge part of the problem here is that most Americans, US politicians included, remain ignorant of the IME conflicts' histories and hold inaccurate perceptions of their protagonists. Common thought is that "Israelis are good; Arabs, Iranians, and Muslims are bad." There is little to no appreciation for important variations among actors on either side. One of my last interviewees hit this nail solidly on the head in summer 2013 while taking stock of his fellow staffers. He said:

> "Most staffers here, they don't know anything about these issues. It's not their fault. Unless you've gone out of your way to study this, then you take what you've been acculturated to know and you know nothing about the other side. You know little to nothing about the human rights violations, the wrongs and injustices committed against the Palestinians. So if you are an early 20s something person from so many parts of the country, no matter whether you're a liberal, conser-

vative, moderate, whatever, why in the hell are you going to go out of your way to tell your boss to take a stand that will put him in a real minority position. You'd have to have knowledge, or a Palestinian friend, or to have experienced something to enlighten you. And even then, it would potentially be like shooting yourself in the foot. Why in the hell would you create trouble for yourself? . . . In other words, even if you know what's right, but your boss doesn't, you'd be taking a risk, and you don't want that; you don't want to jeopardize your own job. So there is a natural tendency toward conformity. So when you ask me where do staffers get their information from—is it from CRS [Congressional Research Services]? The answer is, for the most part, not even from CRS; it's just what AIPAC wants. That's all that really matters. The staffers know AIPAC is the pro-Israel lobby. They're the safest bet."

Unfortunately, this statement also applies all too well to many of the staffers' bosses. Why? In large part because AIPAC, with its massive resources, continues to win the battle for "framing" the IME issues for Congress, as detailed above. If there is a silver lining here, it's that AIPAC's position in Congress is somewhat tenuous because its loyalty among roughly two-thirds of its members is paper thin. The color of that paper is green, and that money could migrate to pro-peace groups backing pro-peace candidates.

The good news is that people can see the light and modify their positions. Prime examples are found among Jewish Americans whose learning and practical experiences have enabled them to reconsider or transcend their childhood and adult socialization and alter once rigid, conservative, unquestioningly pro-Israel perspectives. One former diehard, unflinching supporter of Israel, a former AIPAC employee and Hill veteran, is M.J. Rosenberg. The story of his personal epiphany has been told earlier. Rosenberg had his epiphany, in large part, when a close friend, who was hosting a Palestinian boy, needed to find someone to take care of the boy due to a family emergency. Overcoming his trepidations about letting the enemy into his home, Rosenberg agreed to help his friend, and came to discover that the Palestinian boy, in the way he behaved and spoke of his family, reminded him so much of the love he found in his own family and its proud cultural heritage that he, Rosenberg, felt compelled to reexamine his mind-set. Rosenberg went on to help found the

Israel Policy Forum and later worked for Media Matters. Throughout his time at both organizations and well beyond, his weekly columns pushed for a two-state solution to the I-P conflict. Only in late summer 2014 did Rosenberg bring to an end his years of poignant, pro-peace blogging. He was exhausted, and had given up hope.

But the struggle goes on. The "pro-Israel" lobby is not a monolith. As Dan Fleshler has written, and as I discovered and hopefully have shown in this book, the difference between strong pro–"two-state" groups—like APN, IPF, Brit Tzedek V'Shalom, J Street, and Jewish Voices for Peace—and groups aligned with right wing Israeli positions like AIPAC, ZOA, and the Republican Jewish Coalition is deep and real. And again, all of the groups on both sides of this divide are overwhelmingly Jewish American groups. In discussions about AIPAC's power on the Hill, I heard the dismay, lamentation, and frustration, as well as the expressions of embarrassment, from many Jewish American staffers, and they worked for both Democrat and Republican bosses.

Pro-peace groups like J Street, IPF, and APN are making a difference on Capitol Hill; and organizations like AAI, ADC, and CMEP—and more recently FCNL, NIAC, and Telos—have come to their assistance. These more stridently pro-peace groups did register some significant gains in late 2013 and early 2014. First, they energized an already war-weary American public to oppose Pres. Obama's attempt, for which he explicitly enlisted AIPAC's support, to assume a more aggressive posture vis-à-vis the Syrian regime of Pres. Bashar al-Assad. Second, Pres. Obama did successfully exercise his preference for protracted diplomatic initiatives and engagement with Iran and its newly elected (June 2013), more moderate president, Hassan Rouhani. This despite harsh opposition by Israel's PM Netanyahu and his American supporters, including many leading figures in Congress.

However, neither of these developments has affected core issues, such as Israel's continued occupation and settlement of West Bank territories and Syria's Golan Heights. In fact, the focus on Iran, from a right wing Israeli perspective, has undoubtedly served as a useful distraction from core Palestinian and Arab-Israeli problems. Meanwhile, US aid to Israel continues to flow, even experiencing a certain uptick; Secretary of State Kerry's failure to push the peace envelope buys more time for PM Netanyahu to bury the prospects for a two-state solution; and AIPAC and right wing Israel's US allies repositioned themselves to challenge their congressional opponents and doubters in the 2014 elections. Pro-peace groups have made a dent in AIPAC's armor. But how much and how rapidly AIPAC's competitors will be able to bring about change remains in doubt because they are still so outgunned, not by popular sentiment but by right wing pro-Israel money and the lobbying machinery it put in place long ago.

Over the long run, it could turn out that, as Peter Beinart has argued,[237] the right wing pro-Israel forces are fighting a losing battle for the hearts and minds of the younger generation of American Jews. Most are heavily assimilated and feel completely comfortable in their "American skin," and many are inspired by the humanitarian values embedded in their own faith. In consequence, they cannot abet the aggressive policies of right wing Israeli governments. Again, I saw much evidence of this among my Jewish American interlocutors on and off the Hill. Here too, however, one should remember that, inter alia, Birthright Israel's free trips to Israel comprise an enormous, annual investment to endear young Jews to the country; that AIPAC makes a strong, annual push to ensure youths' participation in its activities; and that the university-based association Hillel makes nationwide efforts to recruit and socialize students for "pro-Israel" engagement. In addition, and perhaps more importantly, great evidence suggests that it doesn't take so many bodies to sustain the power and influence of any special interest group; it takes only a considerable amount of money and a high level of commitment by a very small number—not even "one percent" of the population. Just ask the Koch brothers; or Sheldon Adelson.

On May 24, 2011, Israeli Prime Minister Benyamin Netanyahu spoke to a joint session of Congress. Invitations to foreign dignitaries to speak to Congress are rare privileges, typically granted only to the most cherished friends of the United States. This was Netanyahu's second speech before Congress, his earlier one having occurred some fifteen years earlier. Basking in the warmest of welcomes to the chamber, Netanyahu began his comments by noting that he saw many friends of Israel before him—Democrats and Republicans alike. This, too, elicited its own round of applause, and brought the first in a chain of standing ovations that numbered twenty-nine by the time he completed his speech. After congratulating the US for getting Osama bin Laden, making self-congratulatory comments about Israel's democratic distinctiveness in the Middle East, and thanking America—in a hopefully, self-filling prophetic manner—for pledges to never permit Iran to develop nuclear weapons, the prime minister started addressing issues relating to the Israeli-Palestinian conflict. Using the biblical names for the West Bank, he asserted, "In Judea and Samaria, the Jewish people are not foreign occupiers." He spoke of the bond between the Jewish people and the Jewish land, and how the "fantasy" of the Palestinians' return "must come to an end." He noted that Palestinian Authority Pres. Mahmoud Abbas must say, "I will accept a Jewish state"; that Israel will not return to the indefensible borders of 1967; that the Palestinian refugee problem will be resolved outside the borders of Israel; that Jerusalem must never be divided again; that Israel will maintain a long-term military presence along the Jordan river; and that peace cannot be imposed and must be negotiated. Every one of these statements was highly contentious; several stand in stark contrast to international law, world public opinion, and the expressed position of about 98 percent of the governments on the planet. Yet almost each and every one of these statements was greeted by a standing ovation by nearly all members of Congress, as well as by repeated shouts of hurrah. And when Netanyahu spoke, as he did repeatedly, of the Palestinians' need to be a free, independent people, living in their own state, of Israel's need to compromise, and of Israel's willingness to be the first to welcome a Palestinian state in the United Nations following a negotiated settlement, members of Congress also stood and applauded, albeit in smaller numbers. In essence, Netanyahu held Congress in the palm of his hand.

For many observers, Netanyahu's performance was brilliance personified. The special relationship of the Israeli government with the members of the US Congress was on full display, much to the chagrin of President Obama and his supporters in the White House and State Department. But for most individuals with stronger pro-peace perspectives, Netanyahu's performance was nauseating. As one Jewish American staffer, who was present in the chamber, told me, "The first thing that struck me was the reception that this foreign leader got compared to the US president. It highlights the absurdity of what our relationship with this government [of Israel] has become. I've seen State of the Union speeches, the quickness of congresspersons getting to their feet, the low threshold of standing ovations, etc., but again, on this occasion, most of the members didn't know the issues being brought up. They know this guy [Netanyahu] doesn't like the president, and what he's saying fits their hawkish views, and that there's no cost to it."

When I responded that most of if not the entire chamber had stood, he responded:

"If you get into the heads, the Republicans are seeing this as a black and white issue, most Democrats are seeing gray and nuances. But there was direction from [Democrat] leadership. Some say [Rep.] Debbie Wasserman Schultz was giving hand motions for people to stand.[238] Anyway, Bibi knew this and knew he could exploit the situation. People [House members] did look to others, then jumped to their feet. People [House members] don't know the nuances of 'Judea and Samaria.' What also fed into this atmosphere was that the gallery was filled with AIPAC people . . . [The enormous, annual AIPAC conference, was under way in Washington, D.C., and many congresspersons had given their gallery tickets to big AIPAC donors.] Just about all the people in the seats were 50- to 70-year-old AIPAC Jews who were leaping to their feet even before the members of Congress were. Cantor knew this would play out this way; it's why he invited Netanyahu. Technically it's [Speaker] Boehner's invitation, but it was unquestionably a political stunt. It was timed to coincide and run against Obama's [2009 Cairo, Egypt] Arab Spring speech. It was pure politics."

A time-honored, American political axiom is "all politics is local." When it comes to Middle East matters, interestingly, the axiom holds true in one sense, and yet is simultaneously stood on its head. This was brightly illustrated in a December 31, 2007 interview conducted by Charlie Rose with Akiva Eldar, a sage Israeli journalist who works for the liberal newspaper, Ha'aretz. Near the beginning of the interview, which was dominated by a discussion of the Israeli settlers in the West Bank, the following exchange occurred.

Rose: "So what is the power of the settlers today?"

Eldar: "The power of the settlers is here in the United States; more than in Israel."

Rose: "Here?"

Eldar: "Here in Washington, yes, because of the strong evangelical and Jewish lobby that will not allow the [American] administration to touch them, because in Israel . . ."

Rose (interrupting): "So the administration has no leverage . . . the administration in Washington has no leverage against whatever Israeli prime minister there is . . ."

Eldar: "Because the administration doesn't want to use its leverage; because the administration doesn't want to confront the political lobby. You know, Kissinger used to say that Israel doesn't have foreign policy, only domestic policy. You can say this about this administration when it comes to the Arab-Israeli conflict. It's purely domestic. Israel is not part of American foreign policy; Israel is domestic policy. You know, I'm sure you heard this joke that somebody [an Israeli] was asked if we would like Israel to be the fifty-first state of the United States, and he said, 'No, no! In that case Israel would have only two Senators.'"

Both Rose and Eldar laughed. But who's the joke on?

The range of solutions to the Israel-Palestine conflict is exhaustive. There are Israelis and Israeli supporters who believe Israel should keep all of the occupied territories and eventually take additional territories. Some Palestinians believe they should terminate Israel's existence. In between, one finds advocates for the creation of a binational, unitary state, and others who are comfortable with the status quo. But for decades on end, a two-state solution acceptable to moderate Israelis and Palestinians has been seen as the most plausible way to bring the I-P conflict to an end. Regardless of one's past or current views on the value of that solution, in the estimation of most knowledgeable people, that solution is either moribund or already dead. Should the "two state" solution expire, history will record that the US Congress contributed greatly to its demise.

BIBLIOGRAPHY

Abramoff, Jack. *Capitol Punishment*. Washington, D.C.: WND Books, 2011.

Ahrari, Mohammed E. *Ethnic Groups and U.S. Foreign Policy*. Westport CT: Greenwood Press, Inc., 1987.

Beinart, Peter. *The Crisis of Zionism*. New York: Times Books, Henry Holt and Co., 2012.

Brog, David. *Standing with Israel*. Lake Mary, Florida: Front Line, 2006.

Chafee, Lincoln. *Against the Tide*. New York: St. Martin's Press, 2008.

Curtiss, Richard H. *Stealth PACs: Lobbying Congress for Control of U.S. Middle East Policy*. Washington, D.C.: American Educational Trust, 1996.

Dean, John W. *Broken Government: How Republican Rule Destroyed the Legislative, Executive, and Judicial Branches*. London: Viking; Penguin Books, 2011.

DeLay, Tom. *No Retreat, No Surrender: One American's Fight*. New York: Sentinel, 2007.

Drew, Elizabeth. *Politics and Money: The New Road to Corruption*. New York: Macmillan Publishing Co., 1983.

Edwards, Mickey. *The Parties Versus the People*. New Haven, CT: Yale University Press, 2012.

Etzioni, Amitai. *Capital Corruption: The New Attack on American Democracy*. New York: Harcourt, Brace, Javanovich, 1984.

Feldman, Shai. *U.S. Middle East Policy: The Domestic Setting*. Boulder, CO: Westview Press, 1988.

Findley, Paul. *They Dare to Speak Out*. Westport, CT: Lawrence Hill Books, 1985.

Fleshler, Dan. *Transforming America's Israel Lobby*. Washington, D.C.: Potomac Books, Inc., 2009.

Foxman, Abraham. *The Deadliest Lies*. New York: Palgrave Macmillan, 2007.

Greider, William. *Who Will Tell the People*. New York: Simon & Schuster, 1992.

Hall, Richard L., and Alan V. Deardorff. "Lobbying as Legislative Subsidy," *American Political Science Review*, vol. 100, no. 1 (February 2006), pp. 69–84.

Jackson, Brooks. *Honest Graft: Big Money and the American Political Process*. New York: Knopf, 1988.

Lessig, Lawrence. *Republic, Lost*. New York: Hachette Book Group, 2011.

Lewis, Charles. *The Buying of Congress*. New York: Avon Press, 1998.

Mann Thomas E., and Norman J. Ornstein. *The Broken Branch: How Congress Is Failing America and How to Get It Back on Track*. New York: Oxford University Press, 2006.

Mearsheimer John J., and Stephen M. Walt. *The Israel Lobby and U.S. Foreign Policy*. New York: Farrar, Straus and Giroux, 2007.

Petras, James. *The Power of Israel in the United States*. Atlanta: Clarity Press, Inc., 2006.

Roeder, Edward. *Financing the Elections of the 99th Congress: Pro-Israel PACs*. Washington, DC: Sunshine News Services, 1984.

Sheffer, Gabriel, ed. *Dynamics of Dependence: U.S.-Israeli Relations.* Boulder: Westview Press, 1987.

Slater, Jerome. "The Two Books of Mearsheimer and Walt," *Security Studies* 18:1 (published online February 12, 2009), pp. 4–57.

Smith, Grant F. *Foreign Agents: The American Israel Public Affairs Committee from the 1963 Fulbright Hearings to the 2005 Espionage Scandal.* Washington, D.C.: Institute for Research: Middle East Policy, Inc., 2007.

Tivnan, Edward. *The Lobby.* New York: Simon and Schuster, 1987.

Zuckerman, Edward. *Almanac of Federal PACs: 1986.* Harpers Ferry, West Virginia: Amward Publications, 1986.

_____. Almanac of Federal PACs: 1988. Harpers Ferry, West Virginia: Amward Publications, 1988.

NOTES

1. Frank Newport, "Congressional Approval Sinks to Record Low," *Gallup*, Nov. 12, 2013, http://www.gallup.com/poll/165809/congressional-approval-sinks-record-low.aspx.

2   Jeffrey M. Jones, "42% of Americans Identify as Independents," *Gallup*, Jan. 8, 2014, http://www.gallup.com/poll/166763/record-high-americans-identify-independents.aspx.

3   William Greider, *Who Will Tell the People* (New York: Simon and Schuster, 1992), p. 13.

4   John W. Dean, *Broken Government* (New York: Penguin Group, 2007), p. 14.

5   Thomas E. Mann and Norman J. Ornstein, *The Broken Branch: How Congress Is Failing America and How to Get It Back on Track* (New York: Oxford University Press, 1992).

6   Ibid., 179; and see 179–184.

7   The power of "special interests" is left relatively unchallenged because of a largely compliant, privately owned, and similarly "special interest"–beholden media, and this contributes mightily to the creation of a largely ill-informed public. My assertion about the media merits substantiation, but that could easily fill another book. Allow me to just make two points that relate to Middle East issues: (1) Compare European countries' or Israel's coverage of the Middle East with that of the US to find a greater diversity of views abroad. (2) Major Middle East coverage by entities like National Public Radio, CNN, Fox News, or the *New York Times* tends to provide a much narrower range of views and, with exceptions, less breadth and depth of coverage.

8   Lawrence Lessig, *Republic Lost* (New York: Hachette Book Group, 2011).

9   Ibid., 247.

10 Matt Taibbi, "Wall Street's Big Win," *Rolling Stone*, issue 1111, August 19, 2010, pp. 57–61, 84. See also: Dylan Ratigan, "Is Your Senator a Bankster," *Huffington Post*, May 11, 2010, http://www.huffingtonpost.com/dylan-ratigan/is-your-senator-a-bankster_b_567907.html. MSNBC program host Dylan Ratigan devoted considerable time to decry the influence of special interests in his primary area of expertise—finance. In his sarcastic assessment of congresspersons' efforts to enact financial reforms, Ratigan noted, "The one main benefit to the financial reform effort so far is that it helps further do away with the false paradigms of 'left' or 'right' and 'Democrat' or 'Republican'—fewer and fewer people are falling for those lies anymore. Try to get an ideological conservative to explain why Republicans love spending and so eagerly give welfare to banks. Try to get your local liberal to explain why it was a good idea to make backroom deals with abhorrent corporations and drill, baby, drill. Heck, even try to get a Tea Partier to explain choosing bailout-lover Sarah Palin to keynote their convention, especially when that movement once had at least had some pre-astroturf roots in protesting government giveaways."

11 Lessig, op. cit.

12 One exception was the following work: Dan Fleshler, *Transforming America's Israel Lobby* (Washington, D.C.: Potomac Books, Inc., 2009).

13 John Mearsheimer and Stephen Walt, "The Israel Lobby," *London Review of Books*, March 23, 2006; and John J. Mearsheimer and Stephen M. Walt, *The Israel Lobby* (New York: Farrar, Straus and Giroux, 2007).

14 Ibid.

15 This is the term coined by Prof. Juan Cole of the University of Michigan. It acknowledges the military's role in ousting Pres. Morsy; at the same time, it pays homage to the enormous outpouring of Egyptian citizens—perhaps the greatest per capita outpouring in human history—in support of Morsy's removal from office.

16 Fareed Zakaria, "Are America's Best Days Behind Us?," *Time*, vol. 177, no. 10, March 14, 2011, pp. 28–33, 30.

17 Peter Bachrach and Morton S. Baratz, "Two Faces of Power," *American Political Science Review*, vol. 56, issue 4, December 1962, pp. 947–952.

18 To the organized Arab American community's chagrin, there was no category for Arab Americans in the 2010 census.

19 "AJC 2012 Survey of American Jewish Opinion," American Jewish Committee, http://www. ajc.org/site/apps/nlnet/content3.aspx?c=7oJILSPwFfJSG&b=8479755&ct=12477481.

20 Akiva Eldar, "American Jews Giving Up on Israel," *Ha'aretz*, Nov. 12, 2012. Ten percent stated that Israel was their highest priority in how they voted.

21 "AJC 2012 Survey of American Jewish Opinion," op. cit.

22 Shmuel Rosner, "Election 2012: Does the Jewish Vote Matter?," aish.com; http://www. aish.com/jw/s/Election-2012-Does-the-Jewish-Vote-Matter.html.

23 http://religions.pewforum.org/affiliations.

24 Janet McMahon, "AIPAC, a Night Flower," KabobFest (blog), May 6, 2011, www. kabobfest.com/2011/05/aipac-a-not-so-benign-night-flower.html.

25 Richard Silverstein, "AIPAC's Congressional Lobbying Trips to Israel Endangered?," *Tikun*, Dec. 29, 2006, www.richardsilverstein.com/tikun_olam/2006/12/29/aipacs-congressional-lobbying-trips-to-israel-endangered/, quoting "Proposed Travel Limits on Congress Don't Faze Jewish Nonprofit Groups," *JTA*, Dec. 20, 2006, http://www.jta. org/2006/12/20/archive/proposed-travel-limits-on-congress-dont-faze-jewish-nonprofit-groups. Silverstein continued: "On these trips, they do not hear from Peace Now or Israeli human rights groups. They rarely if ever hear from the likes of Yossi Beilin, Yossi Sarid or parties like Meretz. They rarely if ever hear from Israeli Arabs who represent 25 percent of Israel's population. Sure, they'll see an Israeli air force base or maybe even get a helicopter ride showing them how allegedly vulnerable Israel is to Arab attack (this was a favorite ploy of Ariel Sharon with visiting US presidents and other notables). But will they ever see the inside of Neve Shalom's peace village?"

26 The reader can refer to previous issues of the *Near East Report*, which is AIPAC's primary publication; www.aipac.org/NearEastReport/20101119/112_Congress_ProIsrael.html carries descriptions of numerous candidates who won with references to their "position paper" statements on Israel. Note Sestak's travails in his Senate race against Toomey.

27 Carl Hulse and David D. Kirkpatrick, "Ethics Overhaul Tops the Agenda in New Congress," *New York Times*, Jan. 4, 2007, pp. A1, A16.

28 Joseph E. Cantor, "The State of Campaign Finance," usa.usembassy.de/elections04/cantor.htm.

29 See the Center for Responsive Politics website, OpenSecrets.org.

30   David Knowles, "US Senate seat now costs $10.5 million to win, on average, while US House seat costs $1.7 million, new analysis of FEC data shows," *New York Daily News,* October 28, 2013.

31   See the Center for Responsive Politics website, OpenSecrets.org.

32   Cantor, op. cit.

33   Knowles, op. cit.

34   Bob Biersack, "The Big Spender Always Wins?" OpenSecrets.org, http://www.opensecrets. org/news/2012/01/big-spender-always-wins/.

35   My calculations, based on data from the Center for Responsive Politics (CRP), OpenSecrets.org.

36   Ibid.

37   See the very extensive data available at the CRP website, OpenSecrets.org.

38   Ibid.

39   Ibid.

40   The Center for Responsive Politics, "Pro-Israel and Pro-Arab Interests: The Money," IfAmericansKnew.org, April 24, 2002, http://www.ifamericansknew.org/us_ints/pg-contrib.html.

41   OpenSecrets.org.

42   *Mother Jones,* "The Mother Jones 400: Top 400 Campaign Donors of 2000." Mother Jones website, 2001. On Blankfort, see Israel Shamir, "Blankfort Spills the Beans, http:// mycatbirdseat.com/2010/11/israel-shamir-blankfort-spills-the-beans/. See also Jeffrey Blankfort, "Chomsky's 'Israel Lobby,'" *Global Justice* blog, http://www.indyboy.org/ newsitems/2006/04/04/18131371.php; and Mitchell Plitnick, "Myth and Reality: Jewish Influence on US Middle East Policy", May 24, 2005 online.

43   Blankfort, *Global Justice,* 2005. See also Jeffrey Blankfort, peacepalestine.blogspot. com/2006/07/jeff-blankfort-influence-of-israel-and.html and mondoweiss.et/2009/11/ the-israel-lobby-and-the-jewish-kings.The 50 percent figure corresponded to that esti- mated by the Democratic party itself; however, others say the Jewish American contribu- tions might have been as high as 70 percent.

44   Neve Gordon, "'Pro-Israel Lobbies' in U.S. Urging Agenda Inimical to Israel, Whose Future Lies in a Peaceful Solution," *Washington Report on Middle East Affairs,* January/ February 1998, pp. 51–52.

45   "Price of Admission," The Center for Responsive Politics, https://www.opensecrets.org/ bigpicture/stats.php?display=T&type=A&cycle=2010.

46   Richard Curtiss, *Stealth PACs: Lobbying Congress,* pp. 54–55.

47   Ibid., 55.

48   Ibid., 75. Curtiss says on p. 81 that Robert Kuttner spoke of the appearance of at least 70 such PACs by May 1986.

49   Ibid., 103.

50   Richard Curtiss, *Washington Report on Middle East Affairs,* January/February 1998, pp. 51-52.

51   fccpac.com/upcomingeventsinfo.php.

52   www.ourcampaigns.com/FECCommitteeDetail.html?FECCommitteeID=354.

53   protectourheritagepac.net.

54   Gordon, op. cit., 51–52.

55   Ibid.

56   Neil A. Lewis, "U.S. Jews get a new voice in Washington," *New York Times,* April 24, 2008, www.nytimes.com/2008/04/24/world/americas/24iht-lobby.4.12320195.html.

57 Philip Giraldi, "AIPAC on Trial," *The American Conservative,* Jan. 17, 2011, http://www.
    theamericanconservative.com/articles/aipac-on-trial/.
58 John J. Fialka, "Political Contributions from Pro-Israel PACs Suggest Coordination,"
    Wall Street Journal, June 24, 1987.
59 Dave Levinthal, "OpenSecrets.org Mailbag: Pro-Israel Money, Ethics Inquires and
    More," The Center for Responsive Politics, June 27. opensecrets.org/news/2011/06/
    opensecretsorg-mailbag-1.html.

      "Welcome to the latest installment of OpenSecrets.org Mailbag, where we answer
    your burning questions about the role of money in politics, political influence and the
    work we do here at OpenSecrets.org. So without further ado, this week's questions:

      "QUESTION: What criteria do you use to classify a PAC as pro-Israel? I noticed that
    most of the PACs listed as pro-Israel do not have anything about Israel (or Jews) in their
    titles or in their mission statement filing with the FEC. How do you decide that they
    should be considered pro-Israel PACs?" -- *Susan T. Nicholson, Gloucester, Mass.*

      "ANSWER: Jihan Andoni, the Center for Responsive Politics' research director, is
    here to field this one: 'Classifying pro-Israel political action committees isn't different
    from classifying any other special interest political action committee. The Center's re-
    searchers have been tracking these PACs for more than two decades, and thanks to the
    Internet, their job in the last few years has become much easier. The missions and vision
    statements of various PACs are easily found on most of these PACs' websites.

      "'Additional research and some phone calls by Center staff members are sometimes are
    needed to determine the nature of these PACs.

      "'It is not unusual for people to get confused between political action committees, which
    must register with the Federal Election commission and may donate money to candidates,
    and other lobbying groups, which do not.

      "'A good example of the latter is the American Israel Public Affairs Committee (AIPAC).
    Although AIPAC cannot directly contribute to candidates' committees, political parties
    or political committees—it does not itself sponsor a political action committee—it may
    still spend unlimited amounts of money lobbying the federal government and its different
    agencies.

      "'AIPAC lobbying expenditures in 2010 alone exceeded $2.7 million. . . .

      "'Since corporations and other organizations are prohibited from making direct political
    contributions from their treasuries, our methodology on calculating the influence of any
    group takes into account contributions from people associated with the group. In the case
    of AIPAC, for example, our team of researchers identified about 60 contributions made
    by individuals associated with AIPAC, such as the organization's president and its board
    members.

      "'Motivations behind individuals' political contributions vary. One factor may be the
    ideological beliefs of a donor. Our methodology related to ideological classifications looks
    into the relationship between an individual contributor, ideological PAC and a candidate in
    order to determine whether to count a particular donation toward the "pro-Israel" special
    interest area, or any other special interest area, for that matter.

      "'All numbers attributed to particular interest groups—among them the pro-Israel—are
    conservative. Tens of millions of dollars of contributions in each election cycle are not clas-
    sified by industry at all—either because the original data is incomplete, or because of the
    limitations on the Center's resources.'"

60 "American Israel Public Affairs Committee," The Center for Responsive Politics, www. opensecrets.org/lobby/clientsum.php?id=D000046963&year=2011.

61 "AJC 2012 Survey of American Jewish Opinion," op. cit. Other organizations providing pro-Israel campaign financing included the American Jewish Committee ($150,000), the Republican Jewish Coalition ($80,000), the NephCure Foundation ($40,000), US Israel Science and Technology Foundation ($30,000), Manufacturers Association of Israel ($20,000), and the American Jewish Congress ($14,000). All data from the same source.

62 My many thanks to the staff at the *Washington Report on Middle East Affairs* for this information.

63 See the articles by Theodoric Meyer, "How Much Did Sheldon Adelson Really Spend on Campaign 2012?," ProPublica, December 20, 2012, corrected December 21, 2012, http://www.propublica.org/article/how-much-did-sheldon-adelson-really-spend-on-campaign-2012; Peter H. Stone, "Sheldon Adelson Spent Far More on Campaign Than Previously Known," HUFF POST POLITICS, December 03, 2012, http://www.huffingtonpost.com/2012/12/03/sheldon-adelson-2012-election_n_2223589.html—quoting Stone on the $150 million figure, and the $6.5 to the RJC; and Patrick Temple-West, "Sheldon Adelson Mitt Romney Donation: Billionaire, Wife Give New $10 Million to Restore Our Future," *Reuters*, October 25, 2012, http://www.reuters.com/article/2012/10/26/us-usa-campaign-money-adelson-idUSBRE89P04I20121026—Temple-West wrote that the Adelsons gave at least $47 million to Republican candidates in 2012.

64 Ben Smith, "Soros and J Street," *Politico*, September 24, 2010, http://www.politico.com/blogs/bensmith/0910/Soros_and_J_Street.html.

65 Ron Kampeas, "J Street owns up to Soros funding," *JTA*, September 26, 2010; http://www.jta.org/news/article/2010/09/24/2741032/j-street-owns-up-to-soros-funding.

66 Gordon, op. cit., 51–52, quoting J.J. Goldberg, *Jewish Power: Inside the American Jewish Establishment* (New York: Basic Books, 1997).

67 Curtiss, Stealth PACs, op. cit., 1996, 128.

68 The Center for Responsive Politics, "Pro-Israel and Pro-Arab Interests: The Money," IfAmericansKnew.org, April 24, 2002, http://www.ifamericansknew.org/us_ints/pg-contrib.html.

69 Janet McMahon, "Record Pro-Israel PAC Contributions Failed to Save Senate Minority Leader Tom Daschle's Seat," *Washington Report on Middle East Affairs*, July 2005, p. 26.

70 www.opensecrets.org/pacs/industry.php?txt=Q04&cycle=201.

71 Janet McMahon, "With Massive Help from Pro-Israel PACs, Mark Kirk (R-IL) Ekes Out a Senate Win," *Washington Report on Middle East Affairs*, May-June 2011, pp. 34–35.

72 Interview with Khalil Jahshan in Washington, D.C.

73 Center for Responsive Politics, OpenSecrets.org, April 24, 2005.

74 http://www.snopes.com/politics/obama/donations.asp.

75 Arab American News.com press release, "Arab Americans seek apology from McCain campaign," www. Arabamericannews.com, July 23, 2008, http://www.arabamericannews.com/news/news/id_1006/rp_0/act_print/rf_1/Print.html.

76 "CAIR: Keith Ellison, Maverick or CAIR Bootlicker?" JustPiper.com, November 27, 2010, justpiper.com/2010/11/cair-keith-ellison-maverick-or-cair-bootlicker-timely/.

77 "Keith Ellison's Muslim Brotherhood Support," The Investigative Project on Terrorism, April 22, 2010, www.investigativeproject.org/1913/keith-ellisons-mb-support.

78 Gordon, op. cit.

79   OpenSecrets.org. Data from the Center for Responsive Politics opensecrets.org website; calculation of averages by author.

80   Ibid.

81   Ibid.

82   Janet McMahon, "Record Pro-Israel PAC Contributions . . . ," p. 26.

83   Interview with Khalil Jahshan, spring 2006.

84   Juan Cole, "AIPAC Spy Case Involves Intelligence," Informed Comment (blog), quoting Eric Fleischauer of the *Decatur Daily*, Sept. 7, 2004.

85   Ibid.

86   Ibid.

87   John Nichols, "An Alabama Primary That Went Global," *The Nation*, June 27, 2002, http://www.thenation.com/blog/alabama-primary-went-global#.

88   Jerome Slater, "The Two Books of Mearsheimer and Walt," *Security Studies* 18:1 (published online February 12, 2009), pp. 22–25.

89   Ibid., pp. 25–27

90   Ibid., pp. 25.

91   The American Israel Public Affairs Committee, *AIPAC Insider: Election 2006, Congress, Campaigns and Politics*, volume 2, edition 3, Spring 2006.

92   Ibid., pp. 25–26.

93   Ibid.

94   Ibid., p. 10.

95   The American Israel Public Affairs Committee, *AIPAC Insider: Election 2008, Congress, Campaigns and Politics,* volume 3, edition 1, Spring 2007.

96   James Besser, "Sestak-Toomey Race in Pa. Shaping up Critical Test for J Street," *Jewish Week*, May 27, 2010, http://www.thejewishweek.com/blogs/political_insider/sestak_toomey_senate_race_pa_shaping_up_critical_test_j_street.

97   Ibid.

98   Bryan Schwartzman, "Sestak's Israel Record Goes National," *Jewish Exponent,* July 15, 2010, http://jewishexponent.com/sestak's-israel-record-goes-national.

99   http://www.politico.com/blogs/bensmith/0910/AIPAC_disputes_Sestak_ad.html.

100 Ben Smith, "AIPAC Disputes Sesetak ad," *Politico*, Sep. 29, 2010, www.politico.com/blogs/bensmith/0910/AIPAC_disputes_Sestak_ad.html.

101 Ibid.

102 Ibid.

103 OpenSecrets.org.

104 http://www.examiner.com/article/pollak-and-schakowsky-face-off-at-league-of-women-voters-candidate-forum.

105 Joel B. Pollak, "Schakowski Invokes Anti-Orthodox Stereotypes," *American Thinker*, Nov. 7, 2010. Here's one excerpt from Pollak's article: "[Schakowsky] accused me of making Israel a 'political football' while working throughout her campaign with J Street, which has targeted leaders (even Elie Wiesel, Joe Lieberman, and Alan Dershowitz) who have criticized the Obama administration's policy on Israel. At one stage, J Street even protested a pro-Israel event I held that made no prior mention of J Street or Schakowsky and which had been focused on the media, not politics."

106 Linda Milazzo, "American Midterm Candidates Pandered for Pro-Israel Money and Votes," *LA Progressive*, Nov. 10, 2010, www.laprogressive.com/political-issues/american-midterm-candidates/.

107   Ibid.

108   Ibid.

109   Ibid.

110   Nathan Guttman, "New Foreign Affairs Committee Chairman Draws Praise from All Sides," *The Forward*, April 24, 2008, http://forward.com/articles/13244/new-foreign-affairs-committee-chairman-draws-prais-/.

111   OpenSecrets.org.

112   Richard Mourdock, "Sen. Dick Lugar's History of Harming Israel Must End," *Human Events*, Nov. 17, 2011, http://www.humanevents.com/article.php?id=47573.

113   Ibid.

114   Ron Kampeas, "Lugar Defeat Shows Partisanship on Foreign Policy," *Jerusalem Post*, May 16, 2012, http://www.jpost.com/LandedPages/PrintArticle.aspx?id=270247.

115   Philip Weiss, "Tom Friedman says candidate with AIPAC backing can raise in 3 phone calls what his opponent needs 50,000 calls to raise," Mondoweiss, June 16, 2013, http://mondoweiss.net/2013/06/friedman-candidate-opponent.html.

116   Brooks Jackson, cited in Wright, p. 115.

117   Larry Makinson, *Speaking Freely* (Washington, D.C.: Center for Responsive Politics, 2003).

118   Ibid.

119   Data collected by Hugh Galford for *Washington Report on Middle East Affairs*; see Janet McMahon, "Pro-Israel PACs: 2006 Winners, Losers, and Other Curiosities," *Washington Report on Middle East Affairs*, July 2007, http://www.wrmea.org/2007-july/pro-israel-pacs-2006-winners-losers-and-other-curiosities.html.

120   Michael C. Duke, "Good First Impression: Rep. Bill Flores explores U.S. foreign policy in Israel during AIEF seminar," *Jewish Herald-Voice*, January 26, 2012, http://jhvonline.com/good-first-impression-rep-bill-flores-explores-us-foreign-policy-in-isr-p12441-96.htm.

121   Milazzo, op. cit.

122   www.wrmea.com/component/content/article/369-2011-may-june/10522-election-watch-with-massive-help-from-pro-israel-pacs-mark-kirk-r-il-ekes-out-a-senate-win.html.

123   "Hartzler: Support Israel, Oppose Obama," Free Republic, May 21, 2011, www.freerepublic.com/focus/f-news/2723074/posts.

124   Ron Kampeas, "Ted Deutch, a most Jewish speech from the most Jewish district," *JTA*, April 22, 2012, http://www.jta.org/2010/04/22/news-opinion/the-telegraph/ted-deutch-a-most-jewish-speech-from-the-most-jewish-district.

125   Thomas Francis, "Ron Klein to President: Stop Hurting Israel's Feelings," *Palm Beach New Times*, March 18, 2010, blogs.browardpalmbeach.com/pulp/2010/03/ron_klein_israel_settlements_east_jerusalem_obama_biden.php.

126   "Allen West Rips Obama on Israel," Israel Matzav blog, May 20, 2011, israelmatzav.blogspot.com/2011/05/allen-west-rips-obama-on-israel.html.

127   Neve Gordon, op. cit.

128   David Obey, *Raising Hell for Justice: The Washington Battles of a Heartland Progressive* (Madison, Wisconsin: University of Wisconsin Press, 2007).

129   Laura Rozen, "Shepherd Hotel developer top donor to GOP foreign affairs chair Ros-Lehtinen," *Politico*, January 10, 2011, www.politico.com/blogs/laurarozen/0111/Shepherd_Hotel_developer_top_donor_to_GOP_foreign_affairs_chair_RosLehtinen.html.

130 Robert Naiman, "Jane Harman Weighs In on Israel's Hold Over Congress," *Huffington Post,* May 25, 2011, www.huffingtonpost.com/robert-naiman/jane-harman-weighs-in-on_b_189803.html

131 Michael Massing, "The Storm over the Israel Lobby," *New York Review of Books,* June 8, 2006.

132 Noam Chomsky, "The Israel Lobby?," *ZNET,* March 28, 2006, http://www.chomsky.info/articles/20060328.htm, quoting Zunes, "The U.S. Invasion of Iraq: Not the Fault of Israel and Its Supporters," *Foreign Policy in Focus,* January 3, 2006, http://fpif.org/the_us_invasion_of_iraq_not_the_fault_of_israel_and_its_supporters/.

133 MRA figures from Ida A. Brudnick, "Members' Representational Allowances: History and Usage," Congressional Research Services, January 5, 2011. In 2006, 71.14% of the MRAs were spent on the personnel component, with the percentage spent on personnel ranging from a low of 53% to a high of 90%.

134 http://politicalticker.blogs.cnn.com/2011/07/29/who-is-the-tea-party-caucus-in-the-house/.

135 http://www.congressfoundation.org/projects/communicating-with-congress.

136 http://hobnobblog.com/congress-by-the-numbers/pay-and-perquisites-of-members-of-congress-including-a-history-of-house-and-senate-salaries/.

137 Dan Fleshler, *Transforming America's Israel Lobby* (Washington, D.C.: Potomac Books, Inc., 2009).

138 Ibid., pp. 62–63.

139 Perhaps the best, early work is by Edward Tivnan, *The Israel Lobby* (New York: Simon and Schuster, 1987). Although more polemical, one should also read Paul Findley, *They Dare to Speak Out,* op.cit. One should also read John J. Mearsheimer and Stephen M. Walt, *The Israel Lobby,* op. cit.; Dan Fleshler, *Transforming America's Israel Lobby,* op. cit.; Grant F. Smith, *Foreign Agents: The American Israel Public Affairs Committee from the 1963 Fulbright Hearings to the 2005 Espionage Scanda,* (Washington DC: Institute for Research: Middle East Policy, Inc., 2007); James Petras, *The Power of Israel in the United States* (Atlanta, GA: Clarity Press, Inc., 2006).

140 AIPAC vital statistics chart assembled with data from numerous sources: Mearsheimer and Walt, op. cit.; Fleshler, op. cit.; Tivnan, op. cit.

141 See "Zionist Organization of America Financials," Guidestar, http://www.guidestar.org/organizations/13-5628475/zionist-organization-america.aspx#financials.

142 See "American Jewish Committee," Guidestar, http://www.guidestar.org/PartnerReport.aspx?partner=justgivews&ein=13-5563393

143 Guidestar.org.

144 Telos was founded by Gregory Khalil, a Christian Palestinian American, and Todd Deatherage, a former Hill staffer and State Department employee with an evangelical Christian background. They emphasize that peace and reconciliation is in the best interest of Israelis, Palestinians, and Americans, and seek to convince the American Christian evangelical community in particular that blind support for right wing Israeli governments is destructive to all.

145 Alana Y. Price and Lindsay Blakely, "AIPAC foundation is third largest private sponsor of congressional travel," Medill News Service, www.medilldc.net/power_trips/trips1206_israel.shtml [now expired].

146 Ibid.

147 Linda Gradstein, "U.S. congresswomen see Israel, Palestinians in the eyes of J Street," *JTA,* February 27, 2012. http://www.jta.org/2012/02/27/news-opinion/politics/u-s-congresswomen-see-israel-palestinians-in-the-eyes-of-j-street.

148 "Also rans" included Reps. Frank, Obey, Pence, Weiner, Israel, Kolbe, Issa, Sherman, Schiff, Price, Menendez, Cardoso, Deutch, Wexler, Blumenauer, Crowley, Pitts, and Wolf.

149 Ari Shavit, "You made it big, you jerk!" *Ha'aretz*, September 12, 2006.

150 Jo-Ann Mort, "Scoring Political Points on the Home Front on the Back of Palestinian Poverty," Talking Points Memo, Feb. 15, 2006, http://www.unz.org/Pub/TalkingPointsMemo-2006feb-00159 [now expired].

151 http://www.freerepublic.com/focus/news/2720687/posts?page=56.

152 Pastor John Hagee, "Washington Summit July 18–20, 2011," CUFI, www.cufi.org/site/PageServer?pagename=events_washington_summit.

153 "Positions and Views of Patrick Toomey on Middle East," Vote PA, Nov. 23, 2010, http://vote-pa.org/politicianissue.aspx?state=pa&id=patoomeypatrickj&issue=busmiddleeast, quoting http://toomeyforsenate.com/content/israel [now expired].

154 Interview with the ambassador of Egypt in Washington, D.C., Spring 2013.

155 In no particular order, the group includes Reps. Capps, Lee, Woolsey, Stark, Honda, Waters, Lofgren, (Loretta) Sanchez, (George) Miller, Farr, Filner, Eshoo, Speier, and Issa.

156 Who are they? Among the regulars, one can count (over time) Barbara Lee, Maxine Waters, Lynn Woolsey, George Miller, Pete Stark, Mike Honda, Sam Farr, Lois Capps, Linda Sanchez, Loretta Sanchez, Darrell Issa, Susan Davis, Lucille Roybal-Allard, Zoe Lofgren, Anna Eshoo, Elton Gallegly, and Jackie Speier.

157 Donald H. Harrison, "U.S. Rep. Shelley Berkley urges sanctions on Iran; halt to aid to Palestinian Authority," *Jewish Sightseeing*, April 3, 2006, http://www.jewishsightseeing.com/html/dhh_weblog/2006-blog/2006-04/2006-04-03-aipac-berkley.htm.

FIVE MINUTES WITH CONGRESSWOMAN SHELLEY BERKLEY (D-NEV.)

Following are excerpts from a June 19th interview with Congresswoman Shelley Berkley of Nevada's 1st district. Michelle Labgold, Acting Director of the United Jewish Communities (UJC) Washington Action Office, sat down with Congresswoman Berkley to discuss transportation for seniors, the Middle East peace process, and her legislative priorities for the year.

Michelle Labgold: Congresswoman, what are your top priorities for this year?

Congresswoman Berkley: On the international scene, making sure that the roadmap laid out by the President does not encumber Israel in any way, move towards secure borders free from terrorist attacks, dismantling of the terrorist infrastructure, having the Palestinians account for the millions of dollars that the United States and members of the European Union provided for them, have Israel's right to exist be recognized by all of its Arab neighbors and the Palestinians so they can live within secure borders. [Berkley then went on to discuss the issues of importance to her community, and a top priority for her, like education issues, Medicare, and transportation needs. And then her interviewer returned her to a discussion of matters of significance to Jewish Americans.]

Labgold: Congresswoman, how do you work within your caucus to build support for issues of concern to the Jewish community?

Berkley: I have been a pro-Israel activist for most of my life, very active in Federation, AIPAC, ADL, American Jewish Committee and so forth, and without any fear of contradiction, I would say the United States Congress is very supportive of issues that affect the Jewish community, particularly our strong support of the State of Israel. I realize not every member of Congress has a Jewish constituency and a passion for the issues as I do, but along with the twenty-six other Jewish members of Congress, we do our best to educate other members who may not be as sensitive to these issues as we are about the importance of a strong relationship between the United States and Israel and also trying to explain the difference between a victim of terrorist attacks and a perpetrator.

Labgold: On a personal note, over the years you have been an active member of the Jewish Federation of Las Vegas. Could you share with our readers why involvement in the Jewish community is important to you?

Berkley: I believe as a Jewish people, we cannot afford to sit on the sidelines. This is the first opportunity we have had in our history to truly make an impact in the society in which we live. It is our responsibility as Jews and as citizens of the United States of America to participate fully in the political process. If we do not stand up for ourselves, nobody will stand up for us. We lead the way when it comes to social issues such as education, transportation needs, social security, sensitivity towards our fellow men, and in these trying times with our war against terrorism. It is our obligation not only to our ancestors and the six million Jews that died in the Holocaust, but more importantly for future generations of Jewish Americans and Americans in general, our children, our grandchildren, and unborn children to come." Michelle Labgold, "Five Minutes with Shelley Berkley," Jewish Federation of Atlantic and Cape May Counties, http://jewishbytheshore.org/page.aspx?id=51465.

158   Jason Horowitz, "Eliot Engel Doesn't Like Obama's Israel Policy," *New York Observer News,* May 29, 2009. http://observer.com/2009/05/eliot-engel-doesnt-like-obamas-israel-policy-2/.

159   Jo-Ann Mort, op. cit.

160   Tzvi Ben Gedalyahu, "US Congressman Flunks Mideast 101," Arutz Sheva, May 16, 2012. http://www.israelnationalnews.com/News/News.aspx/155859#.Us19yeBd_Zc.

161   To this end, I decided to use the classification of House members provided in the US scorecards of "That's My Congress," in which congress persons are divided up into camps ranging across the following categories: "Strongly Liberal," "Somewhat Liberal," "Weakly Liberal," the "Mushy Middle," "Milquetoast Conservative," "Reddening Conservative," and "Extremely Conservative." (Later on, I will repeat this exercise for the Senate.) For each category, I calculated percentages based on the number of House members in the 113th Congress whose activism makes them readily identifiable as more aggressive advocates of a two-state solution ("SympA"), more sympathetic to right wing Israeli policies ("SympI"), and the figures combined ("A+I") for the 113th Congress.

ARAB VS. ISRAEL SYMPATHIES BY "THAT'S MY CONGRESS" IDEOLOGICAL CATEGORIES

	Total	SympA	SympI	A+I
Strongly Lib.	23	.48	.11	.59
Somewhat Lib.	74	.14	.04	.18
Weakly Lib.	53	.07	.11	.18
Mushy Middle	47	.05	.06	.11
Milquetoast Cons.	22	.05	.20	.25
Reddening Cons.	138	.03	.07	.10
Extremely Cons.	75	.01	.05	.06

(Only 432 members could be scored.)

162 See the account by Robert Malley and Hussein Agha, *The New York Review of Books*, op. cit.
163 "Sam Brownback," Institute for Policy Studies: Rightweb, http://rightweb.irc-online.org/profile/Brownback_Sam.
164 Here's a look at the array of political ideological camps in the Senate, as informed by the "That's My Congress" scorecard, and matched by their known "pro-Arab" and right wing "pro-Israeli" sympathies. I followed the same approach as above.

SENATORS' IDEOLOGICAL DISPOSITIONS IN 2013

2013 Senators	Number	SympA	SympI	A+I
Strongly Lib.	8	.01	.05	.06
Somewhat Lib.	19	.01	.06	.07
Weakly Lib.	12	.01	.03	.04
Mushy Middle	15	.01	.03	.04
Milquetoast Cons.	6	.01	.02	.03
Reddening Cons.	38	.01	.11	.12
Extremely Cons.	0	0	0	0

(Based on evaluation of 98 senators.)

165 Al Kamen, "In the Loop," *Washington Post*, May 15, 2009.
166 H.R. 3289. Fiscal 2004 Supplemental Appropriations for Iraq and Afghanistan/Vote to Bar Saudi Arabia from Receiving U.S. Financial Assistance, http://www.voterpunch.org/vote.htm;jsessionid=66ACCAFD66670549E6CA379FF-D5502A2?vote=13663&topic=W16&member=400033.
167 House speech by Rep. Barney Frank, "Peace in the Middle East," House of Representatives, February 17, 2005, http://www.gpo.gov/fdsys/pkg/CREC-2005-02-17/html/CREC-2005-02-17-pt1-PgH784.htm.
168 Jennifer Rubin, "Rep. Ed Royce: The New House Foreign Affairs chairman," *Washington Post* Right Turn, Dec. 16, 2012, www.washingtonpost.com/blogs/right-turn/wp/2012/12/16/rep-ed-royce-the-new-house-foreign-affairs-chairman/.
169 Ibid.
170 Ibid.

171 A recent example of this behavior came in fall 2013 when Majority Leader Eric Cantor, backed by a handful of fellow Republicans, held Congress hostage in the debate over the debt ceiling.

172 The same is true, of course, when Republicans have the Majority. With the Republicans, committee chairpersons are chosen by the House Steering Committee, a group of roughly thirty senior Republicans. Each committee member has one vote, but the system is weighted so that the Speaker has five votes and the Majority leader has two votes.

173 Richard Silverstein, "AIPAC Calls Congressional Opponent 'Supporter of Terrorism,'" *Tikkun*, May 26, 2006, http://www.richardsilverstein.com/tikun_olam/2006/05/26/aipac-calls-congressional-opponent-supporter-of-terrorism/.

174 Ibid.

175 Jim Lobe, "U.S. Iran Hawks in Congress in Some Disarray," Inter Press Service, May 17, 2012, http://www.ipsnews.net/2012/05/u-s-iran-hawks-in-congress-in-some-disarray/.

176 Reps. Dingell and R. Paul were two who voted no. Voting present: Woolsey, Lee, Stark, Carson, Edwards, McCollum, Ellison, W. Jones, Blumenauer. Not voting: Donnelly (IN), Burton, Slaughter, Kucinich, Stivers (OH), Eshoo, Filner (CA), Bachmann, Garamendi (CA).

177 Hayes Brown, "Hawkish Senators Ready Backdoor to War with Iran," ThinkProgress, Feb. 28, 2013, http://thinkprogress.org/security/2013/02/28/1650441/graham-menendez-backdoor-war-iran/.

178 Interview with staff at the *Washington Report on Middle East Affairs*.

179 "Moral Majority," Institute for Policy Studies, Right Web, Jan. 2, 1990, http://rightweb.irc-online.org/articles/display/Moral_Majority.

180 Ibid.

181 Ibid.

182 The October Surprise was the alleged delay in the release of the American hostages held by Iran's Hizballah surrogates in Lebanon. Reagan officials had struck a deal with the Iranians. Iran's Lebanese friends in Hizballah were to hold their American hostages beyond the November election in exchange for clandestine arms shipments by a Reagan administration, thus blocking Pres. Carter from achieving their release and benefiting from an "October surprise" just before the November 1980 election.

183 N.B. Talent is well known for his overall hawkish disposition. He took a fellowship at the conservative Heritage Foundation after losing his Senate seat. He is big on maintaining high defense spending and, as regards the Middle East, his aggressive stance against Iran. He is also known to have stated that he would have supported war against Iraq even if it had been known in advance that Saddam Hussein's Iraq did not have weapons of mass destruction because attacking Iraq was the only sound, strategic choice.

184 By 2008, Sen. Evan Bayh had already received over $110,000 in campaign support from pro-Israel PACs.

185 Tzvi Ben Gedalyahu, "Obama Policy Challenges Congressional Law on Jerusalem," Arutz Sheva, March 16, 2010, http://www.israelnationalnews.com/News/News.aspx/136552#.VGsymfnF_GU.

186 Jennifer Rubin, "Hagel, Sestak, and Pro-Israel Groups," *Commentary*, Sept. 2, 2010, http://www.commentarymagazine.com/2010/09/02/hagel-sestak-and-pro-israel-groups/.

187 Jeffrey Blankfort, "Joe Biden: In Israel's Service," CounterPunch.org, June 11–13, 2010, http://www.counterpunch.org/2010/06/11/joe-biden-in-israel-s-service/.

188 http://www.wrmea.org/archives/330-washington-report-archives-1988-1993/july-august-1990/1998-pro-israel-pacs-select-six-senate-incumbents-for-major-support-in-1990.html.

189 Richard Silverstein, "Aipac Calls Congressional Opponent 'Supporter of Terrorism,'" op. cit.

190 Ori Nir, "Israelis Want Aipac-Backed Bill Softened," *The Forward*, March 10, 2006, file:///Users/beattie/Desktop/Israelis%20Want%20Aipac-Backed%20Bill%20Softened%20–%20Forward.com.webarchive.

191 McClatchy, "At least one Republican liked Obama's Iran-AIPAC speech," Planet Washington (blog), March 4, 2012, http://blogs.mcclatchydc.com/washington/2012/03/at-least-one-republican-liked-obamas-iran-aipac-speech.html#storylink=cpy. The article also noted: "Tenn. Sen. Bob Corker, a member of the Senate Foreign Relations Committee, had some nice words to say about President Obama's speech today, calling it a 'good foundation for progress in the Middle East peace process and efforts by the U.S. and Israel to prevent Iran from obtaining nuclear weapons.' . . .Corker noted in a statement he's got 'strong policy disagreements with the president on many issues,' but said he agreed with Obama's 'strong commitment to our alliance with Israel, the right for Israel to defend itself, continuation of the peace process between Israel and the Palestinians, and our shared goal of preventing Iran from obtaining nuclear capability. I thought he was clear and unambiguous, and I thank him for that.'"

192 "Eighty-Eight Senators Condemn Hezbollah," *Philadelphia Jewish Voice*, PJV #15, September 2006.

193 Senate bill 763 was introduced by Sen. Connie Mack (R-FL), along with Lieberman, Grassley, Deconcini, Dole, Lautenberg, Boschwitz, Graham, Gramm, Levin, Coats, Boren, McCain, Helms, and Durenberger.

194 Thune is a strong supporter of Israel. "It's not good for this administration or for members of Congress to step on what is one of America's greatest allies in the world," Sen. John Thune, R-S.D., as quoted in: Ken Dilanian, "US-Israel Riff Adds Tension to AIPAC Meeting," *USA Today*, March 21, 2010, http://www.usatoday.com/news/washington/2010-03-21-aipac_N.htm.

195 Karoun Demirjian, "Harry Reid Cheers Senate Passage of Palestinian Resolution," *Las Vegas Sun*, June 29, 2011, http://www.lasvegassun.com/news/2011/jun/29/harry-reid-cheers-senate-passage-palestinian-resol/.

196 Josh Rogin, "Senators predict massive U.S. withdrawal from international organizations," *Foreign Policy* The Cable, Nov. 2, 2011, http://thecable.foreignpolicy.com/posts/2011/11/01/senators_predict_massive_us_withdrawal_from_international_organizations.

197 Ibid.

198 Ibid.

199 Americans for Peace Now Round-up for Week Ending July 1, 2011, http://archive.peacenow.org/entries/apn_legislative_round-up_for_the_week_ending_july_1_2011.

200 Mairav Zonszein, "US Senate passes resolution against Palestinian statehood," +972, June 29, 2011, http://972mag.com/us-senate-passes-resolution-of-unequivocal-no-to-palestinian-state/17607/. Zonszein is an Israeli-American native of New York City living in Israel since 1999.

201 Maureen Clare Murphy, "Daily Show Takes on US Punishment of UNESCO over Palestine Membership," *The Electric Intifada*, March 16, 2012, http://electronicintifada.net/blogs/maureen-clare-murphy/daily-show-takes-us-punishment-unesco-over-palestine-membership.

202 "After Embracing PLO, UNESCO Lobbies to Circumvent U.S. Funding Penalty," UN Watch, January 13, 2012, http://blog.unwatch.org/index.php/2012/01/13/unesco-officials-frustrated-by-congressional-hold-out-over-funding/.

203 Byron Tau, "W.H. wants UNESCO funded, despite Palestinian statehood support," *Politico*, Feb. 16, 2012, http://www.politico.com/politico44/2012/02/wh-wants-unesco-funded-despite-palestinian-statehood-114702.html, quoting Ron Kampeas, "Obama administration to seek UNESCO funding ban," Feb. 15, 2012, http://www.jta.org/2012/02/15/news-opinion/united-states/obama-administration-to-seek-waiver-on-unesco-funding-ban.

See also Jamie Crawford, website. Two powerful congresswomen have lifted their holds.

As the members of the General Conference had been warned, that action triggered two parts of US law (US Code - Title 22: Foreign Relations and Intercourse / 22 USC 287 - Sec. 287e. Authorization of appropriations; payment of expenses): . . . Pub. L. 101-246, title IV, Sec. 414, Feb. 16, 1990, 104 Stat. 70 . . . and . . . Pub. L. 103-236, title IV, Sec. 410, Apr. 30, 1994, 108 Stat. 454. The first provision is found in the Foreign Relations Authorization Act, Fiscal Years 1990 and 1991, and the second in the Foreign Relations Authorization Act, Fiscal Years 1994 and 1995. These are unusual provisions in that they do not provide the president the ability to waive the provisions if he determines doing so would be in the national interest.

204 Jamie Crawford, "Key Holds Lifted on Most U.S. Aid to Palestinians," CNN, March 23, 2012, http://security.blogs.cnn.com/2012/03/23/key-holds-lifted-on-most-u-s-aid-to-palestinians/.

205 Jarrod Bernstein, "Remarks by Assistant Secretary Esther Brimmer to the American Jewish Committee of Greater Miami and Broward," President Obama and the American Jewish Community, May 1, 2012, https://www.whitehouse.gov/blog/2012/05/01/remarks-assistant-secretary-esther-brimmer-american-jewish-committee-greater-miami-a.

206 Ibid.

207 Victor Kattan, "'UNRWA reform' Effort Will Harm Middle East Peace Effort," Al-Shabaka: The Palestinian Policy Network, May 30, 2012, http://thehill.com/blogs/congress-blog/foreign-policy/230065-unrwa-reform-effort-will-harm-middle-east-peace-effort.

208 See www.unrwa.org.

209 M.J. Rosenberg, "Israeli Settlement Expansion: The Silence of the Lambs," *Huffington Post*, Dec. 14, 2012, http://www.huffingtonpost.com/mj-rosenberg/israeli-settlement-expans_b_2301216.html. "Levin, of course, cares deeply about Israel. In fact, he is one of the few senators (then or now) who actually cares about its survival and security rather than simply viewing Israel and its backers in this country as a cash cow. The other senator of the Levin persuasion is Senator Dianne Feinstein, who also issues criticism when she thinks Israel is going off in a self-destructive direction. The rest, the loudest 'pro-Israel' voices in that body, don't care very much, if at all, which is why they happily accept the dictates of the lobby. What do they care if the end result of the policies they support are calamitous for Israel?"

210 "U.S. Senate Threatens to Halt Aid to Palestinians after Historic UN Vote," *Sign of the Times*, Dec. 1, 2012, http://www.sott.net/article/254279-US-senate-threatens-to-halt-aid-to-Palestinians-after-historic-UN-vote.

211 Jennifer Rubin, "Graham Previews His Iran Resolutions, Including Force Authorization," *Washington Post*, March 4, 2013.

212 Rubin, op. cit.

213 Opensecrets.org. See Rep. Kay Granger.

214 Serge Schemann, "Israelis to Discuss Phasing Out 1.2 billion U.S. Economic Aid," January 27, 1998, http://www.nytimes.com/1998/01/27/world/israelis-to-discuss-phasing-out-1.2-billion-us-economic-aid.html.

215 "Callahan Calls Emergency Israel Aid 'Pork'; Leads Effort to Block Funds," National Jewish Democratic Council website, May 24, 2002, http://www.freerepublic.com/focus/news/688662/posts.

216 Ibid.

217 Hilary Krieger, "Dispute Won't Harm $3b. Aid to Israel," *Jerusalem Post,* March 26, 2010.

218 Ibid.

219 Interview with Jerry Madison, longtime staffer for Mr. Obey, Wisconsin office, fall 2013.

220 OpenSecerets.org.

221 Ibid.

222 Ibid.

223 *Near East Report: AIPAC's Biweekly of American Middle East Policy,* November 19, 2010.

224 Opensecrets.org website. The Center for Responsive Politics. Click on Congress; enter congressperson's name.

225 See Robert Malley and Hussein Agha, "Camp David: The Tragedy of Errors," *The New York Review of Books,* August 9, 2001. It's very interesting to look at the rebuttal presented by Ehud Barak and Benny Morris, "Camp David and After—Continued," *The New York Review of Books,* June 27, 2002.

226 Saad Eddin Ibrahim was an Egyptian professor at the American University in Cairo. He founded the Ibn Khaldun Center, which fought hard to promote democratization in Egypt. The center, among its various activities, acquired and made public information demonstrating the regime's involvement in rigging national elections. Accused and convicted of receiving foreign funding for the center and its pro-democracy objectives, Ibrahim spent many years near the end of his life both in and out of prison.

227 Peter J. Meyer and Mark P. Sullivan, "U.S. Foreign Assistance to Latin America and the Caribbean: Recent Trends and FY Appropriations," *Congressional Research Services,* June 26, 2012, http://fas.org/sgp/crs/row/R43577.pdf.

228 Jeremy M. Sharp, "U.S. Foreign Aid to Israel," *Congressional Research Services,* March 12, 2012.

229 The adjusted figure was presented in the Marker, which is the economics unit of Israel's Ha'aretz newspaper. "US aid to Israel totals $234 billion since 1948," *Memo: Middle East Monitor,* March 22, 2013, https://www.middleeastmonitor.com/news/americas/5558-us-aid-to-israel-totals-234-billion-since-1948-.

230 Brown University's "Costs of War" project has put the figure for the Iraq and Afghanistan engagements alone at $4.4 trillion and counting. See: http://costsofwar.org/.

231 Samuel P. Huntington, "The Clash of Civilizations?," *Foreign Affairs,* vol. 72, no. 3, Summer 1993.

232 Ibid.

233 A.F.K. Organski, *Israel: The $35 Billion Bargain* (New York: Columbia University Press, 1990).

234 Richard L. Hall and Alan V. Deardorff, "Lobbying as Legislative Subsidy," *American Political Science Review,* vol. 100, no. 1 (February 2006), pp. 69–84.

235 Glenn Greenwald, "Unanimous Consent," *American Conservative,* January 26, 2009, http://www.theamericanconservative.com/articles/unanimous-consent/.
236 Ibid.
237 Peter Beinart, *The Crisis of Zionism* (New York: Times Books, 2012). See chapter 9.
238 Ibid., pp. 153–154. I was told about Rep. Wasserman Shultz by House staffers, but Beinart makes reference to this in his book as well. Beinart also notes that about 90% of the gallery seats were filled with "large AIPAC donors." Beinart, p. 154. Another staffer for a progressive House member said, "I was there. It was clear that applause was coming from both sides [R's and D's] even on statements by Netanyahu that were against Pres. Obama's stated policy positions."

About the Author

KIRK J. BEATTIE is the author of two books on Egyptian politics: *Egypt During the Nasser Years* and *Egypt During the Sadat Years*. A professor of Political Science and International Relations at Simmons College, specializing in comparative politics with regional expertise in Middle East and West European politics, Beattie has taught at Harvard, Wellesley, the Fletcher School of Law and Diplomacy, and the University of Michigan. He is a recipient of numerous national scholarships including a Fulbright grant, a Fulbright-Hays grant, an International Rotary Foundation Fellowship, an American Research Center in Egypt grant, and a Center for Arabic Study Abroad fellowship. He lives in Brookline, Massachusetts, and Hazelhurst, Wisconsin.

About Seven Stories Press

Seven Stories Press is an independent book publisher based in New York City. We publish works of the imagination by such writers as Nelson Algren, Russell Banks, Octavia E. Butler, Ani DiFranco, Assia Djebar, Ariel Dorfman, Coco Fusco, Barry Gifford, Martha Long, Luis Negrón, Hwang Sok-yong, Lee Stringer, and Kurt Vonnegut, to name a few, together with political titles by voices of conscience, including Subhankar Banerjee, the Boston Women's Health Collective, Noam Chomsky, Angela Y. Davis, Human Rights Watch, Derrick Jensen, Ralph Nader, Loretta Napoleoni, Gary Null, Greg Palast, Project Censored, Barbara Seaman, Alice Walker, Gary Webb, and Howard Zinn, among many others. Seven Stories Press believes publishers have a special responsibility to defend free speech and human rights, and to celebrate the gifts of the human imagination, wherever we can. In 2012 we launched Triangle Square books for young readers with strong social justice and narrative components, telling personal stories of courage and commitment. For additional information, visit www.sevenstories.com.